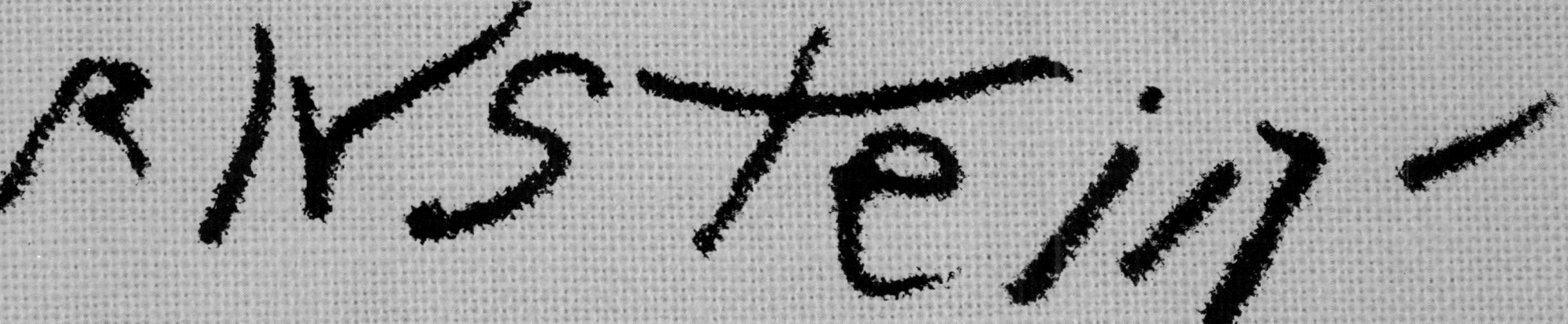

Theresa Bernstein
A Century in Art

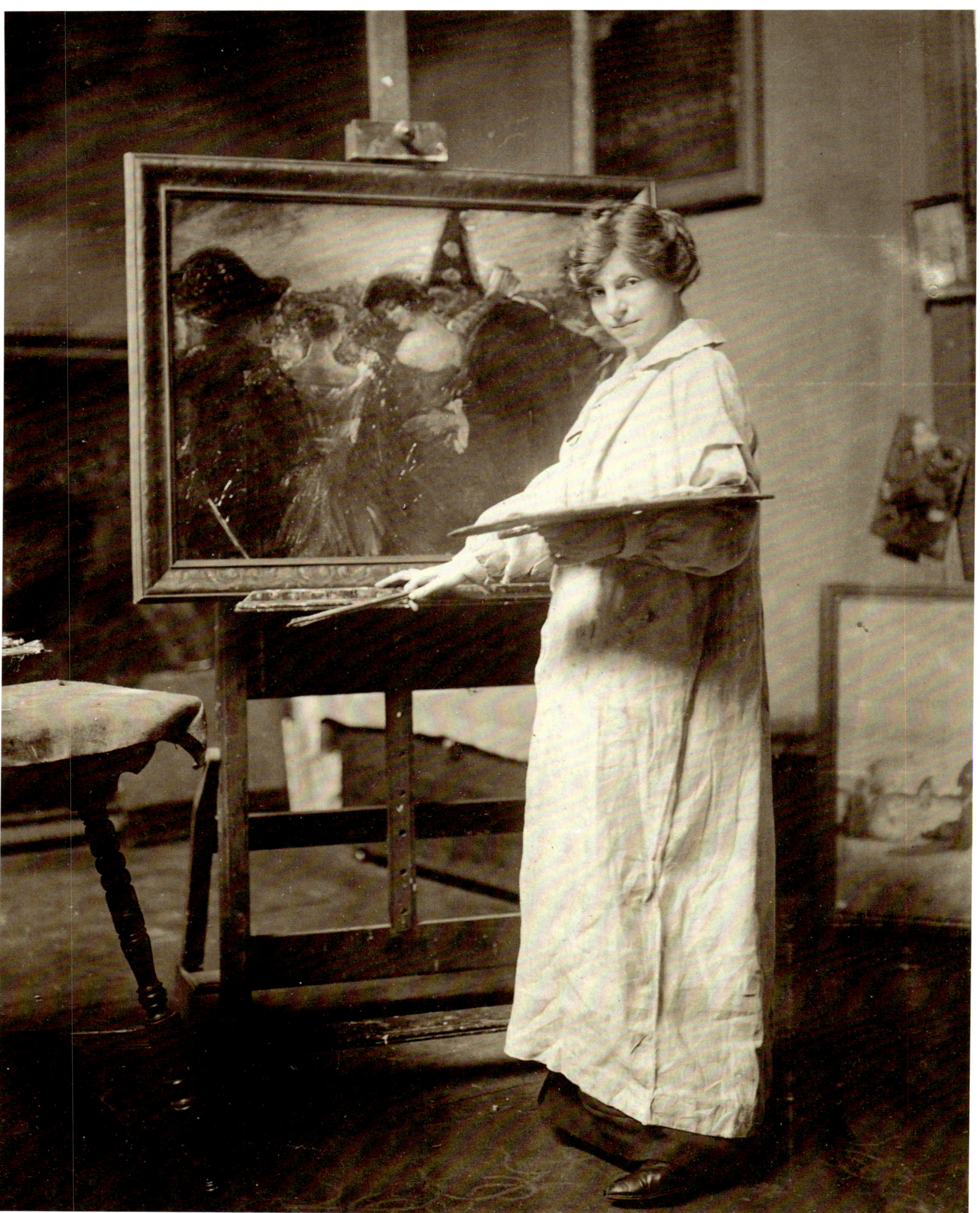

Theresa Bernstein at her easel with the lost painting *Moonlight Masquerade*, 1915

THERESA BERNSTEIN
A CENTURY IN ART

EDITED BY GAIL LEVIN

UNIVERSITY OF NEBRASKA PRESS

LINCOLN AND LONDON

Manufactured in the United States of America

This book accompanies the exhibitions *Theresa Bernstein: A Century in Art* organized by Gail Levin for the James Gallery at the Graduate Center of the City University of New York and *Theresa Bernstein from the Collection of Martin and Edith Stein* organized by Gail Levin for the Sidney Mishkin Gallery of Baruch College of the City University of New York.

∞

Library of Congress Control Number: 2013946624
ISBN: 978-0-8032-4876-2

Set in Garamond and Helvetica by Angstrom Graphics.
Designed by Rolando Zerquera.

Inside back cover: *To New York*. Theresa Bernstein and William Meyerowitz Foundation.

Contents

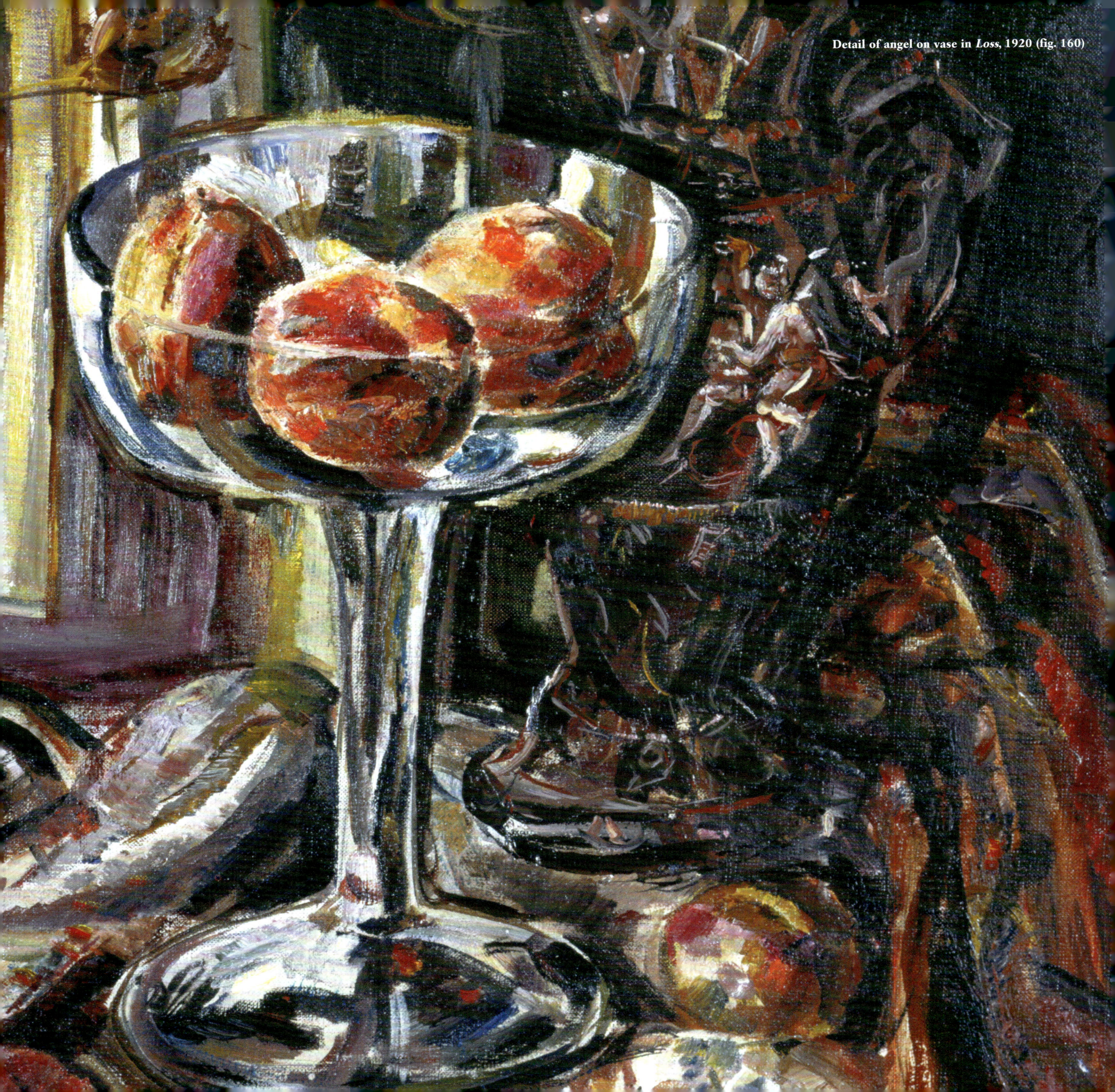

List of Illustrations

ALL WORKS ARE BY THERESA BERNSTEIN, EXCEPT DOCUMENTARY
PHOTOGRAPHS AND WORKS SPECIFICALLY ATTRIBUTED TO OTHERS.

Acknowledgments

The roots of this project go back to the show *Themes of New York: Paintings and Prints by William Meyerowitz and Theresa Bernstein* that I saw at the New York Historical Society in 1983. I subsequently went to meet Bernstein and found that she knew and recalled Edward Hopper on whom I was conducting exhaustive research. I later included her work in an essay that I wrote for the catalogue of the inaugural exhibition at the National Museum of Women in the Arts in 1987. She also had a cameo role in my book, *Edward Hopper: An Intimate Biography*, published in 1995. Only while researching this current project, however, did I come to realize that Bernstein had counted on my writing about her work. In a June 17, 1991, transcript of an oral history in the New York Public Library, Theresa Bernstein told Muriel Meyers of the American Jewish Committee, "Gail Levin, who wrote the book on Edward Hopper....took a great interest in my work. She feels that I haven't as yet reached the appreciation that I deserve for my career. So she has been interviewing me and she's working on a book...."

This book and exhibition project could not have happened without the participation and support of many people and institutions. Theresa Bernstein's collectors are a passionate group who know that she is an artist deserving of a place in history and have rallied to support this effort with both loans of art and financial support. Thus, this project began with a grant from The Bernstein House Foundation arranged by Girard (Jerry) Jackson to support a seminar on Bernstein for doctoral students in the art history program of the Graduate Center of the City University of New York, which I taught in the fall of 2010. Our aim from the start was that this exhibition and publication would grow out of the seminar. Jerry Jackson, who knew both Bernstein and Meyerowitz well, has also shared his knowledge of their art, helped me locate works in private collections, loaned examples from his own collection of her work to our show, donated a painting by Bernstein to the Graduate Center, and provided unconditional support to this project.

No exhibition could happen without the generosity of the lenders who, in order to share their treasures with the world, part for extended periods of time with art that they cherish. In this case, the most extensive collection of Bernstein's work rests with Martin and Edith Stein, who are dedicated to the work of both Bernstein and Meyerowitz. Edith is a graduate of Baruch College, CUNY, making it logical to feature a selection of their collection at Baruch's Sidney Mishkin Gallery simultaneously with the Bernstein show at the James Gallery at the Graduate Center. Thus visitors to both New York shows will have a chance to see Bernstein's work in greater depth. A selection of Bernstein's masterpieces from the Stein collection will tour with the James Gallery show. The extraordinary generosity of the Steins has extended to supporting the exhibition of Bernstein's work at Baruch as well as to sponsoring a related symposium and making possible this lavishly illustrated publication. I wish to thank Judy LeFaive for helping to coordinate the Stein's efforts.

For helping to meet the costs of this project, I also wish to thank Robert Hurst, Walter Manninen, Helen and Edward Ezrick, Willys K. Silvers, Jonathan P. and Margaret S. Harvey, and Sebastian Murken for their generous donations. I also thank Joan Whalen for assistance in fundraising. A personal research award to me from the Hadassah International Research Institute on Jewish Women at Brandeis University also supported this project. Thanks also to those museums, galleries, and collectors who provided photographs of art works in their collections without charge.

Several of the lenders to this show befriended Bernstein. Walter Manninen has given his major collection of Bernstein's work to Endicott College in Beverly, Massachusetts, which will host a stop on our exhibition's tour. Manninen has not only shared his collection of Bernstein's art, but also her letters to him and the stories she recounted. Others who knew Bernstein have been especially helpful, including J. J. and Jackie Bell, Diane Dawson, Helen and Edward Ezrick, Paul Famolari, Jim Fish, Jonathan P. Harvey, Sandy Lepore, Francis Naumann, Pamlyn Smith, Ellen Sragow, and Joan Whalen, as well as some who prefer to remain anonymous. Members of Bernstein's extended family, such as Keith Carlson and Mary Rives; Ken Carlson; Sara Marks, Eta Paransky, Esther, Harold, and Jeffrey and Barbara Marcus, and Janice Carlson Scott, have also shared documents, photographs, art works, and memories.

Acknowledgment and appreciation is also due to The Theresa Bernstein and William Meyerowitz Foundation for the loan of works of art to the exhibition; for access and permission to quote, reproduce, and use art works and writings by Theresa Bernstein and William Meyerowitz.

I thank all of the private and public collections lending to this show for their understanding that by parting temporarily with Bernstein's art, they are allowing a new public to discover and appreciate the importance of her work. Most of Bernstein's major paintings have disappeared from public view and the whereabouts of many remain unknown. Thus, I have tried to include here those major examples that can be located. I also acknowledge help from Jonathan Boos, James B. Hand, and Christie's. It is my hope that this project will result in finding some of Bernstein's important lost works.

My own research on Bernstein benefitted from teaching the seminar at the Graduate Center with six participating students: Sarah Archino, Diana Fischman, Stephanie Hackett, Elsie Heung, Gillian Pistell, and Lindsay Smilow, each of whom contributed research for the list of public institutions and for the chronology published in this volume. As a group we drew up lists of desired works for our projected exhibition, however, the final selection is my own, the result of which works I was able to locate in years between the conclusion of the seminar and the time it takes to stage an exhibition of this scope, as well as from the fruits of my further research into Bernstein's career. Essays by four of the students from the seminar appear in this volume. In addition, Stephanie Hackett and Elsie Heung assisted me on this project in many crucial ways. Hackett, partially funded by the Weissman School of Baruch College, CUNY, has begun compiling a list of all Bernstein's prints and helped to coordinate loans to the exhibition. Since early 2011, Heung has been designing and constructing the Bernstein website that accompanies this show and she has helped me organize the images for this book; her participation has proven essential. Her work has been funded by the CUNY Graduate Center's New Media Lab and facilitated by the Center's Managing Director, Andrea Ades Vasquez and Aaron Knoll, webmaster.

The students in the seminar and I benefitted from two visiting scholars who made valuable presentations to our seminar: Dr. Michele Cohen and Dr. Patricia M. Burnham, both of whom wrote about Bernstein's art during her lifetime, organized a show of her work, and befriended her. Both shared their knowledge and their archives with our project and have researched and written new essays for this volume. This project has been much enhanced by their participation.

Michele Cohen, while working on her Ph.D. in art history at the CUNY Graduate Center in the late 1980s, was also organizing an important show of Bernstein's work for the Museum of the City of New York. Dr. Cohen has generously contributed her expertise to many aspects of this project, serving as an invaluable consultant and a sounding board, helping me with many fundamental tasks from finding lost works to editing this volume. It is my hope that she will continue the important work on Bernstein that she began in the 1980s, as well as lead the next generation of young scholars to pursue further research.

Many other people have helped this project in diverse ways. Scholars Patricia Hills and Alicia Faxon read an early draft of this manuscript and offered useful suggestions. Help with research queries came from the Phillips Collection librarian Karen Schneider; Cape Ann Museum archivist Stephanie Buck and curator, Martha Oaks; Samantha Baskind, who placed Bernstein's work on the cover of her book on Jewish art. In Gloucester, William H. Trayes was most helpful in showing me around.

At the CUNY Graduate Center, I wish to thank President William Kelly (now Interim Chancellor of CUNY) for his early and sustained belief in this project. I also acknowledge help from Chase F. Robinson, Interim President of the Graduate Center; Sebastian Persico, Senior Vice-President for Finance and Administration; Aoibheann Sweeney, Executive Director of the Center for Humanities; Katherine Carl, Curator of the James Gallery, and her assistant, Jennifer Wilkinson. I thank Ray Ring and Chris Lowery for their creative solutions for the installation and other practical ideas; as well as Andrea Appel, Miriam Capua, Tanya Domi, Edith Gonzalez, Marilyn Marzolf, Linda Merians, Margaret O'Garro, Alexandra Robinson, Raymond Soldavin, and Kathleen Stolarski. At Baruch College, I wish to thank President Mitchel Wallerstein; Sandra Kraskin Director of the Sidney Mishkin Gallery; Mark Gibbel, Vice President, Office of College Advancement; Dean Jeffrey Peck, and in the Department of the Fine & Performing Arts Department, Anne Swartz, Chairman, and Charles Dietrich.

For assistance in arranging the tour of this show, I wish to thank the following: Teri Edelstein and Eliza J. Reilly of the Phillips Museum of Art at Franklin and Marshall College, Lancaster, Pennsylvania; at Endicott College, Beverly, Massachusetts, President Richard E. Wylie , Dean Mark Towner, and Kathleen J. Moore, Coordinator of Visual Arts for The Heftler Visiting Artist Gallery at the Walter J. Manninen Center for the Arts; William Valerio, Director and Sally Larson, Deputy Director for Exhibitions at the Woodmere Art Museum, Philadelphia, Pennsylvania; and Steven V. Maklansky, Director and Marisa J. Pascucci, Curator at the Boca Raton Art Museum.

I wish to thank University of Nebraska Press Editor in Chief, Derek Krissoff, for his belief in this project and for shepherding it to fruition. Thanks also to Courtney Ochsner at the press and to David Angstrom, Rolando Zerquera, Barbara Lee, Roberta Boyack, and Sandra Hechavarria of Angstrom Graphics for their care with the design of this book. I wish to acknowledge help with proofreading from Susan Van Sickle, and especially from Benedict P. Duffy, who joined the project as my curatorial intern, just as this book was about to go to press. As always, I thank my husband, John Van Sickle, for his support and editorial acumen as well as for joining me on a trip to visit Theresa Bernstein in Gloucester in July of 1991.

For the contents and conclusions of this book, I am of course responsible. I hope that so many color reproductions of Bernstein's paintings, prints, and drawings published with documentary photographs in an affordable volume will inspire many to examine her important and unrecognized contribution to American art of the twentieth century. In researching and writing my own essay and in compiling this volume, especially the chronology, I have been amazed by the vast amount of newly uncovered information gathered here for the first time. Yet, because of the limitations of both time and the length of this project, this book cannot be definitive. If my work and that of my students and colleagues prompts further study, I will feel that we have succeeded.

Gail Levin

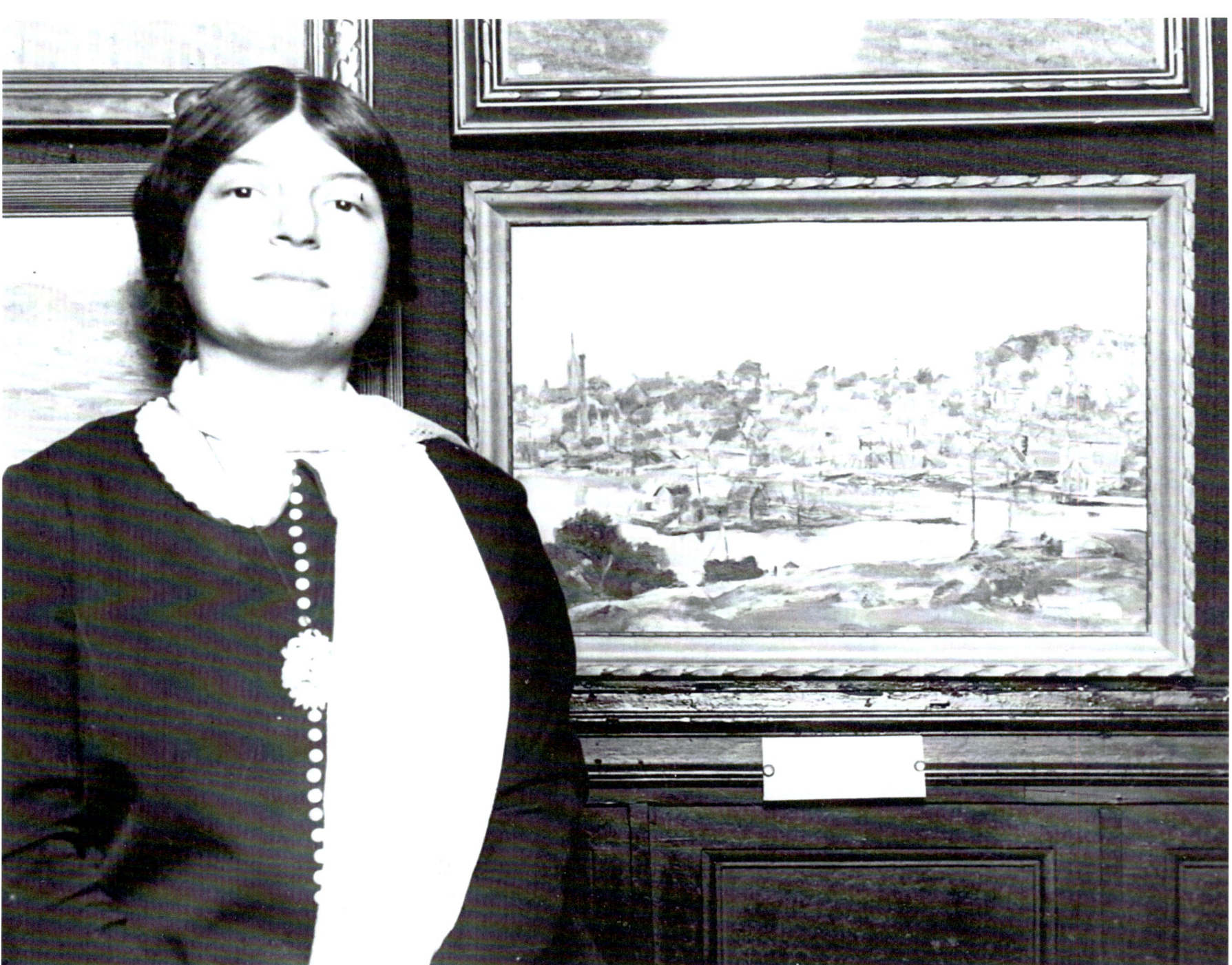

1. Theresa Bernstein upon winning the John Clerici Prize for the best painting with *Sunset Hour* from the National Association of Women Painters and Sculptors, December, 1924.

ONE Forgotten Fame

INSCRIBING THERESA BERNSTEIN INTO HISTORY

Gail Levin

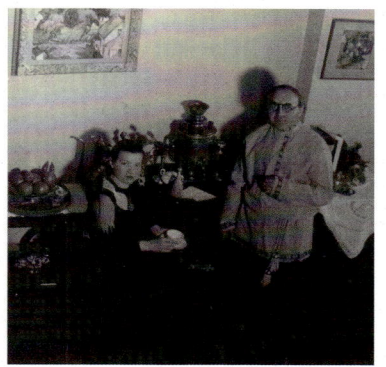

2. Theresa Bernstein and William Meyerowitz. Theresa Bernstein and William Meyerowitz Foundation.

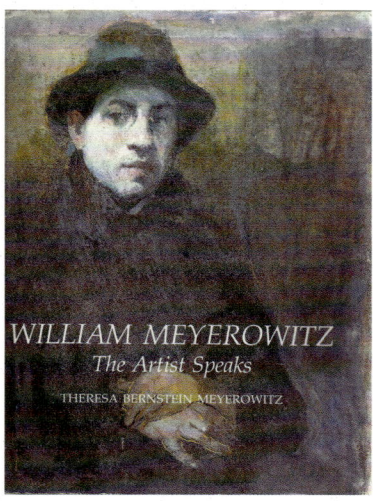

3. Book cover of *William Meyerowitz: The Artist Speaks*, 1986.

Theresa Bernstein belonged to a generation of women artists who had to struggle—not only for recognition but also for the mere chance to show the public their work. Bernstein (1890–2002) was born just three years after Georgia O'Keeffe (1887–1986). Both enjoyed great success in their time, yet only O'Keeffe achieved celebrity and lasting fame. To put their achievement in context, professional women artists of their generation were numerous, yet few made their names as painters, and even fewer reputations have survived, among them Agnes Lawrence Pelton (1881–1961), Marguerite Thompson Zorach, (1887–1968), Alma Woodsey Thomas (1891–1978), Peggy Bacon (1895–1987), and Lucile Lundquist Blanch (1895–1981).[1]

Prejudice against women artists, negative stereotypes of women, and the game of power politics played by men in the art establishment plagued the women of Bernstein's vintage, as she reported in *The Journal*, her book published only in 1991, when she was already 101 years old. She remembered how the art critic Elisabeth Luther Cary had written: "Theresa Bernstein's powerful work has that masculine quality but enough of the feminine to lift it out of that category."[2] To which Bernstein retorts: "In other words, having power in one's work suggests masculinity, but why couldn't it have suggested femininity? After all, the basis of life is in the feminine as well."[3]

Bernstein, O'Keeffe, Zorach, Bacon, and Blanch all married artists, although the relationships of the latter two did not survive. O'Keeffe's husband, the photographer and art dealer Alfred Stieglitz, promoted her work instead of his own at least some of the time. Notably, he made O'Keeffe notorious in 1921, when he exhibited his photographs of her posing nude. O'Keeffe chose to spend a good deal of time living apart from her husband, unlike the traditional marriages of Bernstein and Zorach.[4]

Such traditional relationships placed limits on women's professional and creative pursuits, yet Bernstein tried to sustain both her marriage and her own career as a painter. She was extraordinarily devoted to her husband, William Meyerowitz (1887–1981), himself a painter and printmaker, and she took care not to compete with him. Indeed, she wrote a book about him after his death: *William Meyerowitz: The Artist Speaks*, published in 1986, when she was ninety-six years old. She also continued to insist on including Meyerowitz's art whenever she was invited to show her own work.

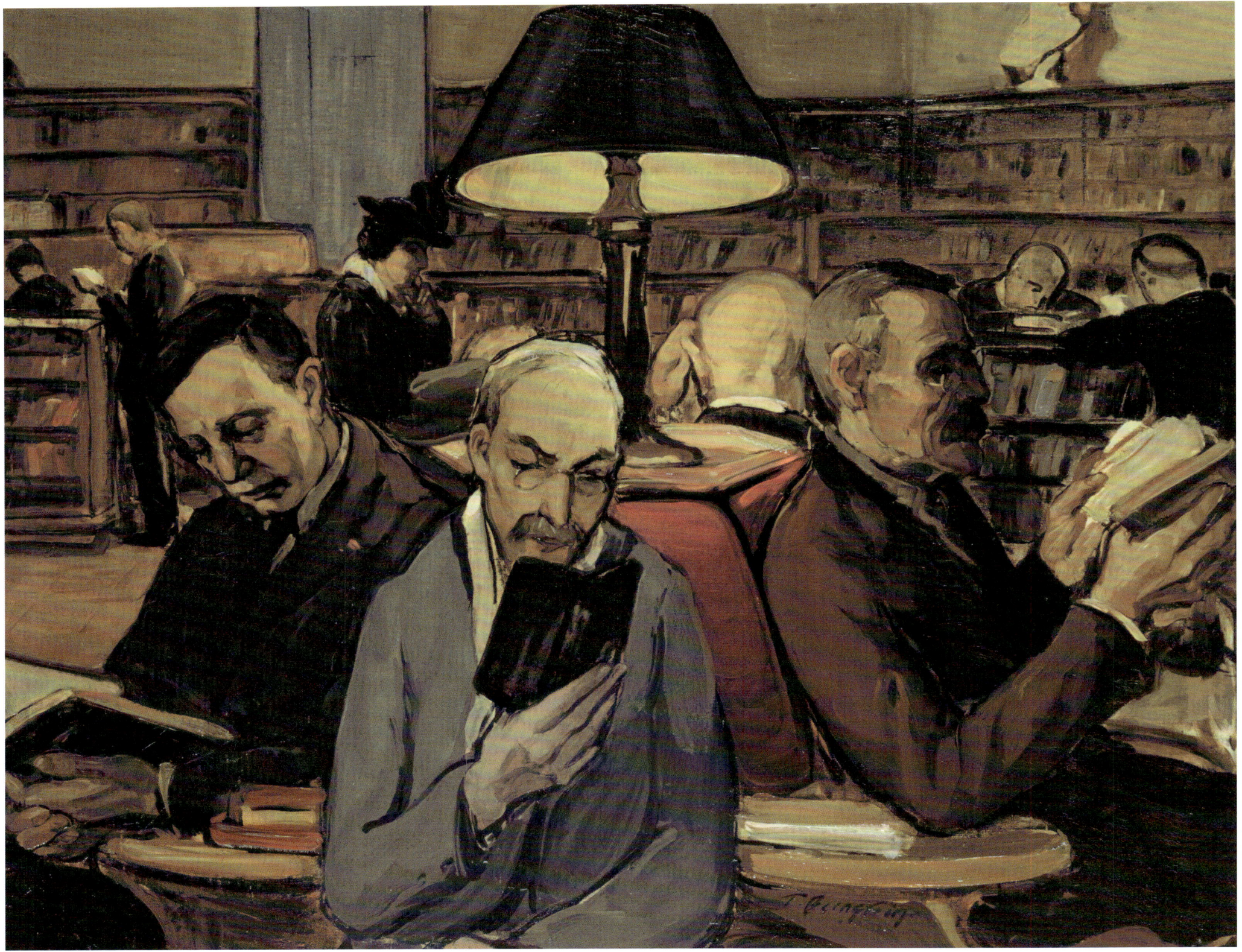

4. *The Readers*, 1914. Oil on canvas, 40 x 50 inches. Martin and Edith Stein Collection.

It remains to place Bernstein's art accurately in the contexts both of her contemporaries and of her own long life. Dates and places have too often been misrepresented, significant events confused or left out, with failures to document some of her many connections to other artists of significance. For example, a recent study, *American Women Modernists: The Legacy of Robert Henri, 1910–1945*, misrepresented Bernstein as Henri's pupil.[5] Instead, as documented by the present project, Bernstein, although she was twenty-five years younger than Henri, never studied with him, though she did show in many exhibitions as his peer.[6]

Bernstein herself caused some inaccuracies, since, like many of her contemporaries, she fibbed about her age, eventually

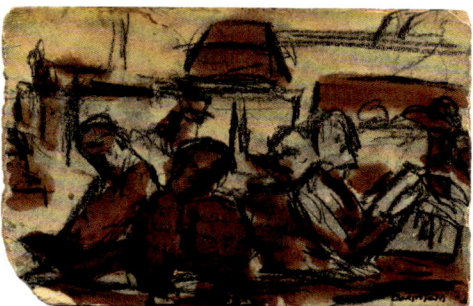

5. Study for *The Readers*, 1914.
Charcoal and watercolor on board, 4 x 6 inches.
Theresa Bernstein and William Meyerowitz Foundation.

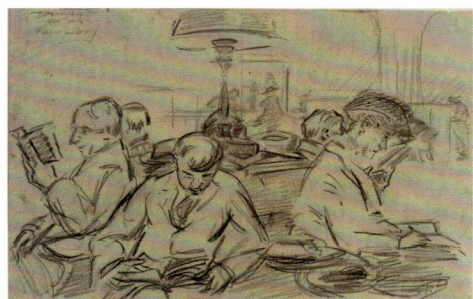

6. Study for *The Readers*, 1914.
Pencil on paper, 7⅛ x 10⅛ inches.
Collection Ervin and Diane Houston.

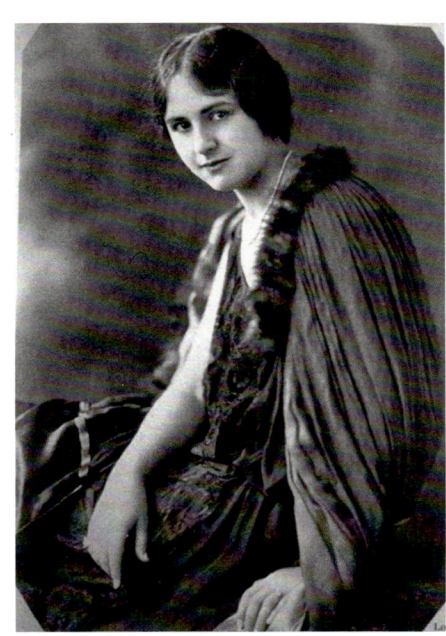

8. Louise Nevelson, ca. 1922,
Theresa Bernstein's most famous pupil.

subtracting a full decade. She thus hid from view some of her most impressive accomplishments and obscured her many early successes. In her own scrapbook, she intentionally did not record the dates of the newspaper and magazine reviews that she clipped out and saved. Making research still more difficult, Bernstein's journals have all disappeared since her death. Late in life she emphasized, "I not only painted but I also wrote and I kept a journal from a very early age."[7]

Although Bernstein wrote her books in old age, she had published a number of earlier articles that some, in writing about her career, have overlooked.[8] "The New York Public Library was my Alma Mater," she declared in the preface to *The Journal*. "I continued to write about art and was often asked to describe other artists whom I knew. Throughout my life I continued to paint and write."[9]

Bernstein was also an avid reader who enjoyed collecting old books. "In my teens I read the English classics, *The Golden Treasury* of English poets. James Joyce fascinated me, and I read Gertrude Stein, T. S. Eliot, and e. e. Cummings in the multinational American literary tradition."[10]

Indeed, *The Readers*, a major canvas of 1914, depicts people in the New York Public Library, where Bernstein made sketches for her large painting. She also portrayed the library in another painting a few years later. Despite her love of books and writing, Bernstein in old age sometimes confused names and dates, though most of what she wrote bears up to scrutiny.[11]

As I began to retrace Bernstein's life and art, I came to realize that her story would also cast light on the plight of other women artists. I also thought about the sculptor Louise Nevelson, one of the exceptions who managed to win a broad market and

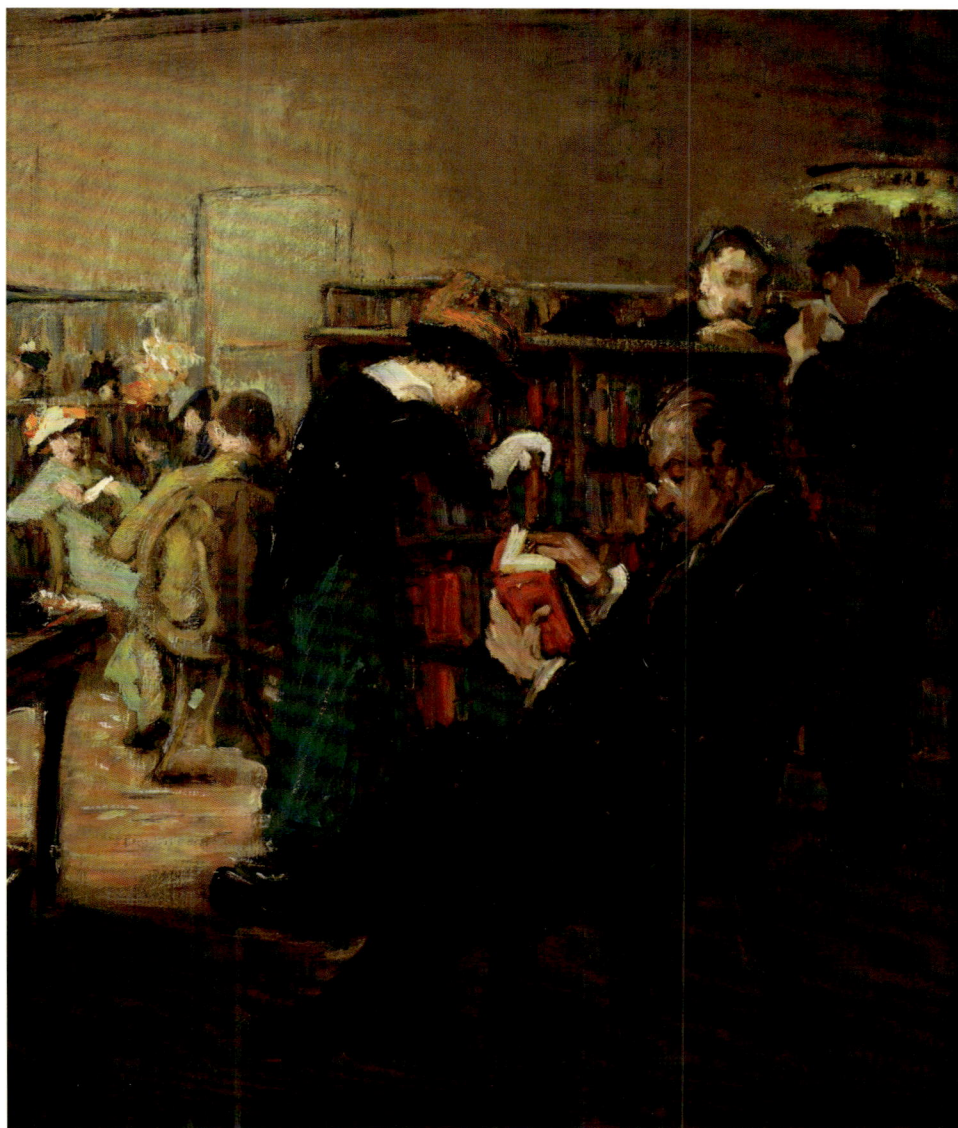

7. *New York Public Library Interior*, ca. 1918. Oil on canvas, 24 x 20 inches. New York Historical Society.

whose artistic reputation is now secure. When Nevelson arrived in New York from Maine, her first art teacher was Bernstein, whose attention she continued to credit.[12] Bernstein also recalled Nevelson as a student, noting that "she had an unusual feeling for form. She was always piling things up on canvas, striving to get structure into her ideas."[13]

Today Bernstein is mostly forgotten, while Nevelson remains a star, her sculpture prominently displayed in public collections and her life and art the subject of many books. We must ask why Bernstein slipped from notice. Why has she so rarely figured in the history of American art? As a young artist, when she first showed her work in the 1910s and 1920s, she achieved incredible momentum and won accolades and prizes. Yet by the 1940s, her reputation had faded. One factor leading to the eclipse of her work may be her continual impulse to promote her husband's art instead of her own. "After her marriage to Bill, she focused on him and pushed his career and not her own," commented Jonathan P. Harvey, who as a child in Gloucester during the 1950s studied with Bernstein and then became and remained a friend. "She kept painting but took a time-out until after his death."[14]

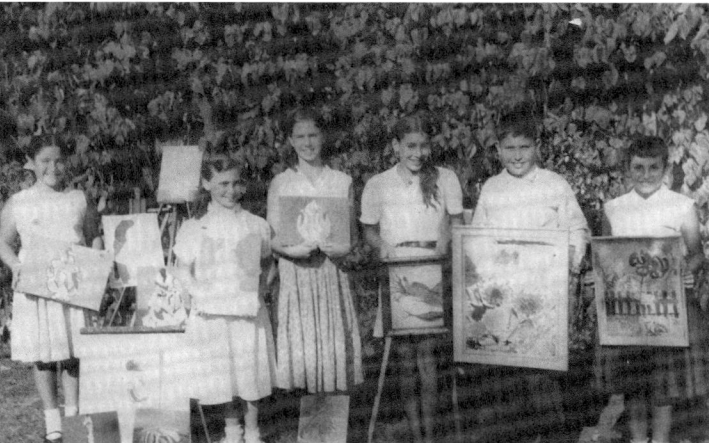

9. "Budding young artists, members of the Theresa Bernstein Meyerowitz junior art class, Gloucester, show off their paintings." *Left to right:* Barbara B. Gold, Susan G. Cohen, Betsy H. Cohen, Nancy A. Lappin, Jonathan P. Harvey, and Eve E. Bernstein, 1953. Photograph courtesy Jonathan P. Harvey.

Nevelson, not saddled with an artist husband, won the support of the young Arnold Glimscher when he was making his mark as a dealer in art. Bernstein did show at major galleries but never bonded with any one dealer. Instead of allying herself with an important gallerist who could have promoted her work, she joined many professional artists' organizations, especially those featuring women and artists like her and her husband, who worked in Gloucester, where she and Meyerowitz spent their summers. Such relatively parochial connections may have been another factor in her career's decline. Nor did Bernstein follow the trend to abstract expressionism that had begun to dominate American art by the end of World War II.

In any event, it was perhaps inevitable that new generations came to overshadow Bernstein, since her life did span three centuries that witnessed many changes both in art and in how art reached the market. If no one factor can explain how and why Bernstein's reputation faded, her remarkable talent, energy, and accomplishment, her ability to navigate the shoals of gender stereotypes, and the fact that she was repeatedly singled out and commended by both male and female critics should earn her a place in the history of American art.

BERNSTEIN'S CHILDHOOD AND EDUCATION, 1890–1911

Theresa Bernstein, like Louise Nevelson, grew up in a Jewish family who had emigrated from Eastern Europe. Nevelson, born in 1899, was already three years old when her parents came, while Bernstein was still an infant when her family arrived in 1890.[15] She captioned a photograph of herself "Theresa Bernstein in New York at the age of 1½."

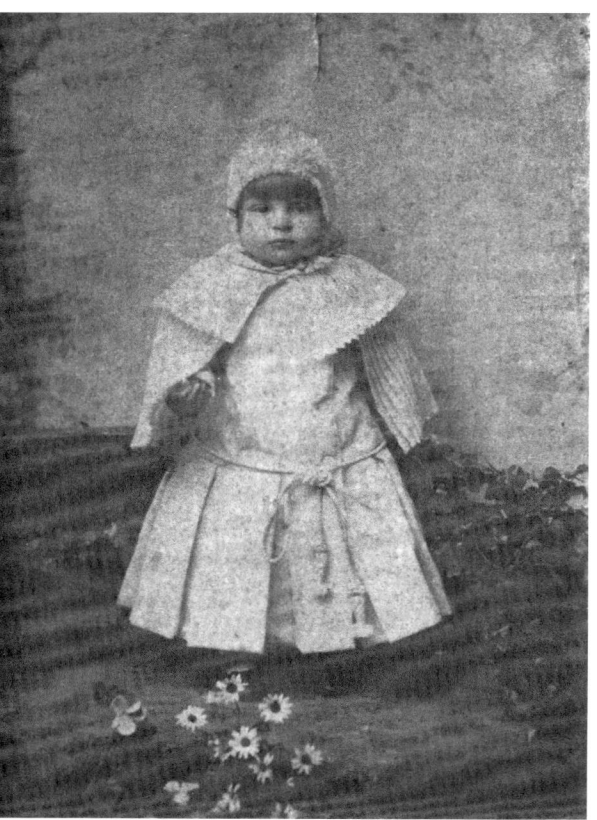

10. Theresa Bernstein at the age of 1½ years.

Born in Cracow on March 1, 1890, but raised in Philadelphia, Bernstein never admitted publicly that Cracow was her birthplace. She preferred to pretend that she was American-born, though late in life she did confide to close friends that she had been born in Cracow.[16] She claimed she was named Theresa because her father's "family originally came from Spain, escaping at the time of the inquisition to Holland and from there to Austria."[17] The Spanish connection would account for a Jewish girl's having a name associated with Roman Catholic saints, especially Teresa of Ávila (1515–1582) in Spain.

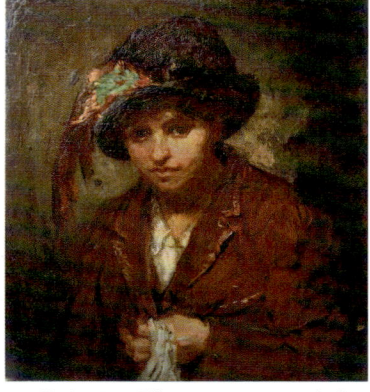

11. *Katie*, 1917. Oil on canvas, 20 x 22 inches. Theresa Bernstein and William Meyerowitz Foundation.

At the time of Bernstein's birth, the city of Cracow had become both a Polish national symbol and a center of art and culture, even while it belonged to the Austro-Hungarian Empire, which had long since granted a degree of autonomy to the entire region of Galicia. Bernstein, however, identified with Polish culture at least to the extent that she painted a number of portraits of Katie Kahlke, the Polish Catholic immigrant whom her family employed as a housekeeper. Bernstein also painted *Polish Church: Easter Morning* in 1916 and the darkly dramatic *Carnegie Hall with Paderewski* in 1914, marking the moment when she heard a performance by Ignacy Jan Paderewski (1860–1941), the Polish pianist, composer, diplomat, and politician.

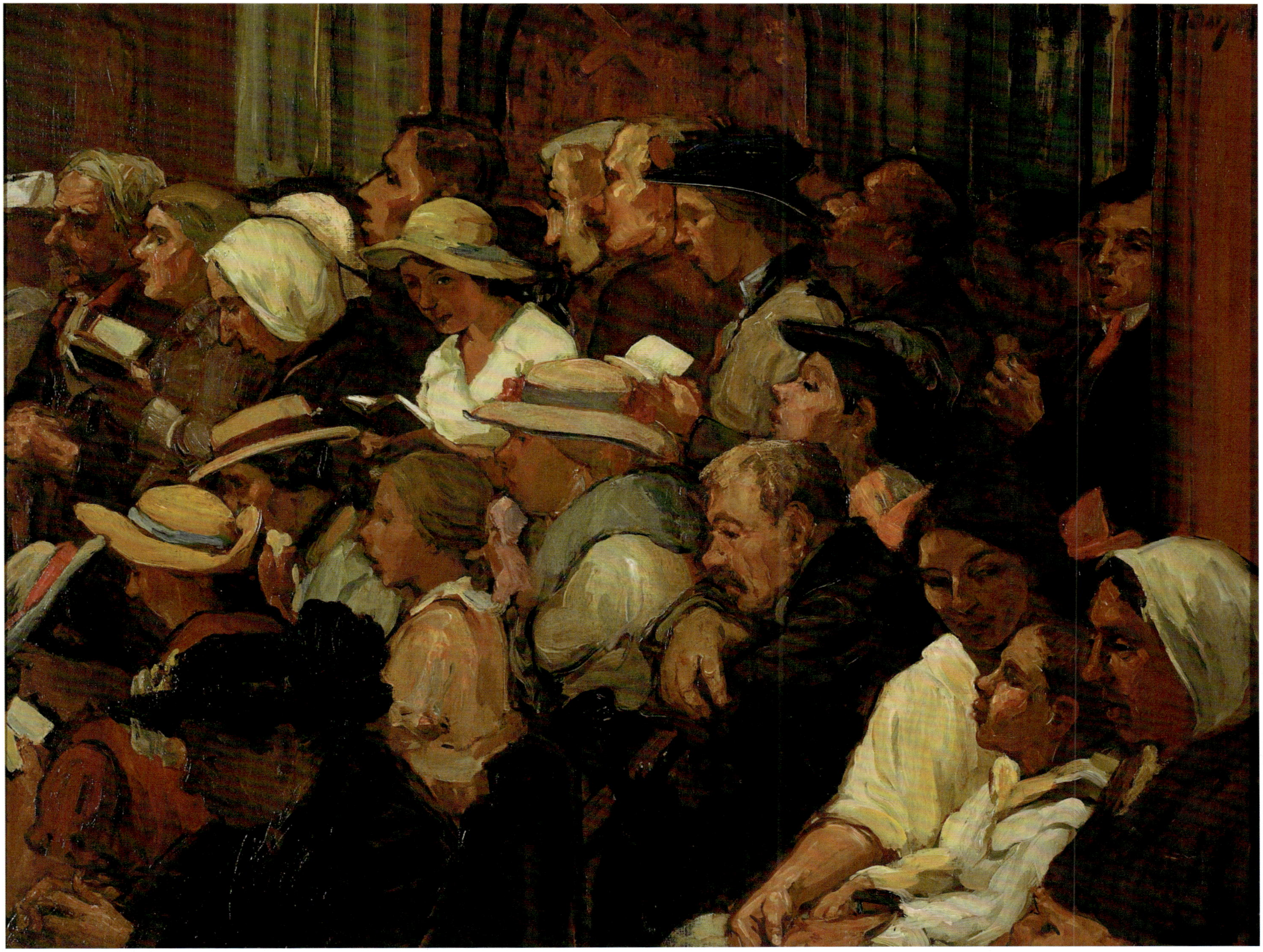

12. *Polish Church: Easter Morning*, 1916. Oil on canvas, 40 x 50 inches. Martin and Edith Stein Collection.

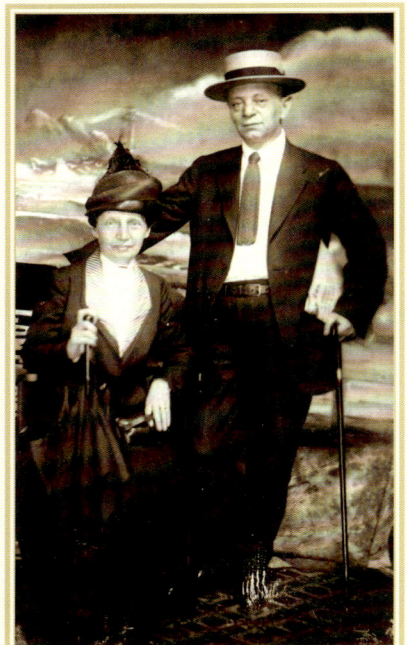

13. Anna and Isadore Bernstein.

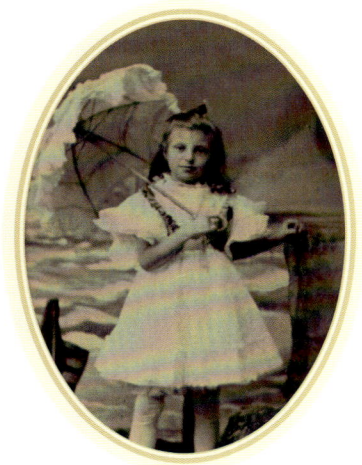

14. Theresa Bernstein with a parasol, ca. 1895.

A clue to Bernstein's decision to claim Philadelphia as her birthplace appears in *The Journal*. In the context of describing games she played as a child, she commented: "Some youngsters used disparaging words against anyone of immigrant background. The insulted answered back by saying, 'Sticks and stones can break my bones, but names will never hurt me.'"[18] Her offhand comment masks the pain she must have felt about prejudice expressed against her own immigrant family, but also suggests a woman who developed the ability to adapt to what life delivered.

Theresa Ferber Bernstein was the only child of Anne Ferber and Isadore Bernstein. Her father was a manufacturer of rayon (then called artificial silk). Her mother, who came from Cernovitz, Bukovina (near Rumania, also then in the Austro-Hungarian Empire and today in Ukraine), had studied at a convent school near Vienna, was "skilled at needlework and embroidery" and played the piano.[19] The family lived in Philadelphia, first on Hollywood Avenue and then nearby at 1631 North Twenty-Ninth Street.[20] Just after Isadore arrived in America, he worked in the Philadelphia factory of his brother, Henry, who manufactured millinery fabrics.[21]

Bernstein attended kindergarten at the Church of the Covenant located on the corner of North Twenty-Seventh Street and Girard Avenue in Philadelphia, where she was known as "Tessa."[22] She graduated from public school in the city.[23] Before 1940, children under the age of twenty-one automatically became naturalized American citizens upon the naturalization of their father, so Bernstein never needed to file for citizenship. Her doting parents sent her to dancing school for ballet lessons, where she recalled drawing some of the dancers at the barre.[24] She recalled, "Both of my parents were very drawn to music and often went to the opera, taking me along with them."[25]

Bernstein liked to tell the story of the family doctor commissioning her when she was only thirteen to paint a copy of an old photograph of his mother. The copy pleased him so that he then asked her to paint a portrait of his three-year-old niece. Since the child insisted upon watching the work, Bernstein put her in front of a mirror so that she could see her portrait being painted.[26]

Theresa's mother kept a journal that documents her pride in her only child and her encouragement of her daughter's talent.

"Whatever choices I made," Theresa herself recalled, "my parents were completely satisfied. They assumed that I had enough sense to do the right thing."[27] During the summer of 1905, when she was just fifteen, Theresa and her mother traveled with family friends to Europe, visiting Berlin, Bremen, Vienna, Munich, Zurich, Cherbourg, and Paris. They also toured Karlsbad, Marienbad, Lucerne (saw Mount Rigi and Mount Pilatus), Frazensbad (in western Bohemia), crossed Lake Constance, and spent time visiting relatives in her birthplace, Cracow.[28]

The culture encountered in Europe clearly won Bernstein's admiration, yet she remained committed to her American identity, which must have pleased her parents. Their religious outlook and worldview were modern, so they provided her with opportunities for both secular and religious education. Bernstein was confirmed at the Jewish Reform Congregation Keneseth Israel in Philadelphia on May 19, 1907. The next month, on June 24, she graduated from the William D. Kelley School, where she was chosen to give the "Address to Undergraduates." Bernstein won a Board of Education Scholarship to attend the Philadelphia School of Design for Women (now Moore College of Art) for the year 1907–8, after competing by making "a charcoal drawing of growing onions seen through a green glass planter."[29] She was admitted to art school for the "Normal Art Course" on October 1, 1907.[30]

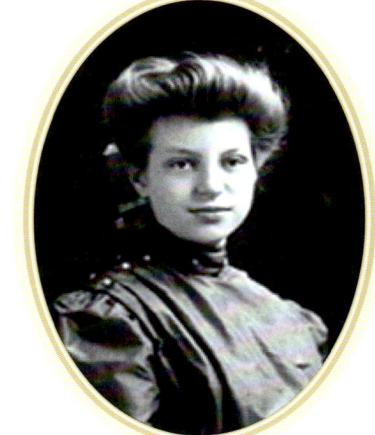

15. Theresa Bernstein at age fourteen.

The story of how Bernstein's talent attracted notice is told in "Discoveries of Genius," a column written by J. P. Glass for the *New York Evening World*.[31] The dramatic occasion was a pre-Memorial Day visit to the school by a Civil War veteran called Dr. Blackwood (William Robert Douglas Blackwood,

1838–1922). Bernstein felt compelled to sketch his portrait in chalk on the blackboard. Her teacher recognized her exceptional talent in the impromptu drawing and brought her to the attention of the principal, Charles S. Boyer. Both her teacher and Boyer then encouraged her to compete for a four-year scholarship at the Philadelphia School of Design for Women. The exam required Bernstein to work in charcoal for the first time ever, but she still won the prize. "Strangely enough," Glass reported, "she didn't know at first if she wanted it. All her life she had possessed an ambition to write. She wanted to go through high school and Bryn Mawr. But finally the diplomatic counsel of Miss Rogers decided her in favor of the brush."[32]

At the School of Design, first-year students in the "preparatory class" learned basic, realistic rendering and technique in pencil, charcoal, and brush. The "Normal" course was intended to educate future teachers in a standard curriculum of drawing from the antique and then from life. Harriet Sartain (1873–1957), a watercolorist known for her landscapes and flowers, taught courses in both watercolor and the history of art. Miss Sartain's first-year course appears in the catalogue as "charcoal drawing in light and shade from geometrical solids and vases with applied perspective, progressing through more difficult casts to the antique."[33]

Bernstein not only studied with Harriet Sartain but also came to know her aunt, Emily Sartain (1841–1927), the principal. Emily Sartain emphasized dedication and ambition to succeed, lamenting the "singular and suggestive fact that we have very few women painters who are entitled to be called great."[34] For women's failure to imagine the "highest genius" within themselves, Emily Sartain blamed discrimination and restrictions imposed by men. She encouraged her students to pursue respect and recognition. "If we have no great woman-artist," she argued, "it is because woman's hour has not yet struck. But the hand already nears the figure twelve on the dial."[35] It would seem that Bernstein was listening carefully.

We know that Bernstein in her first year took art history with Harriet Sartain because her course notebook survives, preserved by Bernstein throughout her long life.[36] The notebook was required and had to be submitted to secure promotion. In a beautiful calligraphic script, Bernstein made notes on the history of art starting with ancient Egypt, Greece, and Rome. She also

attached with paste photographic reproductions called "The Perry Pictures," which were published in Boston and most likely ordered by the school to distribute to students. Bernstein sketched the three kinds of Classical orders—Doric, Corinthian, and Ionic capitals. She noted "the Evolution of Sculpture from Egypt to the Italian Renaissance." On the Renaissance in Venice she referred to "the great men of surpassing imagination," raising the question of just how much she and the other students in this women's art school thought about the absence of women artists in a course that ran from antiquity to Caravaggio.

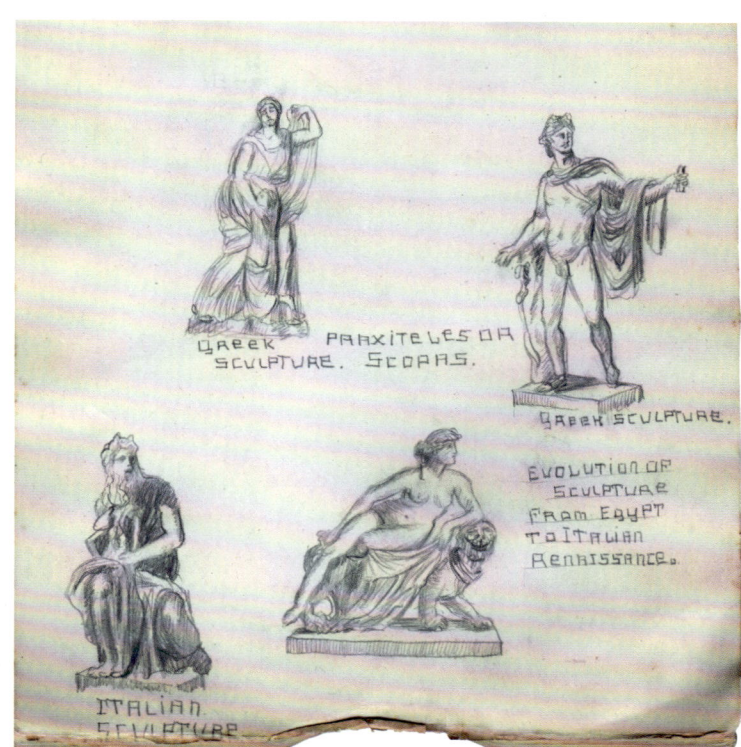

16. Detail of Theresa Bernstein's "History of Art" notebook on the "Evolution of Sculpture." Collection Paul Famolari.

Bernstein recalled her early ambition when she wrote that in order "to gain supremacy over other fields of art," she had studied sculpture with Samuel Murray, whom she remembered as a friend of Thomas Eakins.[37] Murray taught modeling from casts and from life. Bernstein also studied with Elliott Daingerfield, who taught still life, painting flowers from nature, and a full-length portrait from life in oil; and with Daniel Garber, who taught portrait painting from life, while Henry B. Snell, like Harriet Sartain, taught watercolor.

For a brief period, Bernstein also attended lectures on anatomy and architectural design at the Pennsylvania Academy of Fine Arts, a more prestigious coeducational school that aimed to produce fine artists rather than teachers.[38]

Bernstein recalled how Garber would come to observe the drawings on which students had worked for two or three weeks: "If he approved, he would take it away for exhibition. If he didn't approve, he would tear it up, saying, 'do it again.'"[39] She commented on the school's training that "drawing was largely accomplished through the use of charcoal and contrasts were achieved by shading from dark to light. Later, the graphite pen became the vehicle with which most drawings were developed."[40]

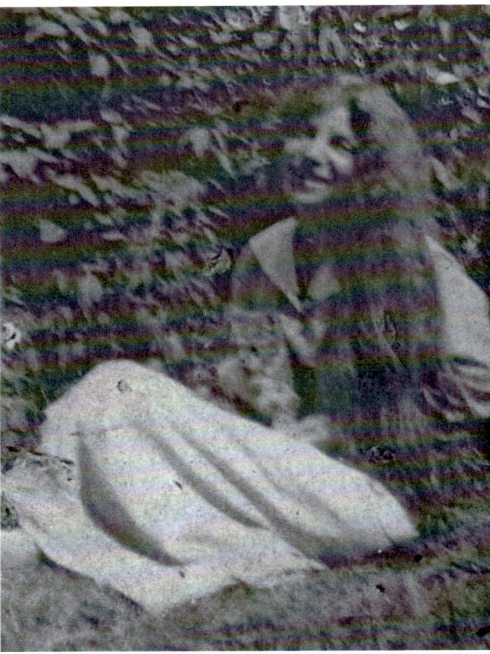

17. Theresa Bernstein with long hair.

While in school, Bernstein won prizes, among them the Sixth Annual Competitive Exhibit of Art Students held in 1909 by Wanamaker's, the Philadelphia department store.[41] She won with her oil painting, *White Roses*. When the School of Design gave out prizes in 1910 for its annual competitive exhibition of student work, Bernstein won one of "three minor prizes of $10 each" for her work in watercolor.[42] She also won a second $10 prize for her work in oils, so that she took two of the eight prizes announced. It was an auspicious start for a young artist about to win early acclaim.

In 1910 Bernstein traveled to Lumberville, Pennsylvania, to paint outdoors with her teacher Daniel Garber and fellow

students Emily Kohler and Leah Ramsey. They visited the New Hope studio of William Lathrop (1859–1938), an American impressionist landscape painter and founder of the art colony at New Hope. She also met visiting artists Robert Spencer (1879–1931) and Edward Redfield (1869–1965), both American impressionists.[43] Her small landscape studies from this trip survive.

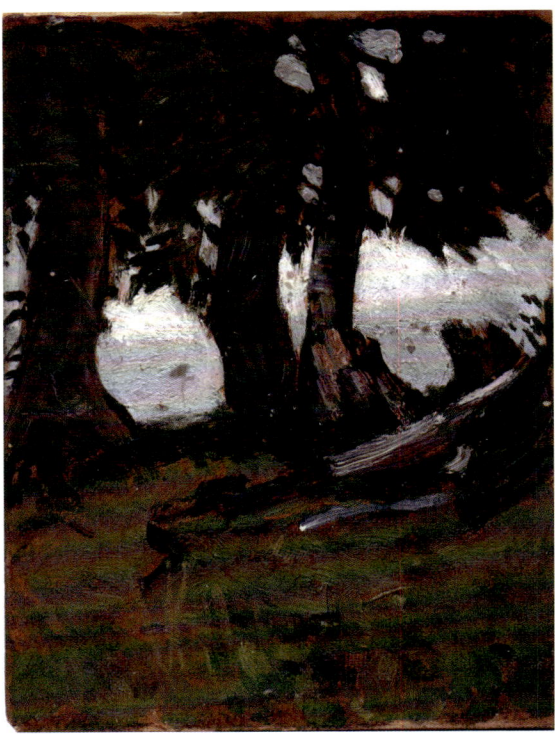

18. *Lumberville*, 1910. Oil on artist's board, 8 x 6 inches. Theresa Bernstein and William Meyerowitz Foundation.

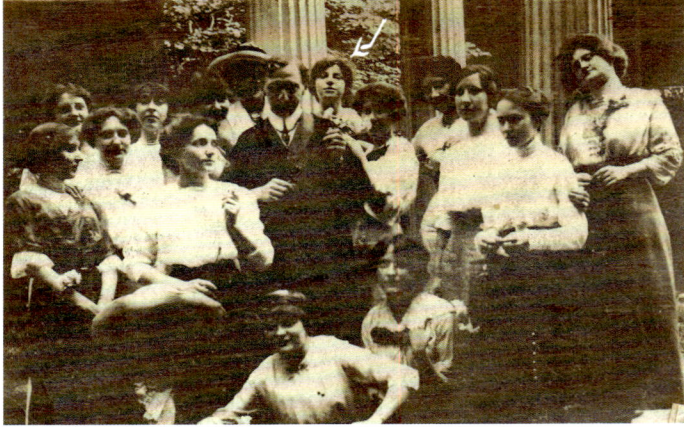

19. Theresa Bernstein with classmates at the Philadelphia School of Design, 1911.

In 1911, when Bernstein graduated from the School of Design, having completed the four-year Normal Art course in teacher training, she won the most important award, the John Sartain Prize "for General Achievement and Ability."[44] Upon graduation, she took a second trip to Europe with her mother, visiting Berlin and Munich. She recalled discovering expressionism and vivid color in the work of Edvard Munch, Vasily Kandinsky, and Franz Marc. Meanwhile, her father suffered the first of his business failures, which may have contributed to her motivation to succeed, resulting in remarkable determination and ambition.

Later that summer, to study further with Elliott Daingerfield, Bernstein traveled to Blowing Rock, North Carolina, a picturesque spot in the Blue Ridge Mountains that attracted artists. Daingerfield she later credited with having "released me into the realm of the Old Masters."[45] It is not clear if she felt she was being "released" from American impressionism or from the expressionism that she had encountered in Europe, but she continued to admire artists such as Michelangelo, Leonardo, Rembrandt, Daumier, Ingres, Rowlandson, Van Gogh, Whistler, and Eakins.[46] She asserted that she followed the examples of the old masters and "made notes of everything–whether it was on the street, in the opera, at a concert, at a parade, or on the beach. I observed people in their unconscious poses–they were my natural guide and the dimensions of my vision."[47]

On August 23, 1911, Bernstein began a month's study at the summer program of New York's Art Students League, located in Woodstock in the Catskill Mountains.[48] Though no instructor is listed on her registration card, the staff then featured Birge Harrison teaching landscape painting. Harrison might have come to Bernstein's attention in 1909, when a book of his lectures called *Landscape Painting* was published and reviewed as "a standard work for students," and "a fine commentary on the technique of the craft."[49] In writing and teaching, Harrison emphasized the creation of tonal harmony.

From October to December 1911, Bernstein enrolled at the Art Students League in the city, where she began to study with William Merritt Chase, then in his last year of teaching. She later recalled going there so that she "could work with a model."[50] Taking both life and portrait classes, she recalled Chase as "a very dapper individual, of average height in a pin-striped suit with a white carnation in his lapel, a grey moustache, and goatee, and the pince-nez with a black ribbon."[51]

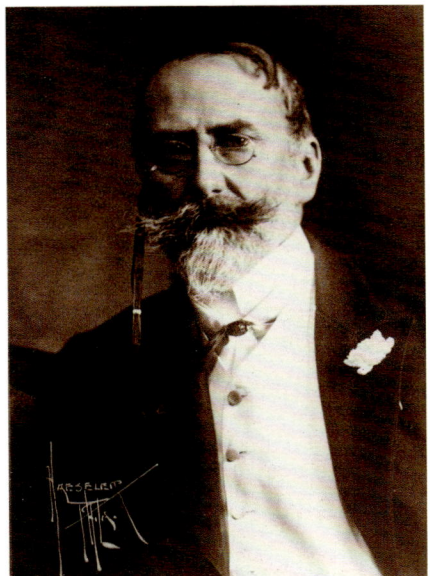
20. William Merritt Chase, 1900.

She found memorable his advice to "Paint a still life before breakfast" and noted how he painted fish "for their silvery gleam and the gold glint of brass and copper objects." Chase told her that she had "a technique like Frans Hals." She felt that Chase had "great courtesy and charm" and "an international art flavor" that she imagined came from his study abroad. From this era, still lifes by Bernstein include one after James McNeill Whistler, whose work Chase had admired.[52] Nonetheless, after her experience of expressionism in Europe, Chase must have seemed old-fashioned.

LAUNCHING A CAREER IN NEW YORK, 1912–1919

Bernstein moved to New York, encouraged by her parents, who had settled at 122 West Ninety-Fourth Street in Manhattan following the reversal in her father's business in Philadelphia. She described her parents as living in "a railroad apartment (little rooms from a hall) and I had one of the little rooms that I could sleep in and use as my cubbyhole. But I didn't do much work in the apartment."[53] It was a mark of her professional commitment that though living with her parents, she rented a place to paint at the Holbein Studio at 145 West Fifty-Fifth Street. It was a tiny windowless space,

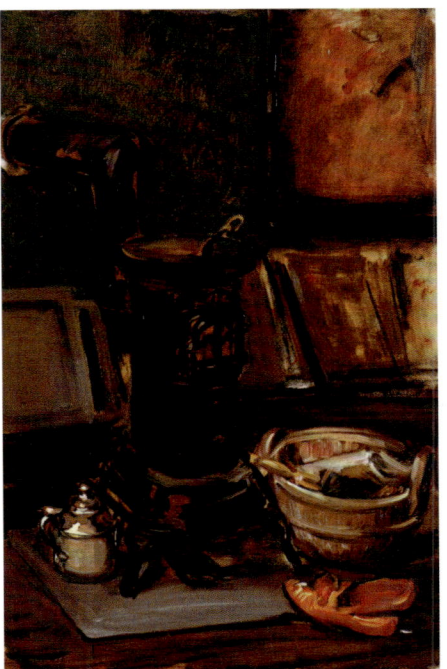

up three steep flights of stairs, with a skylight, but without heat or "sleeping possibilities."[54] The Holbein Studio, which was built in 1888, offered studio spaces above a ground-floor stable and once attracted such artists as Childe Hassam, John Singer Sargent, Cecilia Beaux, and George Inness.[55] Bernstein recorded this space in her painting *Holbein Studio* in 1916.

21. *Holbein Studio*, 1916. Oil on canvas, 37 x 24 inches. Montclair Art Museum, Montclair, New Jersey. Gift of Girard Jackson.

Many recognized Bernstein's talent. Her Philadelphia art school teachers continued their encouragement; Sartain, Daingerfield, and Snell all kept in touch.[56] Her mother's diary for October 1912 records that her daughter had sent a watercolor to the National Academy of Design in New York, as well as some sketches to a dealer named Powell (William H. Powell Art Gallery, located at 983 Sixth Avenue between 55th and 56th Streets, which advertised "A Complete Supply of Artist Materials").[57]

Bernstein herself wrote about "the art supply shop where I used to get my paints. The owner, Mr. Powell, took an interest in the sketches I brought him for framing."[58] Powell, who showed American artists and included women as well as men, bought a few of Bernstein's pictures.[59] It was he who suggested that she enter her work in the juried show at the National Academy of Design. She entered *Open Air Show*, which depicted "a backyard off Broadway" where "a couple of electric bulbs were strung around a greenish screen" used to show early silent movies. She produced a sketch for this painting, noting "Motion pictures were projected onto the sides of buildings."[60] (Later she would make an etching based on this composition, reversing the printed image.)

eventually invited Bernstein to come to England, promising to introduce her work to museums there and on the continent, but she declined, telling him that she was more interested in the American "environment."[62] Despite this attitude, her painting *Russian Ballet (Nudes Dancing in a Forest)* of 1912 suggests that she responded to one of the All-Star Imperial Russian Ballet's performances at New York's Metropolitan Opera in December 1911 or January 1912. Her style shows that she was aware of modernism, particularly of Cézanne and Matisse.

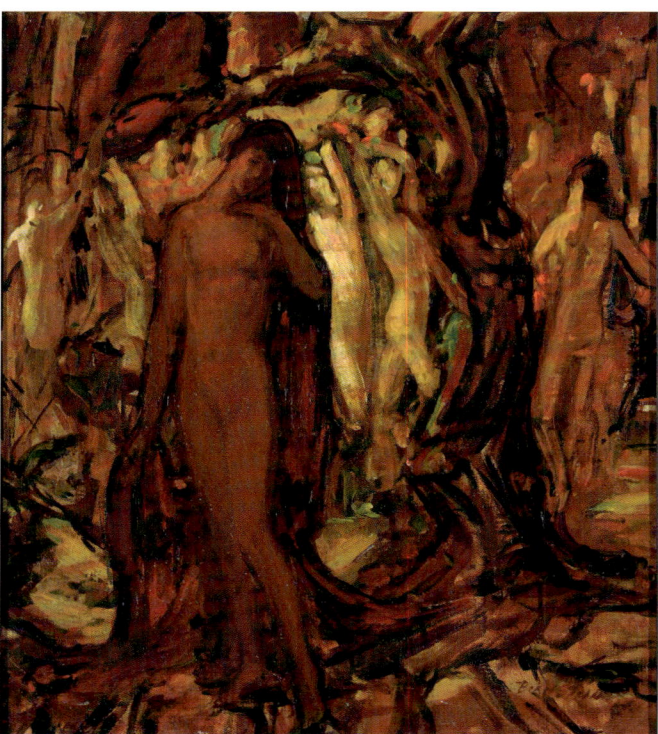

24. *Russian Ballet (Nudes Dancing in a Forest)*, 1912.
Oil on canvas, 26 x 22 inches. Martin and Edith Stein Collection.

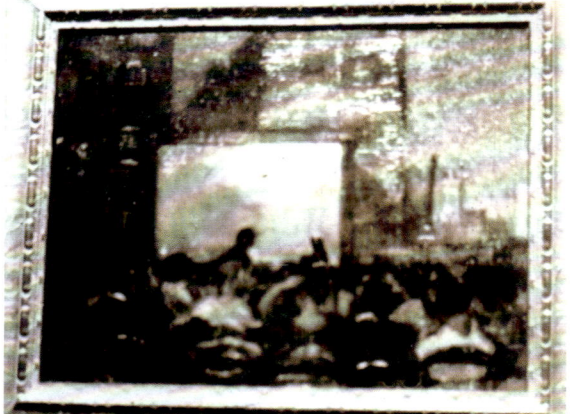

22. *Open Air Show*, 1912-1913.
Photograph of painting bought by John Lane. Now lost.

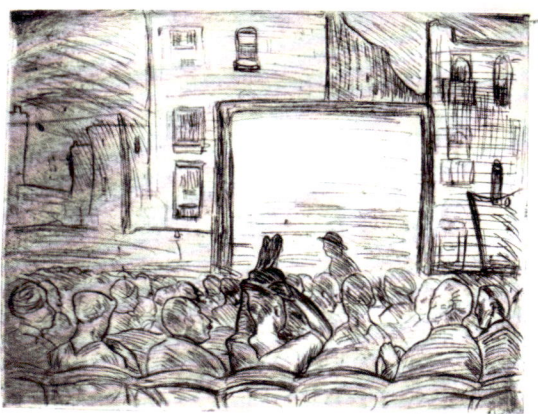

23. *Open Air Show*, ca. 1918. Etching, 7⅛ x 9¼ inches.
Private collection.

Open Air Show was in the academy's Winter Exhibition (December 20, 1913–January 18, 1914), which traveled to the Carnegie Institute, Pittsburgh, and the Art Institute of Chicago. At the latter venue, John Lane, a remarkable English autodidact, collector, and publisher of some controversial literature as well as the journal *International Studio*, purchased *Open Air Show*.[61] Lane

In 1913 Bernstein had visited the Armory Show in New York. She praised "the *Dancing Nude Figures* by Matisse, remarking that despite being hung high up, this work "had such carrying power that you could see it from every part of the Armory."[63] Marcel Duchamp's *Nude Descending a Staircase*, however, provoked her. The painting "was not a nude, there is no staircase, and nothing seems to be descending or ascending," she recorded in her journal.[64] She later recalled how French modernist art became the rage and how this new vogue among collectors affected the recent successes of the American realist painters, who came to be labeled the Ashcan School.

Just after the Armory Show closed in New York, Bernstein's mother reflected in her diary, "To be an artist is nothing but continuous work and worry and it absorbs a person's time, strength and thoughts entirely! And success is not so easy! I believe myself that Thea has lots to learn yet! Very few arrive in a very early age of life. It is a constant struggle for years!"[65]

Yet Bernstein would soon be showing with painters of the Ashcan School in nonjuried, artist-organized shows at the MacDowell Club (100 West Fifty-Fifth Street, nearby her studio). She preferred showing at MacDowell to the more vanguard modernist exhibitions at Alfred Stieglitz's Little Galleries of the Photo-Secession, known as "291" for its address on Fifth Avenue. Although she recalled visiting Stieglitz's gallery in the fall of 1913, Bernstein chose to pursue representation and figuration over modernist abstraction, making only occasional experiments.[66]

By the next year, Bernstein was showing her work regularly, sometimes at MacDowell, where her work appeared along with that of like-minded men and women artists in nonjuried shows such as the one held May 2–17, 1914. Today, like Bernstein, most of those artists are ignored if not forgotten: K. R. Chamberlain, Henry Glintenkamp, C. Bertram Hartman, Ruth Jacobi, Adelaide Husted Long, Frank Montegue Moore, Marjorie Organ, Josephine Paddock, Alethea Hill Platt, Henry Reuterdahl, Gertrude Lundborg Richards, Clara Tice, and Hilda Ward. Only Arthur Young, John Sloan, Stuart Davis, and Robert Henri are well recognized. Both Sloan and Young were active illustrators for *The Masses*, a socialist journal published from 1911 to 1917. Among the women, only Clara Tice is somewhat known today.[67] A reviewer opined that "Theresa Bernstein shows a capital subject," recognizing her originality, "a heavy cloud, brushed out of the way by a swift wind, umbrellas tugging at restraining hands, a youth wading with difficulty against the current, all of these telling the story of a windy day at the seaside as clearly as does the tipsy sail usually made to carry the brunt of such as message."[68]

From the start, Bernstein was confident about the value of her work and also submitted regularly to juried shows, which dominated the scene in this period. In the spring of 1914, her watercolor *Full-Blown Roses* was included in the *Twenty-Sixth Annual Exhibition of Water-colors, Pastels, and Miniatures by American Artists* at the Art Institute of Chicago. Around the same time, she showed another watercolor, *On the Beach*, at the Philadelphia Water Color Club with the Pennsylvania Society of Miniature Painters (see fig. 106). During this same period, Bernstein was also painting figurative watercolors such as *Grape Harvest* and *Celebration of Life*.

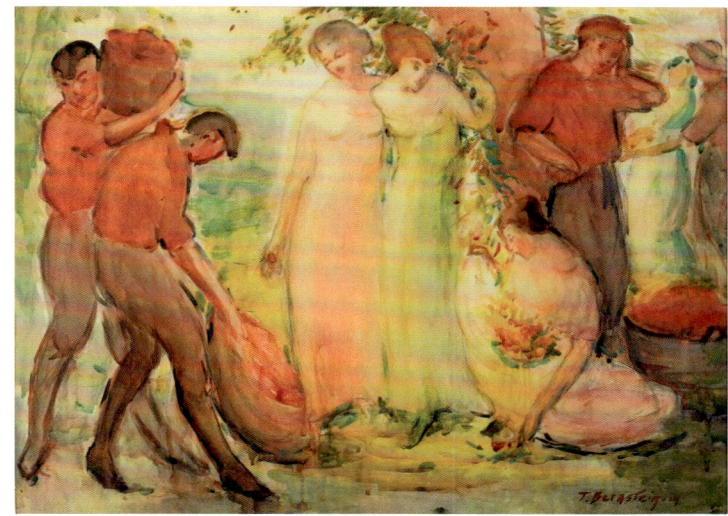

25. *Grape Harvest*, 1914. Watercolor on paper, 18 x 25 inches. Martin and Edith Stein Collection.

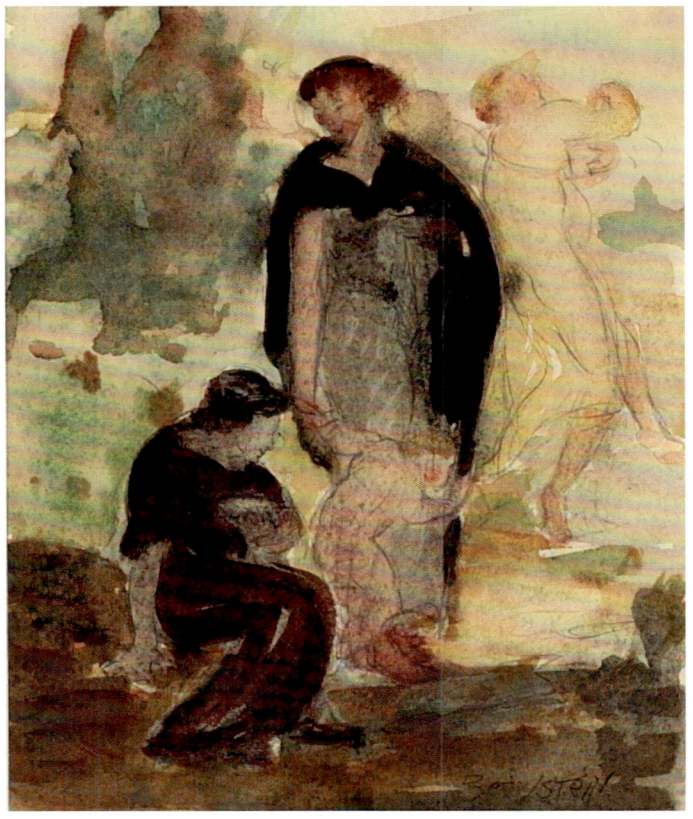

26. *Celebration of Life*, 1914. Watercolor on paper, 7½ x 6¼ inches. Martin and Edith Stein Collection.

While she excelled at still life and landscape, what Bernstein loved most was to paint people, especially if she could catch them unaware. She also said that she was "passionately fond of music, and when I hear it it suggests these pictures to me."[69] Thus she arranged to sketch people listening to Paderewski performing at Carnegie Hall in 1914. "Paderewski was playing," she recalled to a journalist who stopped by her studio, "and there was only standing room in the bal-cony. That is where I always go in Carnegie, and I thought what a splendid thing it would be if I could only sketch the expressions on some of the faces in the audience. I brought along my paints, and for three days sketched along unnoticed. The people were so intent upon the music they simply didn't know what was going on around them."[70] She recounted that she had followed around the man in her painting "until I was afraid I would be arrested as a mad woman."[71]

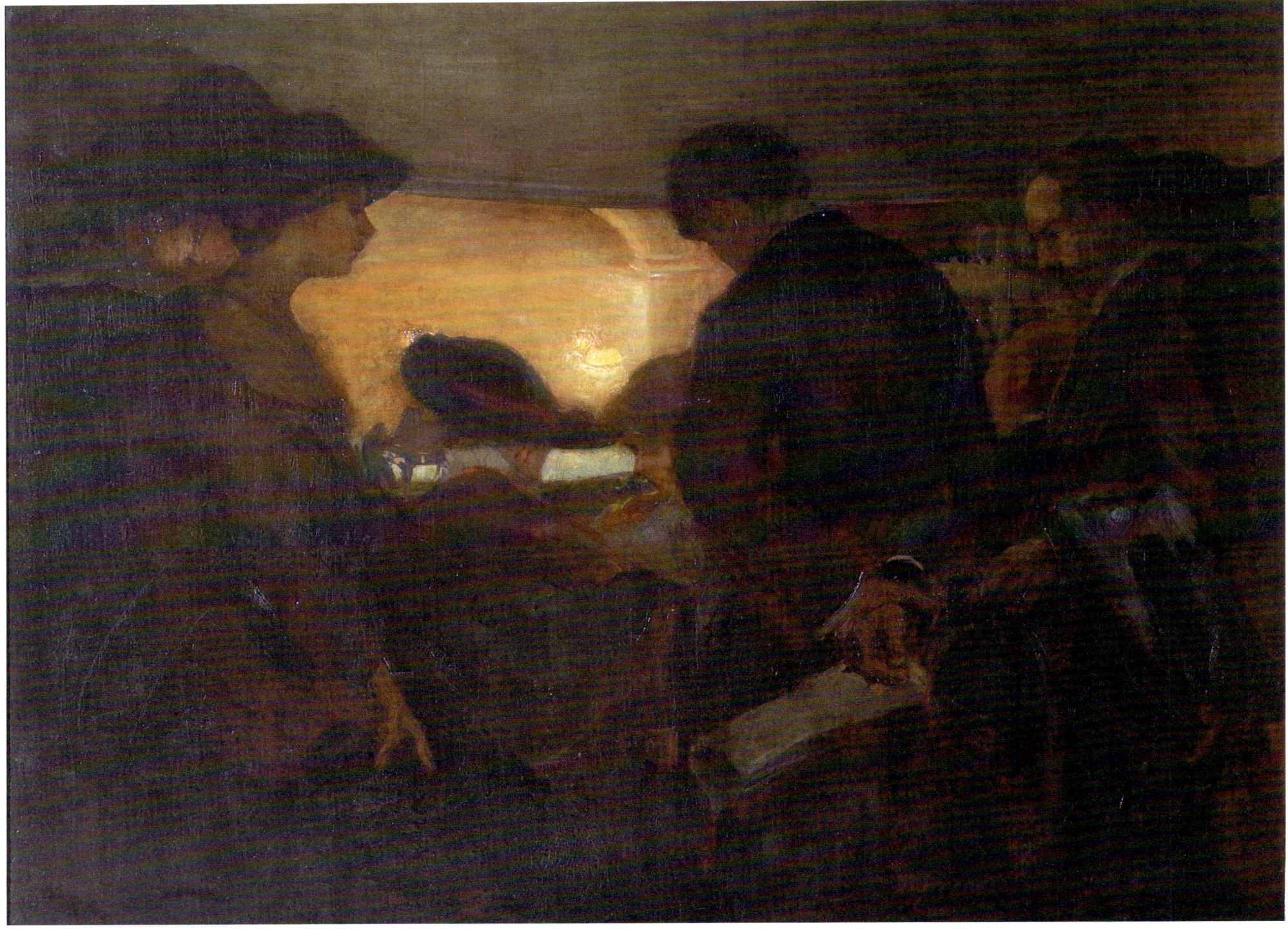

27. *Carnegie Hall with Paderewski*, 1914. Oil on canvas, 54 x 60 inches. Martin and Edith Stein Collection.

Her quip about being perceived as a stereotypical "madwoman" may reflect her awareness that her interest in woman's suffrage might have struck some as mad. By the end of this year, from December 19, 1914, to January, 17, 1915, Bernstein showed her canvases *Opera Night* and *The Suffrage Meeting* at the Winter Exhibition of the National Academy of Design. *The Suffrage Meeting* is a dramatic record of what Bernstein witnessed in women's struggle for the right to vote.

She recalled going night after night to sketch at the meetings, so she must have absorbed a lot of the politics.[72] At the time,

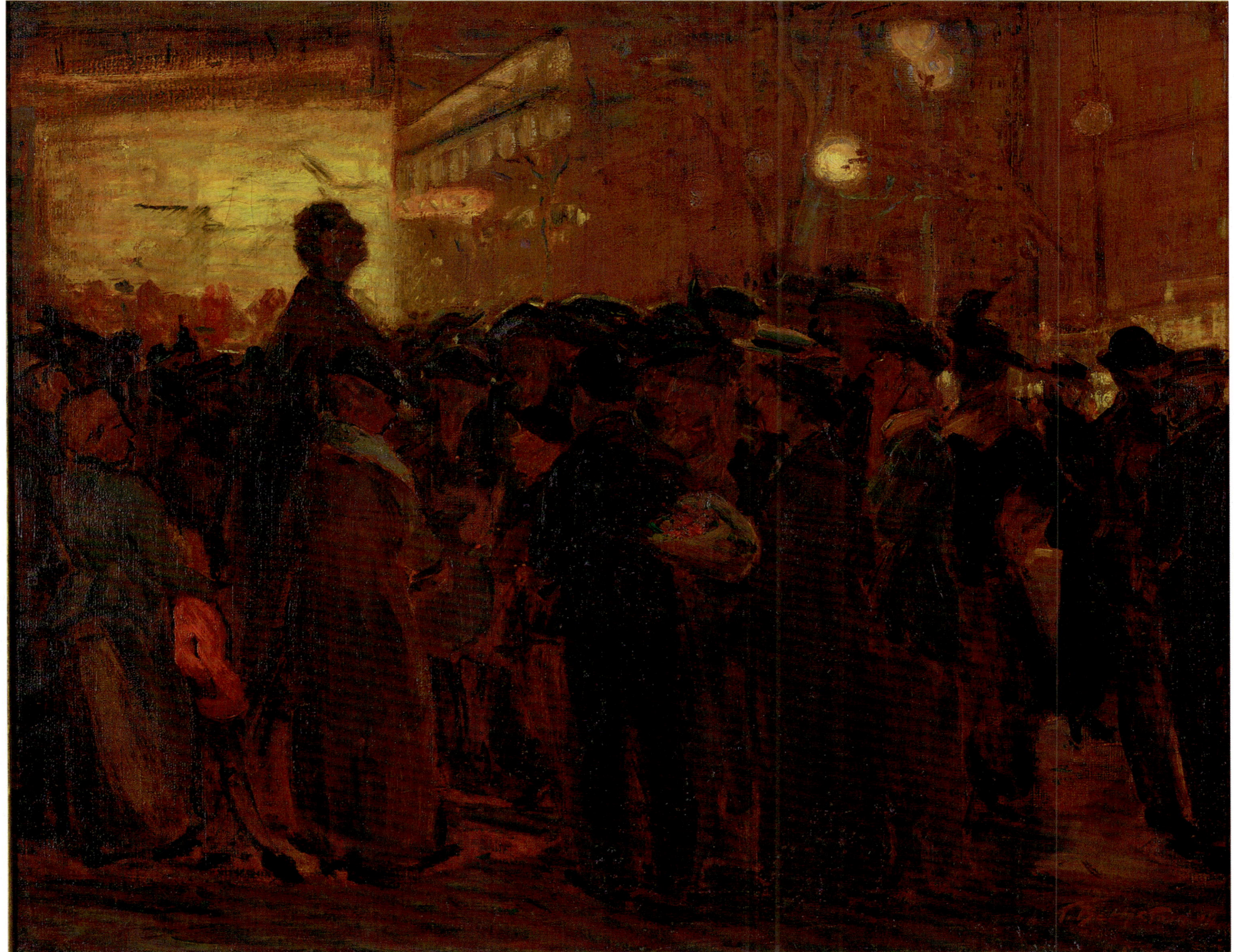

28. *The Suffrage Meeting*, 1914. Oil on canvas, 28 x 35 inches. Private collection.

she was asked to join groups of women artists such as the one that affiliated with the Women's Professional League. At the suffrage meetings, Bernstein remembered seeing three of the most famous activists to campaign for the amendment to the United States Constitution that would give American women the right to vote in 1920: Lillian Wald, the social worker, nurse, and activist for peace; Lillian Russell, the famous actress and singer; and Carrie Chapman Catt, who served as president of the National American Woman Suffrage Association and was the founder of the League of Women Voters.[73]

Bernstein later emphasized the parades and banners, the excitement of the spectacle, recalling, "I would go out at night, make sketches of the crowd, the lights on their banners. They had a banner with a yellow symbol and they would have crowds of women in those very unwieldy suits that they wore to signify their unity: We want the vote!"[74] She said that she made four paintings, all night scenes, about the theme of suffrage. She recalled the scene in one painting as "96th and Broadway . . . the lights would only glimmer on the outline of a figure, a woman carrying a basket of food or a man holding his newspaper would linger while the speaker would cajole them and tell them why it was important for women to have the same point of expression to be able to make a decision."[75]

Bernstein's commitment to the cause is suggested by her small surviving sketch of the British woman's suffrage leader Emmeline Sylvia Pankhurst (ca. 1913), whom Harvard University had banned from speaking on campus just two years earlier and whom others tried to block from entering the United States. Leading up to World War I, Pankhurst identified Germany as a threat, putting the same energy and determination she had previously applied to women's suffrage into patriotic advocacy of the war effort, which also caught Bernstein's attention.

Bernstein's activism for the cause of suffrage may have led to an invitation to participate in the Panama-Pacific International Exhibition, a world's fair held in San Francisco between February 20 and December 4, 1915, since her painting *Open Air Show* was shown in a room featuring only women artists. The stated purpose of the exhibition was to celebrate the completion of the Panama Canal, but it also marked the city's recovery from the 1906 earthquake. Among the older and more established women who took

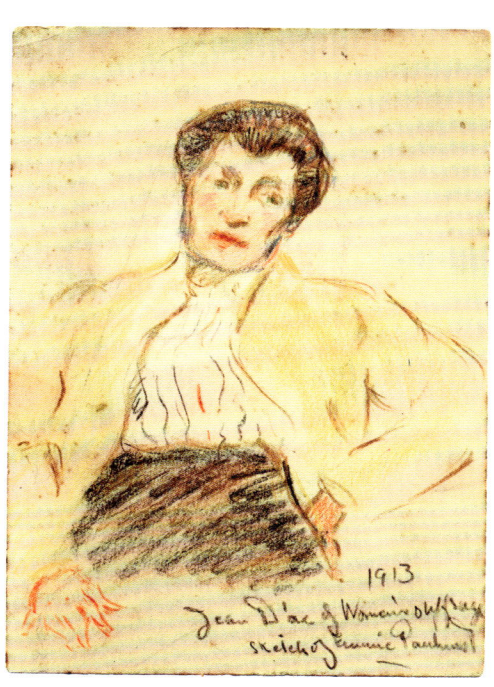

29. *Jean D'arc of Women's Suffrage, Sketch of Emmie Pankhurst*, 1913. Color pencil on paper, 7 x 5 inches. Theresa Bernstein and William Meyerowitz Foundation.

part were the painters Lila Cabot Perry, Lilian Westcott Hale, Mary Cassatt, and Violet Oakley, as well as sculptors such as Anna V. Hyatt, Janet Scudder, and Abestenia St. Leger Eberle.[76] Bernstein's inclusion in this prestigious show is a mark of her growing success.

Also in 1915, Bernstein's excellence won recognition from the women of Philadelphia's Plastic Club, which awarded her its Shillard Gold Medal for *Outing on the Hudson*, which one reviewer described as "quiet and picturesque, if somewhat coarse work."[77] The Plastic Club had been founded by women in 1897, in response to their exclusion from men's clubs. Among the club's founders was Emily Sartain, Bernstein's erstwhile principal. Enhancing communication among women artists and promoting their cause were the club's goals.[78] Thus, they organized shows of women artists with professional standards.

Yet Bernstein kept trying to exhibit her work with men as well as with women. At the Ninetieth Annual Exhibition of the National Academy of Design, from March 20 to April 25, 1915, she showed *The Music Lovers*, causing one reviewer to rave about the "stunning figure pieces of Theresa Bernstein." In this painting, she focused on a group of figures but maintained interest in their individual expressions and gestures. "A young painter hitherto unfamiliar to us who suggests that she may some day make a deep impression is Miss Theresa F. Bernstein," intoned the influential art critic Royal Cortissoz in the *New York Herald Tribune*. "Her canvas *The Music Lovers* shows a good sense of form and an easy, flowing style."[79] (Related is a smaller work on this theme, *Music Lover* [1913], which may have been an oil study for *Carnegie Hall with Paderewski*.)

In May 1915 Bernstein exhibited drawings at the MacDowell Club in a group that included such artists such as Henri, Sloan, George Bellows, and Marjorie Organ. One critic described her offerings as a "highly imaginative set of drawings for the poems of Rabindranath Tagore," a Bengali poet, whose work won the Nobel Prize in 1913.[80]

For the cause of suffrage, Bernstein joined nearly thirty of the same women who had shown earlier that year at the Panama-Pacific Exhibition to participate in a show at the Macbeth Gallery (September 27-October 16, 1915). The artists donated half the

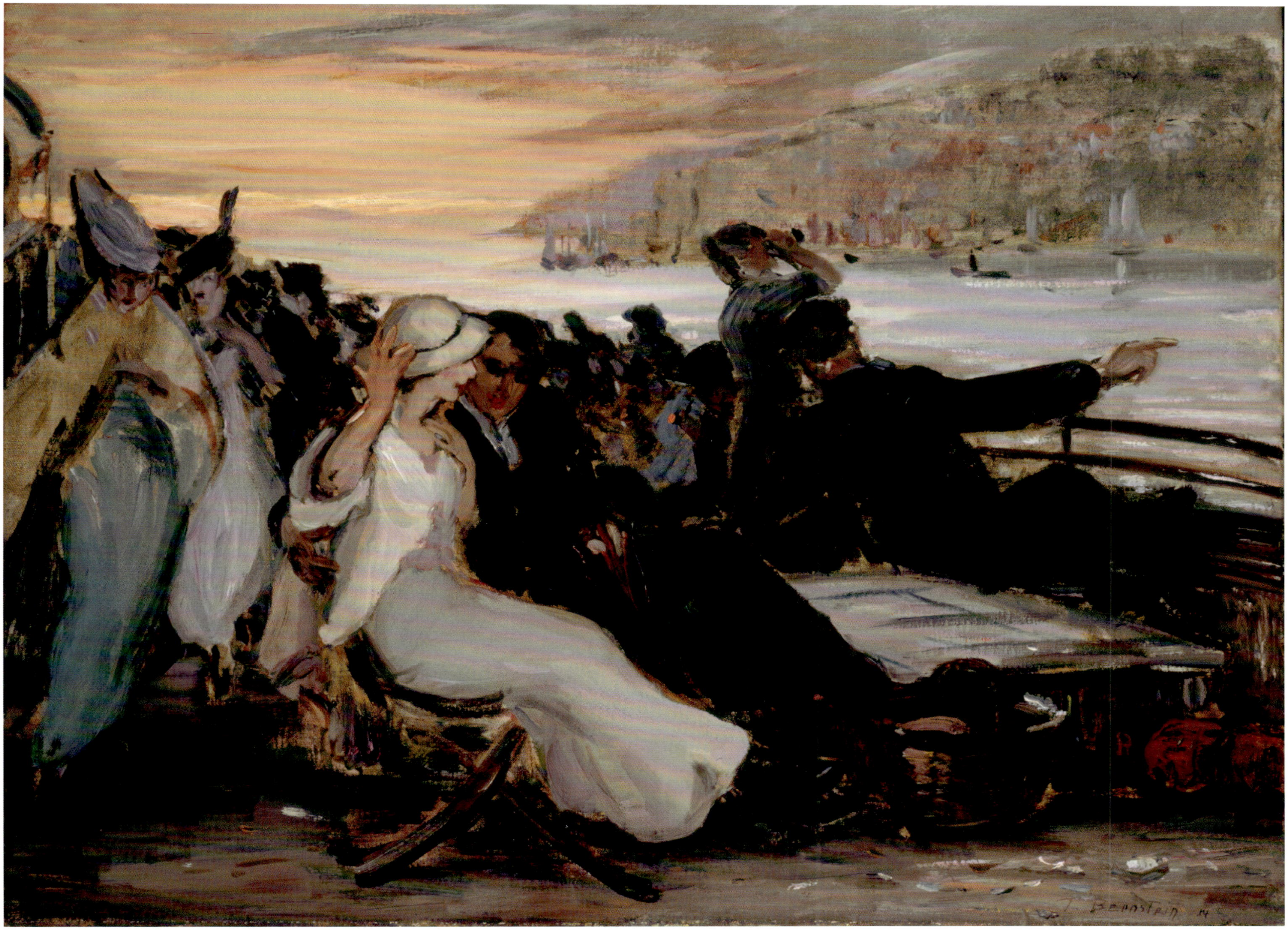

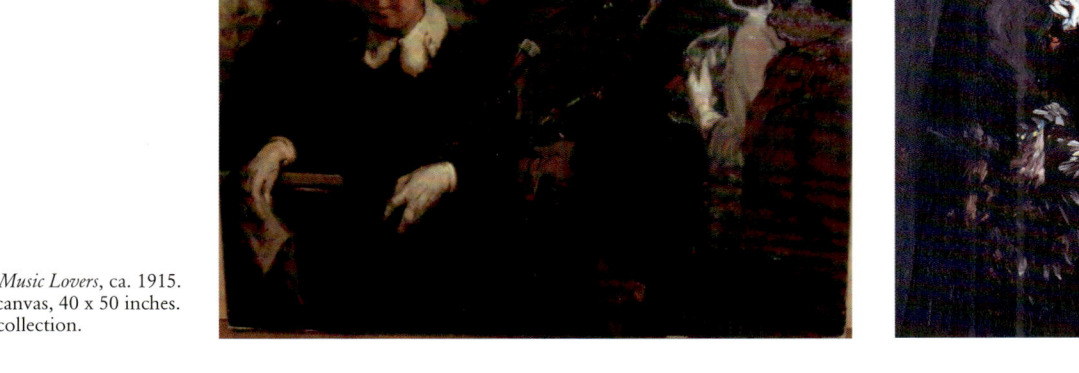

30. *Outing on the Hudson*, 1914.
Oil on canvas, 27 x 34 inches.
Helen and Edward Ezrick Collection.

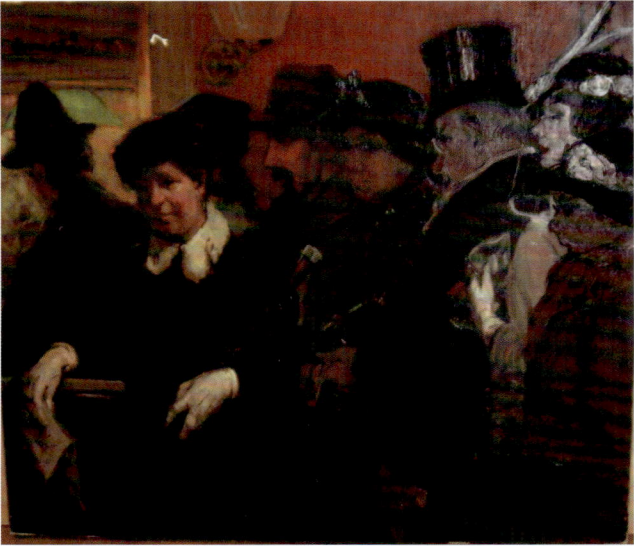

31. *The Music Lovers*, ca. 1915.
Oil on canvas, 40 x 50 inches.
Private collection.

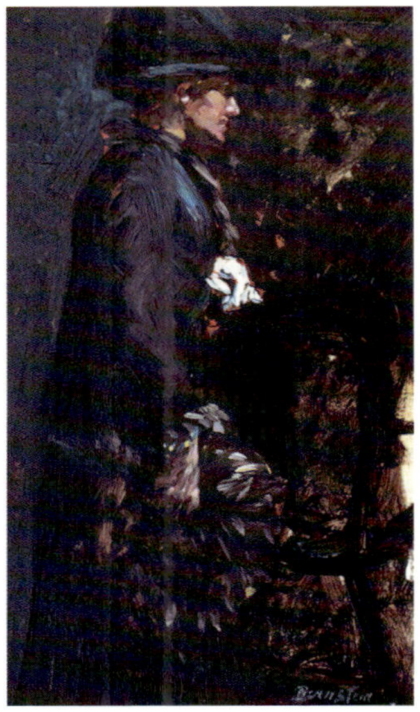

32. *Music Lover*, 1913.
Oil on board, 19¼ x 11⅜ inches.
Private collection, Courtesy Lepore Fine Arts.

proceeds from any sales, but Bernstein and Helena Dayton were the only contributors who addressed the theme of suffrage.[81] "All the contributors are enthusiastic suffragists," noted a reviewer. "Theresa F. Bernstein is in her slap, dashy, artistically effective element in 'The Suffrage Meeting.'"[82] Still another noted how special her painting was: "The movement itself is reflected in only a single canvas, Theresa Bernstein's able 'The Suffrage Meeting,' in which a skirted soap-box orator is at the center of a crowd of humble women of the city, the group being most effectively silhouetted against the yellow light of the street."[83]

Bernstein finished out 1915 by showing with the Association of Women Painters and Sculptors, who held an exhibition of small pictures and sculptures at the Arlington Art Galleries on Madison Avenue.[84] Participating in such all-women shows kept her in that network but apart from the larger male-dominated art world. Of the many other women in this show, only a few are known today: Agnes Pelton, Agnes Schille, and Jane Peterson among the painters, and Harriet Frishmuth, Janet Scudder, Alice Morgan Wright, and Mrs. H. P. Whitney (Gertrude Vanderbilt Whitney) among the sculptors.

Gertrude Whitney provided cash prizes for young painters in an organization called the Society of Young Artists. In June 1915 Bernstein, though passed over for the larger sums, received one of the ten prizes of $25 along with artists such as Louis Bouché and Eugene Higgins.[85] The contest included some 217 paintings all on display at Mrs. Whitney's Galleries (8 West Eighth Street), where the Whitney Studio Club held sketch classes, exhibitions, parties for artists, and where the award ceremony took place. Bernstein later recalled, "We [she and Meyerowitz] were members of the Whitney Studio Club. Gertrude was a very interesting person."[86] Like many struggling artists, Bernstein also praised the plentiful food offered at the Whitney Studio parties.

The young woman from Philadelphia had made the New York scene. Eager and adventurous, she was taking it all in. She later recalled seeing Loie Fuller dance in 1914, and that "her sense of coloring was highly developed."[87] But by the time Bernstein depicted her, the Chicago-born Fuller had long since become famous in America for her *Serpentine Dance* of 1891 and had

retreated to Europe, where she felt she had greater acclaim. In 1915 Bernstein saw Isadora Duncan dance, which inspired sketches on paper and a canvas. Duncan had already captivated painters such as Henri, Sloan, and Abraham Walkowitz, who alone among these artists showed with the more vanguard dealer Stieglitz.

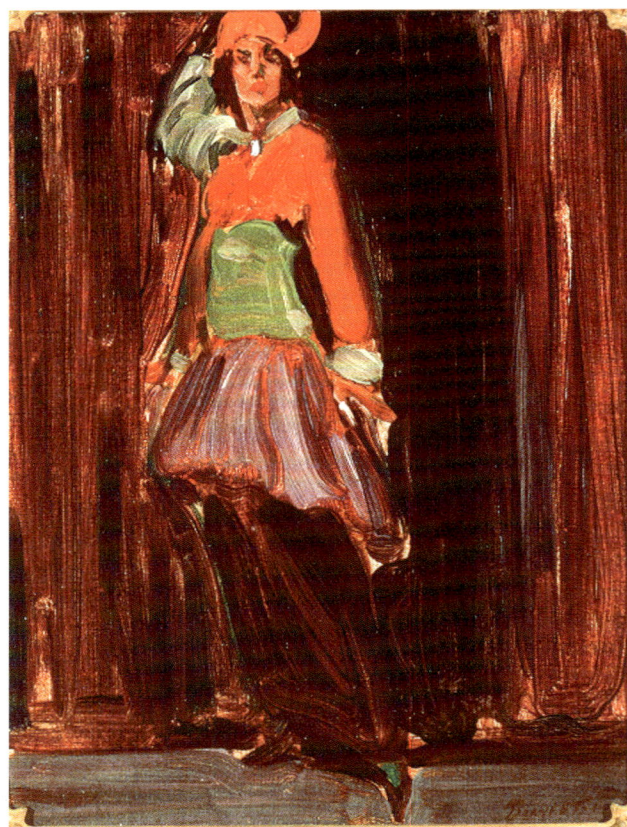

33. *Portrait of Loie Fuller*, ca. 1914, Oil on canvas, 16 x 12 inches. Huntsville Museum of Art, Huntsville, Alabama.

Around this time, Bernstein employed and befriended a Dada poet and artist, the Baroness Elsa von Freytag-Loringhoven, who, having fallen on hard times, was in New York earning her living as an artist's model.[88] Born Else Hildegarde Plötz in 1874 in Germany, she had married and divorced the architect August Endell, then married an archaeology student, Felix Paul Greve, following him to America in 1910. After Greve deserted her, she married the impoverished Leopold Baron von Freytag-Loringhoven in 1913, assuming his noble name. The baron left her in 1914 to enlist in the German army, only to be held as a French prisoner of war. The Baroness went to work as an artist's model at the Art Students League, the Ferrer School, and for various artists, among them Robert Henri, John Sloan, and Marcel Duchamp.

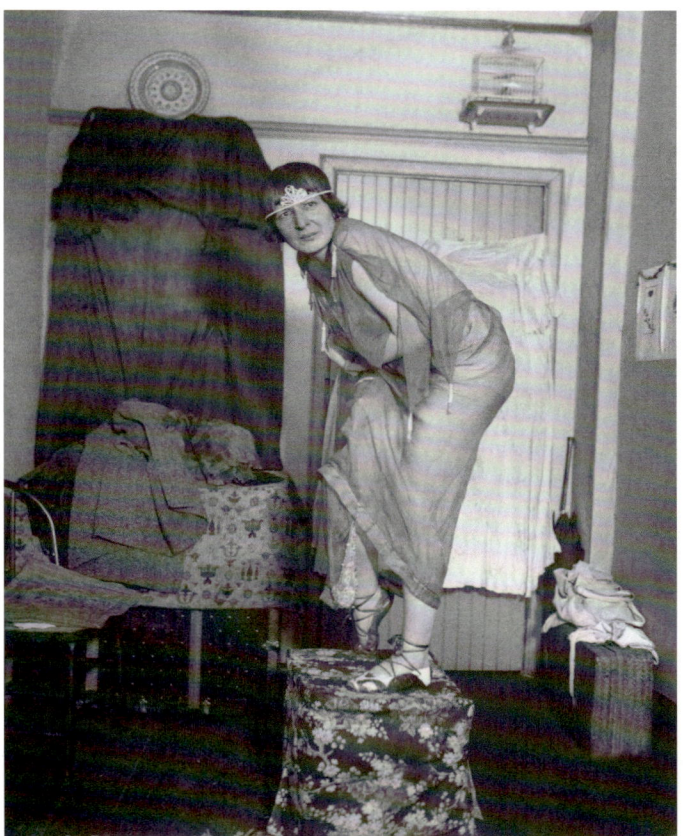

34. Elsa von Freytag-Loringhoven, ca. 1917. Photograph, Courtesy Francis Naumann.

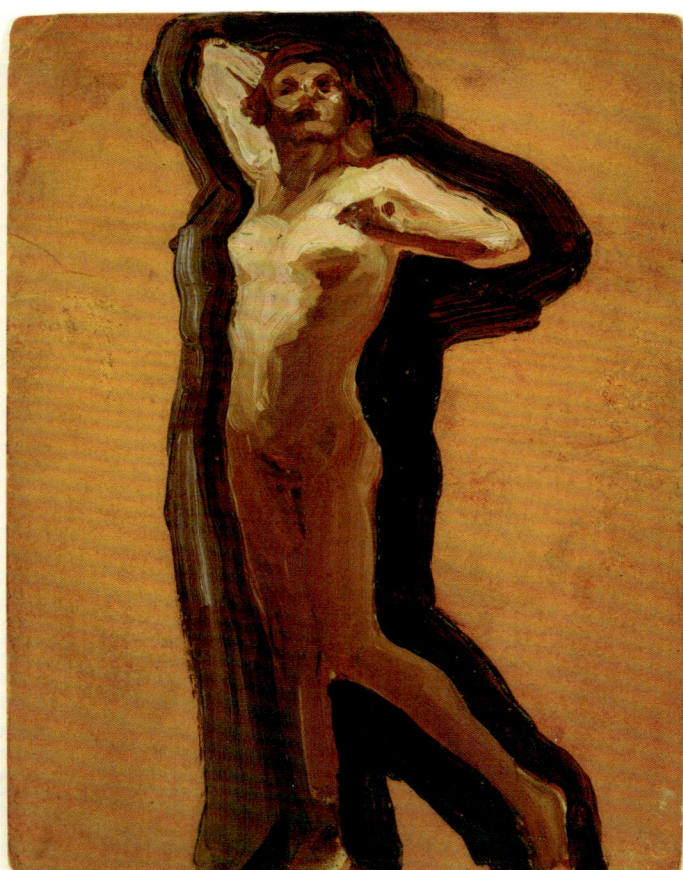

35. *Elsa von Freytag-Loringhoven*, ca. 1917. Oil on panel, 12 x 9 inches. Francis M. Naumann and Marie T. Keller Collection.

Bernstein first met the baroness, whom she described as "a tall, graceful young woman," when she answered a knock on the door of her studio and heard,

"'Do you need a model?'
I said, 'Would you pose?'
She said, 'Yes. Will you pay me?'
I said , 'Yes.'"[89]

"In those days you paid them maybe fifty cents or a dollar or seventy-five cents an hour. This model turned out to be the model that Marcel Duchamp used and he gave her my name.

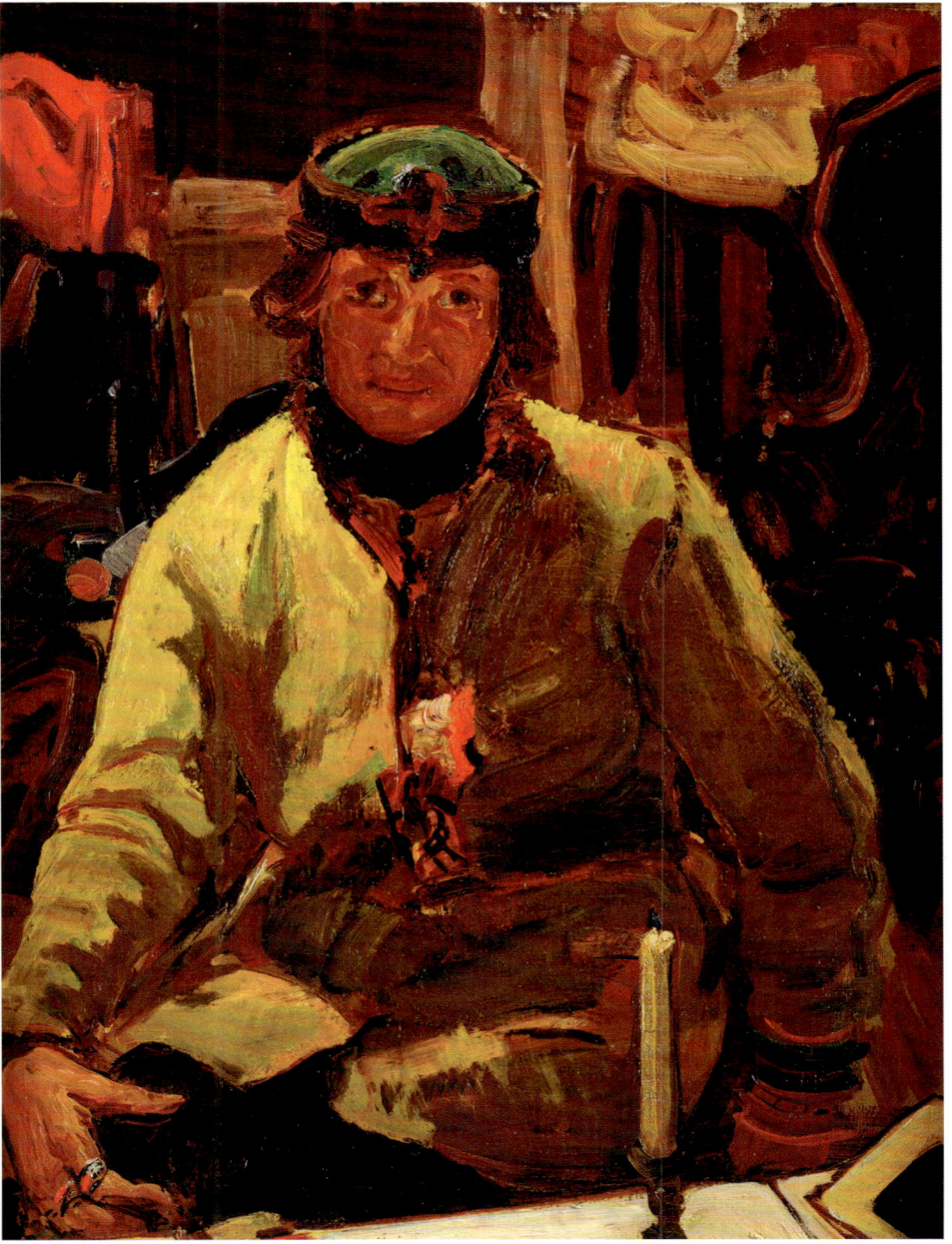

36. *The Baroness*, 1917. Oil on canvas, 35 x 27 inches. Francis M. Naumann and Marie T. Keller Collection.

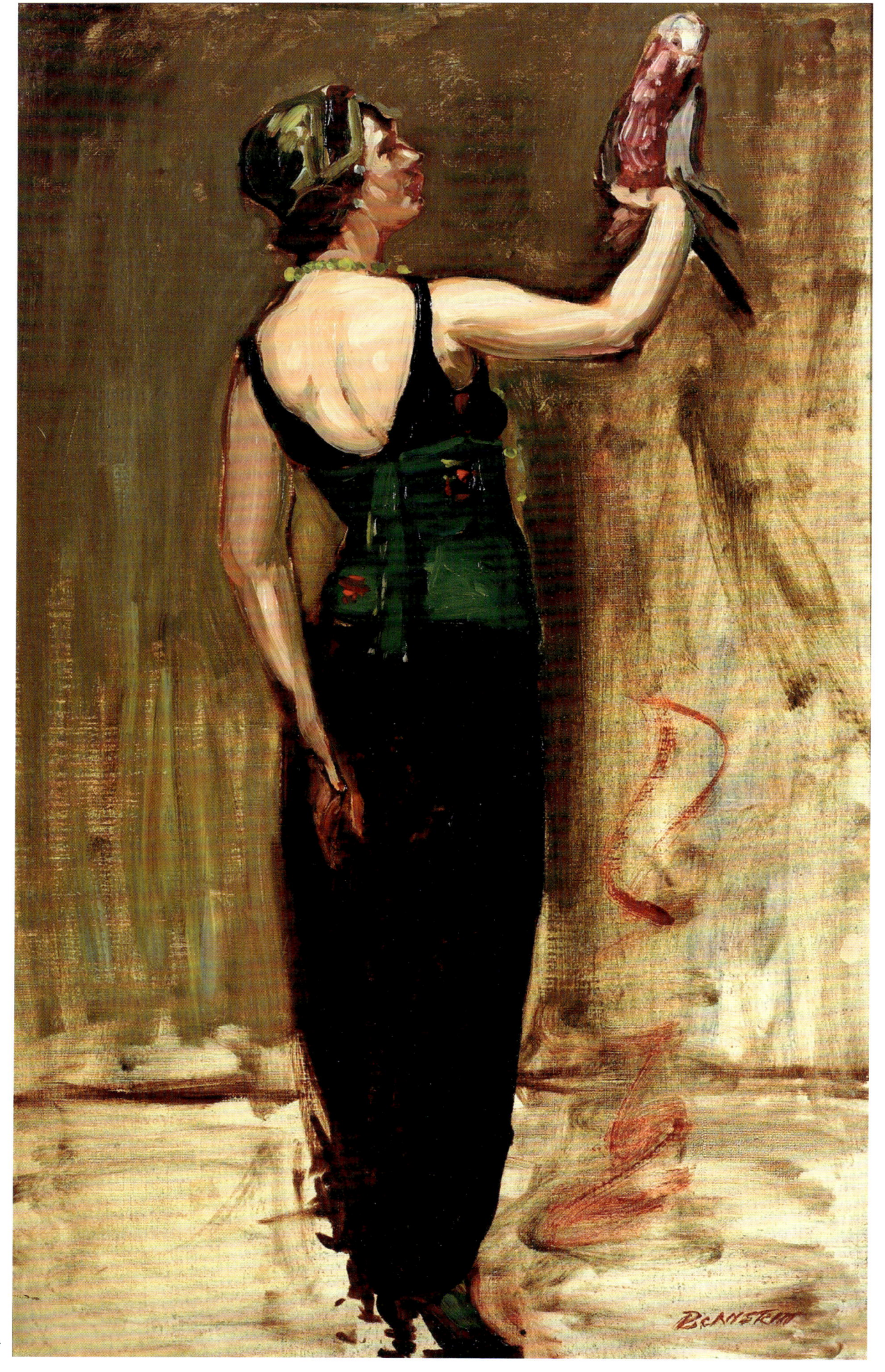

37. *Woman with a Parrot*, ca. 1917.
Oil on canvas, 40 x 25 inches.
Martin and Edith Stein Collection.

He had seen something that I'd done at the Macdowell Club . . . [and] was sending out his model to get more work."[90]

The baroness posed for Bernstein on multiple occasions, including for her portrait and as *Woman with a Parrot* and for the woman holding a parrot in Bernstein's canvas *Lilies of the Field* (1915).[91] According to Bernstein, she was representing "ladies of the night" or prostitutes dressed for work.[92] The women on the left side wear extravagant hats often associated with prostitutes' clothing by artists such as Sloan, who represented one in his cartoon for *The Masses* entitled *The Women's Night Court: Before Her Makers and Her Judge* in 1913.[93] Bernstein's title references Matthew 6:28: "And why take ye thought for raiment? Consider the lilies of the field, how they grow: they toile not, neither doe they spinne."[94] She probably drew upon the Christian text in order to employ with irony some of the same rhetoric that contemporary moralizers were using to condemn women forced to work by the economic oppression that denied them a living wage. Perhaps Bernstein, who had grown up in a comfortable middle-class family, but whose father had lost his business before coming to New York, was also empathizing with the baroness by referring to the need not to be anxious about life's necessities like food or clothing.

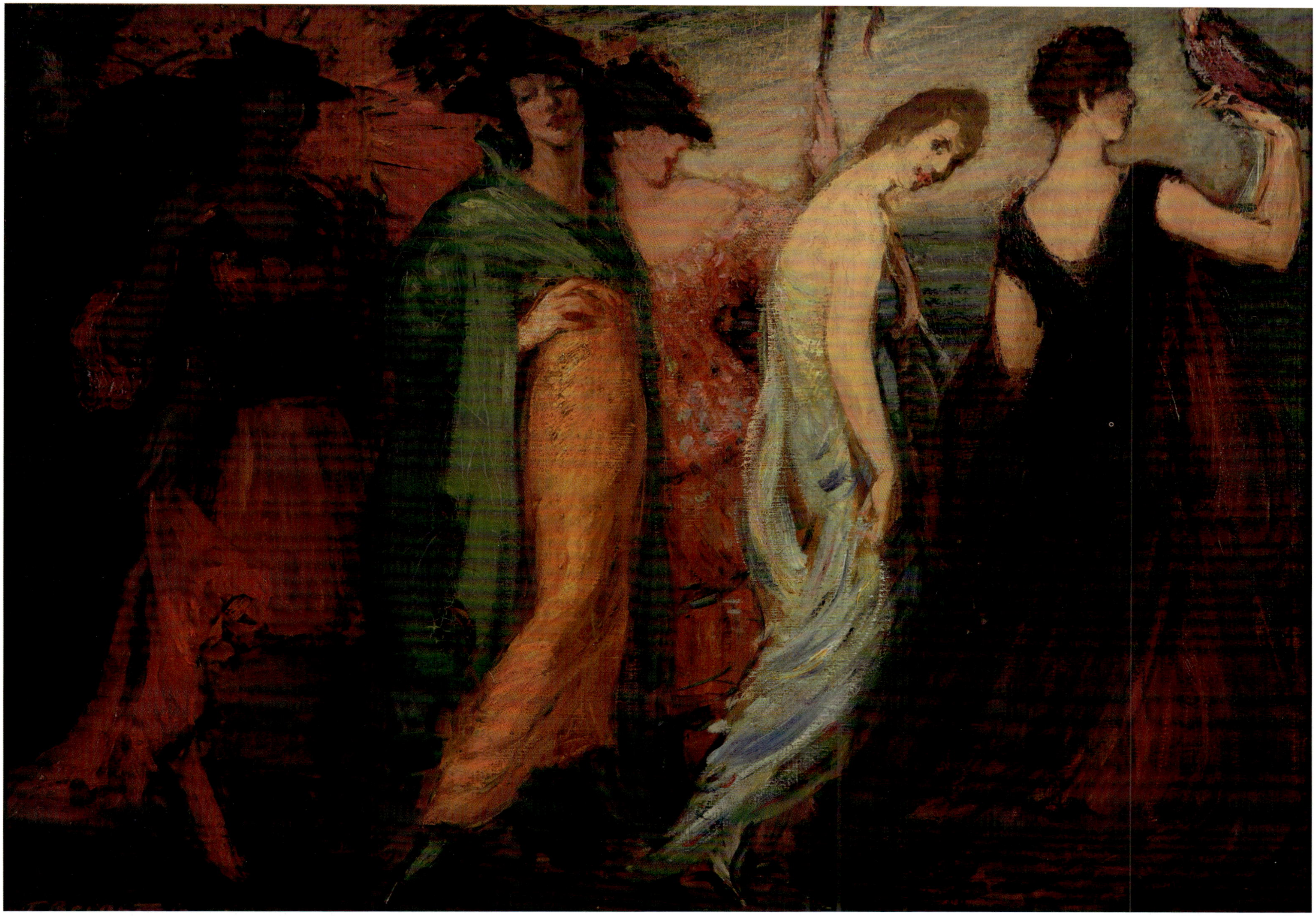

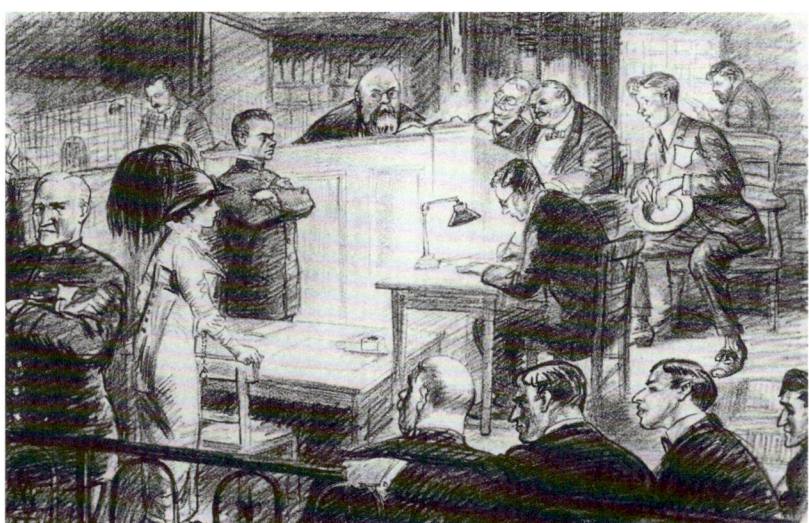

38. *Lilies of the Field*, 1915. 35 x 55 inches.
Endicott College Collection,
Walter J. Manninen Trust.

39. John Sloan's *Women's Night Court:
Before Her Makers and Her Judge*, 1913.
Crayon on paper, 16½ x 25 inches.
Published in *The Masses* 4 (August 1913), 10–11.

Bernstein exhibited *Lilies of the Field* in May 1916 at the
Catharine Lorillard Wolfe Art Club, then located at 802 Broadway.
Founded in 1896 as a national organization dedicated to professional
women artists, it gave Bernstein an award for mural design.[95] None
of the other known entrants in this show is today a household name.[96]

Just twenty-five, Bernstein continued to be very active,
and her work attracted press attention. From December 18, 1915,
through January 16, 1916, her paintings *The Little Merry-Go-Round*
and *The Fleet on the Hudson* were on view in the Winter Exhibition
of the National Academy of Design. A reviewer singled out her

work in the large show and suggested that the influence of "modern illustration" was at work: "Theresa F. Bernstein in her *Little Merry-Go-Round* is doing what Jerome Myers has been doing those many years, but she does it with a more casual air as if nothing matters much except getting color vividly on the canvas and indicating movement by the direction of her brushstrokes."[97] Still, it was remarkable notice for one just starting out.

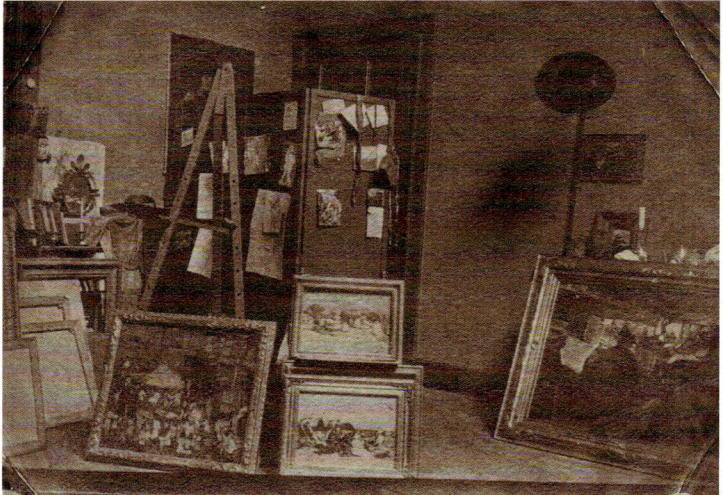

40. Theresa Bernstein's studio with *The Little Merry-Go-Round* ca. 1917 and *In the Elevated* visible.

At the same time, Bernstein showed *Sunset on the Hudson, Opera Night, Fantasy, Little Cafe,* and *Caprice* at the Folsom Galleries in the first exhibition of "The Eclectics," a new group that included, along with Bernstein, the painters Eugene Higgins, Bertram Hartman, Guy Pène du Bois, Robert J. Cole, George Luks, Maurice Prendergast, Robert B. Brandegee, James Britton, Sidney E. Dickinson, Constant Raphael Furyk, Anne Goldthwaite, Philip L. Hale, Henry S. Hubbell, and Martha Walter.[98]

The extraordinary challenge then faced by women artists can be inferred from the story of a group show at the Professional Woman's League, (1999 Broadway, January 1–16, 1916). Apart from Bernstein, Jane Peterson (1876–1965), and Martha Walter (1875–1976), who are somewhat known today, most of the participating women are all but forgotten.[99] Yet an article at the time, captioned "Woman's Work in Art," declared that they were all "well-known artists." Bernstein appears to have been the youngest (at least where the birthdates are traceable) in the group that also included Harriette Bowden, Isabel Vernon Cook, Clara D. Davidson (1874–1962), Marian M. Kerr, Laura V. McClaine,

Clara Mamre Norton (ca. 1853–1930), Lillian Thomas Schmidt (1875–1955), who was listed as Mrs. and the club's "Chairman of Art"), and Elizabeth M. Watrous.[100] According to a review, all the women except for Mrs. Schmidt had just joined the club in order to accept the invitation to show. Of Bernstein, the reviewer remarked only on her painting of a "mass of brilliant nasturtiums in a basket."[101] At the advice of Isabel Vernon Cook, Bernstein first visited the Gloucester artist colony the following summer.[102] Among the works she painted that first summer is a small oil painting of a man working in a garden, which she inscribed "The Twin Trees, To Mamma, Gloucester, 1916."

Her incessant search for venues led Bernstein in 1916 to the German Association for Culture's group show at the Municipal Gallery of the Washington Irving High School on Irving Place. "'The Tango' is a weird and exotic work by Miss Theresa Bernstein," remarked a critic. "[She] also shows a beautiful fantasy called 'Summer.'"[103] At the time, Washington Irving was a public high school for girls and featured instruction in art.[104] A performance in the school's auditorium had been the subject of one of her paintings in 1913.

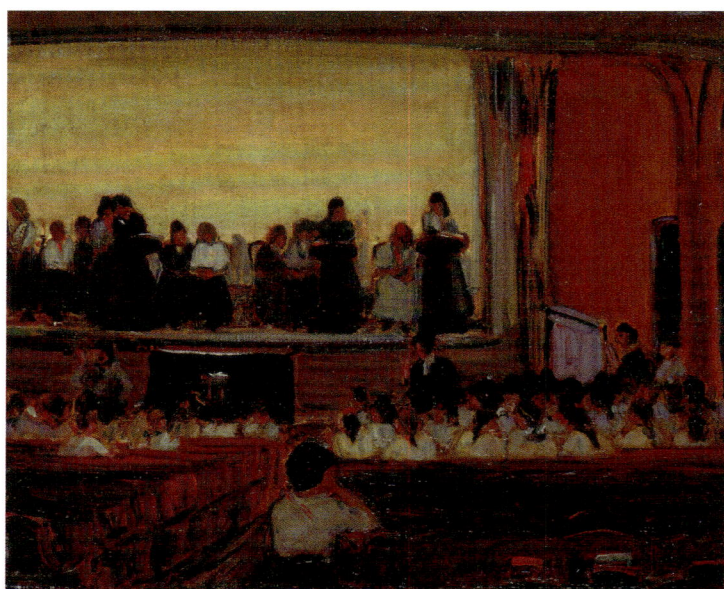

41. *Washington Irving High School*, 1913. Oil on canvas, 20 x 24 inches. Private collection.

Again resorting to a woman's venue, a month later, in February 1916, Bernstein won the National Art Club prize of $100 for *In the Elevated* in the Twenty-Fifth Annual Exhibition of the

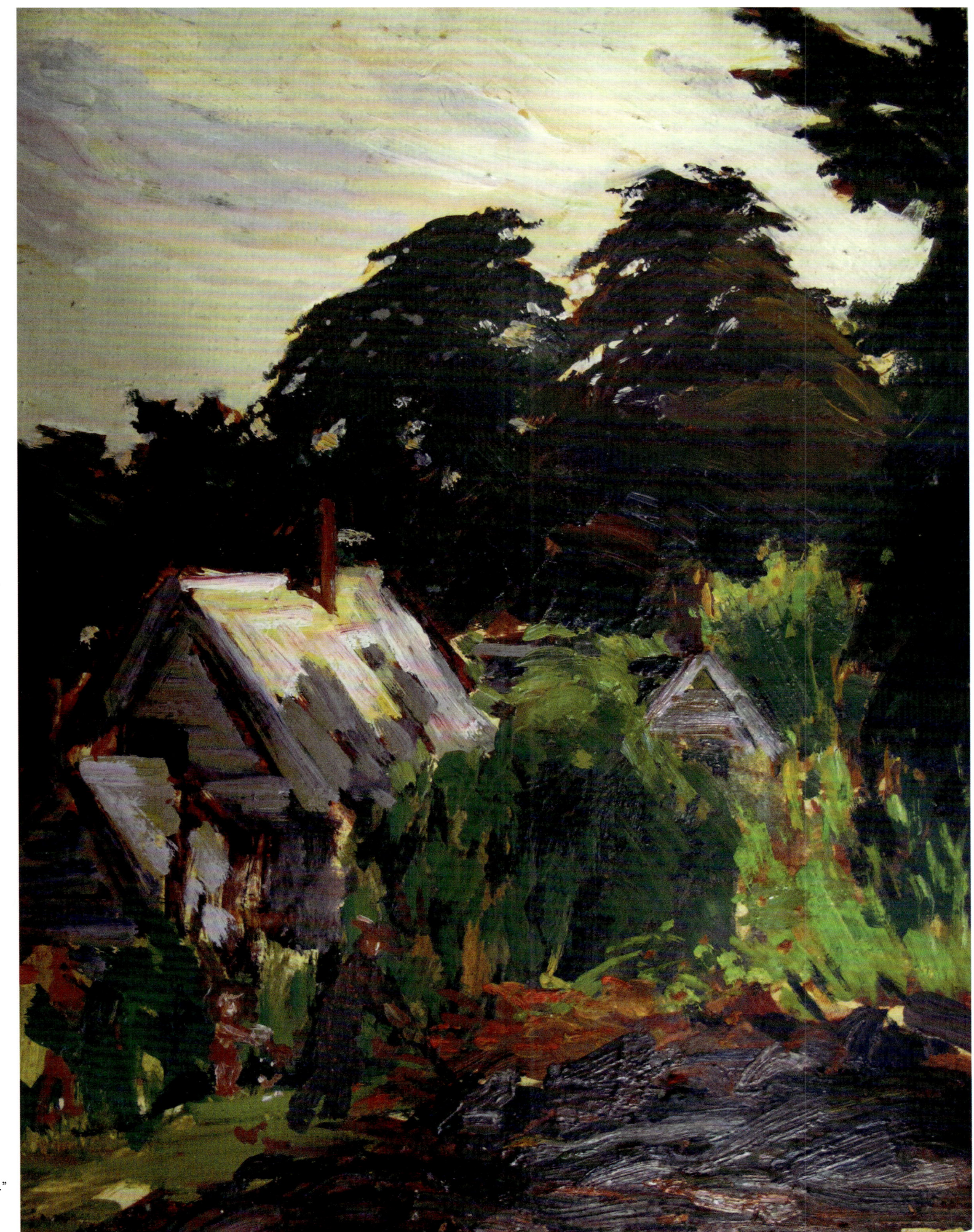

42. *The Twin Trees, Gloucester*, 1916.
Oil on artist's board, 15½ x 12 inches.
Private collection. Inscribed on verso:
"The Twin Trees, To Mamma, Gloucester, 1916."

Women's Association of Painters and Sculptors (at the Women's University Club). *In the Elevated* inspired the comment that it was "an interesting composition obviously based on direct observation. The spots of dark and light are placed in a considered design that becomes slightly confused as you go into the picture. The color is hot, mahogany red and golden yellow playing the principal parts in the scheme."[105] In fact, her colors are vibrant and her paint handling is remarkably sophisticated and forceful.

For this prizewinner, Bernstein later wrote that she drew on her experience riding the Columbus Avenue El along New York's West Side and that she included portraits of her father reading a newspaper and of her mother sitting in the foreground.[106] She could well have known earlier treatments of related subjects such as a small version of Honoré Daumier's 1862 painting *The Third-Class Carriage*, which hung in the Armory Show when she visited in 1913.[107]

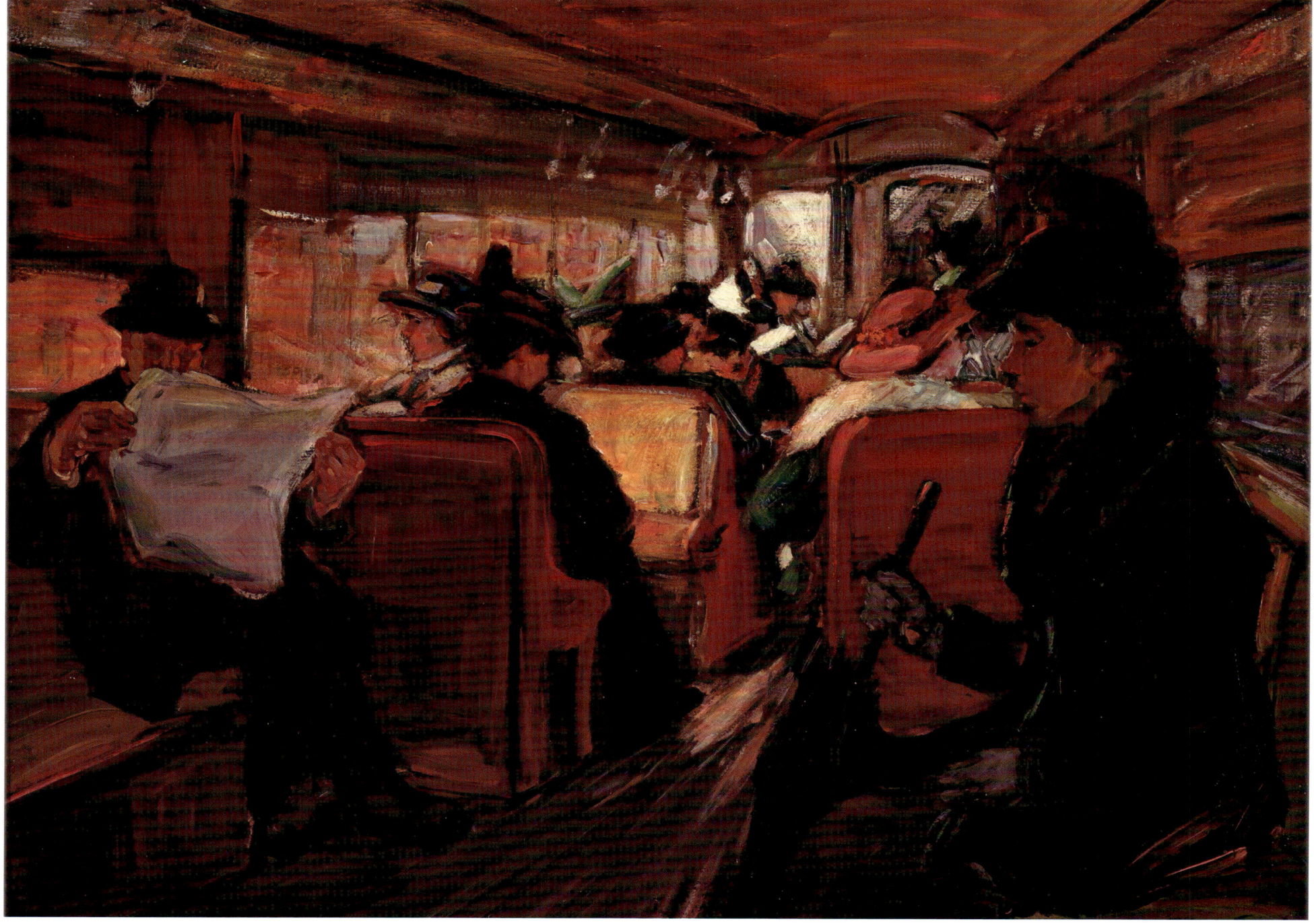

43. *In the Elevated*, 1916. Oil on canvas, 30 x 40 inches. De Young Fine Arts Museum, San Francisco.

She might also have seen the 1893 etching *Omnibus* by Anders Zorn, which depicts Isabella Stewart Gardner in profile in front of windows angled in on the right side of the composition, much as she would pose her mother for her own painting.[108] Bernstein's extant sketch on paper is rough and spontaneous enough to suggest that she made it while riding on the El, but

she also possessed a photograph of her mother in the train striking the pose and wearing the hat that figure in the painting. Since William Meyerowitz appears to be standing behind Bernstein's mother in this photograph, it was probably taken after she first exhibited the painting, rather than as a study for it.

Yet another nonjuried group show at the MacDowell Club

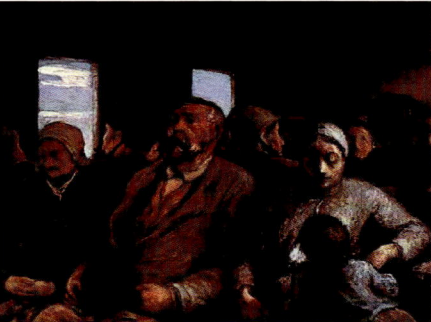

44. Honoré Daumier, *Third-Class Carriage*, 1862, as shown in the New York Armory Show in 1913.

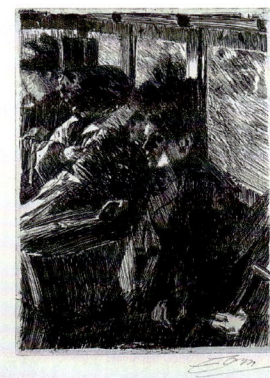

45. Anders Zorn, *Isabella Gardner*, 1892. Etching. Private collection.

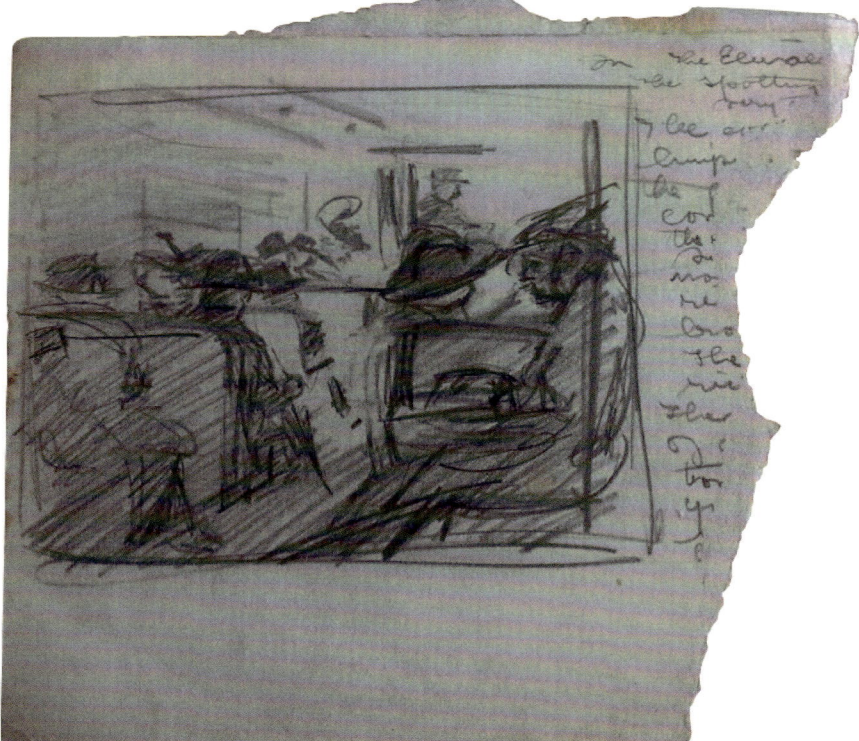

46. Study for *In the Elevated*, 1916. Pencil on paper, 3⅜ x 4½ inches. Sandy Lepore Collection.

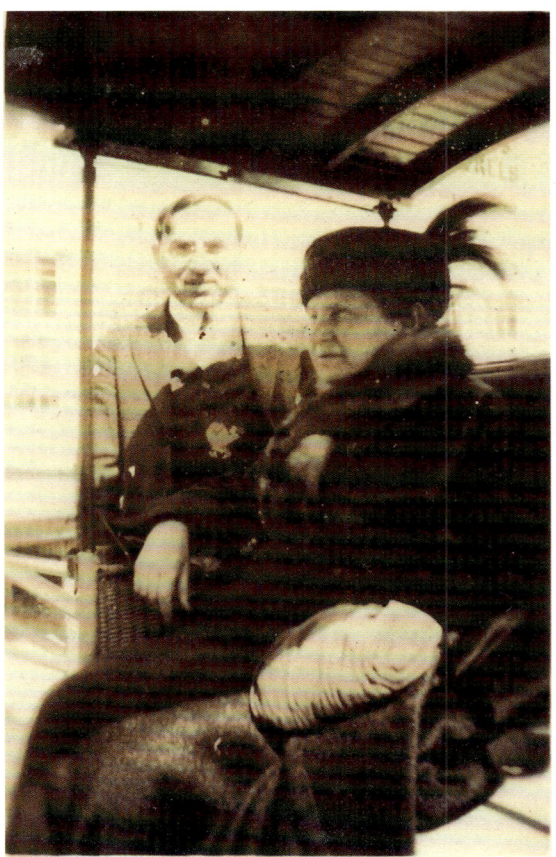

47. Theresa Bernstein's mother posing as if for *In the Elevated*, 1916.

(March 16–26, 1916) allowed Bernstein to exhibit four paintings, among them the political *Suffrage Parade*. Only another work, however, caught the reviewer's notice: "Theresa Bernstein also is at her fortunate best with 'High School Girls,' a well thought out composition devoid of eccentricities. Her decorative portrait has decisive character in design and color."[109] Again, her fellow artists in the group are not now well known; most were women like Annetta St. Gaudens, who married Louis St. Gaudens, younger brother of the sculptor Augustus St. Gaudens; Zulma Steele, a painter who also became a ceramicist and designer at Brydcliff, an Arts and Crafts Colony in Woodstock; Laura Gardin, sculptor and

the wife of sculptor James Earle Fraser; the impressionist and tonalist painter Alexis B. Many; and Maud M. Mason, a painter who studied with Arthur Wesley Dow and Chase.[110]

Bernstein's flurry of accomplishments continued in 1916, when she first showed *The Fleet on the Hudson* in the 111th Annual Exhibition of the Pennsylvania Academy. Her former teacher, Daniel Garber, was then on the painting committee. In the role of "Hanging Chairman," he placed her work with other representational painters including John Sloan, Childe Hassam, John F. Carlson, Ivan Olinsky, and Natalie Peck.

In the Elevated featured again, along with *The Beach*,

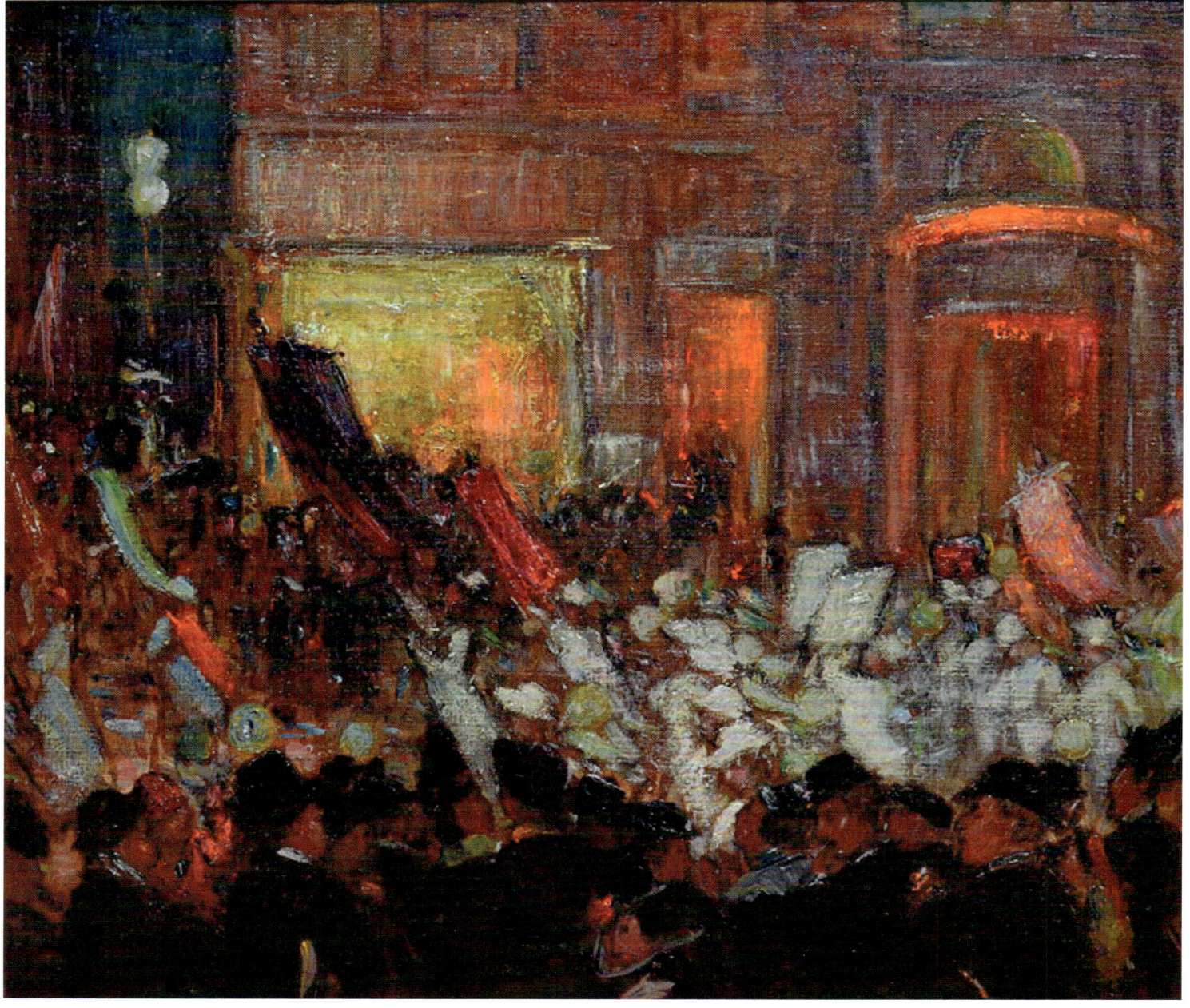

48. *Suffrage Parade*, 1915. Oil on canvas, 17 x 19 inches. Private collection.

Shakespeare Masque, The Mountains, and *Open Air Show,* in another nonjuried group show at the MacDowell (December 1916–January 2, 1917), where a critic singled out *In the Elevated* as "well composed and mellow in color."[111] Another reviewer commented:

> There are 85 pictures in the show, which is dominated by the work of Miss Theresa Bernstein, a young woman with a marked and vigorous talent. This painter belongs artistically with the group of which John Sloan and Randall Davey are conspicuous examples. She has that vital interest in the people of the city and in their social relations that characterizes the group and she paints with a fearless freedom from restraining conventions and a breadth of vigor that is surprising in a young woman. Some fault might, indeed, be found with her unrestraint, but her message is so direct and is given with such intensity of purpose that one prefers to welcome her gladly and leave time to provide what discipline it has for her.[112]

The citation of "fearless freedom from restraining conventions and a breadth of vigor that is surprising in a young woman" tells much about the gender stereotypes of the day.

The gendered conventions defied by Bernstein's style aimed to keep women artists in their place—out of the exclusive commercial galleries that promoted males. The gallery system that was then developing promoted a masculine ideal against rising anxiety in high culture about feminization.[113] So many women were going to art schools and trying to turn professional that they threatened the dominance of male artists in the marketplace. Women had no choice but to organize, founding and joining professional organizations, but these groups could not match the opportunities attained by the art dealers that made close contacts with collectors and dominated the market.

Ambitious women like Bernstein needed to participate in every possible exhibition. She would jump at the chance to donate work for a benefit show with the People's Art Guild at the Jewish Daily Forward Building on East Broadway in May 1917.

The invitation had come sometime during the previous winter in the form of a studio visit from William Meyerowitz, a painter and printmaker.

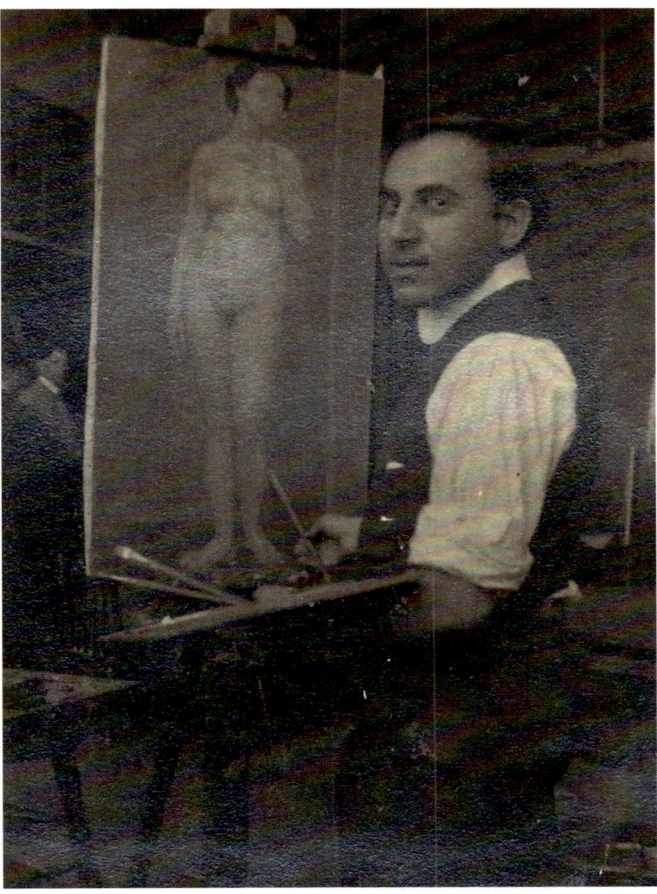

49. William Meyerowitz at the National Academy of Design.

The People's Art Guild, like so many of Bernstein's venues, was an artists' cooperative. It had been founded in 1915 by John Weichsel, who aimed to make art available to the masses and to improve the knowledge of art among the public. Bernstein joined Meyerowitz in the show along with other realists—Sloan, Henri, and George Bellows—as well as such modernists as Walkowitz, Stieglitz, Joseph Stella, Alfred Maurer, Marsden Hartley, John Marin, and Samuel Halpert, but with Meyerowitz she also began a decisive turn in her life.

When the pair met, he was closer to vanguard art and artists than she was. He was involved with the People's Art Guild and he came to know Stieglitz well, since he was living in a building on Fifth Avenue adjacent to Stieglitz's gallery, where Bernstein had seen and rejected abstract art styles in favor of the realism she had studied.

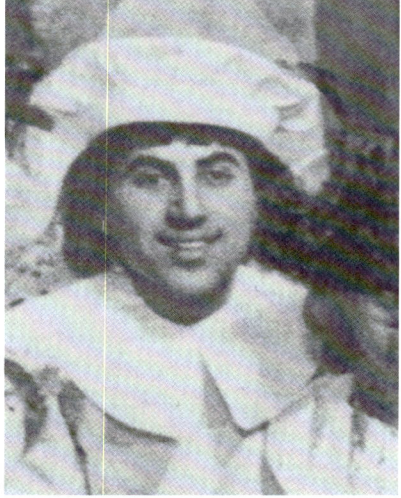

50. William Meyerowitz singing in the chorus at the Metropolitan Opera, 1918.

Meyerowitz, the son of a well-educated Orthodox Jewish cantor, was resourceful and talented, with a passion for music that Bernstein shared.

Meyerowitz supported his immigrant parents and siblings by singing in the chorus at the Metropolitan Opera and by drawing for an architectural firm.[114] Their mutual love of opera facilitated courtship. He wrote to "Miss Bernstein" in April 1918: "Have secured two seats for the opera on Saturday afternoon 'Cavallieria

Rusticana' and 'Le Coq d'Or.' Will call for you at your Studio on Saturday a quarter of two. Sincerely Yours Wm Meyerowitz."[115]

Meyerowitz also spent time in a clapboard shack set high on a bluff in Ridgefield, New Jersey, in an artist's colony begun in 1913 by modernists Man Ray, Samuel Halpert, and Alfred Kreymborg, who in 1915 was one of the founders of *Others: A Magazine of the New Verse*. Bernstein told at least one friend that Man Ray was Meyerowitz's roommate in Ridgefield when she and William first

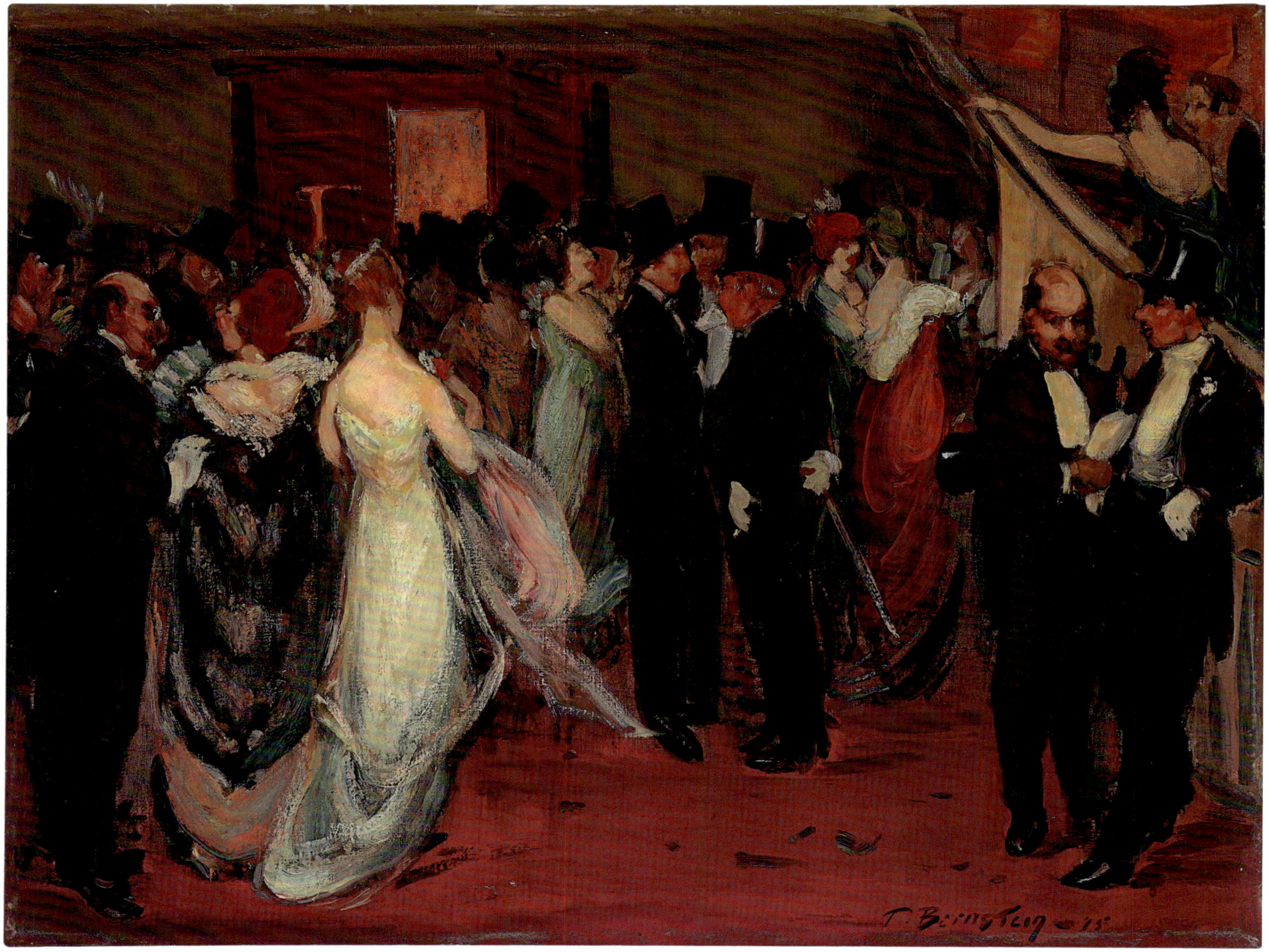

51. *The Opera Lobby*, 1915. Oil on canvas, 27 x 35 inches. Private collection, courtesy of Christie's.

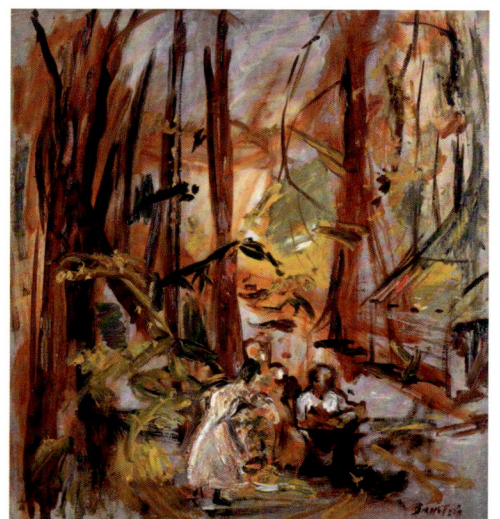

52. *Bill's Shack*, 1918. Oil on tarpaulin, 22 x 20 inches. Girard Jackson Collection.

met.[116] The two men had probably become acquainted through Weichsel of the People's Art Guild, who had written about Man Ray. "On weekends William took me out to his shack in Ridgefield," Bernstein recalled, "with the crackling wood stove and the frequently collapsing stovepipes that had to be adjusted so that we would not choke from the smoke. . . . The view from the rear of the cabin stretched for miles."[117] According to Kreymborg, the participants shared the rent of $8 a month for the modest three-bedroom shack, which stood in an orchard.[118] The area inspired landscapes by both Bernstein and Meyerowitz; hers oils, and his etchings.

In February 1917 Bernstein joined a group of women called the "Philadelphia Ten," with whom she would exhibit until 1931.[119] All the original members of this group had gone to art school in Philadelphia, including nine at Bernstein's old haunt, the Philadelphia School of Design for Women, and two who had studied at the Pennsylvania Academy of the Fine Arts.

Bernstein and Meyerowitz first showed together with a group at the People's Art Guild in May 1917, when the United States had just entered World War I, prompting the British and French war commissioners to parade down New York's Fifth Avenue on May 9 and 11, temporarily renaming it "the Avenue of the Allies." Their slogan, "Show your colors," resulted in a patriotic flurry of Union Jacks, French Tricolors, and Stars and Stripes that caught Bernstein's eye and inspired her to paint *Allies of World War I* (1917), an allegory of costumed figures carrying the flags associated with their countries. In the center of her composition, Joan of Arc stands dressed in armor in front of the French flag, with a Union Jack visible just beyond. On the right side, next to a soldier dressed in the brown of the Allied forces, stands Victory personified. As the model for this figure, Bernstein once again hired the Baroness von Freytag-Loringhoven, whom she depicted before the American flag dressed in a garment reminiscent of that worn by the Statue of Liberty, which, of course, was a gift from France. According to the young French American painter Louis Bouché, when he first encountered the baroness at a Broadway subway station in the midst of the war, she was "wearing a French Poilu's blue trench helmet" and "adored everything French, she a German, and Germany and France in mortal combat."[120]

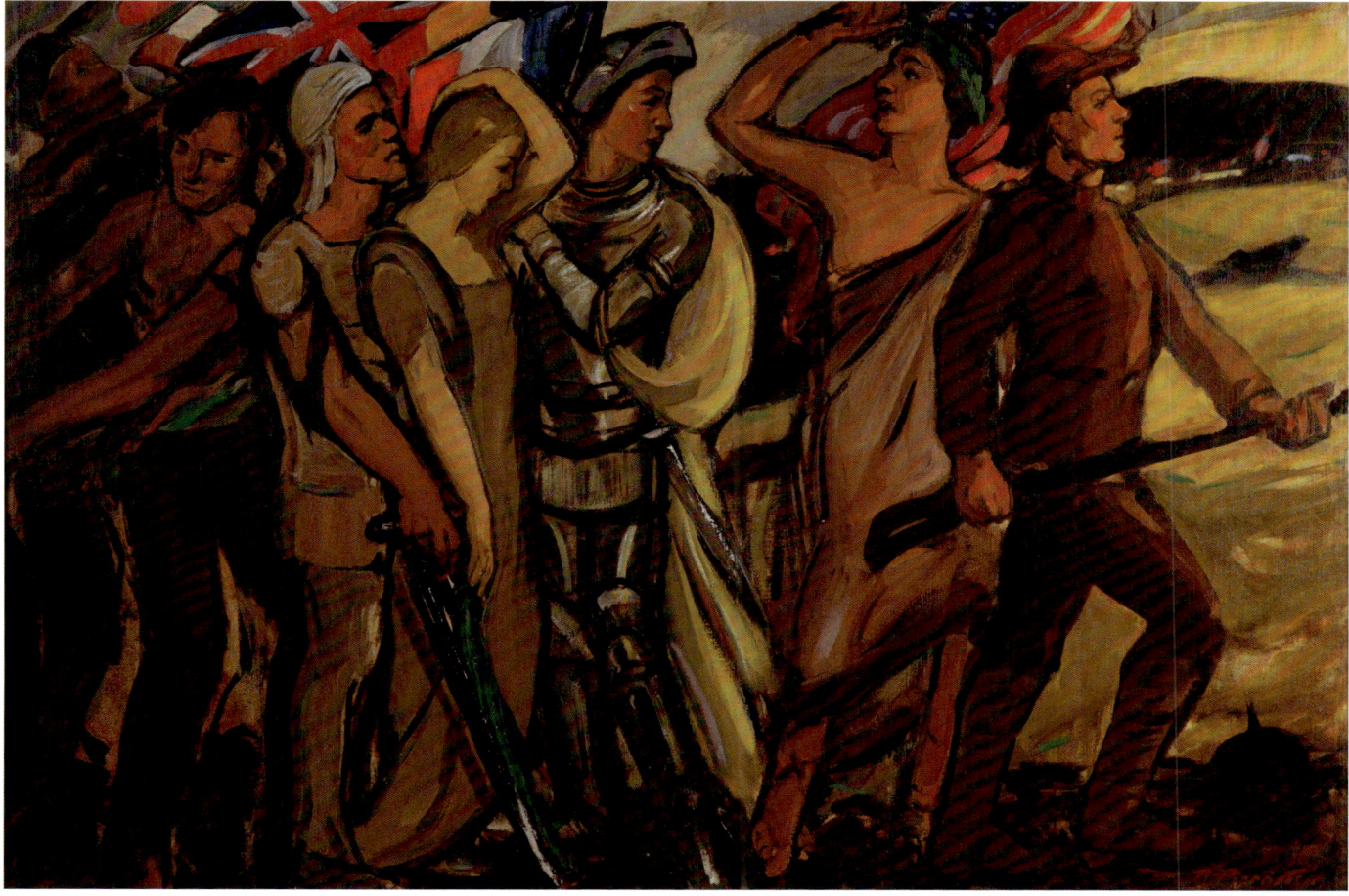

53. *Allies of World War I*, 1917.
Oil on canvas, 40 x 45 inches.
Endicott College Collection,
Walter J. Manninen Trust.

Also in the spring of 1917, Bernstein showed again as one of The Eclectics at the Arlington Galleries on Madison Avenue, where the press noted her "vigorous and gay hued 'Tennis Tournament,' 'Sun, Sand and Sea,' 'Pear Orchard,' etc.," but also commented upon James Britton's "picture of Theresa Bernstein sketching out of doors, which is a pleasing color arrangement."[121] Another critic wrote, "Theresa Bernstein patterns her color with a rich gravity that seems to indicate intelligent study of Oriental carpets."[122]

Bernstein later told of submitting her large canvas *Polish Church: Easter Morning* (1916) to the National Academy of Design's 1917 Annual. She had made sketches for it while attending an Easter service in a church (on Fifth Street between Avenues A and B on New York's Lower East Side) in the company of her mother's assistant, Mary. Bernstein recounted years later that some of the parishioners were annoyed at her sketching on the backs of letters during their service. She then had her mother pose for the figure in the left foreground. Later, the photographer Peter Juley told Bernstein how, while photographing the show, he had overheard that she had won the Shaw Prize of $300 by a unanimous vote of the academy jury. The award was then the only one that could go to a woman. Juley added that he had witnessed Ernest Blumenschein arrive late and protest that the award should go to his wife, Mary, who had been showing there for a number of years without winning the award.[123] According to Juley, the jury then reversed itself, giving Mrs. Blumenschein the prize and rehanging Bernstein's painting concealed behind a group of plants "in the gallery known as the 'morgue.'"[124] Despite the setback, a reviewer singled out the scene: "Theresa Bernstein's 'Polish Church' is one of the positive achievements of a painter who never hesitates to pay with temporary failure for the privilege of adventurous experiment. Every face is carefully studied individually, but each is equally well related to the whole design. Centre the mind upon any of them and the surrounding figures become a coherent background leading up to and away from the one face. And these all, with a few exceptions that serve as accents, are drawn toward a centre of invisible interest."[125]

It was also in 1917 that Bernstein was first included in an important art book—Lorinda Munson Bryant's *American Pictures and Their Painters*, which reproduced *The Opera Lobby* (see fig. 51).

Bryant had interviewed Bernstein who had emphasized "Composition, design, and color . . . as the three necessary attributes for her to see a picture in embryo." Bryant concluded, "Though quite young, she already has a grasp of fundamental principles in art."[126] This book was issued in both New York and London by John Lane, the British publisher who had purchased Bernstein's painting *Open Air Show*. It is worth noting Bernstein's female metaphor for painting, "to see a picture in embryo."

Critics continued to remark Bernstein's work. A review of another group show at the MacDowell Club in May 1918 singled out "Theresa Bernstein . . . [who] is refreshingly herself in her child studies, especially that of the baby sucking candy."[127] She was involved with the organizers, because on April 26, Walter Tittle recorded in his diary that he, Henri, Sloan, Davey, Hopper, Theresa Bernstein, and others had spent most of the day hanging this show.[128]

When Bernstein showed again as one of The Eclectics in a group show at the Babcock Gallery in late 1918, she elicited praise for her "atmospheric effect" in *Gloucester after Sunset*. The same critic wrote: "Most striking of this artist's work is 'Fourth of July, 1918,' with figures and a sweep of the national flag in the foreground."[129] Patriotic themes appealed to Bernstein, who, when she showed again at the National Academy of Design in the Winter Exhibition of 1918, heeded the request that artists submit "subjects pertaining to the late war." Her entry won special notice: "Theresa Bernstein's 'Patriotic Parade,' a strong conception, depicting a scene in front of the public library of recent occurrence, with flags and sunshine and crowds, full of movement and life."[130]

After meeting Meyerowitz, Bernstein had taken up an interest in etching. She participated with him, John Sloan, and Mahonri Young in an exhibition of etchings held by Manhattan Painter-Gravers' Club at the Mussman Gallery, 144 West Fifty-Seventh Street (November–December 1918). One of her etchings resulted from her excitement on November 11, 1918, when New York celebrated the armistice between the Allies and Germany that marked the end of fighting in World War I (see fig. 168). Parades on Fifth Avenue also inspired Bernstein to paint ambitious canvases such as *The Armistice Parade* (1918), *Flags of the Allies* (1918), and *Victory Day: Return of the Army* (1919).

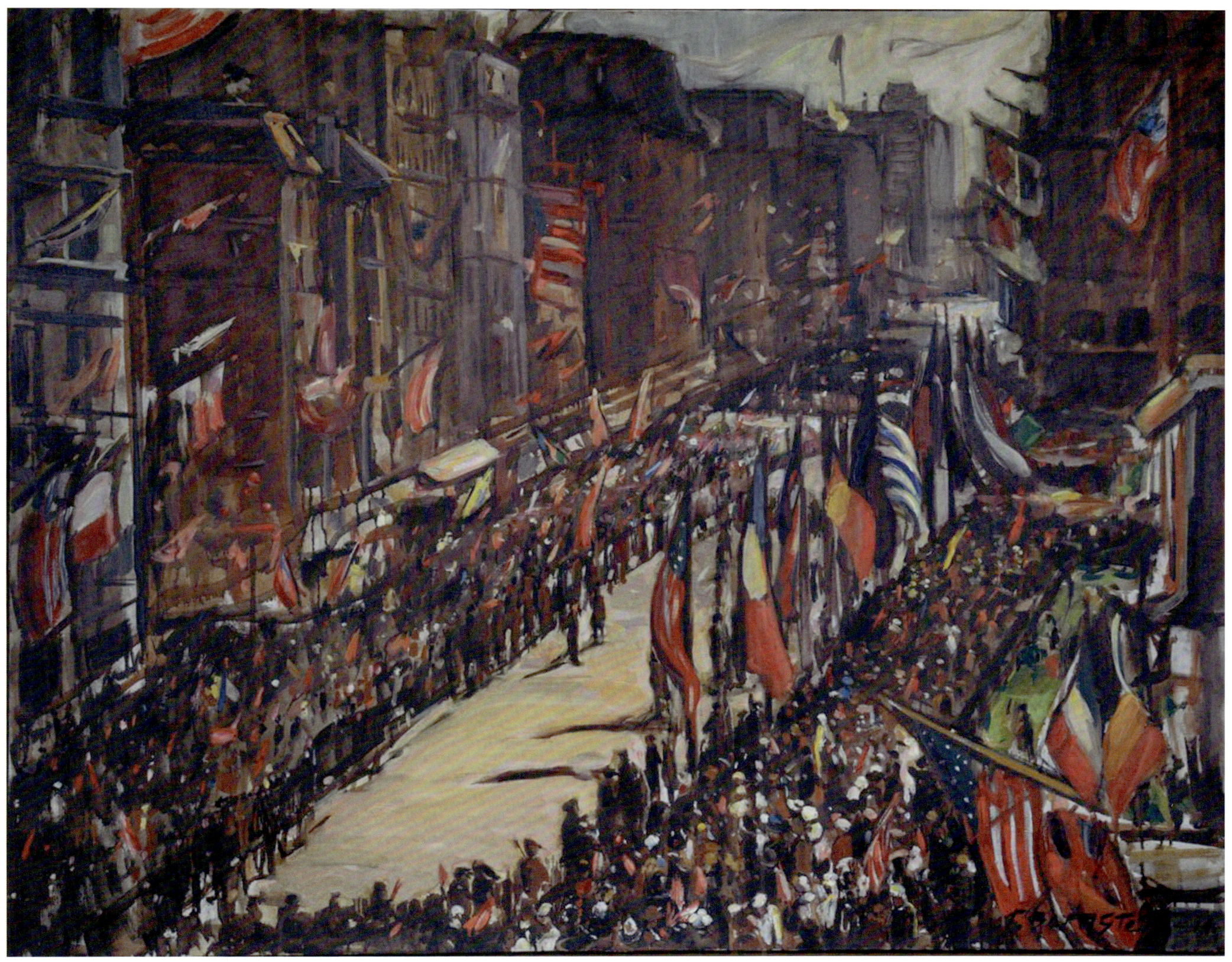

54. *Flags of the Allies*, 1918. Oil on canvas, 40 x 50 inches. J. J. and Jackie Bell Collection.

In *Flags of the Allies*, Bernstein again portrayed the colorful pageantry associated with the war effort at home. Her angle of vision is looking down from the vantage point of a friend's office. Newly engaged, Bernstein and Meyerowitz celebrated the declaration of the armistice, which prevented William from being drafted—at the very moment the army drafted his brother and published William's draft registration number.[131]

Victory Day: Return of the Army depicts a parade in March 1919, which the city sponsored to honor soldiers from New York's Twenty-Seventh Division who forced the German army to retreat by breaking the Hindenburg Line.[132] Although often mistakenly identified as Washington Square, the ceremony took place farther uptown, below a temporary victory arch modeled on the Arch of Constantine in Rome. It was erected in 1918 in Madison Square, which extends from Twenty-Third to Twenty-Sixth Street.[133]

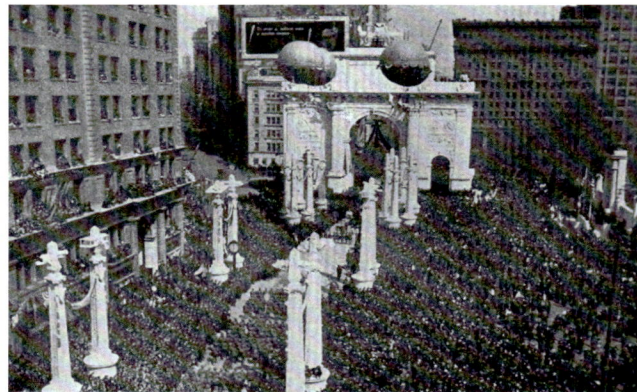
56. Victory arch modeled on the Roman Arch of Constantine erected in 1918 in Madison Square Park, New York City.

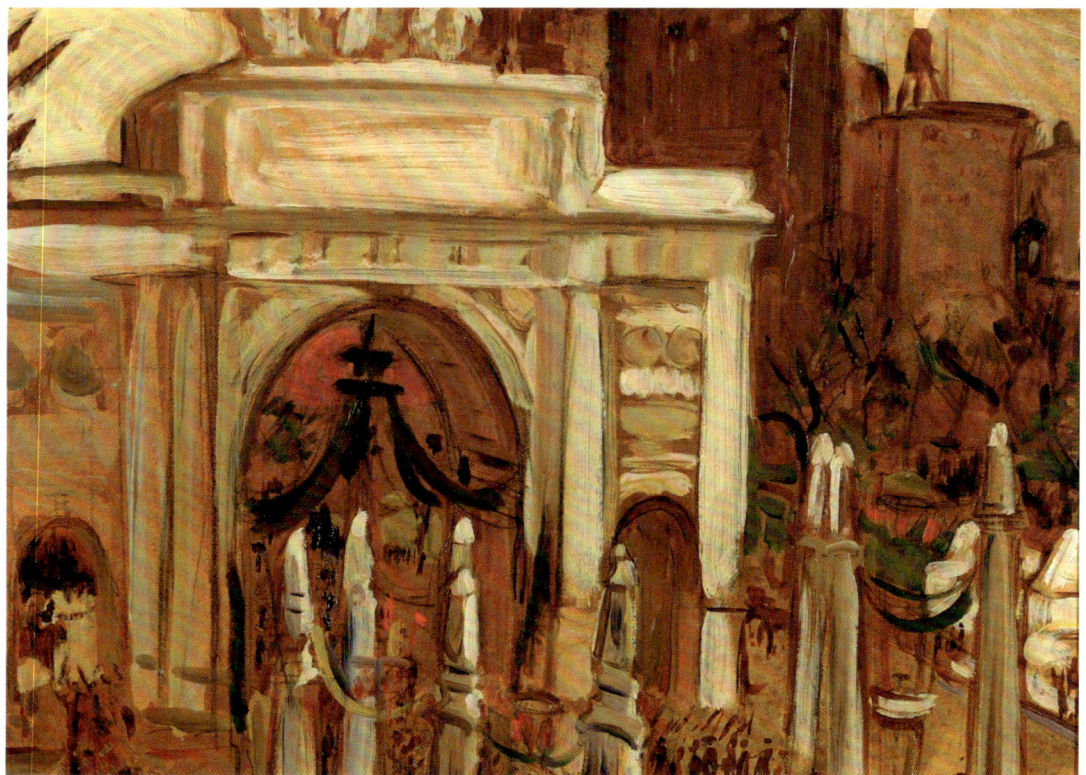
55. *Victory Day: Return of the Army*, 1919. Oil on canvas, 15 x 20 inches. Martin and Edith Stein Collection.

Bernstein showed *Patriotic Parade* and *Polish Church: Easter Morning* at the Sixty-Second Annual show of the Boston Art Club (January 24–February 14, 1919). With *Patriotic Parade*, her approach shifted from concern with individual psychology to explore group dynamics and spectacle.[134] She was showing here in excellent company, with a number of older established men such as Bellows, Henri, Rockwell Kent, Leon Kroll, Luks, Kenneth Hayes Miller, Maurice B. Prendergast, Sloan, many of whom were associated with "the Eight" and the Ashcan School of painting.[135] W. H. de B. Nelson, writing a feature on Bernstein in the *International Studio* in February 1919, described her as "a woman painter who paints like a man," intending this as high praise.[136]

Yet Bernstein's precocious fame and dynamic career were about to suffer. On February 7, 1919, just before her twenty-ninth birthday, she married William Meyerowitz in the Alumni Chapel of the Congregation Keneseth Israel on Broad Street in Philadelphia, with Rabbi Joseph Krauskopf officiating. The marriage certificate records Bernstein's age as twenty-seven (when she was actually twenty-eight) and lists her place of birth as "Cracow, Austria."[137] The groom's age was listed as thirty-one and his place of birth was listed as Kozeletz, Russia, which is a town located in what is today northern Ukraine.[138]

The romance of their relationship infuses Bernstein's lyrical painting *Summer Picnic* of 1919. In conceiving of a metaphor to convey the passion of young love, she placed the two of them out in nature, much as ancient gods and

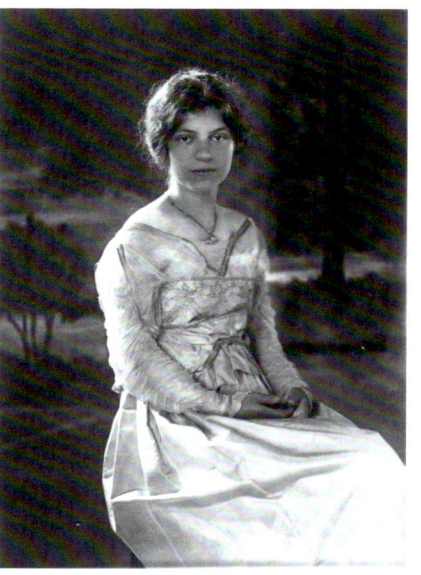
57. Theresa Ferber Bernstein's bridal portrait, 1919.

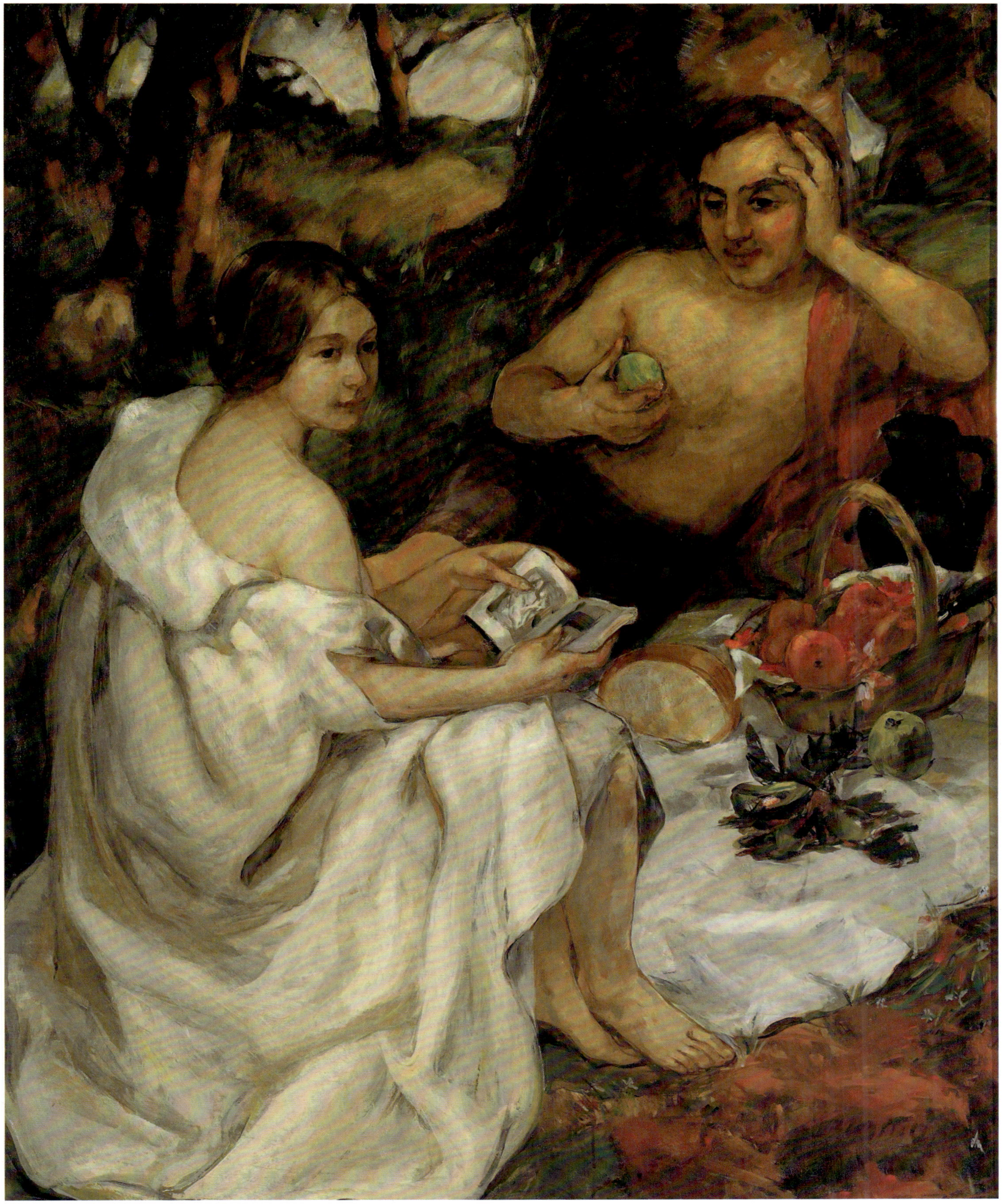

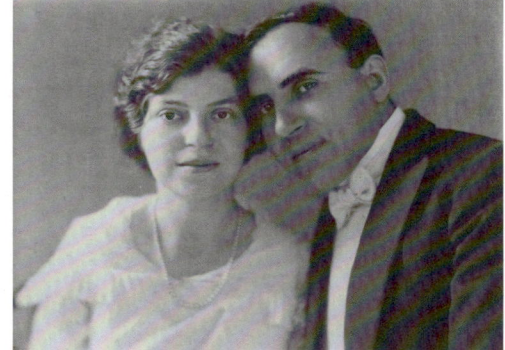

goddesses appear in Renaissance paintings. He holds an apple and she holds an open book, as if reading him poetry or the stories of classical myths. Her billowing white garment falls from her bare shoulder; they are both shown in dishabille—in a kind of egalitarian homage to Edward Manet's *Dejeuner sur L'Herbe*, where only the females were shown in states of undress. By depicting ripe fruit in the basket, which often alludes to fertility, fecundity, and conception, Theresa might have been suggesting the couple's desire to have a child.

By the following December, a newspaper feature about the couple was captioned "Marital Bond Is Doubly Welded by Their Art."[139] The two would be exhibiting together in the museum that was then in the public library in Syracuse, New York, where Bernstein had already appeared in a group show in 1916. "Probably not since the time of the Brownings," commented a local reporter, "has the bond between husband and wife been so solidly welded by art as in the case of Mr. and Mrs. Meyerowitz, whose etchings and paintings will be hung in the art museum at the Public library within a few days."[140] Bernstein would be showing her "wonderful paintings" that

58. *Summer Picnic*, 1919. Oil on canvas, 50 x 40 inches. Martin and Edith Stein Collection.

"are signed with her maiden name" and Meyerowitz would be showing his etchings "which have won such favorable mention in the galleries of various cities where they have been shown." The author of this piece, like many viewers henceforth, chose to see in the two artists "some kind of twinship" despite the fact that "their workmanship" was "so utterly different in execution."

The discussion then shifted to Meyerowitz's heroic story of coming to America in 1905, "bringing his family out of Ukrania because of the revolution and massacres taking place there. He made a fight to become a painter, studying with a sign painter when his parents tried to induce him to study theology. When the family came to America, he helped it to live by working days and studying art at night, studying in the National Academy." In contrast, Bernstein, the article incorrectly reported, "was born half the world away from the man she married." Though she knew about her European birth, she preferred not to disclose it. The feature concluded that "her road was made easy. She was given the opportunity to travel and study the great artists of other days as well as modern art."

In May 1919 Bernstein and Meyerowitz were back from their honeymoon trip to Florida, where she painted works such as *Florida Sky* and *Lake in Florida*. They settled at 39 West Sixty-Seventh Street, where they would remain until 1932. She resumed showing actively, participating in the last group exhibition held at the MacDowell Club, which featured forty-two artists including John Sloan, Edward Hopper, Walter Tittle, and Randall Davey. She was once again in important company. "Among those that claim attention by the freshness of vision and power of expression manifested by the artist," wrote the *Times* critic, "are Theresa Bernstein's Florida sketches. They are strong, well-balanced, original, and remarkably fine in color."[141]

Bernstein also had a solo show at the Milch Gallery, 108 West Fifty-Seventh Street (November 1–15, 1919), which included more than twenty-five pieces. Meyerowitz had a show of his etchings in the adjoining room. Ten of Bernstein's paintings sold on the opening day. Milch Gallery, which had opened in 1911, specialized in American art and at the time showed such leading artists as Henri, who had a solo show there in 1918, just a year before Bernstein's.

For the Milch show the catalogue foreword was written by a fellow member of The Eclectics, Robert J. Cole, announcing that she had "won a place that neither the conservative nor radical will dispute."[142] In the *Brooklyn Daily Eagle*, the painter, writer, and art patron Hamilton Easter Field weighed in with his approval: "Theresa Bernstein has instinct for construction. More frequently than Cezanne she sacrifices the parts for the whole effect. Her paintings are architectural, just as Rachmaninoff's playing of Liszt's First Concerto, is architectural. . . . Theresa Bernstein has this fine sense of arrangement, she is emotional rather than intellectual. . . . Painting should be instinctive."[143] On the same page, Field had reviewed the Exhibition of the Society of American Painters, Sculptors, and Gravers. Now, in addition to praising what he believed to be the best of Bernstein's work, including her painting *Patriotic Parade*, he took the trouble to announce, "Her best canvases, had they been shown at the American Painters, Sculptors, and Gravers, would have added a note of spontaneity to the exhibition. Why oh! why have the A. P. S. and G. been so ungallant, so unjust, to the fair sex? Not a woman painter has gained admission to that 'holy of holies.'"[144]

"There is nothing feminine about the paintings of Theresa Bernstein," opined Frederick James Gregg, reviewing for the *New York Herald*. "It is with a man's vision that this artist looks at her subjects in the streets, the elevated railroad trains, at the beaches, in the parks, in the lobbies of theatres, in the seaport places or in a church. Then, having found what she wants, it is with a man's vigor that she gets it down to stay."[145]

This line of praise was especially ironic since Bernstein was already in her sixth month of pregnancy at the time her show opened. On January 29, 1920, she gave birth to a daughter, Isadora G. R. Meyerowitz. It was a joyful time for the parents. Meanwhile, their show together that April (her paintings and Meyerowitz's etchings) with paintings by both Henri and Charles Bittinger opened in Rochester, New York, at the Memorial Art Gallery.[146]

But on May 11, 1920, their daughter died suddenly from pneumonia at the age of only three months and twelve days. Bernstein told of both the birth and the death of their only child in her book, *William Meyerowitz: The Artist Speaks*.[147]

She based the pose in her painting *Mother and Child* on a photograph of herself holding Isadora. She also recorded her feelings in paintings such as *Joy of Life* (1920) or *Loss* (1920), where she depicted the Angel of Death of Talmudic lore, seen as a figure dressed in a black cloak with a hood, carrying a large scythe (see fig. 160). In *Loss,* a white angel on a vase commemorates the child (see page 6).

About six months later, Bernstein began to give private art lessons to Louise Nevelson, who, newly married, had just moved to New York City. Bernstein taught her to paint in watercolor and served her as a strong role model of a dedicated woman artist, which the Sartains had earlier been for her.

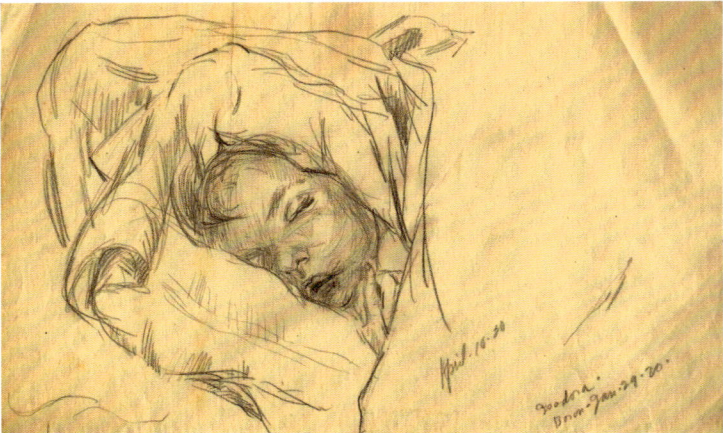

60. *Isadora*, April 10, 1920. Pencil on paper.
Theresa Bernstein and William Meyerowitz Foundation.

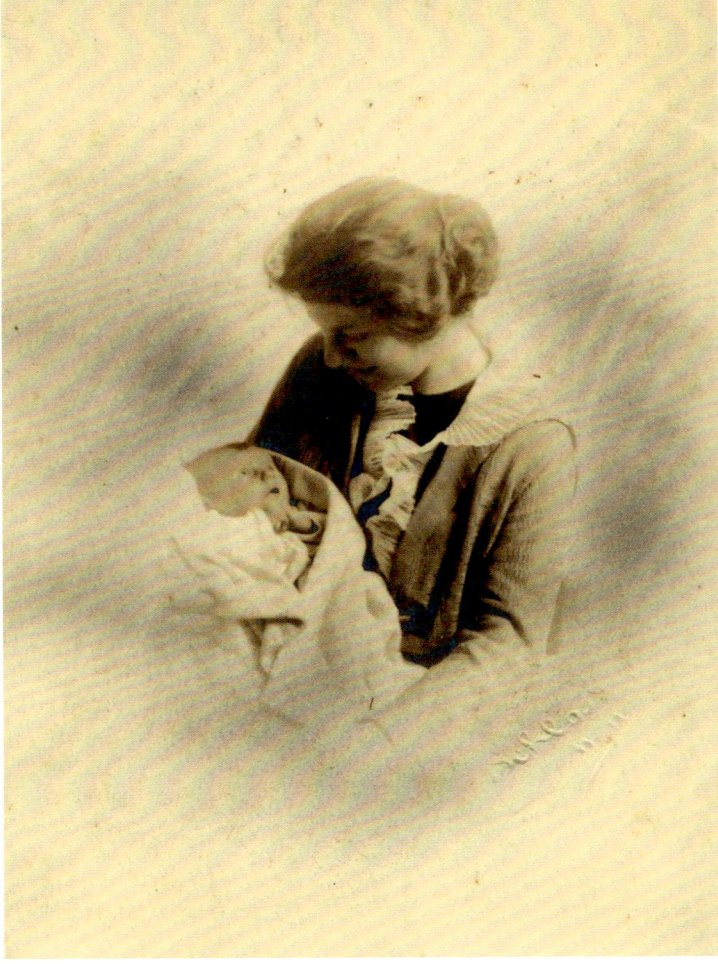

61. Theresa Bernstein with her baby, Isadora, 1920.
Theresa Bernstein and William Meyerowitz Foundation.

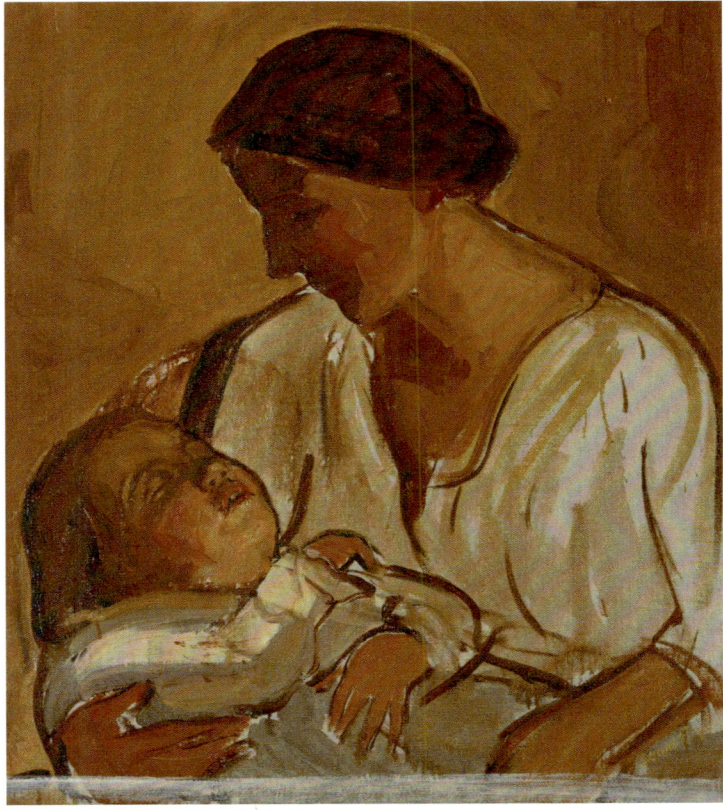

62. *Mother and Child*, 1920. Oil on canvas, 25 x 22 inches.
Martin and Edith Stein Collection.

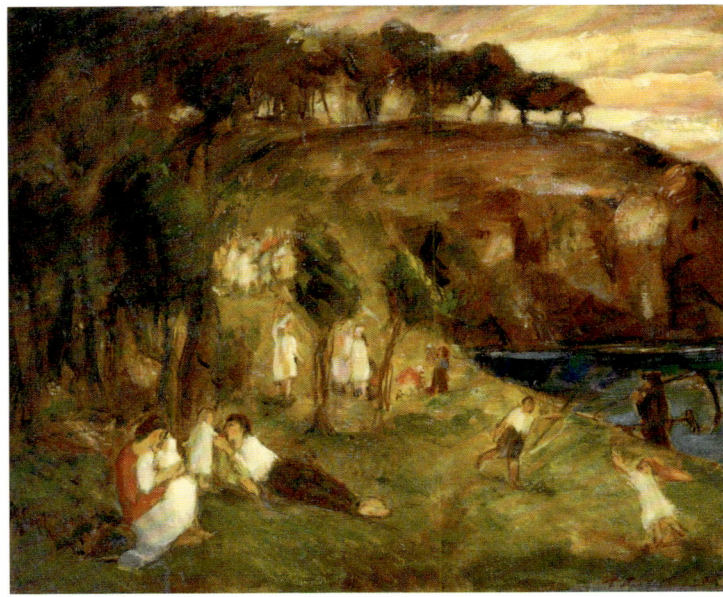

63. *Joy of Life*, 1920. Oil on canvas, 25 x 22 inches.
Martin and Edith Stein Collection.

47

ADVENTURES OF AN ARTIST COUPLE IN NEW YORK, 1921-29

Bernstein and Meyerowitz were invited to make portraits of Albert Einstein at the first Zionist meeting in America, held in New York in the spring of 1921, on the occasion of Einstein's first trip to America.[148] In Russia, Meyerowitz's father had been a member of a group called "Lovers of Zion," which continued in America as "Friends of Zion." After his father's death, William joined the group.[149] Einstein came to help raise money for the Jewish Development Fund to build Hebrew University in Jerusalem. "We were seated on either side of him on the stage." Bernstein recalled: "The leading Zionists of the period were there." Among others, she remembered the biochemist and future president of the state of Israel, Chaim Weizmann, reading the Balfour Declaration: "The speakers spoke of their dreams for the establishment of the new state, although it could not be said for certain that it would ever become a reality. Einstein's presence had an electrifying effect on everyone."[150] Bernstein and Meyerowitz sat near Einstein, who she recalled asked them to translate because he did not yet understand English that well.[151] At least three of Bernstein's sketches of Einstein on paper survive as well as an etching and a painting. In her painting, she depicted him standing before a chalk-board with one of his formulas inscribed, managing to capture his intensity and his singular creativity.

Not long after her Einstein series, Bernstein painted a portrait in oil of one of her husband's three sisters, which she called *Girlhood*. She later described the painting as "a portrait of this blonde girl contemplating the peaches which symbolized the three stages of life—youth, development and maturity. The green peach, the partly blooming peach and the fully ripened peach represented the full cycle of the fruit's ripening. The sitter was my husband's sister, Minna. She was visiting us at our studio in 1921 when we were guests of the Hale family in Folly Cove [Gloucester], Massachusetts."[152] Bernstein exhibited *Girlhood* in 1921 in the Winter Exhibition at the National Academy of Design and then again in 1922, in Philadelphia, at the Annual Exhibition of the Pennsylvania Academy.

In May 1922 Bernstein participated in the seventh group show of The Eclectics, this time at the Dudensing Galleries. "Theresa Bernstein's flowers and her beach scene alike smolder with autumnal color under the heat of a September atmosphere," wrote the *Times* critic. "Her palette gathers up all the richness of complete maturity whatever subject she paints."[153]

Later in 1922, Bernstein and Meyerowitz, perhaps seeking a change of scene after losing their child, decided to make a trip to

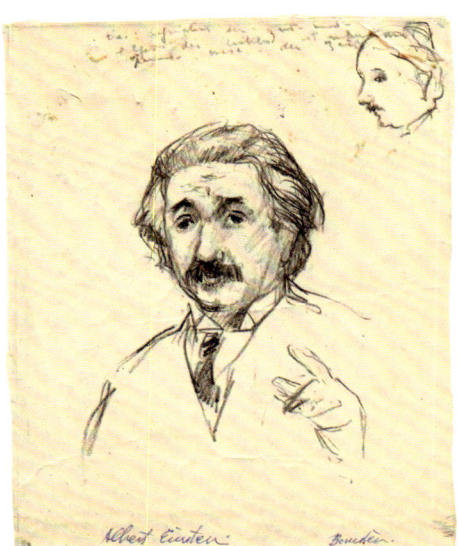

64. *Albert Einstein 1*, 1921. Pencil on paper, 10 x 8 inches. Theresa Bernstein and William Meyerowitz Foundation.

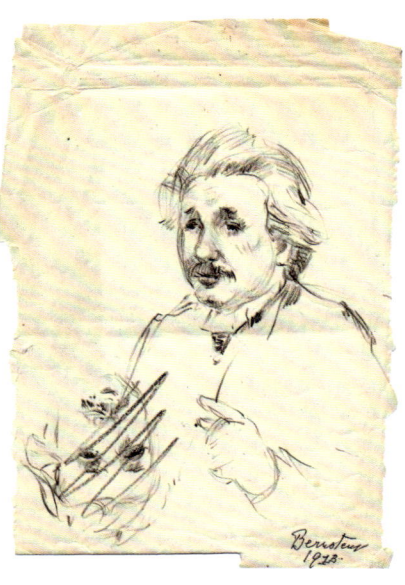

65. *Albert Einstein 2*, 1921. Pencil on paper, 10 x 7 inches. Theresa Bernstein and William Meyerowitz Foundation.

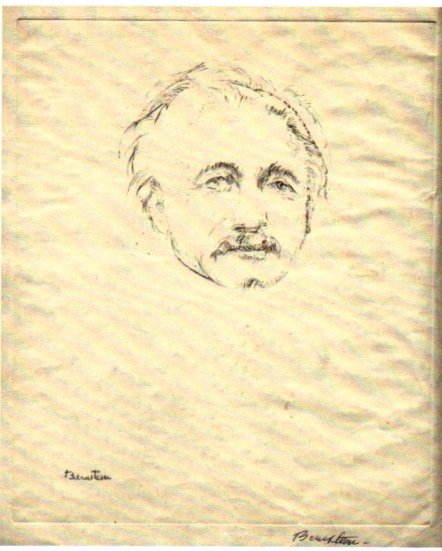

66. *Albert Einstein*, 1921. Etching on paper, 9¾ x 8 inches. Theresa Bernstein and William Meyerowitz Foundation.

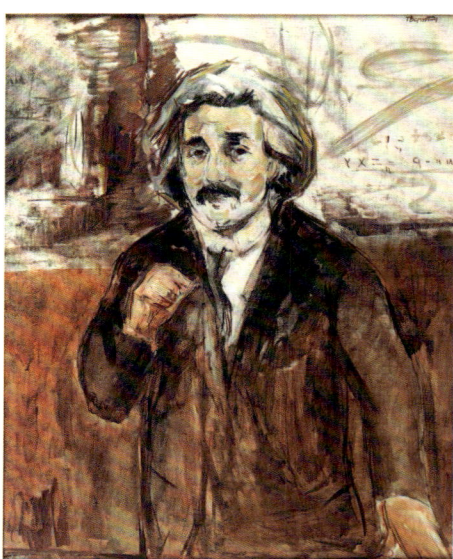

67. *Albert Einstein*, 1921. Oil on canvas, 23 x 19 inches. Private collection.

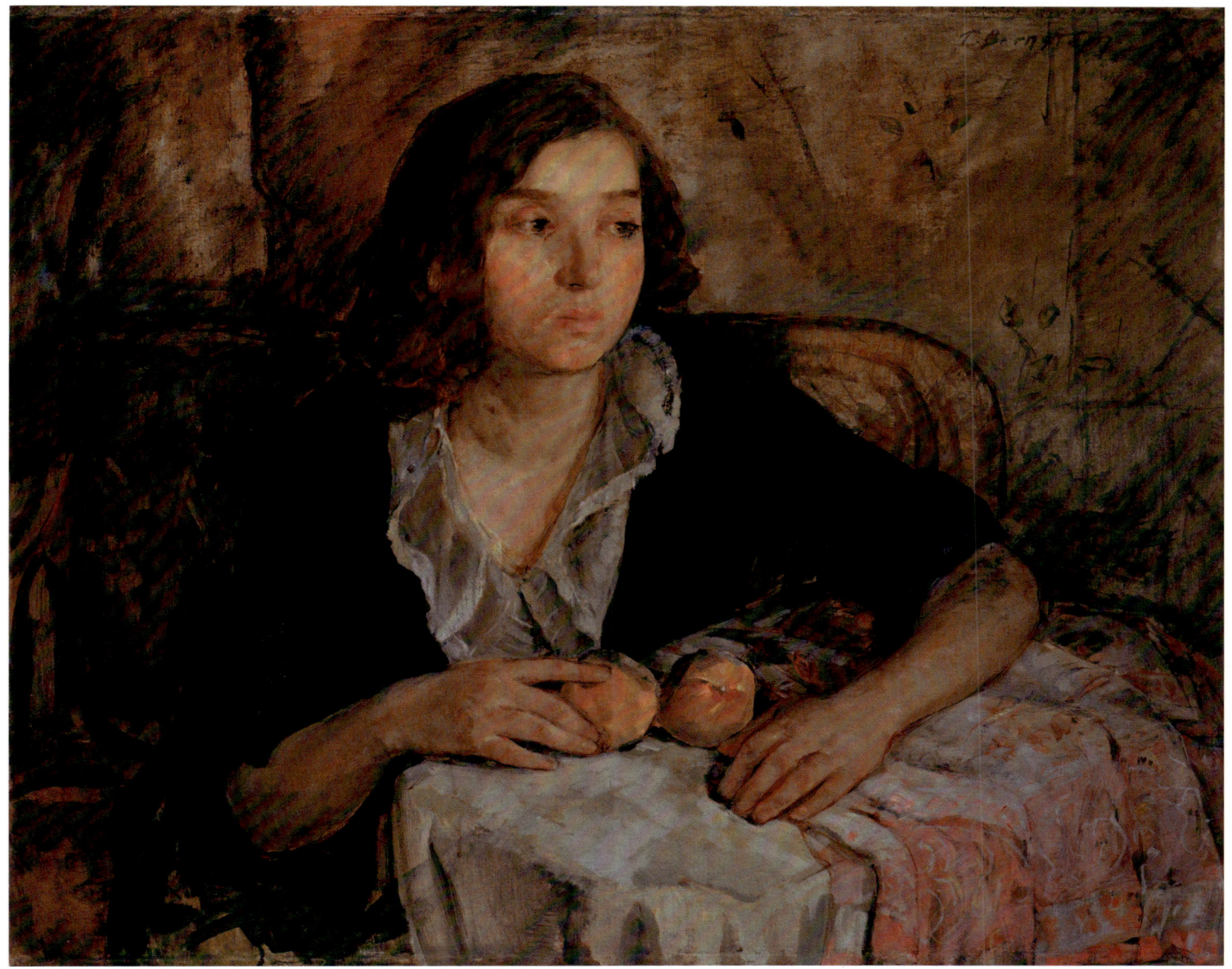

68. *Girlhood*, 1921. Oil on canvas, 29 x 35⅛ inches. The Phillips Collection, Washington, D.C.

Europe, where their funds enabled them to stay for five months. They visited London, Holland, Berlin, Poland, Vienna, Venice, Florence, Rome, and Paris. In Venice, they splurged for a brief stay at the Hotel Europa because it offered a great view, which she recalled painting from a small balcony (see fig. 89): "the sun in all its glory, radiating across of the arch of the Venetian scene. The little island and the Santa Maria della Salute, a great antique church in the center of the canal, and all the gondolas with their sweeping curves, like lilies on the water, were dancing in the sunlight."[154]

In October 1923 Bernstein showed her large canvas *The Milliners* (1919) at the Exhibition of the National Association of Women Painters and Sculptors, where it won the John Clerici prize of $100. To an interviewer, Bernstein explained her method: "I find that I can paint almost anything I have seen, provided I make sketches of it immediately, before any other impression superimposes itself in my thoughts. When I am creating a group, I conceive it as a unit, and then seek out my types. Perhaps I find them among my friends, as I do not like to work from people who pose. They seem unnatural."[155]

In *The Milliners*, Bernstein incorporated portraits of her mother, William's mother, his sisters Sophie, Bessie, and Minna, along with Katie, her parents' housekeeper. All her models were born

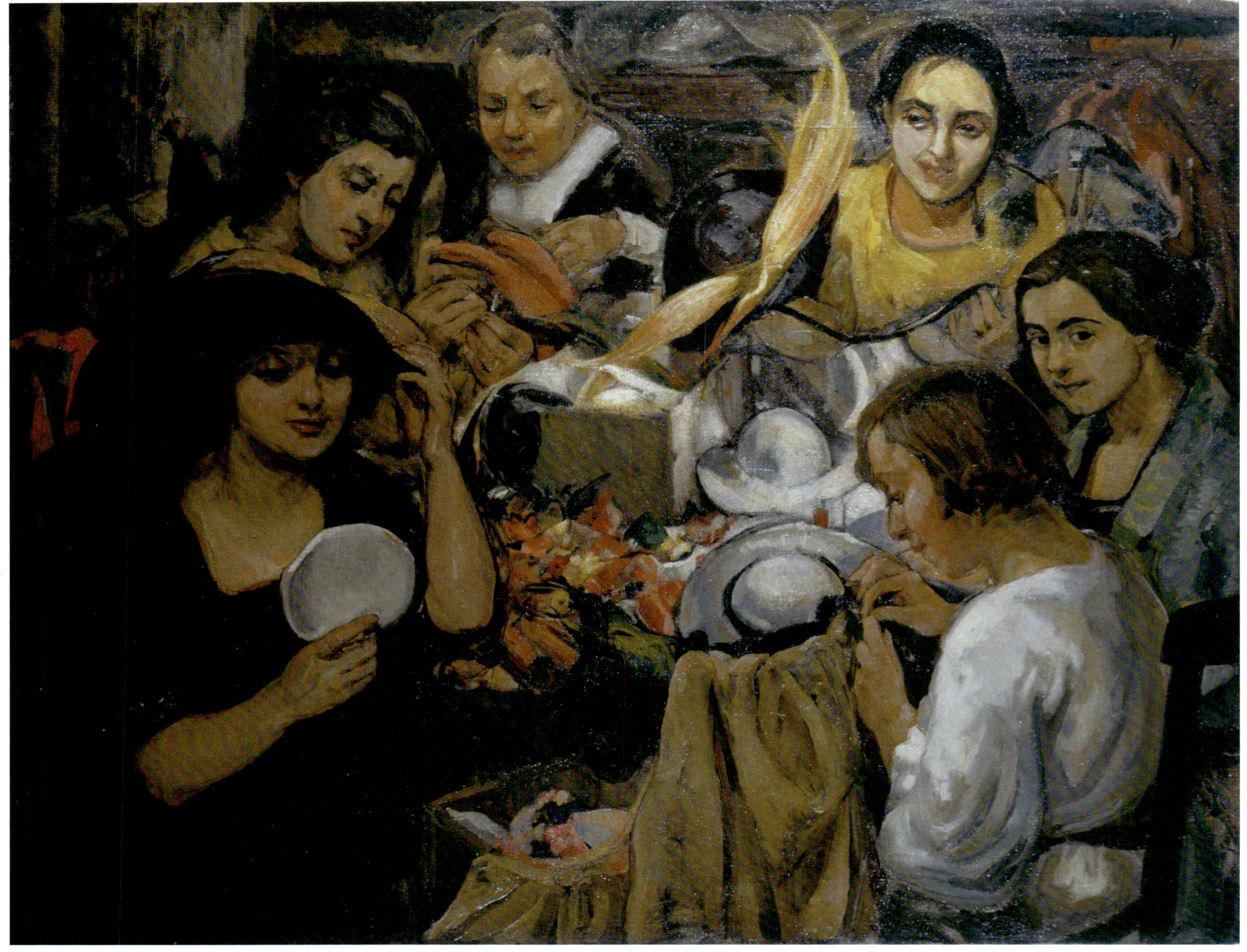

69. *The Milliners*, 1918. Oil on canvas, 40 x 50 inches. Private collection.

in Europe, and all but Katie were Jewish. At the time Bernstein painted *The Milliners*, Jewish immigrants populated the garment trades in New York City, where many, including Bill's sister Sophie, worked as hatmakers or made the artificial flowers that decorated hats, often doing some of the skilled labor at home.[156] Thus, Bernstein can paint a slice of immigrant life with empathy, knowing both the scene and the personal subjects firsthand.

Bernstein finished 1923 with a flurry of activity. In November, the Art Institute of Chicago's juried show of painting and sculpture included *The Music Lovers*. None of the medals awarded went to women; two of the winners, George Bellows and Charles W. Hawthorne, have earned a secure place in history. The all-male jurors for paintings are today at least as obscure as Bernstein, with the exception of Ernest Lawson, who was a member of "The Eight." Meyerowitz, who was busy with etchings, was not in this show.

The next month, Bernstein again showed her canvas *Girlhood* in the Ninth Exhibition of Contemporary American Oil Paintings at the Corcoran Gallery of Art. At the opening reception, Duncan Phillips and his wife, Marjorie, attended and briefly met Bernstein, who was shy and did not recognize who they were. She was later surprised to learn later that Phillips had purchased *Girlhood* for his Washington DC museum, making it the first museum to purchase one of her paintings.[157]

In 1924 Bernstein became a founding member of the New York Society of Women Artists. She recalled colleagues in this group such as Marguerite Zorach, Dorothy Varian, and Anne Goldthwaite. By now, she had become acutely aware of the challenges for women artists. She had been exhibiting with the National Association of Women Artists since 1916. When asked in 1923 to speak at the University Club in Washington DC, she chose "to talk about how women have minimal representation in annuals throughout the country. Juries don't accept the work of women; and if it isn't hanging on the wall, it isn't seen. Women have to assert themselves."[158] Such outspoken activism cannot have endeared her to the men whose approval she needed in order to enter mixed exhibitions.

Bernstein did not shy away from painting themes that featured women's concerns. Around this time she painted *Baby Carriages Laundry Day, Park Slope, Brooklyn*.[159] In the foreground a mother in a red dress is shown minding her own and the others' baby carriages while in the background another mother hangs out her wash. Clotheslines drooping with garments fill the middle

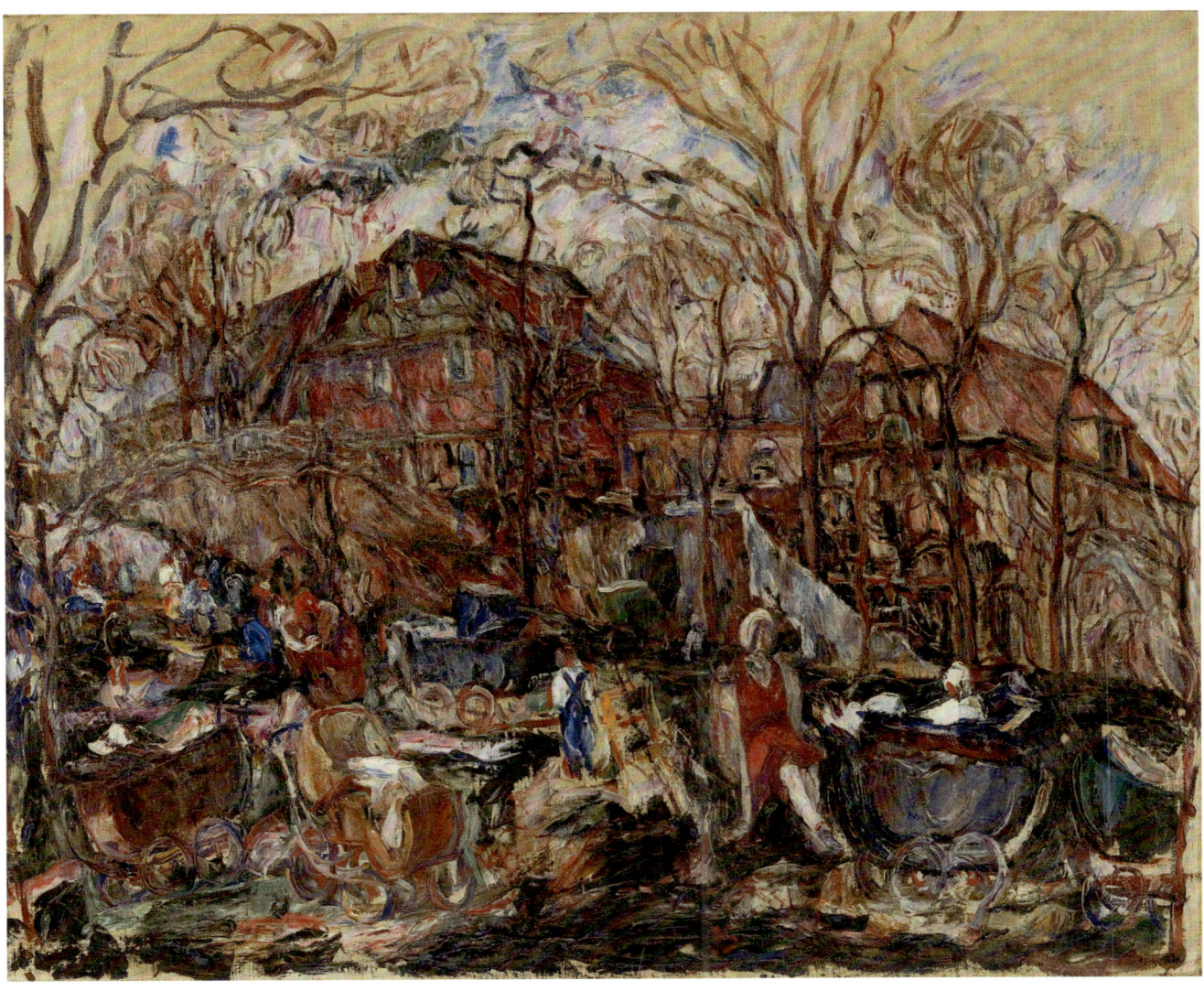

70. *Baby Carriages Laundry Day, Park Slope Brooklyn*, ca. 1923. Oil on canvas, 36¼ x 43¼ inches. Collection Girard Jackson.

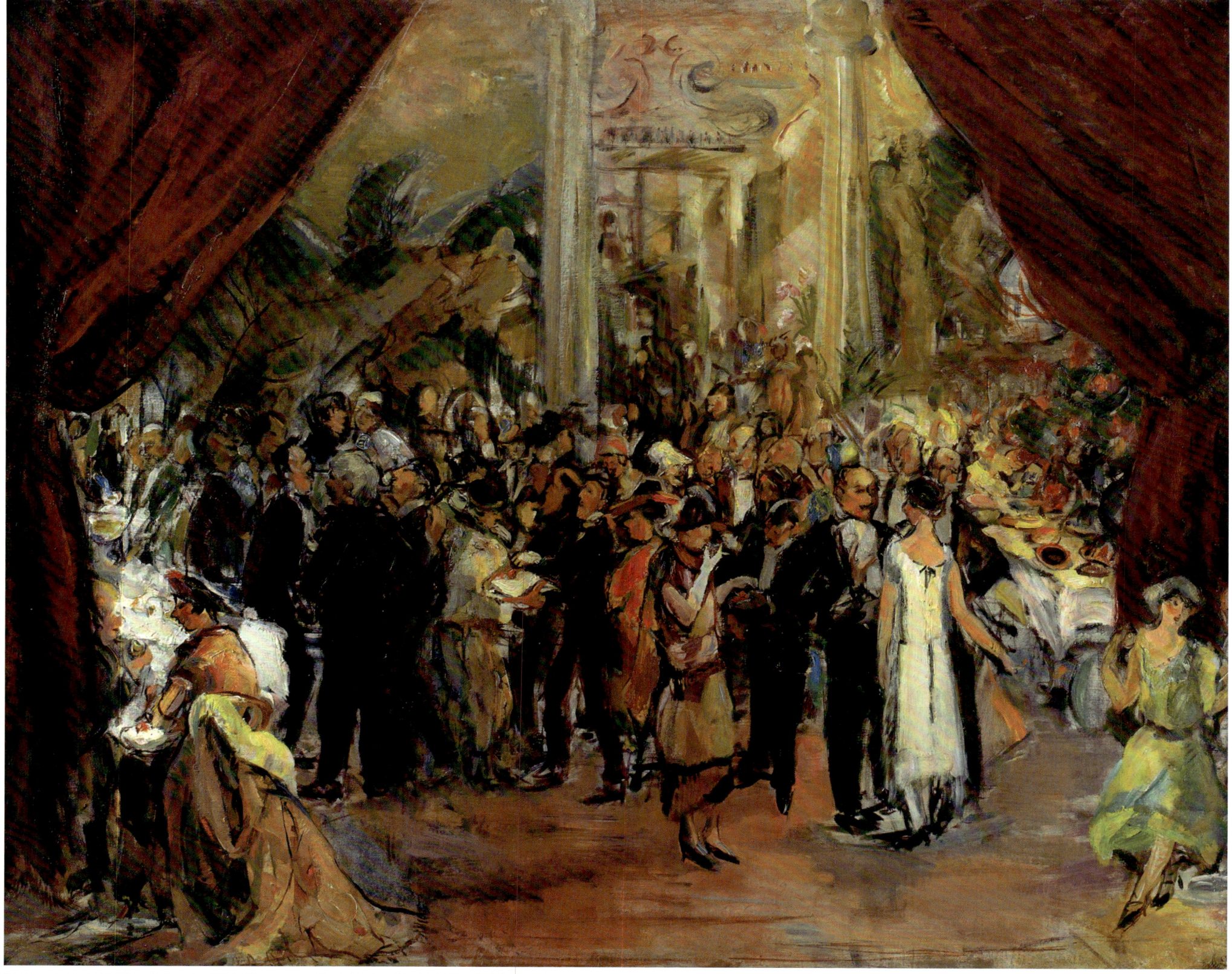

71. *Gertrude Vanderbilt Whitney's Reception*, 1924. Oil on canvas, 29 x 36 inches. New York Historical Society, New York.

ground. The theme, expressing Bernstein's empathy for the many chores of mothers of young children, is especially poignant considering her own loss.

In 1925 Bernstein showed her canvas *Mrs. Whitney's Reception* (now known as *Gertrude Vanderbilt Whitney's Reception*) at the tenth annual exhibition of the Whitney Studio Club held at the Anderson Galleries.[160] By making one of Mrs. Whitney's soirees her subject, Bernstein appears to have tried to get the patron's attention and persuade her to purchase a painting. The problem was that although Mrs. Whitney paid the bills, she employed Juliana Force to oversee the shows at the Studio Club, select works for purchase, and define the direction of the Whitney Museum after its opening in 1931.

Bernstein later wrote about attending one of the masquerade balls at the Whitney Museum on Eighth Street. She recalled that she, dressed as Catherine the Great, was dancing a waltz with the artist Reginald Marsh, who was dressed as a lifeguard. Meanwhile, her husband, dressed as a French cab driver, had just finished dancing with Peggy Bacon, who came as "a lady suffragette." Meyerowitz was relaxing on a chair "in the hall when Mrs. Juliana Force came in, sat on his lap, put her arms around his shoulders, and said, 'Kiss me, kiss me.' William looked at her and said, 'You're not my cup of tea.' She got off."[161] Bernstein would have agreed with Edward Hopper's wife, Jo, who explained, "I came right along with my husband, not leaving him for their devices—Mrs. Force always ready to grab & do her Circe act on him—naturally she'd hate me. She hated wives."[162] Force had conducted a well-known affair with the art critic Forbes Watson while acquiring several examples of his wife Nan's work for the Whitney.[163] Neither Theresa nor Jo was willing to sacrifice her husband for the sake of her career.

From February 27 to March 15, 1926, Bernstein had a successful solo show of paintings at the Civic Club (14 West Twelfth Street). The show won considerable press attention, headlining a set of reviews in the *Times*, but then the anonymous critic rambled, interjecting a sexist tone into his analysis: "Theresa Bernstein's attitude toward her work seems to be circuitous rather than direct. This is, in itself, a baffling feminine quality, but dependable. . . . The state of mind has nothing to do with method of painting. That is direct and contemporary." He also cited her "intellectual bent" and her "intense emotional state."[164] The result of this and other reviews were sales of about half the show.[165]

Later in 1926, both Bernstein and Meyerowitz figured in a show of "younger American artists" chosen to inaugurate the new wing of the Brooklyn Museum. The installation featured artists grouped around "the art colonies of Provincetown, Woodstock, Gloucester, Taos, and New Hope." The art critic for the *Brooklyn Daily Eagle*, Helen Appleton Read, noted: "The Gloucester group numbers many well-known names—Theresa Bernstein, William Meyerowitz, Hayley Lever, Eben Comins, Edward Hopper and Tod Lindenmuth. There appears to be no predominant point of view or mannerism."[166]

Read singled out Hopper's work for praise at a time when he was not yet well established. Hopper had just two years earlier had his first commercial success, showing watercolors at the Frank K. M. Rehn Gallery, which continued to represent him until the end of his life. Although the Rehn Gallery did take some of Meyerowitz's work on consignment, it rarely ever showed work by women.[157]

Hopper's long overdue success resulted at least in part from help he had gotten from the artist Josephine Nivison, whom he had married in 1924, the year after she got him included in a watercolor show to which she had been invited at the Brooklyn Museum. Hopper won the purchase prize and benefitted from resultant publicity.[168] Bernstein was eight years younger than Hopper, whom she knew in both Gloucester (where she and Meyerowitz bought a summer house in 1924) and New York. She had won many prizes and received press attention for her paintings at a time when Hopper had been obliged to work as a commercial illustrator. Juries at the National Academy of Design regularly accepted Bernstein's paintings, at least thirty by her own count. But, she recalled, "I was not elected to be a member. I was nominated five times with a majority of the votes, but two-thirds was required for membership. The few women who belonged were not inclined to vote for another woman."[169] While accepting Bernstein's paintings, the academy had so often rejected Hopper's canvases that he turned down his election as an associate member in March 1932, provoking an outburst of press attention.[170] Now Hopper's and Bernstein's career trajectories would shift dramatically—perhaps in part the result of their marriages to other artists, which might reflect a gender difference in the effect of marriage on an artist couple.

Yet on at least one occasion, Bernstein's marriage to Meyerowitz seems to have worked to her advantage. Duncan Phillips had already purchased William Meyerowitz's *Still Life*

Window for his Washington DC museum when in December 1923 he encountered Bernstein, who was there to show her husband's painting to a friend. It was after hearing her speak to her friend about key works in his collection that Phillips introduced

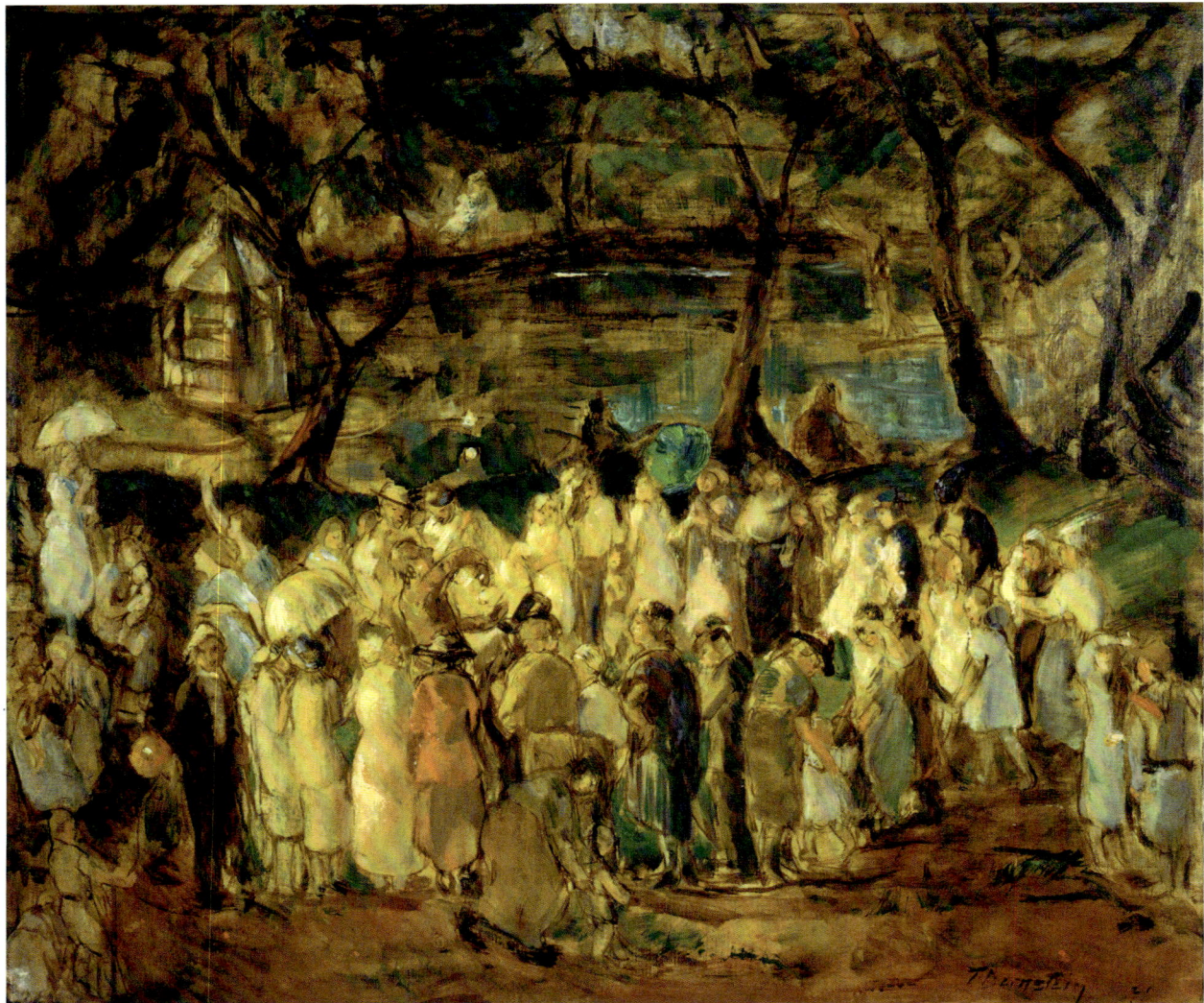

72. *Garnersville*, 1921. Oil on canvas, 29 x 35⅛ inches. The Phillips Collection, Washington, D.C.

himself to her at the Corcoran Biennial's opening party. He went on to purchase from the show her painting *Girlhood*.[171] This purchase preceded his purchase of Hopper's painting *Sunday*, which he had bought in 1926, not long after its completion.[172]

In his 1926 book *A Collection in the Making*, Phillips called Bernstein "a painter of appealing individuality and commendable courage for difficult undertakings. She seems to be enamoured of the effect of color and light simplifying a throng of people and often she attempts, from a safe distance, to

suggest the movement of a crowd." He praised *Girlhood* in his own collection, writing that it "without sentimentality, observes the day dreams of youth and lingers tenderly over the sensitive drawing of the face, the arms, the hands. Miss Bernstein within a remarkable range gives evidence of considerable ability and promise of important achievement."[173]

In 1927 Phillips purchased a second work by Bernstein from Grand Central Galleries, an artists' cooperative exhibition space in New York, which was founded as a nonprofit association in 1922.[174] His pick, *Garnersville*, depicts a small New York town of which Bernstein wrote: "It had a large crowd of picnickers watching a juggler and various performers."[175] Phillips wrote to Meyerowitz,

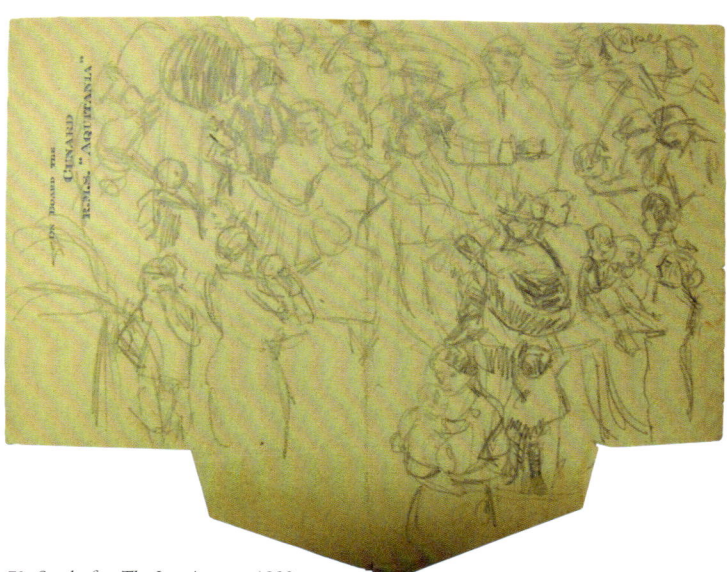

73. Study for *The Immigrants*, 1923.
Pencil on paper envelope, 8 x 10½ inches.
Theresa Bernstein and William Meyerowitz Foundation.

"By the way, I have a little picture of Theresa Bernstein's sent on by the Grand Central Galleries. Am I to send the check to Mrs. Meyerowitz or to the Galleries? Tell her please that I like it very much, it is a lovely thing in color."[176]

Crowds appealed to Bernstein. In 1923 she painted *The Immigrants*, showing people standing exposed on the deck of the Cunard RMS *Aquitania* as it arrived in New York. From a bird's-eye view, she focuses on one mother's tender embrace of her infant, while many other adults and children animate the open space. She

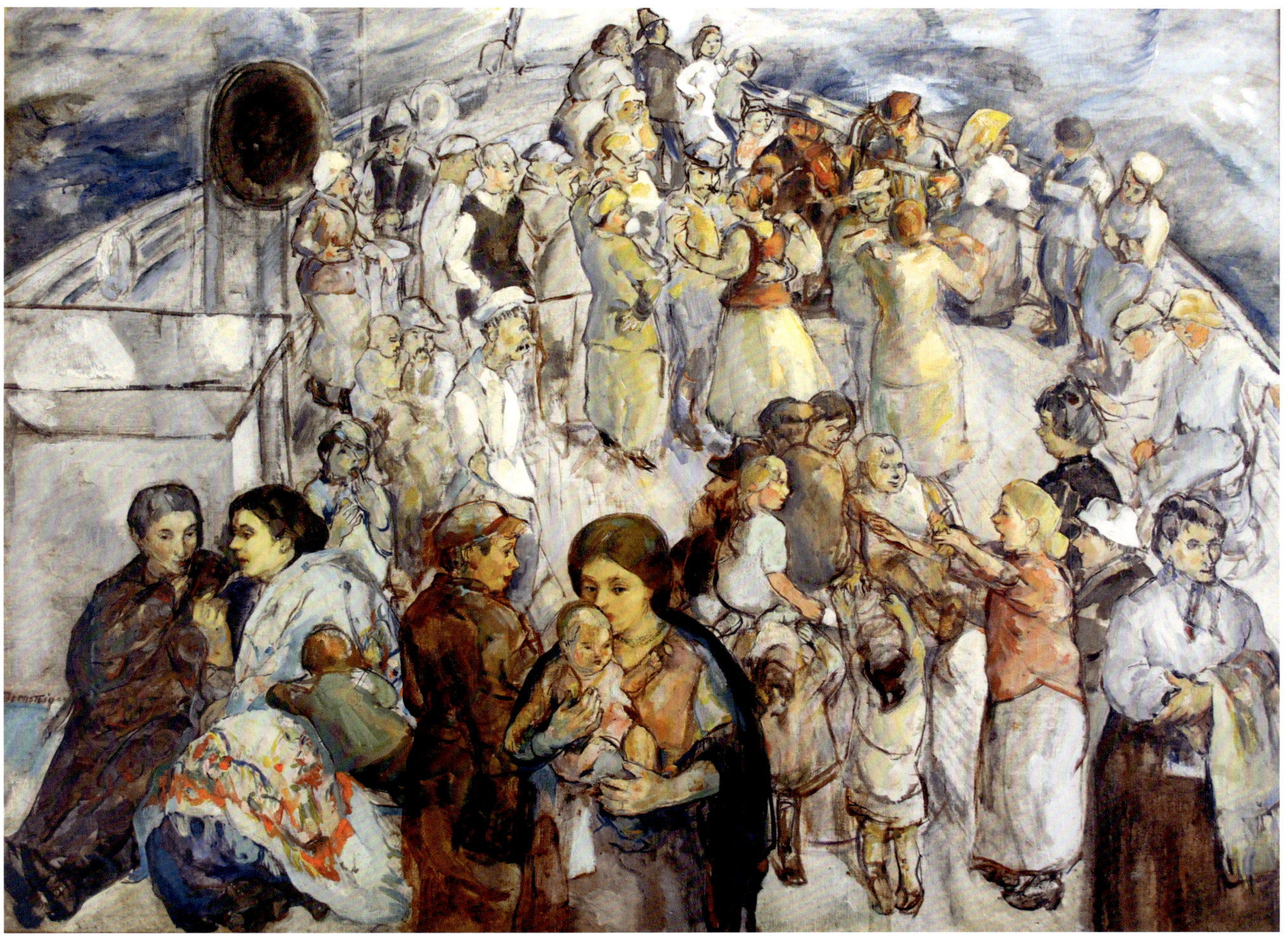

74. *The Immigrants*, 1923. Oil on canvas, 40 x 50 inches. Thomas and Karen Buckley.

emphasized their humanity just as America enacted laws to limit immigration during the early 1920s, restricting, among others, Jews who since the 1890s had been migrating in large numbers from the Russian Empire to escape persecution. An extant sketch on an envelope from the ship documents her presence.

At this time Bernstein also painted individuals, including a portrait of the modern dancer and choreographer Martha Graham. She posed for Bernstein in 1927, less than a year after "Martha Graham and Dance Group" made its debut in New York City. Though it is not known how the two women met, they were near contemporaries in the city, where Bernstein had earlier depicted modern dancers Isadora Duncan and Loie Fuller.

Other significant figures appear in Bernstein's pictures. In *The Chess Players* (1926), she depicted William playing chess with the Massachusetts champion while the artist Stuart Davis watched, and in the background she showed herself playing the piano. The

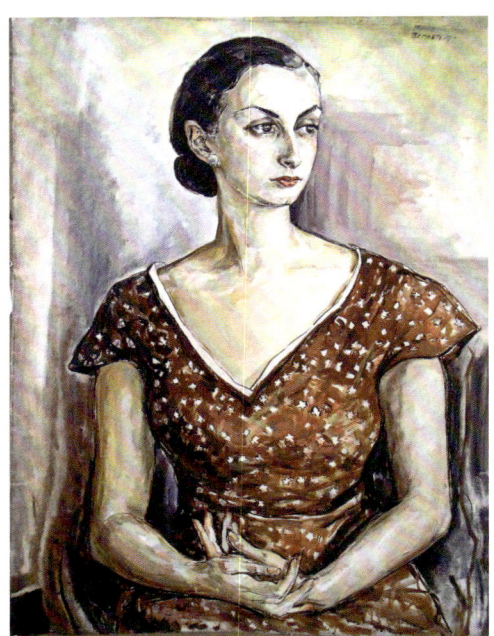

75. *Martha Graham*, 1927.
Oil on canvas, 35½ x 27 inches.
Theresa Bernstein and William Meyerowitz Foundation.

following year, Bernstein painted *Cribbage Players*, probably depicting Gloucester fishermen at leisure (see fig. 200).

Success continued for Bernstein when she placed ahead of Hopper in the critical response to her show of twenty-six paintings at Arnold Constable's, an upscale department store on Fifth Avenue in January 1929: "International and Other Exhibitions from Pillar to Post but Theresa Bernstein Makes It Worth While— Paul Burlin, Hopper, and Harman." The art critic Edward Alden Jewell noted that "The honor of having the most thronged show was carried off by Miss Bernstein. . . . The portraits have body. . . . Above all, there is room left for character."[177] In popularity and publicity, Bernstein still trumped Hopper.

By this time, however, Bernstein had already begun to change her style, possibly in response to her enjoyment of jazz music, which she liked to listen to together with Stuart Davis, her neighbor in Gloucester. There were recordings in Gloucester as well as excursions to favorite clubs in Harlem. Bernstein shared Davis's enthusiasm for African American jazz and culture.[178] Yet she had already shown this interest with her painting *Dance Hall* (1911), an African American nightspot that caught her attention while she was studying in Blowing Rock, North Carolina.

Later, Bernstein recalled mingling with George and Ira Gershwin at the Whitney Studio Club during the 1920s, when they too embraced the influence of jazz. Bernstein's interest in jazz coincides with that of many visual artists and composers who were seeking to develop an original "American" art in the 1920s.[179]

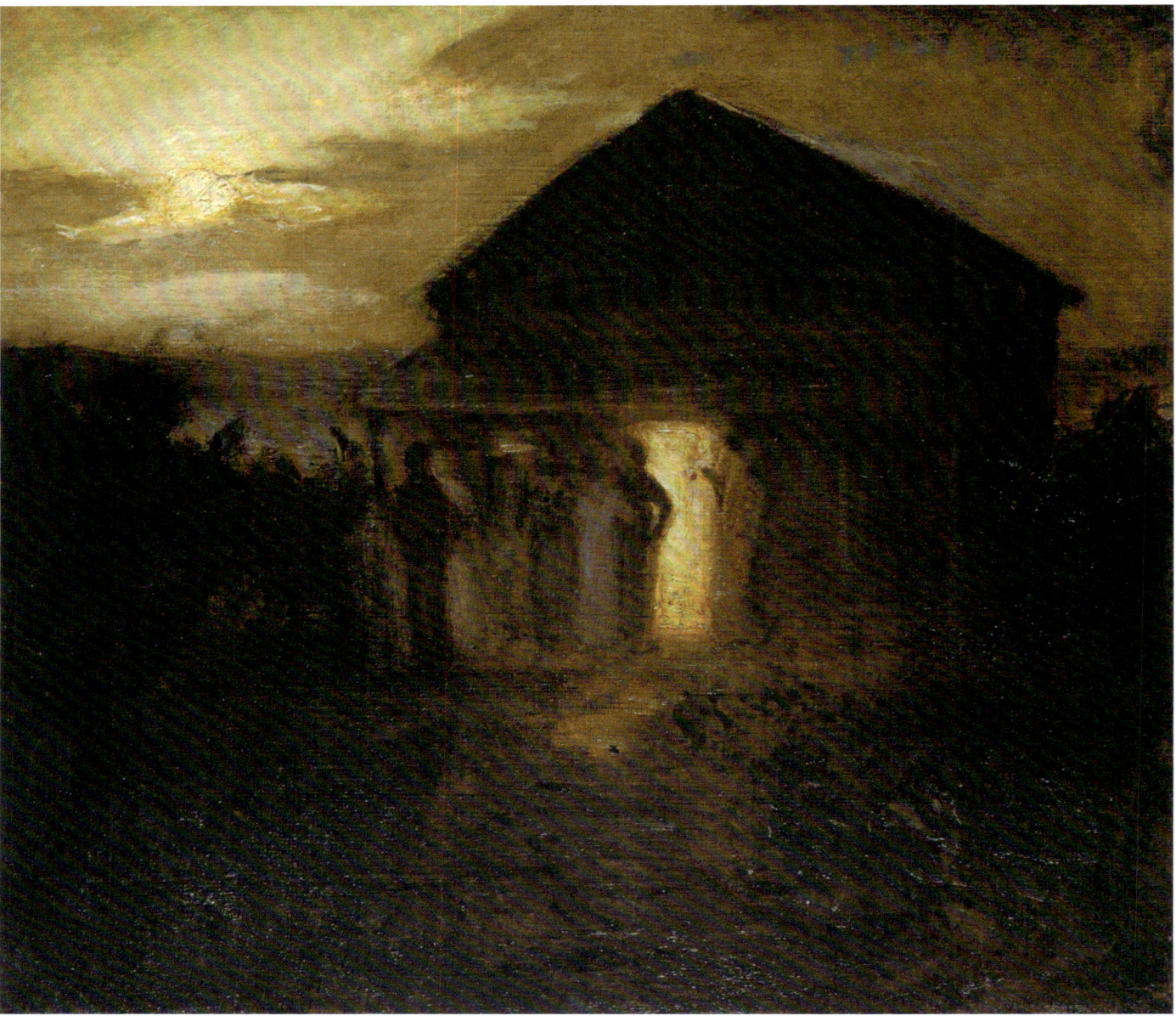

76. *Dance Hall*, 1911.
Oil on canvas, 22 x 25 inches.
Martin and Edith Stein Collection.

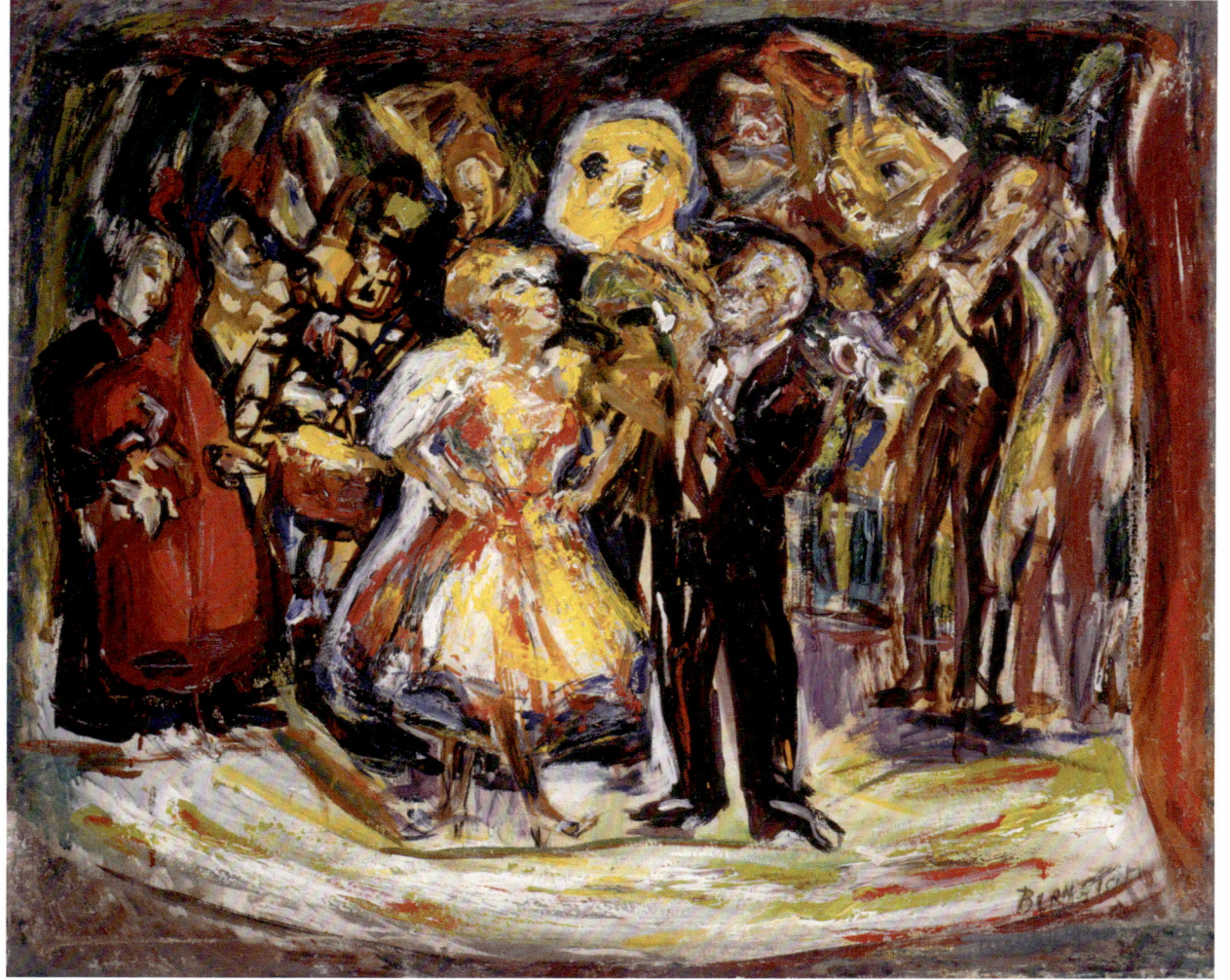

77. *Lil Hardin and Louis Armstrong*, ca. 1927. Oil on canvas, 27 x 30 inches. Girard Jackson Collection.

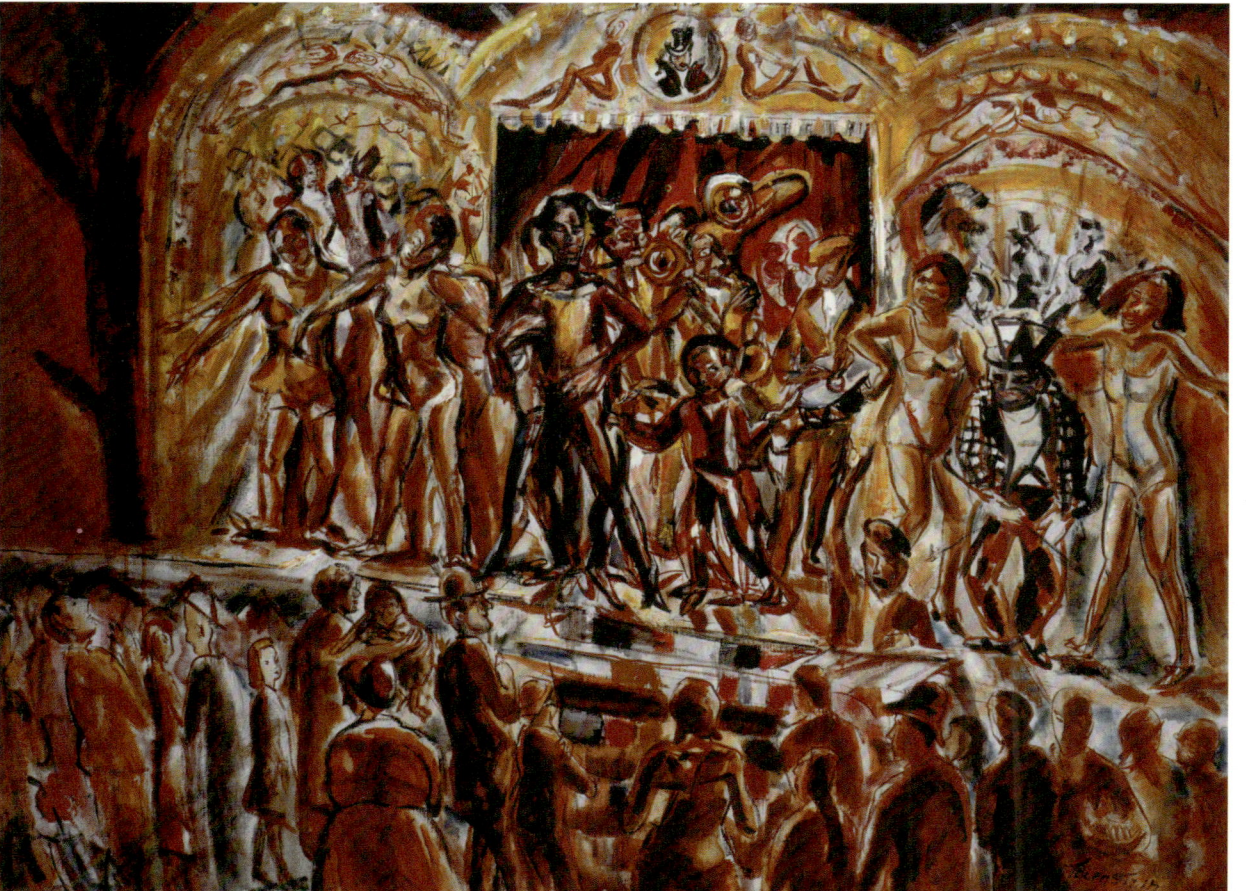

78. *Hot Chocolates*, 1929. Oil on canvas, 30¼ x 40 inches. Smithsonian American Art Museum, Washington, D.C. Gift of Girard Jackson.

In 1927 she painted *Lil Hardin and Louis Armstrong* at the time when the trumpeter was married to the singer. Here, Bernstein's style can be seen as "a painter's innovative solution to the synesthetic challenge of converting aural perception into visual form."[180]

A "noisy, high-spirited and fast moving show" called the *Hot Chocolates*, an African American musical revue with words by Andy Razaf and music by Fats Waller, became the theme of a painting by Bernstein in 1929.[181] Billed as a "Senegambian song-and-dance theatre," the revue appeared on Broadway in June 1929, after having been performed since February at "Connie's Inn, a Harlem cabaret known to tourists from downtown."[182] Since Bernstein moved to Gloucester each summer, she might have painted this canvas after one of the excursions she made to her favorite clubs in Harlem, before the revue reached Broadway.[183]

Yet 1929 would be hard on Bernstein. The carefree excursions to jazz clubs would not last. Her mother died. In late October, the stock market crashed and her father lost his Brooklyn business, which involved new machines to knit designs on sweaters. Once again he found himself without a means of earning his living. Bernstein recalled, "The Depression engulfed us all with its economic doldrums. Artists faced a challenge every day. There was no such thing as established [Social] security. One had to grapple with the elements or be overpowered by them."[184]

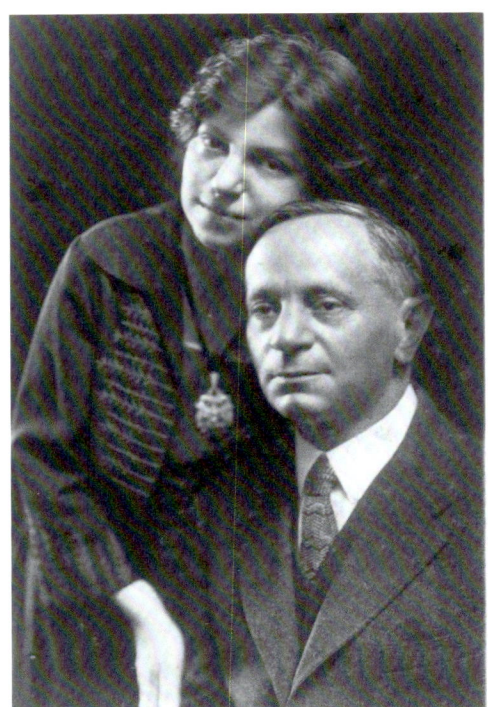

79. Theresa Bernstein with her father, Isadore Bernstein.

BERNSTEIN IN THE 1930S: FURTHER CHANGES TO HER STYLE DURING THE GREAT DEPRESSION

In 1930 Bernstein and Meyerowitz had simultaneous shows at the Baltimore Museum of Art. They met there the sisters Claribel and Etta Cone, who were patrons of modern art and then actively collecting work by Matisse and other artists in Paris. Using loose expressionistic brushwork, Bernstein painted a lively double portrait, *The Cone Sisters*.[185] As early as 1911, while painting in Blowing Rock, North Carolina, Bernstein had met their sister-in-law, Mrs. Sydney Cone, who purchased one of Bernstein's paintings.[186] Bernstein wrote that the Cone sisters "continued to buy several of our works for their collection."[187]

Also in 1930, Bernstein had a solo show at the nonprofit Grand Central Galleries in New York. In a review, Elisabeth Luther Cary compared Bernstein's early style, evident in her inclusion of *Polish Church: Easter Morning*, with the newer style in her more recent canvas, *The Chess Players*, which she described as executed "in a somewhat loose design. The warm color is also loosely woven across the canvas background, much of which is seen between the brush strokes."[188] Cary praised Bernstein's "extraordinary freedom and daring," even as she noted the change from her earlier successful realist style.

Economic hardship may have contributed to Bernstein's stylistic change during the 1930s, from using especially thick paint to working in a style that utilized much less pigment, for example, *Toscanini at Carnegie Hall* of 1930. Since money was in short supply, she may well have wished to save on the high cost of paint. In an interview, she recalled an earlier moment when her aesthetic

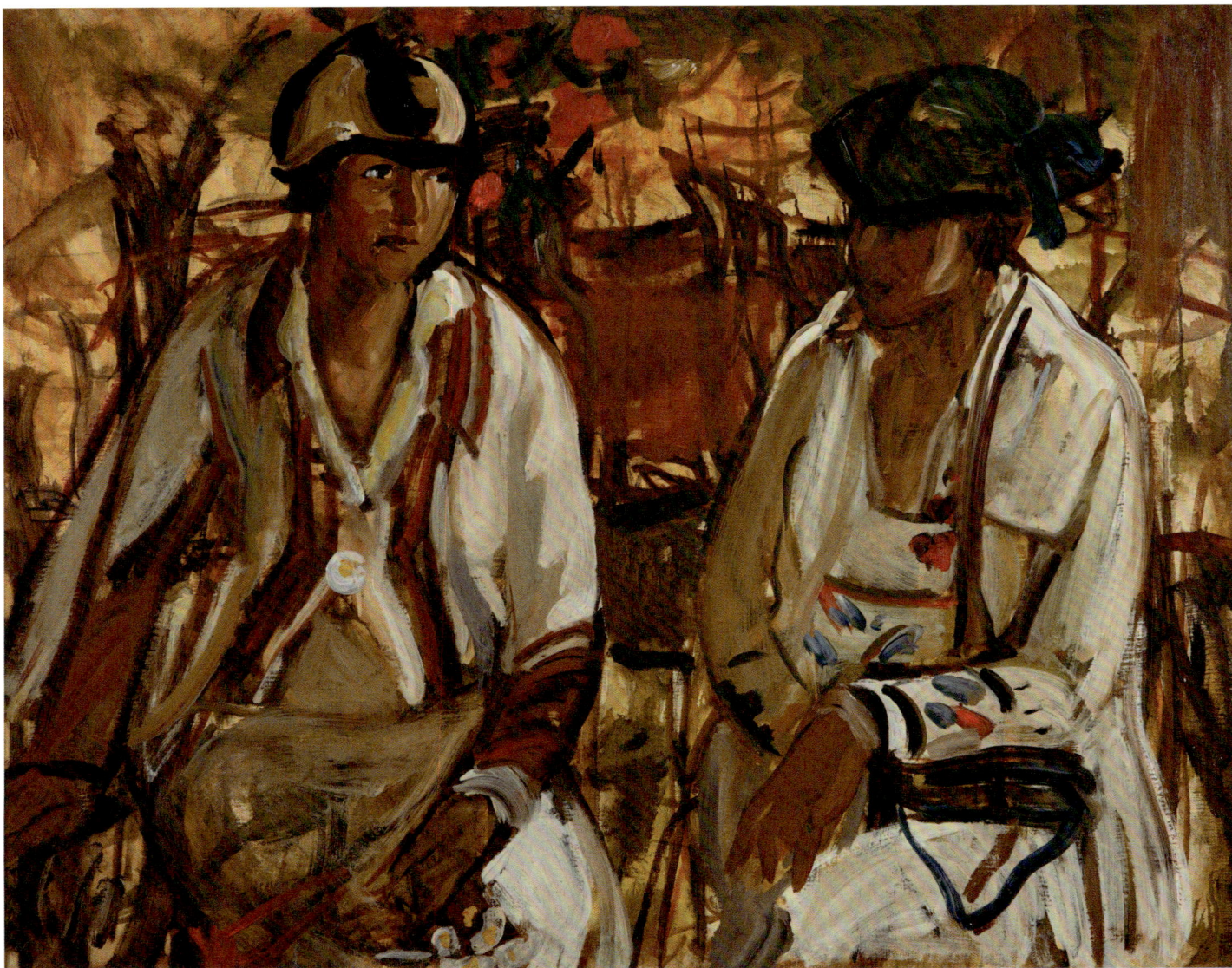

80. *The Cone Sisters*, 1930.
Oil on canvas, 40 x 50 inches.
Endicott College Collection,
Walter J. Manninen Trust.

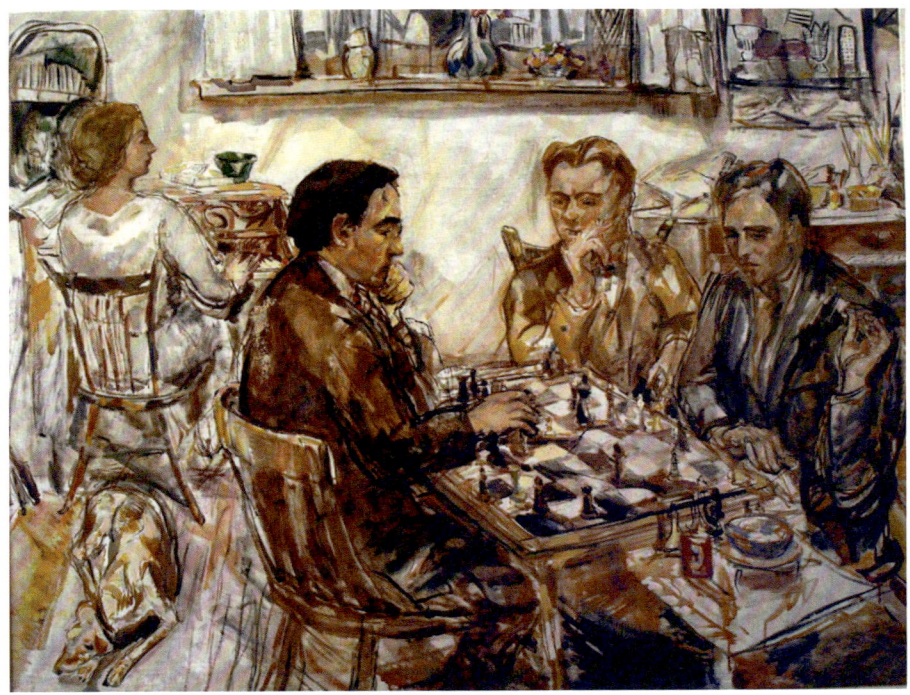

81. *The Chess Players*, 1932. Oil on canvas, 40 x 50 inches. Jim Fish Collection.

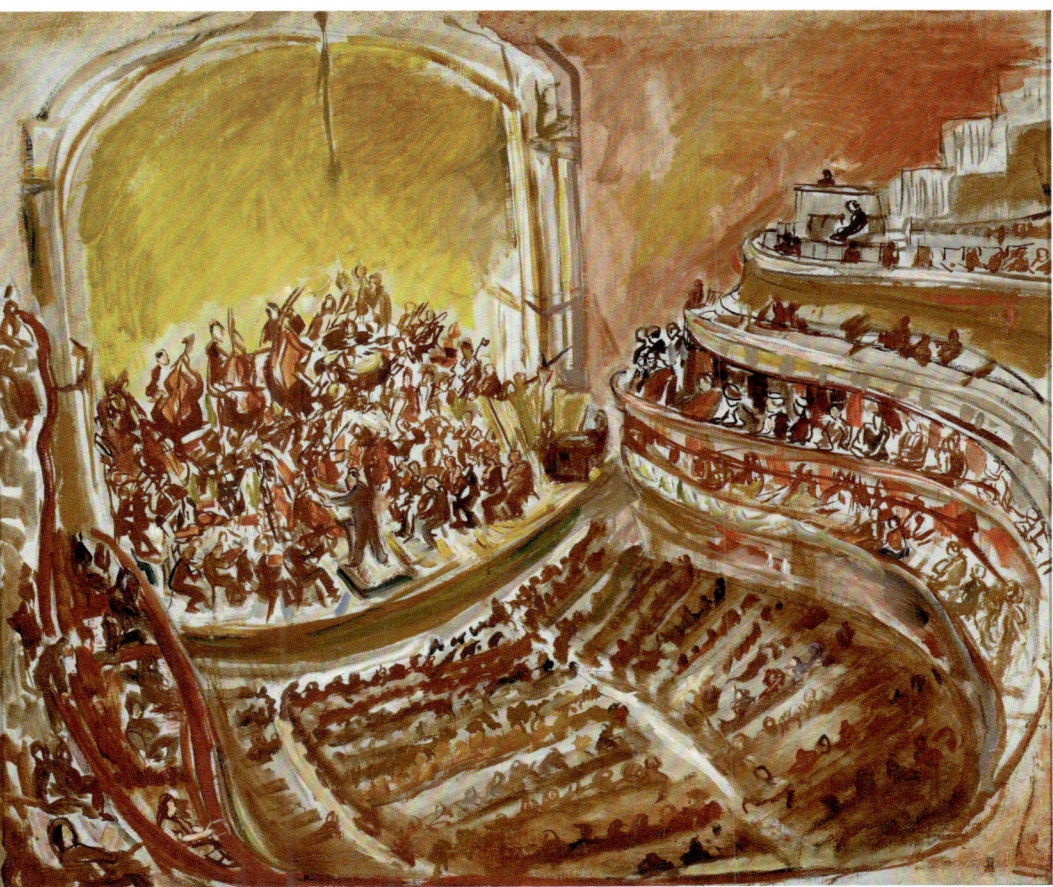

82. *Toscanini at Carnegie Hall*, 1930. Oil on canvas, 30 x 40 inches. Martin and Edith Stein Collection.

choices had been limited by her finances: "I was a struggling unknown, and I had to work with the few tubes of paint [that I] managed to scrape together during the hard winter. Naturally my range of colors was limited!"[189]

To save money, she and Meyerowitz moved in 1932 to 54 West Seventy-Fourth Street, a modest raw space that he renovated himself, constructing a sleeping loft to increase their work area. He produced a painting of the two of them in their new home and studio. They continued to teach and to show, but sales of their work suffered. When her father died in 1932, after undergoing a kidney operation in Boston, she arranged to pay the doctor with art.

When Bernstein was showing with the New York Society of Women Artists in 1932, a critic saw her as "a sort of twentieth century impressionist. The 'snapshot' quality of her work, its informal composition and broken prismatic color all look back to the nineteenth century. Unlike the luminists, however, she draws rather than paints with her brush. . . . The canvases are as thinly painted as watercolors."[190] Yet following her change in style, reviews were mixed.

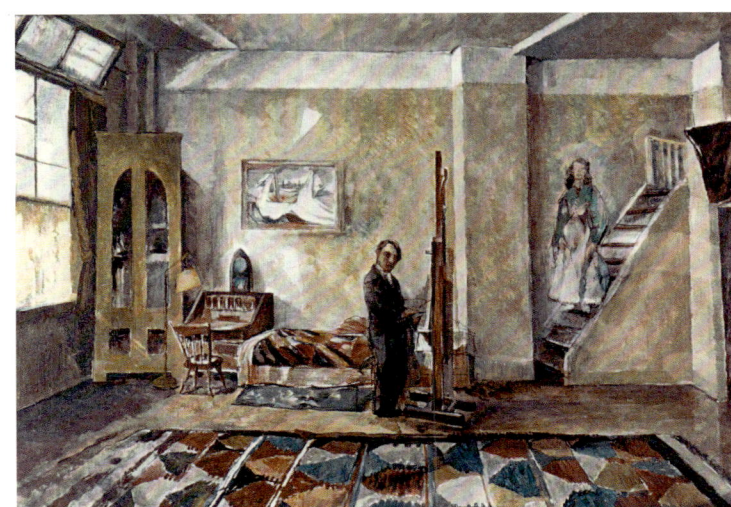

83. William Meyerowitz, *The Studio* (54 West 74th Street), 1935. Oil on canvas, 30 x 40 inches. Private collection.

Sometimes, as when reviewed together with Meyerowitz, Bernstein seemed to be "going lame."[191] To another critic, her work had "a delightfully sketchy quality."[192] She was accused of "formula-ridden persuasiveness" but also lauded for "a new and much bolder manner."[193]

Both the dire economic situation and her continued

interest in jazz appear to have contributed to the change in style. In 1935 Bernstein painted another image of a jazz singer, *Cab Calloway–Minnie the Moocher*, taking for her title his most famous song, remarking, "I began to listen to Cab Calloway to relieve my mind."[194] For this composition she used a looser, more improvisational style with bold colors reflecting jazz rhythms.

Meanwhile, in an ominous sign for the future, "Mr. and Mrs. William Meyerowitz (the former Theresa Bernstein)" were reported as attending a preview and tea for Brooklyn Museum members and their guests on January 7, 1935, for a show, "The Fine Prints of the Year, 1934," that included Meyerowitz but not Bernstein, although she, too, made prints (see figures 165–172).[195] This phrasing probably reflected the larger society's customs rather

than the Meyerowitz-Bernstein household, but even as Bernstein had learned to take care not to overshadow her artist husband, she was beginning to be eclipsed by him.[196]

In October 1935 the couple were among more than one hundred artists and critics who signed the call to artists for a congress to be set in New York City early in the winter. The American Artists' Congress, which took place in February 1936, intended to unite artists and enlist them to help combat fascism.[197] Their friend and Gloucester neighbor, Stuart Davis, took a lead in organizing the congress.

The congress would focus upon federal, state, and municipal projects: the Federal Art Bill, the rental of pictures, the economic plight of the artist, museum policies, fascism, and

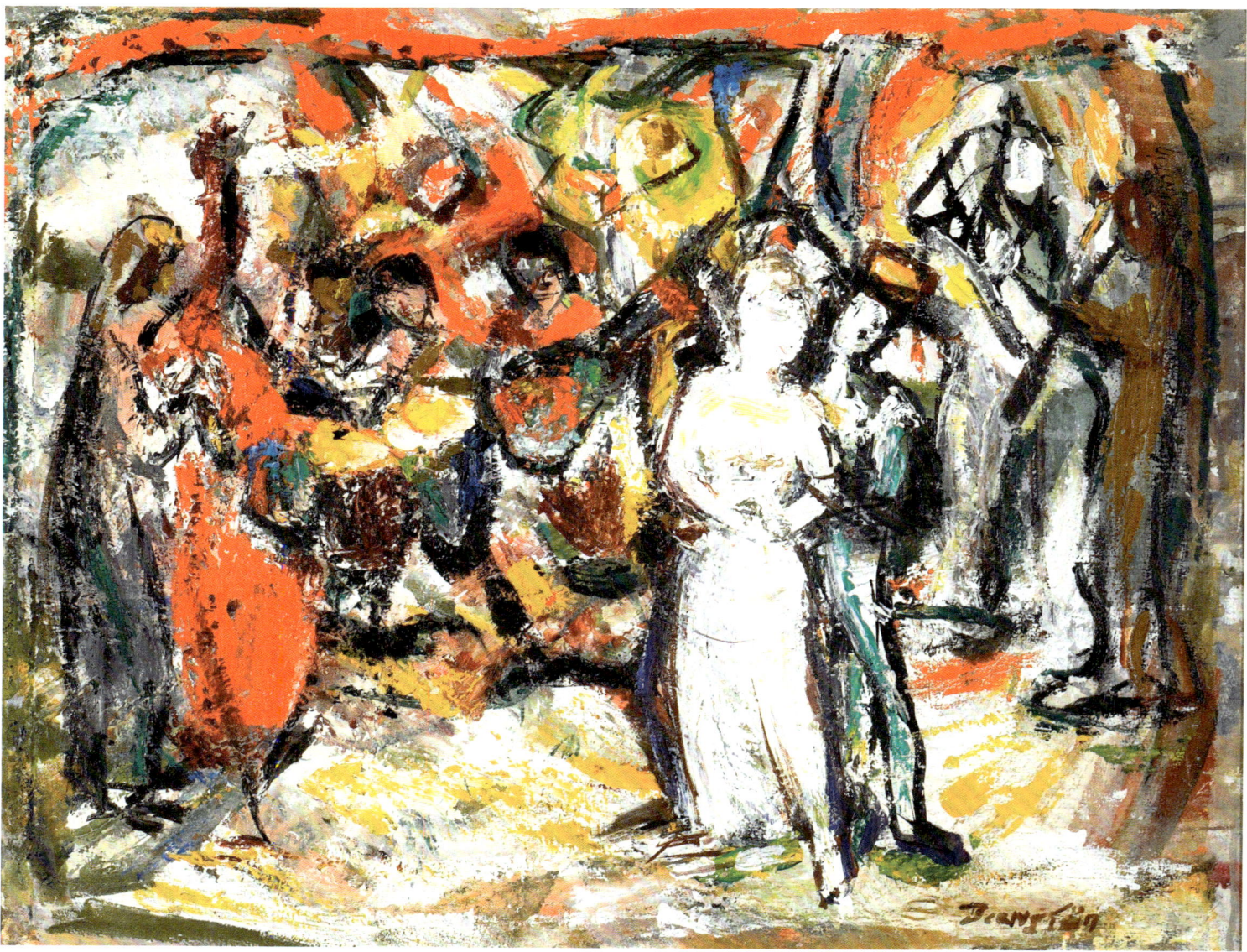

84. *Cab Calloway–Minnie the Moocher*, 1935.
Oil on canvas, 20 x 25 inches.
Martin and Edith Stein Collection.

war. Among the many other signers were Peggy Bacon, Lucile Blanch, Arnold Blanch, Peter Blume, Aaron Bohrod, Margaret Bourke-White, Ben Shahn, and Moses and Raphael Soyer.[198] The next month, for a print sale held at ACA Galleries in New York to aid the Artists' Congress, Bernstein and Meyerowitz joined a host of contributors, among them, Davis, Marsh, and Bourke-White, as well as Harry Gottlieb and Bertram Hartman.

In keeping with the left-leaning sympathies of the Artists' Congress, Bernstein also joined a committee to gather art for a museum in the Jewish autonomous region in the Russian Far East promoted by Stalin as a solution for the Jews. For the projected Birobidzhan Museum, the committee collected more than one hundred works of contemporary American art. An exhibition in an improvised space on Fifth Avenue in March 1936 featured donated works from artists such as Yasuo Kuniyoshi, Peggy Bacon, and William and Marguerite Zorach.[199] The committee, along with Bernstein and Stuart Davis, included others active on the political left, such as Nicolai Cikovsky, Minna Harkavy, Eugene Higgins, Frank C. Kirk, Louis Lozowick, Philip Reissman, Sol Wilson, and Adolf Wolff.[200]

Bernstein also participated in 1936 in an exhibition of contemporary art held at the New School for Social Research, 66 West Twelfth Street, and arranged as a benefit for the Little Red School House on Bleecker Street. Though the school was founded as a joint public-private educational experiment that tested principles of progressive education advocated by John Dewey, political conservatives forced it to go private. Its patron list was headed by Mrs. Franklin D. Roosevelt and Mayor Fiorello La Guardia.

During the 1930s, Bernstein continued to show her work in such large group exhibitions as the Carnegie Institute's International, the Corcoran Gallery's Biennial, as well as the annuals at institutions such as the Pennsylvania Academy, the National Academy of Design, the Salons of America, the Society of Independent Artists, and the Art Institute of Chicago.[201] She still received notice from the critics. She also showed regularly in New York, at the Uptown Gallery at 249 West End Avenue, directed by Robert Ulrich Godsoe, who also worked as a critic.

His stable of artists included Mexican muralist Diego Rivera, and Mark Rothko and Adolph Gottlieb, just before the latter two withdrew to show together as part of "The Ten." Established people commissioned portraits by Bernstein, often for presentation to institutions like Harvard University.[202] Museums occasionally purchased her paintings; for example, the Dayton Art Institute acquired *Girl in Old-Fashioned Bonnet* for $300 in 1936. She later told how Dayton requested her painting, but she told her husband that she could not send it because she had no frame. He offered to lend her one that he had just made for his own landscape, having spent an entire week carving it. When the museum acquired the painting, they got the frame too.[203]

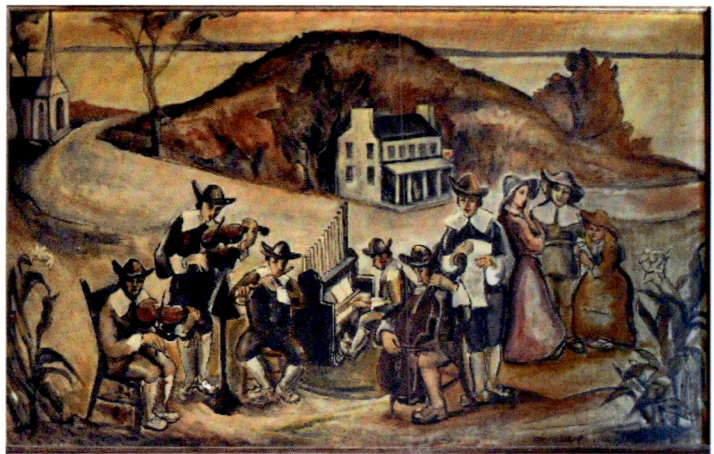

86. *First Orchestra in America*, U.S. Treasury Department mural for the Post Office in Manheim, Pennsylvania. 1938.

During the lean years of the Great Depression, Bernstein received some support for her work from the U.S. Treasury Department, which commissioned a mural from her for the Post Office in Manheim, Pennsylvania. She produced *The First Orchestra in America* in 1938, depicting a group of musicians in old Moravian dress playing their instruments in front of the home and church of Manheim's founder in the eighteenth century, Baron Wilhelm Stiegel.[204] She also made studies for two other murals for the Treasury Department: *Women of America* and *The Elevated Station*, but these were not executed. This commission represented much-needed income since few private individuals were buying art during the depression years.

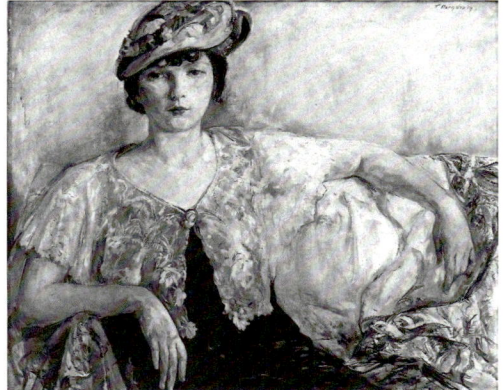

85. *Girl in Old-Fashioned Bonnet*, 1936. Oil on canvas. Deaccessioned from the Dayton Art Museum, Dayton, Ohio, now lost.

From the 1940s to 2002: Still Working but Overlooked

During World War II, Bernstein was apprehensive about the situation of her aunt, uncle, and cousins who were still living in Cracow, where she and Meyerowitz had visited them in 1922. As the reality of the Holocaust began to reach the United States, Bernstein and Meyerowitz, helpless to intervene in Europe, participated on the home front by donating art works to the fundraising efforts of the Joint Distribution Committee, a leading Jewish humanitarian assistance organization that rescued tens of thousands of Jews.[205] On January 5, 1942, an advertisement in the *New York Times* headlined "Jews Fight for the Right to Fight," campaigning to permit stateless Jews in Palestine to form an army "to fight side by side with the American people and her allied nations."[206] In December 1942 she and Meyerowitz attended a dinner for distinguished American public figures in support of the Committee for a Jewish Army of Stateless and Palestinian Jews. Among the prominent figures in the arts who supported this cause were the writer Ben Hecht, the critic Waldo Frank, the composer Arnold Schoenberg, the architect Eric Mendelsohn, and the sculptor William Zorach. She later reported that her aunt and uncle in Cracow "were annihilated by the Nazis in 1942."[207] Though she did not make overt references to the fate of the Jews in Europe in her art, she soon renewed her engagement with Jewish themes that had begun when she painted the *Portuguese Synagogue* in 1919 (see fig. 87), as well as with Zionist history, inspired by her chance to meet and sketch Einstein in 1921.

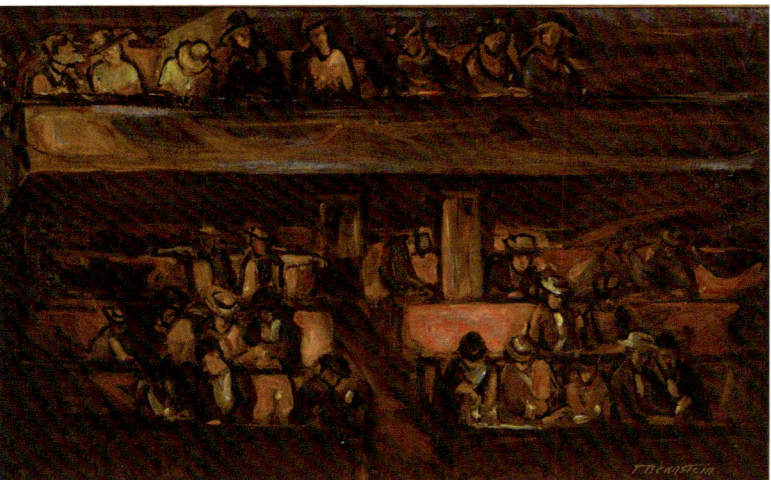

87. *Portuguese Synagogue*, 1919. Oil on canvas, 20 x 30 inches. Endicott College Collection, Walter J. Manninen Trust.

In April 1943, in the midst of the war, Bernstein and Meyerowitz served together on a jury for an exhibition of paintings to benefit the British War Relief Society, held at the American British Art Center in New York and sponsored by Local 91 of the Ladies' Garment Workers Union. The other jurors were Edward Hopper, Isabel Bishop, Luigi Lucioni, and Otto Soglow.[208] In the past, when she and Hopper had shown together, she had garnered more attention. Now he had become well established while her fame was in decline.

With the war, art dealers like Peggy Guggenheim, avant-garde European artists such as Fernand Léger, Piet Mondrian, and Marc Chagall, and surrealists like Yves Tanguy, André Breton, and Max Ernst, all fled Europe for the United States. Their presence set the stage for younger American artists like Jackson Pollock and Robert Motherwell, who were beginning to attract attention. Their experimental works made Bernstein's painting look dated, even though it had evolved into a looser, less realistic mode of representation. New York critics occasionally carped at her work, but mostly they began to ignore her while focusing on the younger, hipper artists who were vying for attention.

When Dorothy Grafly reviewed the Annual Exhibition of the North Shore Arts Association in Gloucester in 1944, she announced that Bernstein won the $100 Anne Baker Lewis prize for the "best picture" in the show. She then wrote: "Mrs. Bernstein, with her husband William Meyerowitz, may be credited with the most stimulating group of paintings on view. These two artists, whose choice of pigments and approach to the subject matter are so closely akin, bring to their Gloucester impressions the flavor of the wharves, not a mere reproduction of what a color camera might interpret with equal success. . . . The art of these two painters has behind it a genuine sympathy for human beings."[209] Even though it was Bernstein who won the prize, the critics often viewed her in the role of artist wife, which meant that she played second fiddle to her male partner.

Louis Lozowick included Bernstein and Meyerowitz in his 1947 book, *One Hundred Jewish American Painters and Sculptors*.[210] Since the time they had portrayed Einstein and the Zionist meeting in New York, the couple had become ever more ardent Zionists.

In 1945 they met the attorney Bartley Crum, who was one of the six United States representatives on the Anglo-American Commission of Inquiry on Palestine that advised President Harry Truman to support the opening of the British Mandate of Palestine to unrestricted Jewish immigration, and to allow the creation of a Jewish state.[211] Bernstein expressed her enthusiasm for the founding of the state of Israel in 1948 with her painting *The Menorah* (1948) (see fig. 152). She and Meyerowitz made thirteen visits to Israel beginning in 1951. She recorded scenes of daily life, made portraits of people they met and admired, and recorded her recollections in a memoir, *Israeli Journal*.[212] Although Bernstein and Meyerowitz got to meet such distinguished Israeli artists as the

what was then called the United States National Museum of the Smithsonian Institution in Washington DC.[213] Three years later, she won the Margaret Cooper Prize of $100 from the National Association of Women Artists. Attention for her work in graphics continued throughout the 1950s, which was otherwise a quiet time for Bernstein. In 1954 she won an Honorable Mention from the Society of American Graphic Artists for her monoprint *Venice* (ca. 1922–1953), which she based on her oil painting of 1922. The next year, the Society of American Graphic Artists donated *Venice* to the permanent collection of the Metropolitan Museum of Art. It was the kind of honor that her precocious success had portended but seldom delivered.

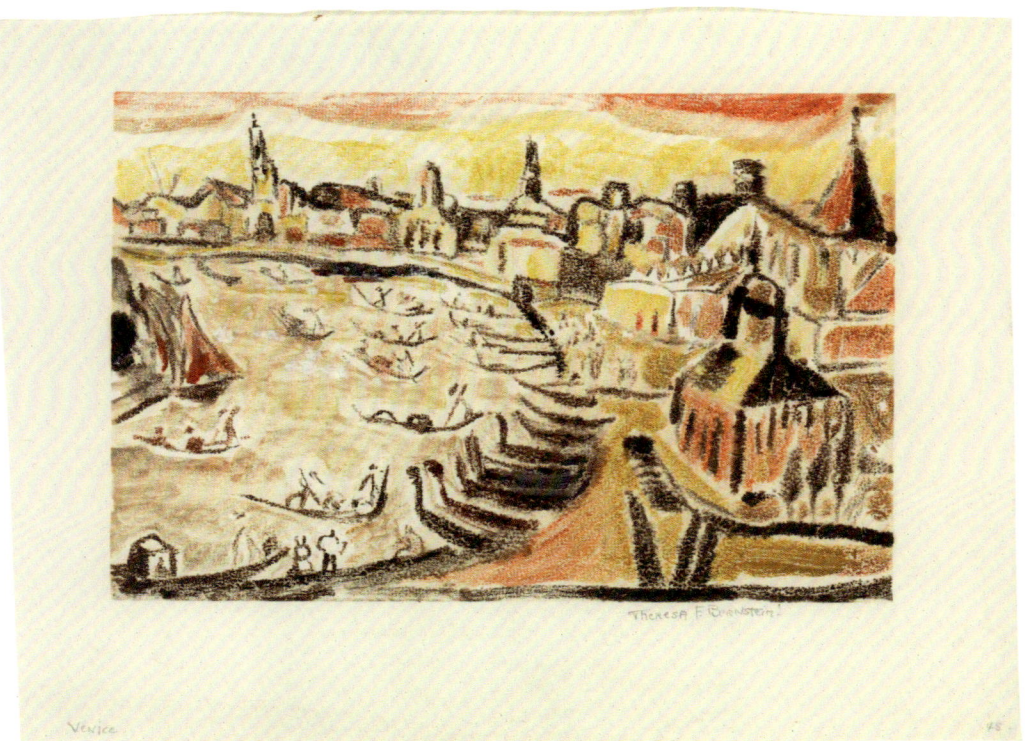

88. *Venice*, ca. 1922–55. Monotype, 8½ x 12⅞ inches. Metropolitan Museum of Art, Gift of the Society of American Graphic Artists, Dorothy Noyes and John Taylor Arms Collection, 1955.

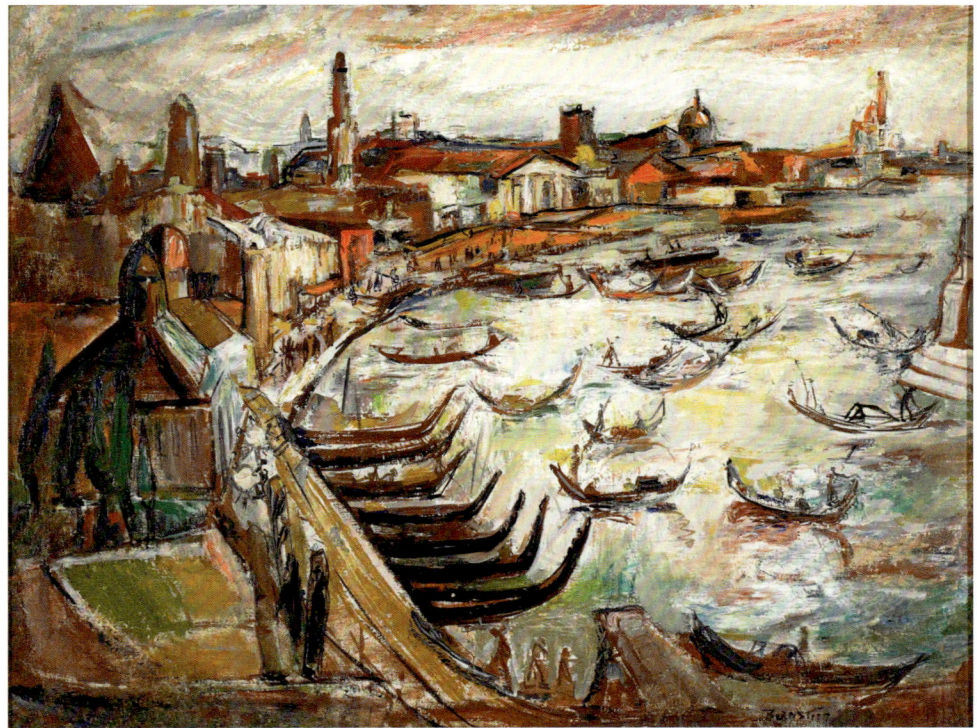

89. *Venice*, 1922. Oil on canvas, 28 x 36 inches. Martin and Edith Stein Collection.

Rumanian-born Reuven Rubin (1893–1974) and Marcel Janco (1895–1984), these new social connections did not take the place of alliances that might have helped their careers progress in the United States.

Bernstein had the honor of an exhibition of thirty-six of her prints, etchings, and monotypes in the spring of 1948 at

When Doll and Richards Gallery in Boston gave a joint show to Bernstein and Meyerowitz in April 1949, Dorothy Adlow, the art critic for the *Christian Science Monitor*, which had earlier featured Bernstein's work, privileged Meyerowitz over Bernstein, mentioning her as his wife.[214] Perhaps this editorial decision reflected gender stereotypes prevalent during the postwar period, when society at large encouraged women to stay at home and to give up the jobs they had filled while men were in the armed forces. Adlow contrasted Meyerowitz's painting, which she linked to "the post-Impressionist trend" and saw as emphasizing "inner structural design," with Bernstein's "more expressionist manner of painting. . . . She has the gift of description."[215]

Interviewed in Gloucester in 1950, Bernstein commented on stylistic change: "The artist is still searching and growing, continually learning and trying to increase his power, and is not afraid to change his approach."[216] Though she speaks of "the artist" with the male pronoun, she described her own picture, *Cosmic Harbor* (now lost), then on view in her show at the Bass Rocks Theatre in Gloucester, as "surrealistic in concept," pointing out that she wanted to express forces of nature beyond fact: "The artist tries to extract the truth below the surface and make it cohesive in his work."

In 1953 Doll and Richards gave another joint show to Bernstein and Meyerowitz. Dorothy Adlow again focused on Meyerowitz and introduced Bernstein as "his wife." After writing three complimentary paragraphs about Meyerowitz's work, she noted, "Miss Bernstein shows a group of landscapes, some still lifes, and a portrait. The latter work finds her at the top of her talents."[217]

In April 1960 Bernstein had a solo show at the Cober Gallery in New York that was reviewed in *Art News* as the work of "an older artist, showed last in New York over eight years ago. The current show of recent work is done loosely in the style of the non-abstract expressionists. Her subjects are jazz and the New York scene, with a few still-lifes and landscapes thrown in."[218] The use of "older" was not a term of endearment; it suggests prejudice against older artists. At seventy, Bernstein already had ample cause to conceal her age, which became even more acute as she would approach and pass the centennial of her birth.

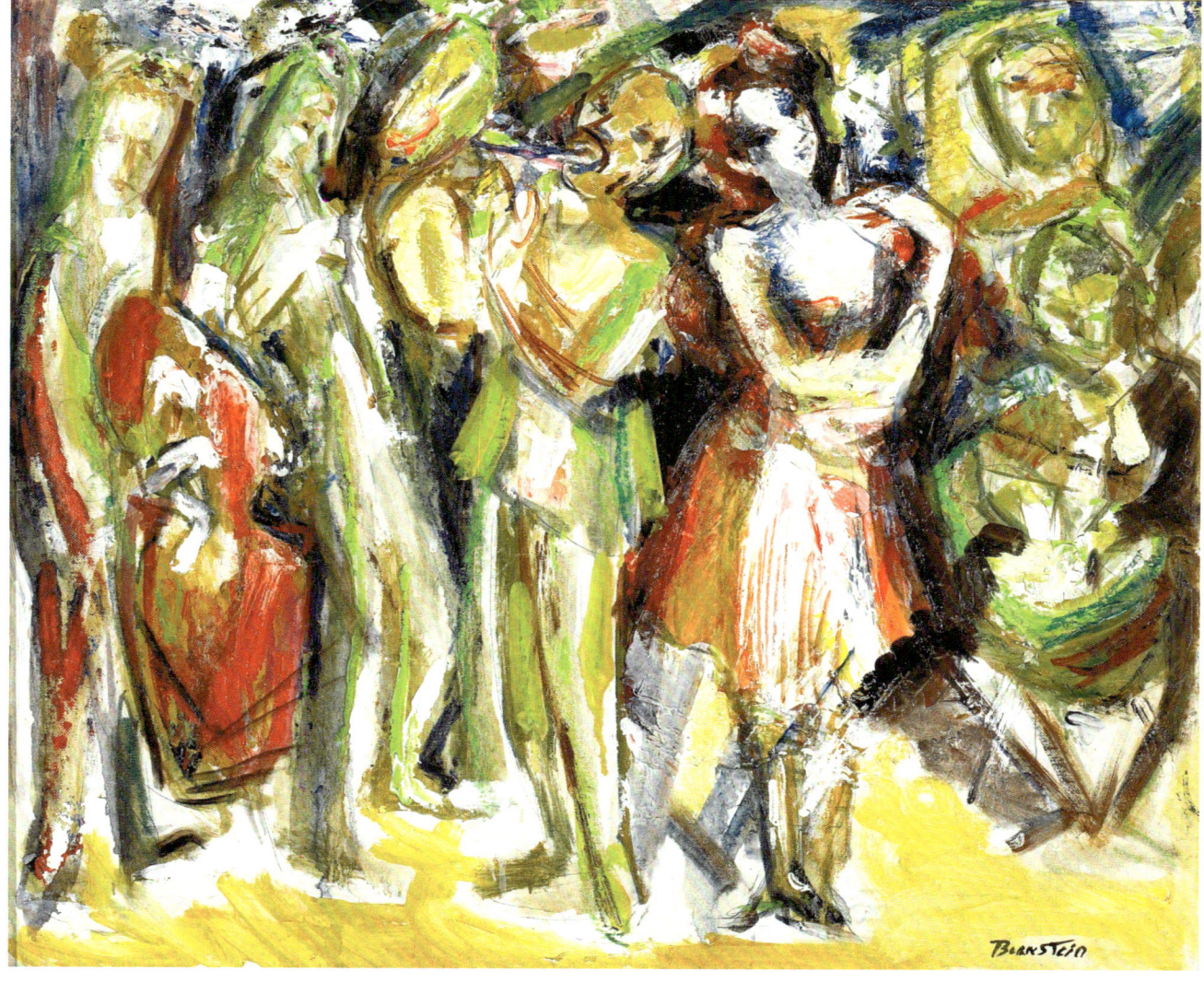

90. *Charlie Parker*, 1953.
Oil on canvas, 20 x 24 inches.
Martin and Edith Stein Collection.

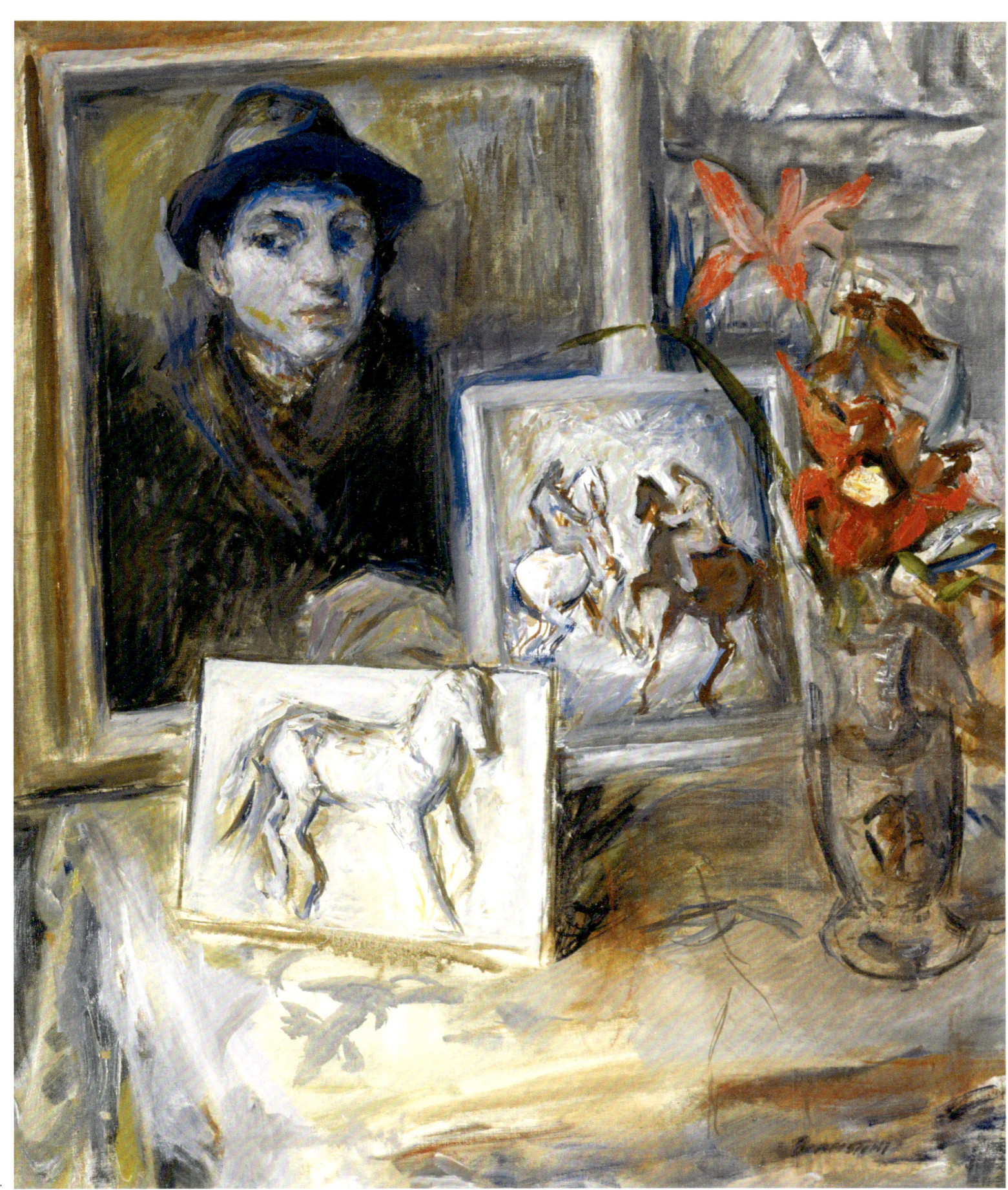

91. *William in Blue*, 1962.
Oil on canvas, 30 x 25 inches.
Martin and Edith Stein Collection.

As late as 1963, when Bernstein was seventy-three years old, she and Meyerowitz were both honored by being included in the *Exhibition of Paintings Eligible for Purchase Under the Child Hassam Fund* at the American Academy of Arts and Letters. Both showed still lifes; hers was called *Green Pears*. Though her entry was not one of the works chosen to be purchased and presented to a museum, she was included in a show with artists who were mostly more than a generation younger: for example, George Tooker (1920–2011), Jimmy Ernst (1920–1984), and David Aronson (born 1923).

Bernstein and Meyerowitz continued making art, traveling, and enjoying life together. He remained an important portrait subject for her. Slowed by a heart attack in 1961, he died on May 28, 1981, at the age of ninety-three. His last words to Theresa were "You must go on–I love you."[219] Married for more than sixty years, they were devoted to one another and to art. She took his command seriously and survived for more than two decades, until just two weeks short of her 112th birthday. The attention Bernstein gave to promoting Meyerowitz's work after his death evidences her love for him. If she compromised any career opportunities by marrying, she never regretted it. She wrote with satisfaction in her book about him: "The devotion he lavished on this portrait [of me] in his final days has served as a testament of all the love he felt for me."[220]

Bernstein described how she felt after Meyerowitz's death: "It was two weeks after the loss of my life's companion. The walls were echoing with his spirit. The large horse panel still hung near the table where we ate in the loft that was transformed into a studio by his ingenuity, possibly the first of that kind in New York. . . . I must write this book [about William] now."[221] She described a friend giving her a tape recorder and the problems she had to contend with: "my age, and the fact that I had broken both my hips, although I was able to learn to walk again. My left eye had a cataract that had to be operated on, and I learned to see again. But my mental process remained intact. I figured, as long as I could walk and talk, I could write the book."[222]

Bernstein shared with her late husband the show *New York Themes: Paintings and Prints by William Meyerowitz and Theresa Bernstein*, presented from October 5, 1983 through April, 29, 1984, at the New York Historical Society.[223] James B. Bell, the society's director, wrote the foreword to Bernstein's 1989 book, *The Poetic Canvas*, noting, "The New York Historical Society has had a long relationship with William Meyerowitz and Theresa Bernstein Meyerowitz. As neighbors, William and Theresa attended Sunday afternoon concerts at the Society for many years."[224] He then noted that the couple had had a popular "special exhibition at the Society."

Seeing that exhibition prompted me to look up and interview Bernstein. I discovered that she had known Edward Hopper, a subject that had long preoccupied me as a scholar.[225] When asked to write an essay for the inaugural show at the National Museum of Women in the Arts, which opened in April 1987, I remembered Bernstein and included a brief mention and a reproduction of her painting in my essay but was unable to convince the curator to add an artist whose work she did not yet know.[226]

Meyerowitz's work caught the eye of Girard Jackson, a Texas attorney who first purchased a painting out of a show while vacationing in Maine in 1964. After meeting the couple in 1972, he continued to purchase art by Meyerowitz and bought just one watercolor by Bernstein. After Meyerowitz's death, Jackson began to collect and promote Bernstein's art, becoming a close and devoted friend. By the mid-1980s he was selling Bernstein's work out of his home in Stamford, Connecticut, and had begun to donate examples of her work to public collections.[227] Eventually, Dorothy Mayhall, director of the Stamford Museum and Nature Center, heard about Bernstein and decided to present "A Centennial Exhibition" that opened in Connecticut in November 1989 and then traveled to Boston in 1990. In Jackson's catalogue essay for this show, he quoted an art dealer as sighing and remarking, "I wish she hadn't changed her style," as well as Bernstein's rejoinder, "I didn't change; the times did."[228]

In 1988 the art historian Patricia Burnham accepted an assignment to write an article on Bernstein's work for *Woman's Art Journal*, prompted by some requests that its editor Elsa Honig Fine had received from some interested women artists including Elsie Driggs (1898–1992).[229] Bernstein was thrilled with the attention, and she and Burnham became friends. Burnham organized the 1995 exhibition *Theresa Bernstein—People and Places, A Retrospective*, at the Philadelphia Museum of Judaica.[230]

It was images of New York from the 1910s and 1920s, however, that inspired a show called *Echoes of New York: The Paintings of Theresa Bernstein* at the Museum of the City of New York (November 20, 1990–March 31, 1991), organized by Michele Cohen, then a young art historian, drawn to Bernstein's work on suffrage. Cohen met Bernstein while viewing her 1983 exhibition at the New York Historical Society.[231] Affected by feminist scholarship, Cohen recognized that despite Bernstein's remarkable talent, she had not received scholarly attention, a state of affairs that Cohen determined to change. Bernstein befriended Cohen, whose efforts eventually helped to generate interest in her early work among other scholars. A *New York Times* feature prompted by Cohen's show described Bernstein as "100 years old (or 101 or 102—she never will really say)" and quoted

her: "I never got frustrated, because I didn't expect anything. I enjoyed painting the works I did. I didn't do it for public acclaim." Bernstein "spent several hours at the Museum of the City of New York talking about her work to graduate students from the City University of New York," said the *Times*. The students in question were my graduate seminar, which I had brought to interview Bernstein. She was effervescent, obviously enjoying the attention. The *Times*' Bill Cunningham took many pictures, printing one of me seated on the floor at Bernstein's feet with the caption, "Bernstein speaking to a student before one of her paintings at the Museum."[232]

The Women's Caucus for Art, founded in 1972, responded to all the recent attention that had been coming to Bernstein and chose her in 1991 to receive one of its five annual Honor Awards for Outstanding Achievements in the Visual Arts. Previous honorees had included such notables as Bernstein's

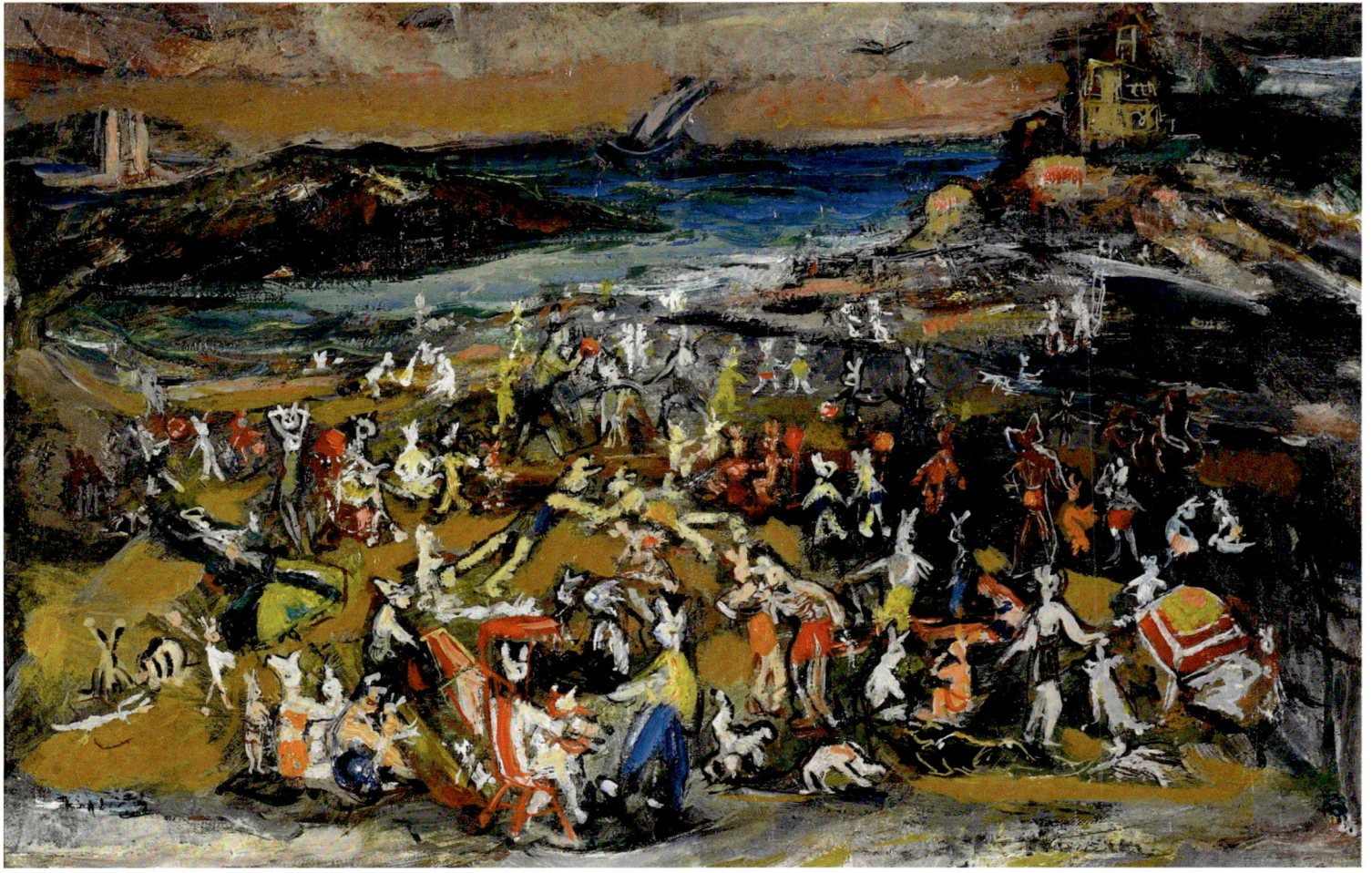

92. *Rabbits, Good Harbor Beach, Gloucester*, ca. 1980. Oil on board, 12 x 18 inches. Martin and Edith Stein Collection.

student Louise Nevelson, Georgia O'Keeffe, Louise Bourgeois, and Lee Krasner.[233]

In 1998 Bernstein began to have solo shows with Joan Whalen Fine Art at 24 West Fifty-Seventh Street in New York. She was well enough to attend the openings as late as 1999, when she was the subject of a feature story in *Antiques and Art Weekly* captioned: "Oldest Living American Artist Marks 109th Year." This article included a photograph of Bernstein holding a copy of *Rabbitville*, her illustrated book for children, based on a tale that she had been telling for decades and illustrating in later years.[234] She was proud of the book, published by a group of devoted friends.[235] She had also found a dedicated dealer in Whalen, who adored both the artist and her work and gave Bernstein a chance to interact with the public in her last years.

"This century has seen great changes. . . . As for my own work, I made no attempt to push it forward," wrote Bernstein in 1991, near the end of *The Journal*.[236] "Possibly my greatest talent has been my will power to overcome the hurdles of physical handicaps and to gallop away from unpleasant situations into the field of love, of friendship, and of cooperation."[237] Indomitable, when she fell and broke her right arm, she taught herself to draw and paint with her left.

Bernstein demonstrated amazing ability and determination to persist as an artist and even to fend for herself in later years. Looking again at her record reminds us not only of her extraordinary talent but also of the tough context in which she labored with its entrenched biases against women. Despite some frustrated efforts to promote her work and her own perception of gender bias, she remained content with her accomplishments. She took pleasure in making art until shortly before her death in 2002.

Uncovering just some of Bernstein's remarkable record of exhibitions, reviews, and prizes reveals her high level of accomplishment before the Great Depression and the postwar shift in fashion eclipsed her early reputation. Having had an early exposure to European modernism much richer than that of Edward Hopper, Bernstein, like him, rejected avant-garde and abstract art, remaining attached to figuration. And like Hopper, she chose to emphasize her American identity. Yet critics celebrated his identity as American, while overlooking hers, even when she painted patriotic themes, which did not figure in Hopper's art.

Despite her early prominence, Bernstein did not make it into the new Museum of Modern Art's 1929 show, *Paintings by Nineteen Living Americans*. The museum's director, Alfred H. Barr, Jr., and the trustees, packed the show with artists they collected. Beside Hopper, Sloan, Ernest Lawson, and other men, the sole woman picked was Georgia O'Keeffe.

Nor was Bernstein acquired by the new Whitney Museum of American Art, as might have been expected given her activities at its predecessor, the Whitney Studio Club. The Whitney Museum, which identified itself as "American," did feature Hopper, whom it promoted as "the most inherently Anglo-Saxon painter of all times" notwithstanding the fact that his distant ancestors were French and Dutch.[238] To such stereotyping, Bernstein, as a daughter of recent immigrants, did not lend herself. Nor did her Jewish and immigrant themes fit the Whitney's mold.

Bernstein's career reveals shifting fashions and evolving stereotypes. "People want to make comparisons between a woman's work and the work of a man," she commented late in life. "Of course, I don't think sex has much to do with it, except that few women in history were able to be outstanding. There's no real encouragement for either sex, but for a woman there was less in every respect."[239] It is now time to begin to reconstruct her long and productive career, and to look for the full story of what became of her early prominence.

NOTES

1. For an important and relevant discussion of "The Gendered Making of a Modern Market System" for art, see Kirsten Swinth, *Painting Professionals: Women Artists and the Development of Modern American Art*, 1870–1930 (Chapel Hill: University of North Carolina Press, 2001), especially pp. 99–130. Swinth included Bernstein in her study and interviewed her.

2. It has not been possible to locate this quotation in the *New York Times*, where Bernstein recalled reading it, but her recollection about this comment is worth consideration.

3. Theresa Bernstein Meyerowitz, *The Journal* (New York: Cornwall Books, 1991), p. 40; noted hereafter as Bernstein, *The Journal*.

4. Bernstein met O'Keeffe. Bernstein and Zorach knew each other since both were members of the New York Society of Women Artists. See Bernstein, *The Journal*, p. 57. They were both showing in *Imaginative Paintings by Thirty Young Artists of New York City*, held in the spring of 1917 at Knoedler Galleries, New York.

5. See Erika Doss, "Complicating Modernism: Issues of Liberation and Constraint among the Women Art Students of Robert Henri," in *American Women Modernists: The Legacy of Robert Henri, 1910–1945*, ed. Marian Wardle (New Brunswick NJ: Rutgers University Press, 2005), p. 117. The original source for this error appears to be Robert R. Preato, *The Genius of the Fair Muse: Painting and Sculpture Celebrating American Women Artists, 1875 to 1945* (New York: Grand Central Art Galleries, 1987), p. 11, which states: "Bernstein, who had studied for six months with Chase (then with Henri), painted scenes of everyday urban life." Though Bernstein was still alive when this was published, she was ninety-seven years old. For Bernstein's relationship to Henri and the Ashcan School, see Michele Cohen, *Echoes of New York: The Paintings of Theresa Bernstein* (New York: Museum of the City of New York, 1990), and Elsie Heung's essay in this volume.

6. For a list of shows with both Bernstein and Henri beyond those discussed in this essay, see the chronology in this volume.

7. Theresa Bernstein Meyerowitz to Muriel Meyers, Oral History, American Jewish Committee, Dorot Jewish Division, New York Public Library, July 17, 1991, pp. 1–8 (hereafter as Oral History, AJC).

8. This distortion persists. See Judith A. Curtis, *Rocky Neck Art Colony, 1850–1950, Gloucester, Massachusetts* (Gloucester MA: Rocky Neck Art Colony, Inc., 2008), p. 107, which claims, incorrectly: "In later life, when *William Meyerowitz* passed away in 1981, loneliness crowded in unrelieved, until Bernstein took up writing to help the grieving process and discovered a new creative outlet. At the age of 91, the artist became a writer, publishing at least six books including children's books and poetry." She ignored Bernstein's earlier published articles on Gloucester, prints, and other topics. Her published and unpublished essays still need to be collected; a list of her known writings is in Appendix 1.

9. Bernstein, *The Journal*, p. 9.

10. Bernstein, *The Journal*, p. 16. See Francis T. Palgrave, ed., *The Golden Treasury of the Best Songs and Lyric Poems in the English Language* (London: Macmillan, 1875).

11. For example, in Theresa Bernstein Meyerowitz, *William Meyerowitz: The Artist Speaks* (Philadelphia: Art Alliance Press, 1986), pp. 47–48 (hereafter as Bernstein, *William Meyerowitz*), she confused names, substituting Dali in describing Duchamp's "entry called The Fountain" in the Society of Independent Artists show of 1917, describing it as "a new toilet" that "represented his 'ready-made' objects."

12. Some published accounts, including Bernstein's in *William Meyerowitz*, p. 53, have stated that Nevelson studied with both Bernstein and Meyerowitz, but Nevelson insisted that she studied only with Bernstein. Laurie Wilson, conversation with author, 2012. Wilson is Nevelson's biographer who knew her subject.

13. Bernstein, *William Meyerowitz*, p. 53.

14. Jonathan P. Harvey, telephone interview with author, August 20, 2012. When Harvey studied with Bernstein in the 1950s, he was photographed in a newspaper feature, "Art Students Complete Course," September 10, 1953, clipping in Theresa Bernstein's scrapbook.

15. This is according to the U.S. Census for 1900, when the family was living in Philadelphia.

16. Bernstein told Suzanne Laurier, who from 1978 was her accountant, that she had been adopted as an infant (Laurier, interview by author, August 23, 2012). Jerry Jackson, conversation with author, 2012, also says that Bernstein told him she had been adopted, but both her birth certificate and her close physical resemblance to her mother make this unlikely.

17. Theresa Bernstein, "The Review," June 4, 1996, unpublished nineteen-page typescript memoir, a copy in the author's private collection, gift of Patricia M. Burnham.

18. Bernstein, *The Journal*, p. 19.

19. Bernstein, *The Journal*, pp. 24, 36.

20. The Hollywood Avenue home is mentioned in Bernstein, "The Review."

21. Bernstein, "The Review," p. 1.

22. A receipt for her tuition survives from December 1894.

23. From 1903 to 1907 she attended William D. Kelley School on North Twenty-Eighth. A school still exists in this location.

24. Bernstein, *The Journal*, pp. 21–22.

25. Theresa Bernstein, *The Sketchbook* (Woburn MA: privately printed, 1992), p. 80.

26. Bernstein, Oral History, AJC, pp. 2–32.

27. Bernstein, *William Meyerowitz*, p. 24.

28. Bernstein kept a tiny travel diary of this trip that she gave to Michele Cohen, curator of *Echoes of New York*.

29. Bernstein, *The Journal*, p. 22.

30. According to information in the ledger book in the archives at Moore College of Art, Philadelphia, Bernstein was recommended by Charles S. Boyer.

31. J. P. Glass, "Discoveries of Genius: The Finding of Theresa Bernstein," *New York Evening World*, undated clipping, c. 1925, Bernstein's scrapbook.

32. Glass, "Discoveries of Genius." It appears that Bernstein was already trying to make herself appear younger than her actual age. She certainly finished high school and gave the graduation address.

33. *The Philadelphia School of Design for Women, 1907–1908*, course catalogue now in the archives at Moore College of Art, the successor school.

34. Emily Sartain quoted in Swinth, *Painting Professionals*, p. 156.

35. Sartain, quoted in Swinth, *Painting Professionals*, p. 157.

36. Bernstein's "History of Art" notebook from her first year of art school narrowly survived among papers auctioned off from her house in Gloucester. It was saved by Paul Famolari.

37. Bernstein, *The Journal*, p. 24.

38. Bernstein, Oral History, AJC, pp. 2–34, Bernstein insisted that she studied briefly at the Pennsylvania Academy of Fine Arts PAFA. She might have attended lectures without registering formally, especially since some of the faculty, such as Daniel Garber, taught at both the academy and the Philadelphia School of Design. Since the PAFA's archives have no proof she ever registered, Page Talbott says that Bernstein never attended the Pennsylvania Academy. Page Talbott and Patricia Tanis Sydney, *The Philadelphia Ten: A Women's Artist Group, 1917–1945* (Philadelphia: Galleries at Moore and American Art Review Press, 1998), p. 30, n. 2. Though sometimes difficult to verify, Bernstein's other claims have generally turned out to be true.

39. Bernstein, *The Sketchbook*, p. 1.

40. Bernstein, *The Sketchbook*, p. 1.

41. This undated catalogue page is pasted in Bernstein's scrapbook, but I have confirmed that the date was 1909.

42. "Art Students Win Prizes," *Philadelphia Inquirer*, November 8, 1910, p. 8.

43. Bernstein, *The Journal*, p. 35.

44. The prize was named for Emily Sartain's father, John (1808–1897), an artist and printmaker who had taught at the school before his death.
Harriet Sartain was John's granddaughter and the daughter of John's son, Henry Sartain (1833–1895), a master printer.

45. Bernstein, *The Journal*, p. 9.

46. Bernstein, *The Sketchbook*, pp. 1–2.

47. Bernstein, *The Sketchbook*, p. 2.

48. Student Registration Records, Archives of the Art Students League, New York.

49. *New York Times*, November 14, 1909.

50. Bernstein, Oral History, AJC, pp. 1–2.

51. Bernstein, claims that she studied "the nude form" with Chase at the Art Students League in 1912, *The Journal*, p. 39. Quotation: Theresa Bernstein, "William Merritt Chase (1849–1916)," in pamphlet "Etchings and Paintings: *William Meyerowitz*/Theresa Bernstein," June 10, 1984–October 20, 1984, Paterson Public Library, Paterson NJ, n.p.

52. See Patricia Burnham's essay on Bernstein's still life paintings in this volume.

53. Bernstein, Oral History, AJC, pp. 1–2.

54. Bernstein, *The Journal*, p. 40.

55. See Christopher Grey, "Streetscapes: Holbein Studio; Art Came Alive Over a Stable," *New York Times*, December 20, 1987.

56. See the diary of Bernstein's mother, which cites studio visits from Daingerfield and Snell as well as correspondence from Daingerfield and Sartain.

57. See *Art and Progress* 3, nos. 1–2 (1912), which ran an advertisement for William H. Powell Art Gallery. Artists such as Leon Dabo (1864–1960) and Paul Cornoyer (1864–1923) also showed with Powell around this time.

58. Bernstein, *The Journal*, p. 39.

59. Powell advertised his shows in the *New York Times*.

60. Bernstein, *The Sketchbook*, p. 41.

61. John Lane published the periodical *The Yellow Book* (1894–1897) and Keynote Series, which was linked to fin-de-siècle decadence. The series, aimed at the "New Woman," included Grant Allen's novel *The Woman Who Did* (1895), Victoria Crosse's immediate reaction to it, the novel *The Woman Who Didn't* (1895), and H. G. Wells's novel about his affair with Amber Reeves, *The New Machiavelli* (1911).

62. Bernstein, *The Journal*, p. 42.

63. Bernstein, *The Journal*, p. 40. Bernstein referred to Matisse's *Nasturtiums with the Painting Dance, I*, of 1912, now in the collection of the Metropolitan Museum of Art. At over 75 inches in height, this work towered over the petite Bernstein.

64. Bernstein, *The Journal*, p. 40.

65. Anna Ferber Bernstein, diary entry of March 19, 1913, four days after the Armory Show closed in New York City on March 15, 1913.

66. Bernstein, *The Journal*, p. 39.

67. Clara Tice (1888–1973) would attract the attention of Marcel Duchamp in 1915, when the anti-vice crusader Anthony Comstock raided an exhibition of her work at Polly's Restaurant on Washington Place in Greenwich Village. She eventually illustrated for magazines such as *Vanity Fair* and *Rogue*. Marjorie Organ (1886–1931) became a newspaper cartoonist and married Robert Henri.

68. "Art at Home and Abroad: At MacDowell Club," *New York Times Magazine*, May 3, 1914, p. SM11.

69. Theresa Bernstein quoted in "Inspiration for Pictures Found in Musical Themes," *Brooklyn Daily Eagle*, n.d., n.p., clipping in Bernstein's scrapbook.

70. Bernstein quoted in "Inspiration for Pictures."

71. Bernstein quoted in "Inspiration for Pictures."

72. "Paintings, Sculptures, Etchings and Miniatures by Eighty Women Artists Placed on View to Aid State Campaign–Works Fill Whole Gallery," *Evening Post*, September 25, 1915, MacBeth Gallery Papers, Archives of American Art, Smithsonian Institution.

73. Bernstein, *The Journal*, p. 41.

74. Bernstein, Oral History, AJC, pp. 2–56.

75. Bernstein, Oral History, AJC, pp. 2–56.

76. See *Official Catalogue of the Department of Fine Arts, Panama-Pacific International Exhibition* (San Francisco: Wahlgreen Co., 1915), p. 61, #2082, as Open-Air School.

77. Unidentified clipping in Bernstein's scrapbook.

78. See Swinth, *Painting Professionals*, pp. 120–22; and Helen Goodman, "The Plastic Club," *Arts Magazine* 59 (March 1985), pp. 100–103.

79. Royal Cortissoz, *New York Herald Tribune*, unidentified clipping in Bernstein's scrapbook.

80. "News of New York Art Exhibitions," Drawings at MacDowell Club, *Christian Science Monitor*, April 3, 1915, p. 22.

81. "The Exhibition of Painting and Sculpture by Women Artists for the Benefit of the Woman Suffrage Campaign." See Maria Caudill Dennison, "Babies for Suffrage: 'The Exhibition of Painting and Sculpture by Women Artists for the Benefit of the Woman Suffrage Campaign,'" *Woman's Art Journal* 24, no. 2 (Autumn 2003–Winter 2004), pp. 24–30. The exhibition committee included Mrs. John W. Alexander, Mrs. Albert Herter, Abastenia St. L. Eberle, Anne Goldthwaite, Alice Morgan Wright, and Ida Proper.

82. "Joyous Art of Suffragettes," Bernstein's scrapbook.

83. "Women Artists Give Suffrage Benefit Exhibit," *Christian Science Monitor*, October 2, 1915, p. 21.

84. This group began as the Woman's Art Club in January 1889, changing its name in 1913 to the Association of Women Painters and Sculptors. Three years later, it became the National Association of Women Painters and Sculptors. This show was from November 20 to December 24, 1915.

85. "Young Artists Get Prizes, *New York Times*, June 24, 1915, p. 11.

86. *Theresa Bernstein*, DVD produced for the New-York Historical Society show by J. Wright and B. Maturo, Wright Brothers Production, 1986.

87. Bernstein, *The Journal*, pp. 39–40.

88. See Irene Gammel, *Baroness Elsa: Gender, Dada, and Everyday Modernity—A Cultural Biography* (Cambridge MA: MIT Press, 2002), pp. 189, 198, 206.

89. Bernstein, Oral History, AJC, pp. 2–40.

90. Bernstein, Oral History, AJC, pp. 2–40.

91. Gisi Baronin Freytag von Loringhoven, in a letter to Walter Manninen of December 28, 1990, wrote: "Mrs. Theresa Bernstein Meyerowitz told me that Elsa was the model for one of the figures in the painting 'The Lillies of the field' you have."

92. Theresa Bernstein stated this to Walter Manninen. Manninen, interview with author, August 2012.

93. Such attire is widely discussed in art historical literature. See, for example, Rachel Schreiber, "Before Their Makers and Their Judges: Prostitutes and White Slaves in the Political Cartoons of *The Masses* (New York 1911–1917)," *Feminist Studies*, Spring 2009, vol. 35, pp. 176–78.

94. Matthew 6:28, King James Version (1611).

95. See Theresa Bernstein to Walter Manninen, letter of July 1984.

96. Others entrants were Ida Becker, Lillian Crittenden, Caroline Geiger, Emily Dunham Hall, Anna F. Morse, Katharine Milmoe, Therese Milmoe, Clara Mamre Norton, Marjorie Pegram, and Sylvia Rafter.

97. "Contrasts and Sculpture at the Academy," *New York Times*, December 26, 1915.

98. Clipped reviews in Bernstein's scrapbook. There were also four sculptors: Marie Apel, A. H. Kitson, Sonia Rosenthal, and Mahonri Young.

99. Martha Walter, born in Philadelphia, studied with William Merritt Chase at the Pennsylvania Academy of Fine Art and in Paris at the Académie de la Grande Chaumière. She became an American impressionist painter and taught at the New York School of Art.

100. This show is listed in the *American Art Annual*, vol. 13, published in 1917 by Macmillan for the American Federation of Arts, Washington DC. Elizabeth N. Watrous (1858–1921) was listed with the wrong middle initial. McLaine may be Laura V. McLean.

101. "New Art Members Exhibit at League: Ten Painters Show Their Work at Professional Woman's Clubrooms," *New York Times*, January 2, 1916.

102. For Bernstein and the Gloucester artist colony, see Michele Cohen's essay in this volume.

103. "Meritorious Display of Art: German Society Opens Exhibition in Municipal Gallery—War Inspires Paintings," clipping in Bernstein's scrapbook.

104. For a description of the art, architecture, and educational program of Washington Irving High School, see Michele Cohen, *Public Art for Public Schools* (New York: Monacelli Press, 2009), pp. 59–65.

105. "Art Notes: Association of Women Painters Opens Twenty-fifth Exhibition," anonymous undated newspaper clipping, Bernstein's scrapbook.

106. Bernstein, *The Journal*, p. 61.

107. Bernstein might also have already seen the larger version of Daumier's *Third-Class Carriage*, now in the Metropolitan Museum Collection, since it was auctioned in New York in 1913. After Matthew C. D. Borden of New York died in 1912, the painting was in his estate sale, which took place at the American Art Association, New York, February 13–14, 1913 (no. 76, sold to Durand-Ruel for Mrs. H. O. [Louisine W.] Havemeyer, New York).

108. Stephanie Hackett suggested to me the possible influence of Zorn's etching.

109. "Art Notes: Interesting Pictures in the Macdowell Club's Exhibition," *New York Times*, March 24, 1916, p. 10.

110. Others in the group were Charles C. Cook, W. C. Emerson, Ossip L. Linde, Mary Nicholina McCord, F. Ledyard Towle, and James Weiland.

111. "Art Notes: A Notable Collection of Photographs from Spain," *New York Times*, December 24, 1916, p. E2. It is not clear if *The Beach* is the same work as the 1914 watercolor *On the Beach*.

112. "News of New York Exhibitions," *Christian Science Monitor*, May 1, 1915, p. 22. Unattributed clipping in Bernstein's scrapbook reviewing MacDowell Club show with Thomas G. De Laurier, Walter Farndon, Robert Hamilton, Frank M. Moore, Leonora Morton, John F. Parker, E. E. Richards, and C. W. Swenson. Others showing were Le Roy Barnett, Horace Brown, Laura Gardin Fraser, Ossip L. Linda, Mary N. MacCord, Athea Hill Platt, Karl F. Skoog, and Maria and Judson Strean.

113. I base my discussion on the analysis of Swinth, *Painting Professionals*, pp. 104–5.

114. Bernstein, Oral History, AJC, pp. 1–2. She stated that Meyerowitz was a baritone, that he could "read any script," and that he had "perfect pitch."

115. *William Meyerowitz* to Theresa Bernstein, letter collection of Keith Carlson. This double bill debuted in New York on March 6, 1918. Two Saturday performances occurred in April, on the 13th and 20th; thus, this note can be dated.

116. Girard Jackson, *Theresa Bernstein: Expressions of Cape Ann and New York, 1914–1972* (Stamford CT: Stamford Museum and Nature Center, 1990), n.p. By the time that Meyerowitz met Man Ray, he had married Adon Lacroix in Ridgefield in May 1914. In December 1915, the couple had moved to a studio near Grand Central Station in Manhattan. Evidently, Man Ray sublet one of the rooms in his shack to Meyerowitz but retained one for his own use. The best source for Man Ray's early chronology does not include Meyerowitz. See Francis M. Naumann, *Conversion to Modernism: The Early Work of Man Ray* (New Brunswick NJ: Rutgers University Press, 2003), p. 135.

117. Bernstein, *William Meyerowitz*, p. 26.

118. Alfred Kreymborg, "Man Ray and Adon La Croix, Economists," *Morning Telegraph*, March 14, 1915, cited by Gail Stavitsky, "Artists and Art Colonies of Ridgefield, New Jersey," the afterword to Naumann, *Conversion to Modernism*, p. 222.

119. See Talbott and Sydney, *The Philadelphia Ten*.

120. Louis Bouché quoted in Gammel, *Baroness Elsa*, p. 165.

121. "Art and Artists: 'Eclectics Again'–Exhibition at Museum of French Art," New York, April 19, 1917, Bernstein's scrapbook.

122. "Art Notes: Garden Subjects, Lecture by Maratta," *New York Times*, April 22, 1917, p. E2.

123. Mary Greene Blumenschein (1869–1958) married Ernest Leonard Blumenschein in 1905.

124. Bernstein, *The Journal*, pp. 43–44.

125. "Studio and Gallery," Friday March 30, 1917, Bernstein's scrapbook, year filled in by author.

126. Lorinda Munson Bryant, *American Pictures and Their Painters* (New York: John Lane Company, 1917), pp. 278–79.

127. "American Industrial Art Shown in Textiles: Art at Home and Abroad," *New York Times Magazine*, May 5, 1918, p. 83. This show divided into four groups of which hers also included Martha Baxter, Isabel Cook, Aline Davis, May Fairchild, Ruth Hammerslough, Stetson Humphrey, Alice Judson, Eleanor Laroque, Vance Swope, and James Thompson.

128. See Gail Levin, *Edward Hopper: An Intimate Biography* (New York: Alfred A. Knopf, 1995), p. 115.

129. "Eclectics at Babcock Galleries," *Brooklyn Daily Eagle*, December 15, 1918, p. 7.

130. See *American Art News* 17, no. 10 (December 14, 1918).

131. Bernstein, *William Meyerowitz*, p. 24.

132. See "O'Ryan Marvels at City's Tribute: Commander of 27th Says . . . ," *New York Times*, March 26, 1919. For further discussion of Bernstein's response to World War I, see the essay by Sarah Archino in this volume.

133. *Victory Day: Return of the Army* has the notation "From Edward Hopper's Studio New York" written (not in Bernstein's hand) on a sticker pasted on the verso. Since Bernstein never told me of this connection to Hopper when I interviewed her about him for my biography of Hopper, and she never put this account in any of her books, someone probably invented this story to sell this painting for more money. Not only was Hopper's studio then in the back without a view of Washington Square, but the arch in Bernstein's painting

with the notation is not Washington Square Arch but a temporary monument then located at Madison Square (23rd to 26th Streets) and definitely not visible from Hopper's building. Among those confused by this fake notation are Paula E. Calvin and Deborah A. Deacon, *American Women Artists in Wartime, 1776–2010* (Jefferson NC: McFarland and Co. Publishers, 2011), pp. 88, 194.

134. Patricia M. Burnham, "Theresa Bernstein," *Women's Art Journal* 9, no. 2 (Autumn 1988/Winter 1989), p. 23, viewed parades as Bernstein's "signature subject."

135. The Ashcan artists did not constitute an organized "school," but they were all urban Realists who supported Robert Henri's credo, "art for life's sake," rather than "art for art's sake."

136. W. H. de B. Nelson, "Theresa F. Bernstein," *International Studio* 66, no. 265 (February 1919), p. xcviii.

137. See the Theresa Bernstein website at CUNY for these and other documents.

138. Although Meyerowitz was later said to be younger than Bernstein, it seems unlikely that he lied on this document to make himself older than he was. This age is consistent with the date of birth on his death certificate, which was July 15, 1887, indicating he was ninety-three at his death on May 28, 1981.

139. "Marital Bond Is Doubly Welded by Their Art," *Syracuse Herald*, December 28, 1919, Bernstein's scrapbook. Subsequent quotations are also from this reference.

140. The reference is to the English poets Robert Browning (1812–1889) and Elizabeth Barrett Browning (1806–1861).

141. "Comments on Several Exhibitions: Art at Home and Abroad," *New York Times*, May 4, 1919, p. 85.

142. Robert J. Cole, foreword to *Paintings by Theresa F. Bernstein*, Milch Galleries, 108 West Fifty-Seventh Street, New York. The paintings that sold were *Opera Lobby*, *Sun, Sand, and Sea*, *Portrait of a Lady*, *Outing on the Hudson*, *The Hill Town*, *The Connoisseurs*, *Atlantic City*, *Late Summer Afternoon*, *Hill Top*, *Sunset*, *Lake in Florida*, and *Promenade*.

143. Hamilton Easter Field, "Exceptionally Interesting Art on Exhibition: At the Milch Galleries," *Brooklyn Daily Eagle*, November 9, 1919, p. 4.

144. Field, "Exceptionally Interesting Art," p. 4.

145. Frederick James Gregg, "Theresa Bernstein a Realist in the Old Sense of the Word," *New York Herald*, November 2, 1919, sec. 3.

146. Catalogue of an exhibition of paintings by Robert Henri, Charles Bittinger, Theresa Bernstein, and etchings by *William Meyerowitz*: Memorial Art Gallery, Rochester NY, April 1920. Charles Bittinger (1879–1970) had served with the U.S. Naval Camouflage Section at Eastman Kodak Laboratories in Rochester.

147. Bernstein, *William Meyerowitz*, p. 32.

148. Meyerowitz also made an etching of the Zionists' meeting, held at the Metropolitan Opera House, which Bernstein later conflated with Einstein's 1930 meeting at Madison Square Garden. Bernstein, too, later made a painting of the convention, which was last listed as the property of the Jewish National Fund in New York but is now missing.

149. Bernstein, *William Meyerowitz*, p. 69.

150. Bernstein, *William Meyerowitz*, p. 69.

151. Bernstein, Oral History, AJC, pp. 1–14.

152. Theresa Bernstein Meyerowitz to Richard Rubenfeld, letter of May 27, 1991—a remarkably detailed letter written when Bernstein was already 101 years old—copy in the archives of the Phillips Collection, Washington DC.

153. "Art: Exhibitions of Portraits; Exhibition of the Eclectics," *New York Times*, May 7, 1922, p. 86.

154. Bernstein, *The Journal*, p. 69.

155. Theresa Bernstein in Dorothy Grafly, "A Bernstein-Meyerowitz Conversation," *Christian Science Monitor*, September 1, 1923, p. 12.

156. Bernstein, Oral History, AJC, pp. 2–44.

157. Bernstein Meyerowitz to Rubenfeld, letter of May 27, 1991.

158. Bernstein, *The Journal*, p. 57.

159. Bernstein sold this painting in 1925 and must have painted it in the period just before.

160. "The World of Art: The Mingling of May; Currents in Art Exhibitions," *New York Times*, May 17, 1925, p. SM16.

161. Bernstein, *William Meyerowitz*, p. 47.

162. Jo Hopper quoted in Levin, *Edward Hopper*, p. 534.

163. On Juliana Force and Forbes Watson's affair, see Avis Berman, *Rebels on Eighth Street: Juliana Force and the Whitney Museum of American Art* (New York: Atheneum, 1990), p. 166.

164. *New York Times*, March 7, 1926, p. X12. See also review by Margaret Breuning, *New York Post*, clipping in Bernstein's scrapbook.

165. The works in the Civic Club show were *Stormy Sea*; *Beach Group*; *Opera Night Metropolitan*; *New England Village*; *Tapestry*; *Portrait of a Young Woman*; *Nude*; *Pine Brook, Winter*; *Trees*; *Fisherman's Cottage*; *Portuguese Synagogue*; *Sunset*; *Ostend*; *Early Morning Gloucester*; and *Venice*.

166. Helen Appleton Read, "Brooklyn Museum Inaugurates New Wing with American Exhibition," *Brooklyn Daily Eagle*, November 22, 1926, unidentified, undated clipping in Bernstein's scrapbook.

167. The Rehn Gallery did show the work of Ruth Gikow, the wife of Jack Levine, though she is not in the study of the gallery. See Edna M. Lindemann, *The Art Triangle* (Buffalo NY: Burchfield Art Center, 1989). The Rehn Gallery Papers are in the Archives of American Art.

168. See Hopper's story in Levin, *Edward Hopper*, pp. 171–73, 185–87.

169. Bernstein, *The Journal*, p. 57. Between 1900 and 1930, only eight women were elected academy members, and twenty-two were made associates. See Laura R. Prieto, *At Home in the Studio: The Professionalization of Women Artists in America* (Cambridge MA: Harvard University Press, 2001), p. 179; and Julie Graham, "American Women Artists Groups, 1867–1930," *Women Artists Journal* 1, no. 1 (Spring–Summer 1980), p. 8.

170. See Levin, *Edward Hopper*, pp. 242–43.

171. Bernstein to Rubenfeld, letter of May 27, 1991.

172. The Corcoran awarded its Gold Medal and $2,000 to George Bellows (Hopper's classmate, in Robert Henri's class).

173. Duncan Phillips, *A Collection in the Making: A Survey of the Problems Involved in Collecting Pictures Together with Brief Estimates of the Painters in the Phillips Memorial Gallery* (New York: E. Weyhe; Washington DC: Phillips Memorial Gallery, 1926), p. 73.

174. Bernstein, Oral History, AJC, pp. 1–19, states that she was "elected a life member in 1930 and the membership was still going on until '40 or '50."

175. Bernstein, *The Journal*, p. 90.

176. Duncan Phillips to *William Meyerowitz*, letter of November 17, 1927, courtesy of the Phillips Collection archives.

177. Edward Alden Jewell, *New York Times*, January 20, 1929, p. 13, reproduces *Portrait of Princess Greyhound*.

178. For Davis's engagement with African American culture and jazz, see Patricia Hills, *Stuart Davis* (New York: Harry N. Abrams, 1996), p. 127.

179. Bernstein, *William Meyerowitz*, p. 47. On the influence of jazz on Gershwin and American visual artists, see Gail Levin in Gail Levin and Judith Tick, *Aaron Copland's America* (New York: Watson-Guptill, 2000), pp. 55–59.

180. Sharyn R. Udall, *Sensory Crossovers: Synesthesia in American Art* (Albuquerque, NM: Albuquerque Museum, 2010), p. 76.

181. "'Hot Chocolates' Is High Spirited: New Negro Revue, the Best of Its Type Since 'Blackbirds,' Early Introduces a Novelty," *New York Times*, June 21, 1929.

182. "'Hot Chocolates'" *New York Times*, June 21, 1929.

183. The show, however, was renamed *Hot Chocolates* only after it appeared on Broadway, making the revue more famous.

184. Bernstein, *The Journal*, p. 89.

185. Bernstein dated *The Cone Sisters* 1929 in *The Journal*, but a more logical date for this painting is 1930.

186. Bernstein, *The Journal*, p. 37.

187. These works have not shown up in the Cone Collection at the Baltimore Museum of Art, but the Cone sisters gave some works to their relatives in North Carolina.

188. Elisabeth Luther Cary, "Mature Work Is Shown; Time Element Makes It Difficult to "Bet on The Winner"–Some Outstanding Items," *New York Times*, April 27, 1930, p. 126.

189. Theresa Bernstein in Dorothy Grafly, "A Bernstein-Meyerowitz Conversation," *Christian Science Monitor*, September 1, 1923, p. 12.

190. "Modern Work by Women," *New York Times*, February 22, 1932, p. 22.

191. Edward Alden Jewell, "Subject Matter and the Abstract; Debate at the Whitney Museum–The Society of Independent Artists and G.R.D.–The Manship Exhibition–Other Events," *New York Times*, April 16, 1933, p. x8.

192. Howard Devree, "In the Galleries: The Week's Shows," *New York Times*, June 4, 1933, p. xx4.

193. Edward Alden Jewell, "Less Pseudo-Modernism at Gloucester and Rockport Than at Provincetown," *New York Times*, August 27, 1933; "Group Shows," *New York Times*, February 4, 1934, p. x12.

194. Theresa Bernstein, interview recorded in 1981 for the New York Historical Society; see Bernstein CUNY website.

195. The Brooklyn Museum Fine Prints of the Year, 1934. See Stephanie Hackett's essay on Bernstein's prints in this volume.

196. See Gillian Pistell's essay on Bernstein and Meyerowitz in this volume.

197. The Artists' Congress was part of the popular front of the Communist Party USA, which hoped to encourage artists to help combat the spread of fascism.

198. "Calling All Artists," *New York Times*, October 13, 1935, p. x9.

199. "Show Displays Art Given Biro-Bidjan: Improvised Gallery Is Setting for Paintings, Prints, and Sculpture of 100 Artists," *New York Times*, February 28, 1936, p. 17. The fate of these artworks is unknown.

200. "Art Works to Be Shown: Exhibition Here to Precede Shipment to Biro-Bidjan Museum," *New York Times*, March 7, 1936, p. 17.

201. See Peter Hastings Falk, ed., *The Annual Exhibition Record of the Pennsylvania Academy of the Fine Arts*, vol. 3, 1914–1968. The PAFA Annual Exhibition Record, p. 90, also documents that Bernstein showed in the annuals of 1916–28. See also, for example, the Carnegie Institute's International (1931), the Corcoran Gallery's Biennial (1937, 1939), as well as the annual juried exhibitions of both oils and watercolors at institutions such as the Pennsylvania Academy of the Fine Arts (1930–1934, 1938) and the Art Institute of Chicago (1930, 1931, 1932, 1937, 1938, 1939).

202. For example, in 1934, her portrait of Professor David G. Lyon, the first curator of the Semitic Museum, was presented at Harvard University, for whom she also painted a portrait of Professor Harry Austryn Wolfson in 1932. Bernstein, *The Journal*, p. 94.

203. Bernstein, Oral History, AJC, pp. 1–18; Siegfried R. Weng, Dayton Art Institute, to Theresa Bernstein, letter of December 8, 1936, confirming this purchase, original at Theresa Bernstein and *William Meyerowitz* Foundation, New York City. According to Sally Kurtz, registrar of the Dayton Art Institute, in an e-mail to the author, October 3, 2012, the museum sold this work at Garth's, a small-town Ohio auction house in 1999 for $6,000. The museum's rationale for deaccessioning this work (and thirteen other works by different artists) was that they had not been "on exhibit" either at all or very much since accession "and/or condition." This museum made the classic mistake by deaccessioning just before interest in the artist revived. See, for example, the purchase in 2011 by the De Young Fine Arts Museum of San Francisco of Bernstein's *In the Elevated* and their prominent publication of this work.

204. She also depicted Benjamin Franklin and Declaration of Independence signer Robert Morris.

205. Edith Bry, Chairman of the Joint Distribution Committee Artists' and Sculptors' Division, to Bernstein, letter of May 3, 1938, thanking Bernstein. Bernstein had sent money to her aunt in Europe, but she and her family did not escape (*The Journal*, p. 107).

206. "Jews Fight for the Right to Fight," *New York Times*, January 5, 1942.

207. Bernstein, *William Meyerowitz*, p. 36.

208. "Art Notes," *New York Times*, April, 20, 1943, p. 19.

209. Dorothy Grafly, "More Than 400 Exhibits Shown By North Shore Association," *Christian Science Monitor*, July 13, 1944, p. 4.

210. Louis Lozowick, *100 Contemporary Jewish American Painters and Sculptors* (New York: YKUF, 1947).

211. Bernstein, Oral History, AJC, pp. 1–15.

212. Theresa Bernstein, *Israeli Journal* (New York: Cornwall Books, 1994).

213. This is now the Smithsonian American Art Museum in Washington DC.

214. Dorothy Adlow, "Husband and Wife Show Paintings and Prints," *Christian Science Monitor*, April 18, 1949, p. 4. Dorothy Grafly, "East Gloucester Annual Is Conservative in Mood," *Christian Science Monitor*, July 1, 1946, p. 4, had already referred to Bernstein as Meyerowitz's "painter-wife." Dorothy Grafly (Mrs. Charles Drummond), was the daughter of American sculptor Charles Grafly, who followed her father into the world of art, working as an art critic, editor, and feature writer.

215. Adlow, "Husband and Wife Show Paintings and Prints," p. 4.

216. Bernstein quoted in Jean Elwell Sharfman, "Theresa Bernstein Comments on Works," *Gloucester Daily Times*, August 1, 1950.

217. Dorothy Adlow, "Oils by Husband and Wife Seen at Doll and Richards," *Christian Science Monitor*, April 3, 1953, p. 6.

218. A.S., "Theresa Bernstein," *Art News*, April 1960, p. 58. For Bernstein's comment in the brochure for this show, see the essay by Gillian Pistell in this volume.

219. Quoted in Jackson, *Theresa Bernstein: Expressions of Cape Ann and New York*, 1914–1972.

220. Bernstein, *William Meyerowitz*, p. 84.

221. Theresa Bernstein Meyerowitz, "How I Wrote the Book '*William Meyerowitz*, the Artist Speaks,'" July 1985, unpublished ms., copy collection of the author.

222. Bernstein, "How I Wrote the Book."

223. See Grace Glueck, "New York through the Eyes of Artists," *New York Times*, October 14, 1983, pp. C1, C24. Originally scheduled from October 5, 1983, through February 26, 1984, this show was extended to April, 29, 1984.

224. James J. Bell, foreword to *The Poetic Canvas* by Theresa Bernstein Meyerowitz (New York: Cornwall Books, 1989), p. 7.

225. I included Bernstein in Levin, *Edward Hopper*, pp. 115, 167, 203, 265, 295, 418, and 439.

226. The curator was Eleanor Tufts. See Gail Levin, "The Changing Status of American Women Artists, 1900–1930," in *American Women Artists, 1830–1930* (Washington DC: The National Museum of Women in the Arts, 1987), pp. 13–16, a show that traveled to four other venues. My article featured a reproduction of Bernstein's *Waiting Room Employment Office*, 1917, now in the collection of the Jewish Museum, New York City.

227. For example, Bernstein's *Self-Portrait* is in the Jewish Museum in New York City; *Grecian Pageant* went to the National Museum of Women in the Arts, Washington DC; in 1994 both *Holbein Studio* and *Billie Holiday and Louis Armstrong* along with two figure drawings went to the Montclair Art Museum, Montclair NJ; in 1996 *New York Street* went to the Jack S. Blanton Museum of Art, Austin TX; in 1998 *Hot Chocolates* as well as two drawings and the etching *Mexican Market* went to the National Museum of American Art, Smithsonian Institute, Washington DC, and *Gaviota* went to the Moore College of Art, Philadelphia. See Bernstein, *The Journal*, p. 11, where she acknowledged "Jerry Jackson for his interest."

228. Jackson, *Theresa Bernstein: Expressions of Cape Ann and New York*, n.p.

229. Burnham, "Theresa Bernstein," pp. 22–27.

230. The Philadelphia Museum of Judaica is located in Congregation Rodeph Shalom.

231. Only an abbreviated essay by Cohen published in brochure form served as the exhibition catalogue for *Echoes of New York*, even though Cohen had written a longer text. The exhibition featured over forty canvases and was on view from November 20–March 31, 1991, coinciding with Bernstein's one hundredth birthday.

232. Trish Hall, "A Painter Wins a New Lease on Fame," *New York Times*, February 17, 1991, p. 61. I recorded an interview with Bernstein on December 20, 1990.

233. The WCA Honor Awards brochure for 1991 featured an essay on Bernstein by Patricia M. Burnham.

234. "Oldest Living American Artist Marks 109th Year at Whalen Fine Art," *Antiques and The Arts Weekly*, April 9, 1999, p. 92-H. Theresa Bernstein Meyerowitz, *Rabbitville: Stories and Illustrations* by Theresa Bernstein Meyerowitz (Lunenburg VT: Stinehour Press, Inspired by the Friends of Theresa Bernstein, 1998).

235. See Bernstein, *Rabbitville*, for the list of those who worked on this book, including Diane Dawson, Sylvia Selfridge, and Suzanne Laurier.

236. Bernstein, *The Journal*, p. 125.

237. Bernstein, *The Journal*, p. 128.

238. See Levin, *Edward Hopper*, p. 238; Guy Pène du Bois, *Edward Hopper* (New York: Whitney Museum of American Art, 1931).

239. Bernstein, *The Journal*, p. 56.

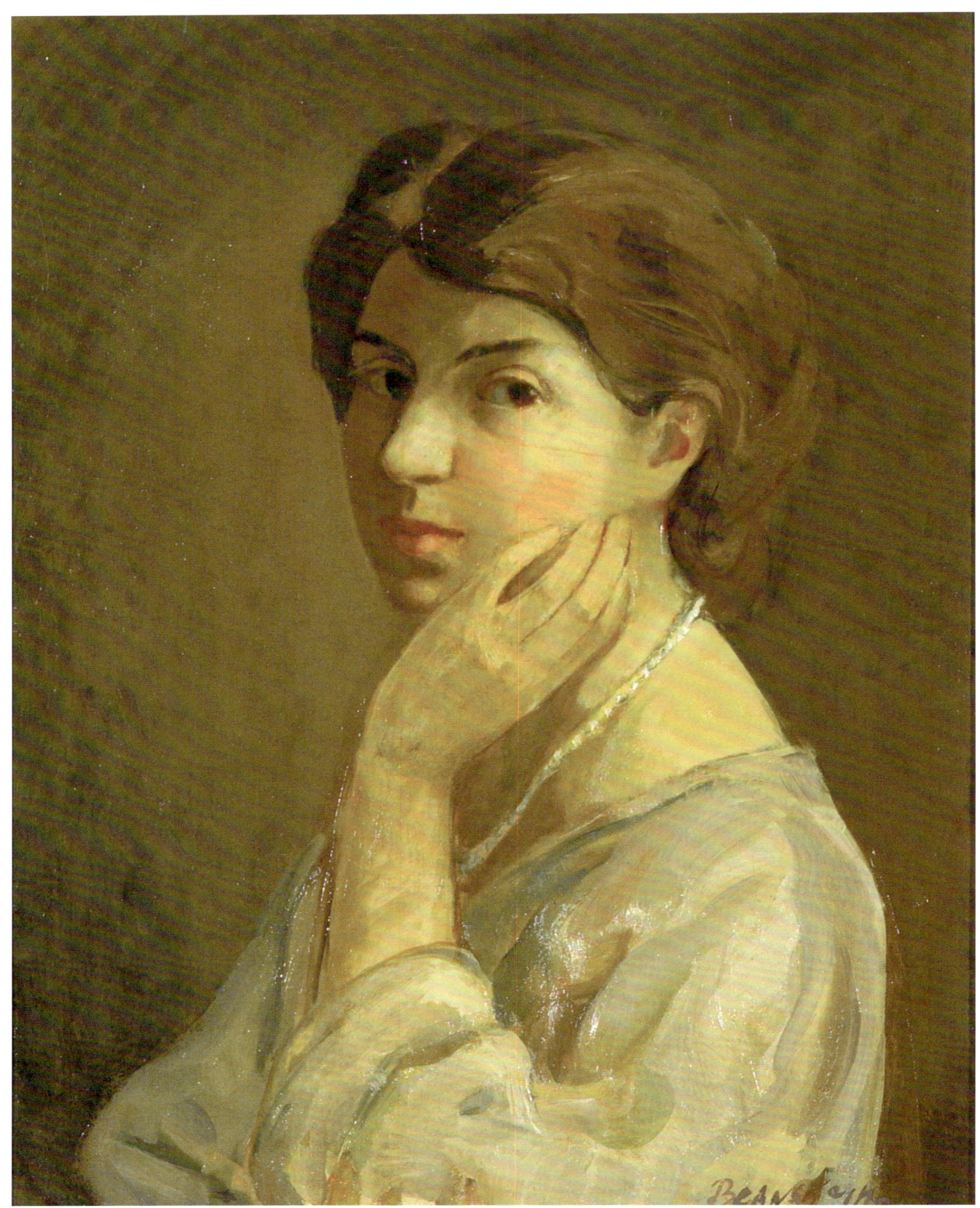

93. *Self-Portrait*, 1914. Oil on canvas, 23 x 18 inches. Martin and Edith Stein Collection.

TWO

The Ashcan School?

Theresa Bernstein and Her Vision of New York

Elsie Heung

Around 1912, and shortly after moving to New York City from Philadelphia, Theresa Bernstein painted *New York Street*. With a dark, muted palette of browns, grays, and ochre, she captures people, tenement buildings, and the ever-present elevated railroad (the "El") under a charged and painterly moonlit sky.

To anyone familiar with the urban realist paintings of the Ashcan School, Bernstein's work will undoubtedly be reminiscent of any number of cityscapes by Robert Henri, John Sloan, William Glackens, George Luks, and Everett Shinn. By the time Bernstein had completed her painting, these artists had already secured their reputations as painters of urban life three years earlier in the notorious show *Eight American Painters* ("The Eight") held at the Macbeth Gallery in Manhattan. *New York Street*, as well as many of her works from the 1910s, enthusiastically embraced the themes and stylistic tendencies that preoccupied her male counterparts of the Ashcan School. This, along with the fact that she frequently exhibited with members of the group, both in New York and in Gloucester, Massachusetts, led to frequent misidentifications of Bernstein as a student of Henri, and as an Ashcan artist.

In her book *The Journal*, which Bernstein published in 1991, she reports that a critic from *Art News* wrote, "Theresa Bernstein might as well have been labelled a Henrietta and elected as the ninth member of The Eight."[1] Even as recently as 2005, Bernstein was repeatedly misrepresented as Henri's student in *American Women Modernists: The Legacy of Robert Henri, 1910–1945* (2005), a catalogue published in conjunction with an exhibition at the Brigham Young University Museum of Art.[2] Further facilitating this misrepresentation is the fact that throughout her career, critics characterized her works as masculine (masculine vitality being a central component of the Ashcan rhetoric). "It is with a man's vision that this artist looks at her subjects. . . . Then, having found what she wants, it is with a man's vigor that she gets it down to stay," as one critic famously wrote in 1919.[3] Bernstein's connection to the Ashcan School, though valid and undeniable, has at the same time overshadowed her status as an artist with her own unique vision that separated her from her contemporaries.

Since the 1990s there has been renewed scholarly interest in the Ashcan School, placing the movement within the specific social and cultural context of New York in the early

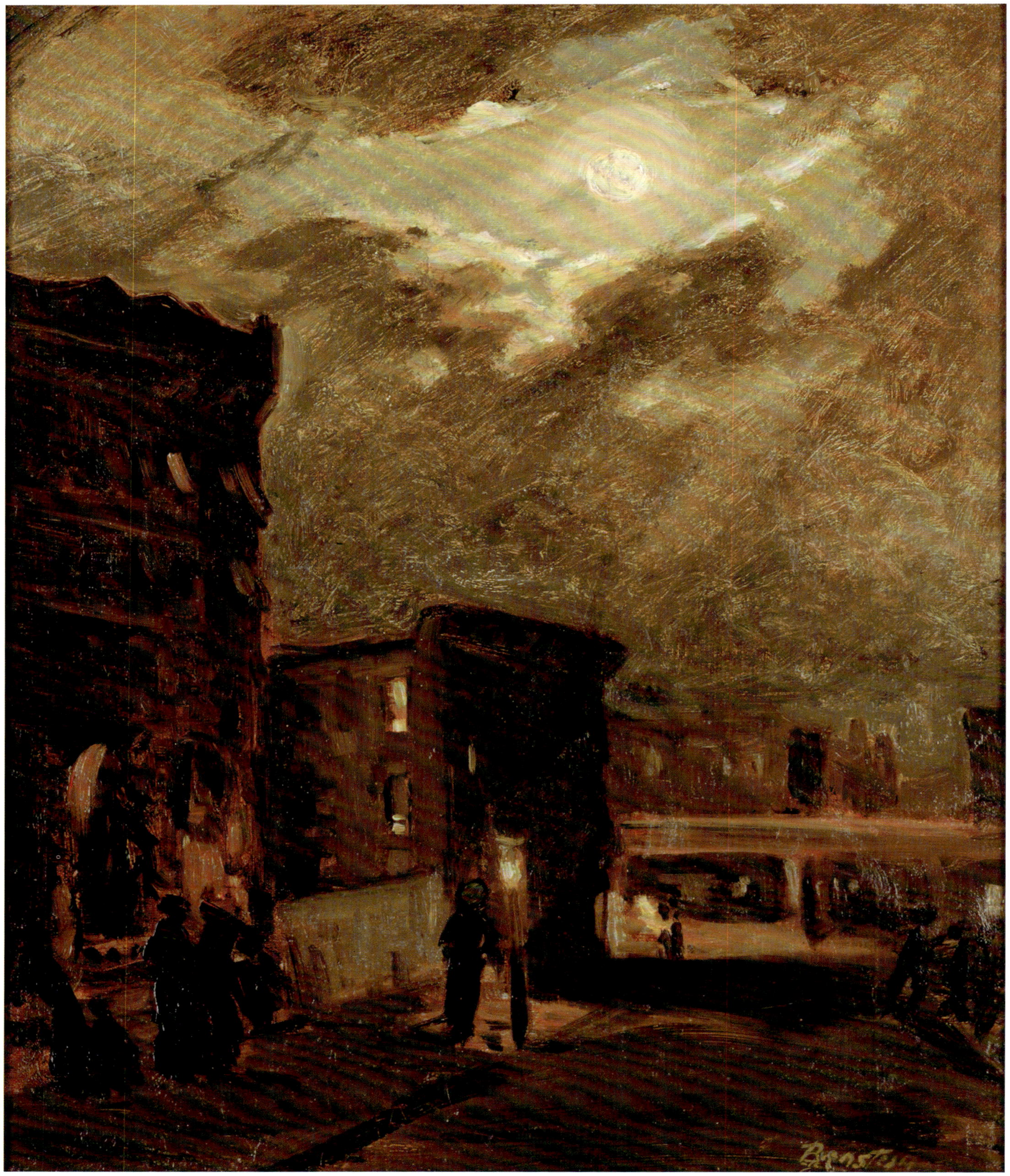

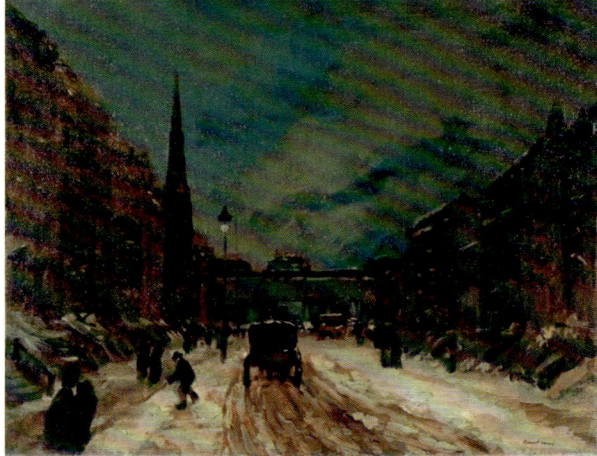

95. Robert Henri, *Street Scene with Snow*, 1902. Oil on canvas, 26 x 32 inches. Yale University Art Gallery.

twentieth century, and thus providing models for us to expand upon the existing scholarship on Bernstein, which has remained for the most part formal and biographical.[4] A close analysis of Bernstein's works from her "Ashcan period," and an examination of her professional relationship with her realist contemporaries, not only offer an opportunity to reconsider her position in relation to the Ashcan School but also allow us to reassess the school itself. Rather than being the token female Ashcan artist, Bernstein must be viewed as an artist who added her individual voice to the mix, while still participating in the realist trends of the moment. Though the "Ashcan period" constitutes only a few early years in her lengthy career (ca. 1911–1920), her status as a female artist, and as someone who received an artistic training different from many of the Ashcan artists, provides us with a richer picture of the urban scene during the 1910s.

Though the extent of Bernstein's relationship with members of the Ashcan

94. *New York Street*, ca. 1912. Oil on canvas, 24 x 20⅛ inches. Jack S. Blanton Museum of Art, Austin, Texas. Gift of Girard Jackson.

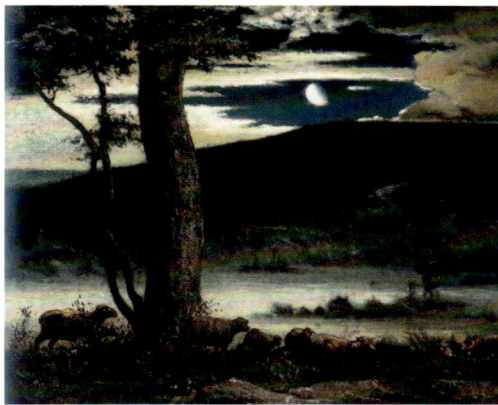

96. Elliot Daingerfield, *Midnight Moon*, ca. 1906.
Oil on canvas, 30⅛ x 36 inches.
Brooklyn Museum, John Woodward Fund.

School is not fully documented, we do know that she frequently exhibited with them, including in the MacDowell Club exhibitions between 1914 and 1919, with the People's Art Guild in 1917, with The Eclectics beginning in 1915, and in the 1918 *American Paintings and Sculptures Pertaining to the War* exhibition held at the Knoedler Gallery in New York. Moreover, she maintained a lasting friendship with John Sloan, whom she likely met around 1918, when she and her husband, William Meyerowitz, joined the Society of Independent Artists.

In *The Journal*, Bernstein recalls meeting Robert Henri for the first time in front of *Carnegie Hall with Paderewski* (see fig. 27), which she showed at a MacDowell Club exhibition around 1914. "He was a tall, dark haired man with Oriental expressions," she describes.[5] Apparently, the origin of her painting, signed "T. Bernstein," caused Henri some confusion until he actually met her, as he had a student by the name of Aline Bernstein, an artist who went on to become a highly regarded set and costume designer.[6] Though neither a student of Henri's nor a member of the Ashcan group, Theresa Bernstein "was philosophically closest to Robert Henri, whose aesthetic she readily grasped," as Michele Cohen points out.[7] At least on the surface level, Bernstein's *New York Street* seems to demonstrate her understanding of Henri's aesthetic; one cannot avoid drawing visual parallels to his cityscapes from 1902, *Street Scene with Snow* and *Snow in New York*, particularly with respect to palette, composition, and subject matter.

It is thus easy to understand why Bernstein has so frequently been misidentified as Henri's student or a "Henrietta." A consideration of Bernstein's artistic training at the Philadelphia School of Design for Women offers a way in which to reevaluate her works from the 1910s and early 1920s as not merely derivative of Ashcan art, but rather as products informed by her schooling.

During the time Bernstein spent at the School of Design between 1907 and 1911, Elliott Daingerfield's influence on her early paintings is particularly evident, including such works as *New York Street*.[3] Here, she reenvisions her teacher's dark, atmospheric landscapes—for instance, *Midnight Moon*—as a cityscape silhouetted against a highly charged moonlit sky,

97. *Moon Over Cityscape*, ca. 1913. Oil on canvas, 17 x 14⅛ inches. Theresa Bernstein and William Meyerowitz Foundation.

dramatized by shifting, painterly clouds. Bernstein's emphasis on the effects of nocturnal light against expressive clouds is again demonstrated in *Moon Over Cityscape*, an oil sketch that bears some formal affinities to Daingerfield.

Before moving to New York in 1911, Bernstein and several fellow art students traveled to Blowing Rock, North Carolina, where Daingerfield was spending the summer. In *The Journal*, she recalls watching black workers from her window as they sang spirituals by their bonfires. She writes: "On Saturday nights they dressed up, and I followed them in the dark in the shadows of the trees. They went to a small house far down the road, a meeting place where they danced and sang. I watched through the door and made a painting of the scene."[9]

This observation resulted in *Dance Hall*, with its dark, sober palette and eerily moonlit sky that suggest Daingerfield's influence (see fig. 76). When painting in New York, Bernstein recreates the same dark atmosphere in *New York Street*, *Carnegie Hall with Paderewski*, and *Searchlights on the Hudson* (see fig. 129). In short, *Dance Hall* indicates that the artist arrived at the dark palette that is so much associated with Henri's paintings before she even began exhibiting with the Ashcan artists. Though Bernstein is associated with the tradition of American Realism, the formal correlations between her works from the 1910s and Diangerfield's situates her in the artistic lineage of tonalists Ralph Albert Blakelock and Albert Pinkham Ryder, both of whom inspired Daingerfield. Another of her teachers, the impressionist painter Daniel Garber, also had a notable role in connecting Bernstein to earlier movements in American art. Though Garber's bucolic landscapes awash in the bright pastel tones of Impressionism bear little obvious resemblance to Bernstein's urban realism, the artist acknowledged her teacher as a vital link to the American realist painting tradition. She states, "[He was a] pupil of Anshutz who was a pupil of Eakins. And I was a pupil of Garber's, so I was kind of the grandchild of Eakins."[10] While Bernstein's commitment to urban realism might suggest that she came to it through a connection with Henri, who, like Garber, was also a student of Anshutz, one can alternatively argue that this focus emerged from her association with Garber.

The notion of artistic backgrounds is essential to reassessing Bernstein's relationship to the Ashcan School. Like her, some of the Ashcan artists had their start in Philadelphia. Indeed, Henri even taught at the Philadelphia School of Design from 1892 to 1895, leaving when Bernstein was still a young child. However, one important difference is the fact that Sloan, Glackens, Luks, and Shinn began their careers as illustrators for Philadelphia (and later New York) newspapers. The training and practical experience they gained while working for these papers remained with them throughout their careers and manifested in various ways within the context of their artistic output. In other words, these artists (some more so than others) viewed their subjects with a reporter's eye, which distinguished them from the more traditionally trained Bernstein.

Remembering the time he spent working for the *Philadelphia Press*, Shinn writes, "The Art department of a newspaper in 1900 was a school far more important in the initial training of the mind for quick perception than the combined instruction of the nation's art schools."[11] Shinn, more than any of his Ashcan colleagues, carried this training into his fine art practice. His paintings and pastels of city streets, urban disasters, and tenement life, combined with his gritty and quickly executed style, evocative of newspaper illustrations, testify to his background in the press. Sloan likewise looked back upon his days in journalism with fondness, and as an experience that offered better training than the stultifying lessons of the Pennsylvania Academy of the Fine Arts, in which he enrolled in 1892.

As an artist who never participated in the world of journalism, which was so central to the Ashcan identity, and who received her artistic training through more traditional means, Bernstein's overall output during her so-called Ashcan period demonstrates a broader range of genres than that of her contemporaries. Without question, her urban realist paintings are as an Ashcan artist.

Bernstein's painting *In the Elevated* (see fig. 43) offers an interesting contrast to Shinn's much earlier pastel, *Sixth Avenue El After Midnight*. Both works portray a similar scene and display a similar composition: a view of the interior of an El and its passengers, who are absorbed in solitary activities (reading the newspaper, sleeping, gazing out the window, etc.). One essential difference, of course, is that Shinn sets his work after midnight, as indicated by the title, the dark

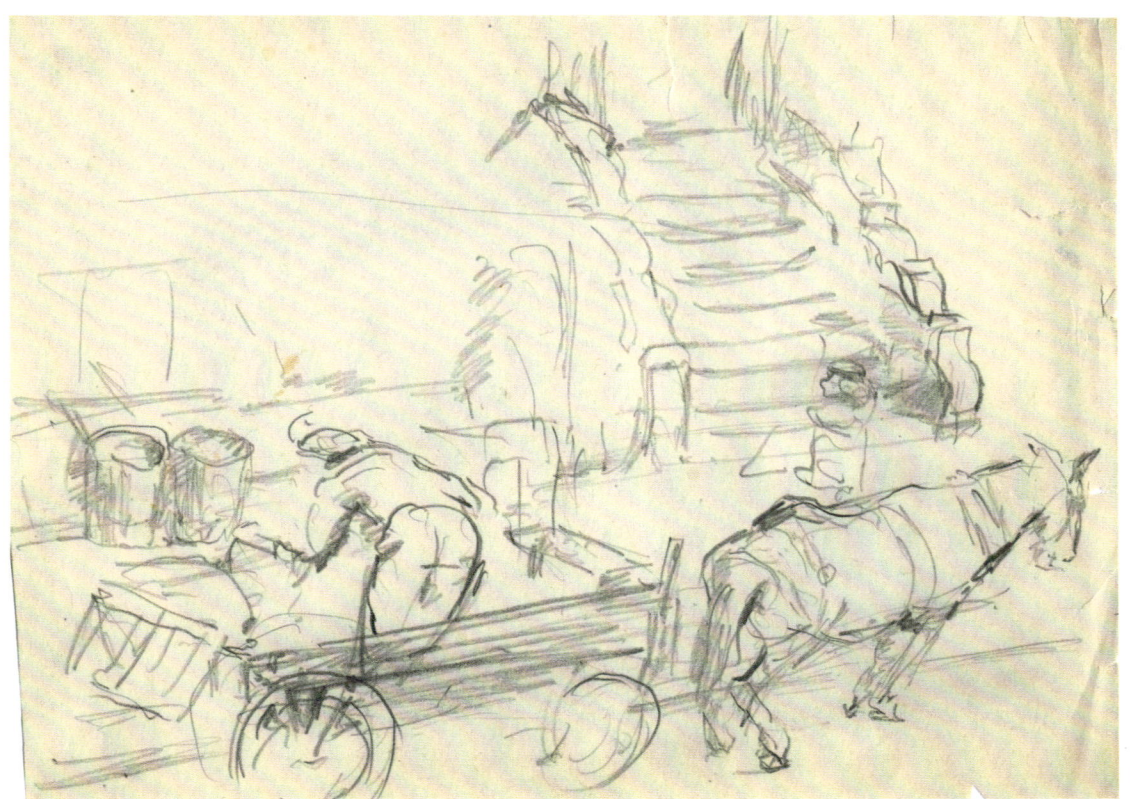

98. *Street Scene with Horse and Cart*, ca. 1912. 7¾ x 10⅜ inches. Theresa Bernstein and William Meyerowitz Foundation.

and were the most well known and the most frequently reproduced and discussed. At the same time, it is also important to acknowledge that even while she was capturing scenes of contemporary urban life, she also painted a number of mythological themes during the same period—a remarkable though overlooked body of work that certainly warrants investigation by future scholars. Bernstein's interest in fictitious subjects and her lack of involvement with the press challenges her incorrect labeling

atmosphere, and the sleeping passengers. Bernstein's painting, in contrast, is set during the day, as suggested by the sunlight filtering through the windows. As a respectable, middle class woman, it is likely that neither she nor the women she depicts in the painting would set foot in the El after midnight.

Subject matter aside, a consideration of style provides insights into the idea of the popular press as a training ground for Shinn. Sylvia L. Yount points out that while working for the newspapers in Philadelphia, Shinn developed a prodigious skill in sketching quickly from memory. A focus on "human interest, topicality, and quickness of perception and execution" necessary for the task of creating illustrations for the popular press remained with him for the duration of his career, allowing him to develop his own "particular brand of realism in both style and subject matter."[12] In addition, Shinn's use of pastel, his preferred medium, allowed him to work more quickly and to convey the sense of spontaneity and immediacy associated with illustrations in the popular press.

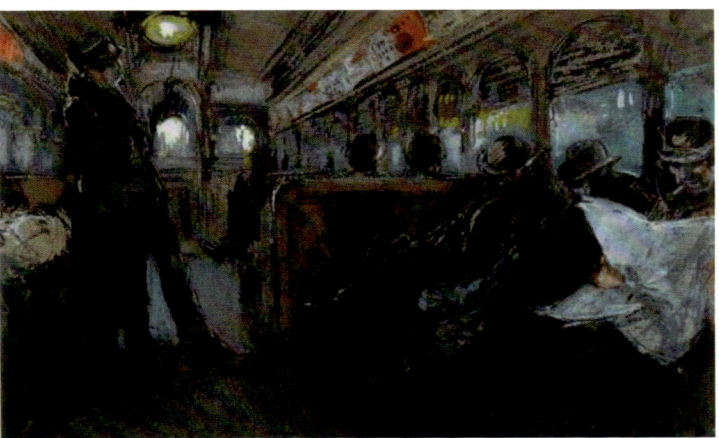

99. Everett Shinn,
Sixth Avenue El after Midnight, 1899.
Pastel, gouache, and watercolor on paper,
8 x 12⅜ inches. Private collection.

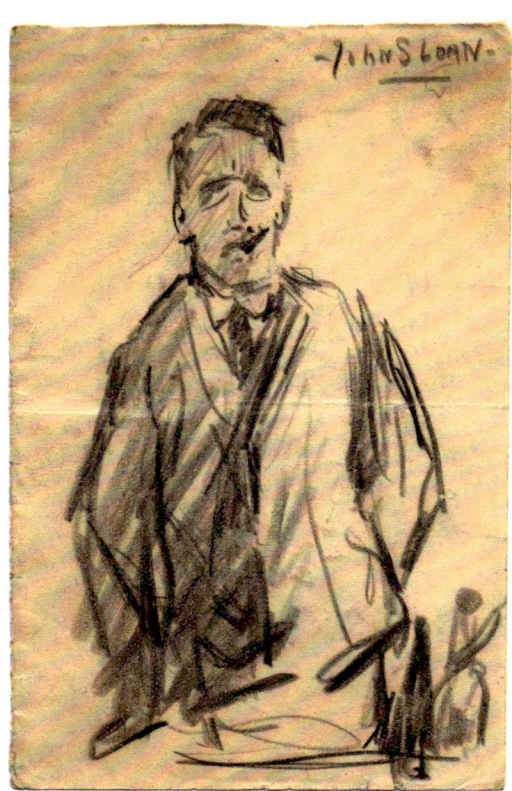

100. *John Sloan*, ca. 1918. Pencil on paper.
Theresa Bernstein and William Meyerowitz Foundation.

Though *Sixth Avenue El* is not a newspaper illustration, it still displays a sketch-like quality in the quickly drawn lines that constitute the figures. Bernstein's painting, at first glance, also suggests a similar quality through the energetic application of paint. However, close examination of the painting shows a great deliberateness in her rendering of the figures, particularly in the female figure in the foreground; indeed, the use of slow-drying oil paint does not lend itself quite as well to the rapid execution we see in Shinn's work. Furthermore, two figures in the painting are portraits of Bernstein's parents: the man reading a newspaper is her father, while the woman in the foreground is her mother.[13] In knowing that she modeled her figures on family and friends, we lose some of the sense of immediacy that we recognize in Shinn's pictures. In other words, *In the Elevated* is a carefully thought out and composed painting; her extant preparatory sketch also supports this assessment (see fig. 46). As Bernstein's career progressed, her painting would become increasingly sketch-like and linear, but in the 1910s she worked in a manner closer to her art school training.

Despite their obvious differences and diverging artistic backgrounds, Bernstein frequently crossed paths with various members of the Ashcan School in multiple venues, including the MacDowell Club exhibitions, the Society of Independent Artists, the Eclectic exhibitions at the Folsom Galleries in New York, and the Gallery-on-the-Moors in East Gloucester, which helped pave the way for earning her status as the token female Ashcan painter. Of the artists in the Ashcan School, Bernstein's relationship with Sloan is perhaps the best documented. While it is not entirely clear when the two artists met, they must certainly have been aware of one another by 1914, when Bernstein began exhibiting at the MacDowell Club in New York. Initiated by Henri in 1911, these nonjuried exhibitions were meant to provide artists with the opportunity to show their works to the public in artist-organized groups. Speaking to the *New York Times*, Henri stated, "My desire is to see a great big place where artists can hang their pictures—a place where they will be judged, but not judged wrongly, and where every artist can have a fair chance."[14]

In addition to meeting Henri around 1914, as Bernstein describes in *The Journal*, she also exhibited at a MacDowell Club exhibition in May of that same year, which included, among others, Sloan, Henri, and Stuart Davis. Though there is no particular evidence to document that Bernstein and Sloan had actually met at the exhibition, each must have been aware of the other, especially since it was a small artist-organized show, and they were reviewed together in the *New York Times*.[15] Certainly, Bernstein would have known about Sloan, given the reputation of the Ashcan circle, which had been established in the 1908 exhibition of The Eight at the Macbeth Galleries.

Bernstein claimed that in 1914, Sloan wrote, "We should all keep our eyes on Theresa Bernstein." Though this quote is impossible to document, it is not altogether implausible that her works caught Sloan's attention as early as 1914.[16] Around this time, critics also compared Bernstein to Sloan. In viewing an exhibition at the MacDowell Club, one critic remarked that the display of eighty-five works "is dominated by the work of Miss Theresa Bernstein, a young woman with a marked and vigorous talent," who like Sloan and Randall Davey "has that vital interest in the people of the City and in their social relations that characterizes the group."[17] The two artists would have been personally acquainted by 1918, when Sloan became president of the Society of Independent Artists, which held annual nonjuried exhibitions. Both Bernstein and Meyerowitz were members of the society (with Meyerowitz as treasurer), participating in nearly every exhibition until it ended in 1944. "John Sloan, who continually railed against a nation that neglected its artists, helped to found the Society of Independent Artists," Bernstein writes in *William Meyerowitz: The Artist Speaks*. "William and I became charter members of the society. William was elected treasurer, but there wasn't much treasure to spend."[18]

Bernstein's friendship with Sloan was long lasting, and

she showed her support for the society, to which Sloan stayed fiercely loyal. She remained one of the "very few artists of note" to participate regularly in the 1940s, when it "had become a largely amateur, ragtag operation."[19]

Among the numerous drawings Bernstein made over her lifetime is a casual sketch of Sloan, which she likely drew around 1918, when she joined the Society of Independent Artists. With a few quickly executed and abbreviated lines, Bernstein manages to capture a fairly convincing likeness of Sloan in this sketch. The work can be placed in the tradition of portraits of artists by artists, as a sign of respect and shared values. Though within her overall oeuvre, it may not be her most significant nor her most accomplished sketch, it is nevertheless important as a marker for the beginning of a friendship that would span decades. Bernstein remembers Sloan as "a good friend [. . .] who, incredible as it may seem, didn't actually sell a painting until he was sixty years old." However, he sold etchings before then, Bernstein explains, including *The Barber Shop*, which she purchased.[20]

Though the two artists maintained an important relationship, there is as yet no evidence to suggest that they shared the same politics. In 1912 Sloan became the art editor of *The Masses*, a radical leftist periodical. In addition to dealing with the typical socialist subjects of workers' rights and poverty, *The Masses* also focused on birth control, suffrage, sexual liberation, prostitution, economic freedom for women, racial equality, religion, and other controversial issues of the time. Importantly for Sloan, as well as for fellow artists Bellows, Davis, and others, *The Masses* accorded with the progressive tendencies of urban realism. As Rebecca Zurier points out, "Frustrated by the difficulties of exhibiting their unorthodox art and by the conservative taste of magazine editors, they saw in *The Masses* a potential outlet—a new kind of art gallery—as well as an alternative to conventional publications."[21] Moreover, it gave Sloan further opportunities to explore the lives and activities of the New York's working class. Although he insisted throughout

his career that his status as a socialist never manifested in propaganda, one cannot deny the fact that many of his works contain social commentary.[22]

Though Bernstein supported woman's suffrage and empathized with the economic plight of women, her work contrasts with Sloan's, since she maintained an interest in urban crowds in all its variations rather than capturing small vignettes of urban life that contain social commentary. With Sloan's background in newspaper and journal illustration, and in the social activism of *The Masses*, creating narratives through his works seems a natural outcome. Bernstein, on the other hand, "rarely let her work slip into story telling, which is sometimes a predominant motive in paintings by Sloan, Glackens, Luks and Shinn," as Michele Cohen points out.[23] Moreover, the facets of urban life that she chose to portray (opera houses, Carnegie Hall, the New York Public Library, and churches) were quite often more respectable than the sites that Sloan and the other Ashcan artists turned to (bars, vaudeville, tenements, and the Bowery). Indeed, unlike Sloan, who lived in the seedier neighbourhoods of Manhattan with his alcoholic wife, Bernstein lived uptown, where the neighbourhoods were considered more respectable.

This question of respectability arises when we consider Bernstein's 1917 canvas *Waiting Room Employment Office* in relation to Sloan's *Sixth Avenue and 30th Street, New York City*. *Waiting Room*, which depicts a group of working class women, is based on Bernstein's teenage memory of going to the employment office with her mother to hire their housekeeper, Katie. The canvas suggests Bernstein's opinion of her family as belonging to a more privileged socio-economic class.

Unlike her portrayal of crowds where people are merely anonymous masses, Bernstein captures the different facial features, gestures, and clothing of these women. As Patricia Burnham describes, "Although she does not comment on the larger society forces that governed the destiny of the women, by particularizing them Bernstein gives their lives dignity and

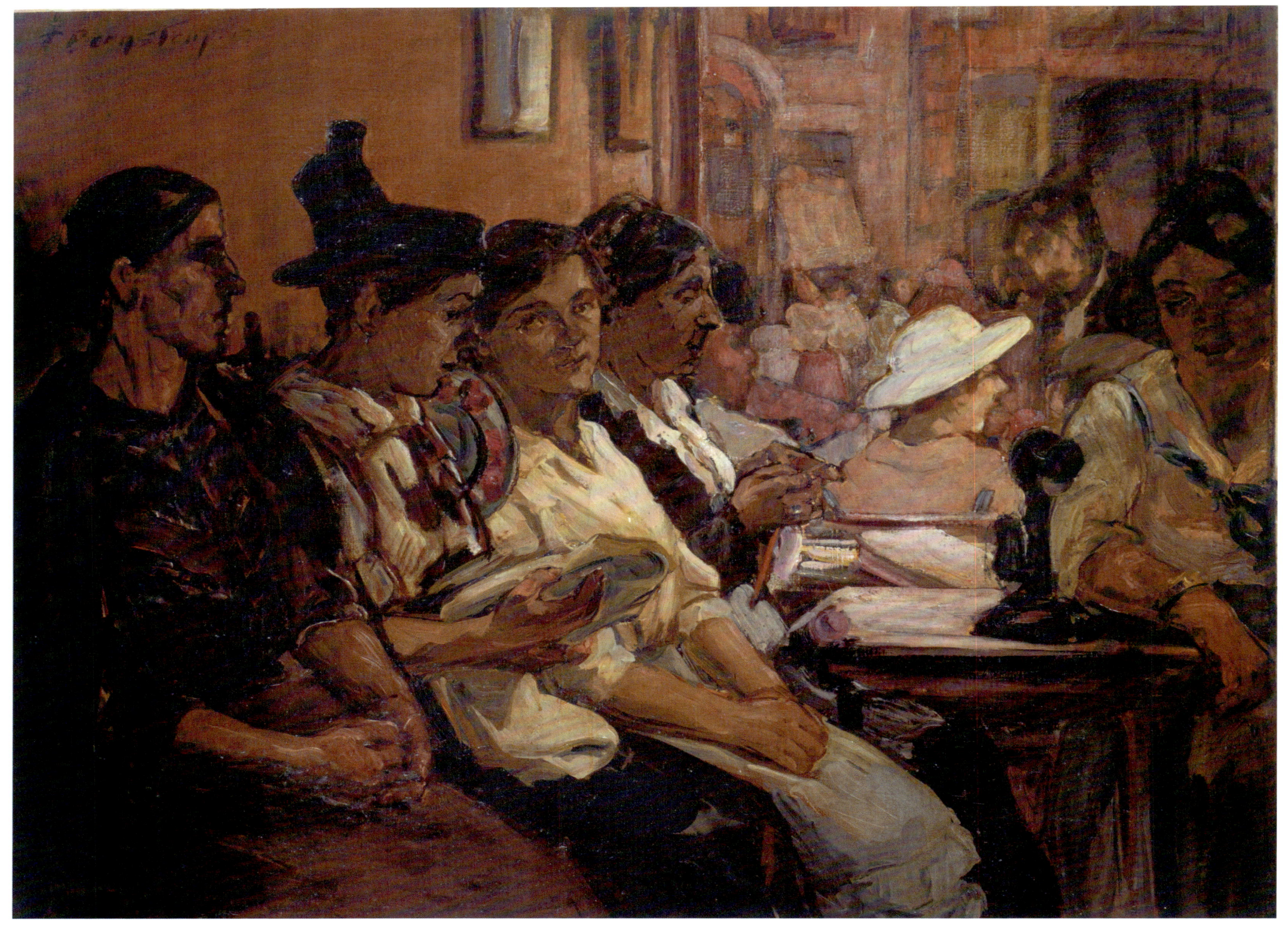

101. *Waiting Room Employment Office*, 1917. Oil on canvas, 30 x 40 inches. The Jewish Museum, New York, New York. Gift of Soledad and Robert Hurst, 2011-8.

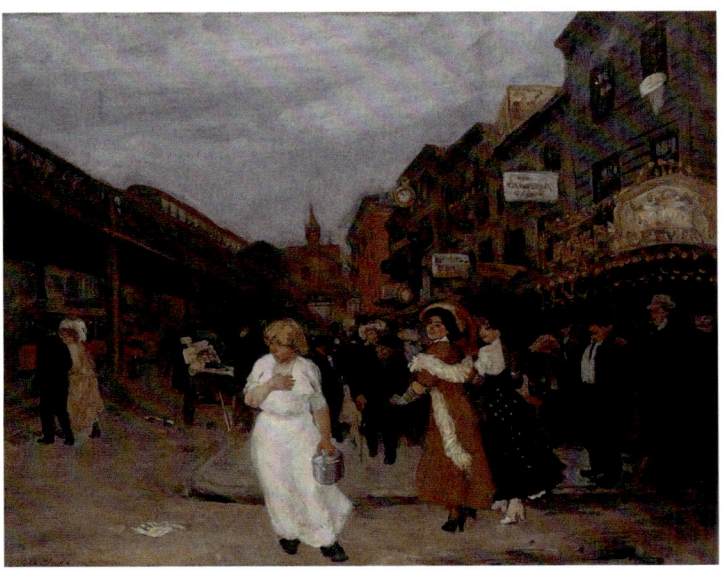

102. John Sloan, *Sixth Avenue and 30th Street, New York City*, 1907.
Oil on canvas, 26¼ x 32 inches. Philadelphia Museum of Art.

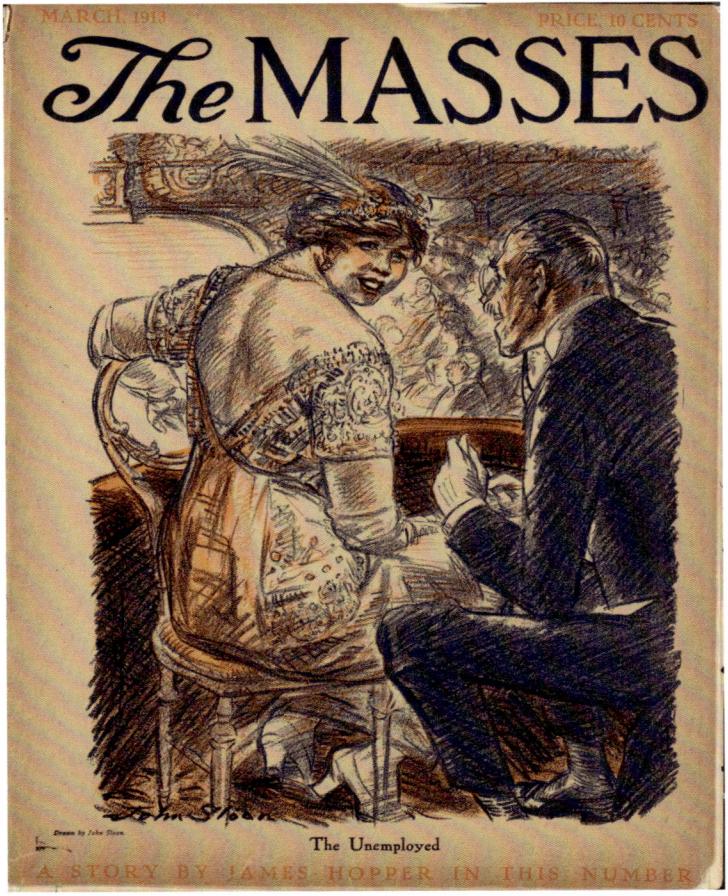

103. John Sloan, *The Unemployed*, cover of *The Masses*, vol. 4 no. 6, March 1913.

purpose; they are much more than the picturesque poor depicted by many of her contemporaries."[24]

While we cannot necessarily characterize the figures in Sloan's *Sixth Avenue* as "picturesque poor," they certainly represent a contrast to Bernstein's figures. The individuals depicted in her painting are unemployed, yet she lends them a sense of dignity, as they are shown looking for honest employment. The women in Sloan's painting, on the other hand, are prostitutes and alcoholics who coalesced in the notorious Tenderloin District near his studio.

When he does depict the "respectable" classes of society, he is less than complimentary. In a work such as *Gray and Brass*, Sloan portrays the city's affluent class as "snob, cheap, 'nouveau riche,'" and idle—the truly unemployed.[25] For the March 1913 cover of *The Masses*, he satirically repeats this theme in his illustration of a wealthy couple attending the opera, captioning it *The Unemployed*. Ostensibly, these are the same individuals who would attend the opera houses and symphony halls that interested Bernstein in such works as *Carnegie Hall with Paderewski* and *The Music Lovers* (see figs. 27 and 31). Unlike Sloan, however, she makes no obvious social judgment, preferring to capture the atmosphere, energy, and spectacle of these spaces and the rapt attention of the spectators.

Despite the great differences between Bernstein and Sloan's respective approaches to representing contemporary urban life, the two artists, as well as the other Ashcan artists, were connected by a shared commitment to asserting their identities as American painters. By responding to Henri's prescription for equating art with life in order to express "the virile ideas of their country," the Ashcan artists found the authenticity of the United States in the vitality of New York's urban life and activities.[26] Indeed, Bernstein even acknowledges the desire to assert their identity as American artists. She writes: "The Ashcan group, as they were called, got together and had shows of considerable importance, saying, 'We're Americans.

We live here, and the French are coming and taking money out of the pockets of our American collectors.'"[27]

Bernstein, too, asserted her identity as an American painter, taking the life of the city—its crowds, spectacles, and places—as her subject.[28] In 1915 she turned down the invitation of John Lane, editor of *International Studio*, who had purchased her painting *Open Air Show* (see fig. 22), to go to England. "I declined," she states in *The Journal*. "I felt that the environment that most interested me was my own country."[29] Though she traveled abroad a number of times, Bernstein's commitment to the American scene can be observed in her sustained interest, over the course of her long career, in painting New York City. The subject matter of her paintings from the 1910s, such as *New York Street* and *In the Elevated*, parallels and sometimes even resembles the works of the Ashcan School, yet we need to recognize that the urban environment was not the exclusive domain of these artists.

Wanda M. Corn describes the early twentieth century as a moment when artists "had begun to identify New York as something indigenously American."[30] They saw the metropolis as a place that allowed them to mine subject matter they considered unique to America, thus providing them a means by which to differentiate themselves from their European contemporaries. Considering Corn's assessment of New York as a source of national identity that artists tapped in order to assert themselves as American artists, we can begin to see Bernstein as one who operated under this broader trend in the early twentieth century. Whether it was the urban realists who explored the everyday life and spectacles of the metropolis or the vanguardists who saw the bridges, skyscrapers and machines as indigenous American forms, New York—as the epitome of modernity—became an endless source of fascination for numerous artists.

In his 1916 essay, urban sociologist Robert E. Park observes that the emergence of new forms of transportation and communication changed the way in which a city organized itself and affected the dispersal of its population, while simultaneously altering the social interaction of the urban dweller. The large city, he points out, transforms formerly intimate associations into ones that are "more transitory and less stable." Hence, under such circumstances, social intimacy is reduced to the act of looking, and to "a scrupulous study of style and manners."[31] In essence, the city evolves into a theater, in which the urban citizen becomes a passive spectator of the drama and spectacle of everyday life.

In her analysis of the Ashcan School in *Picturing the City: Urban Vision and the Ashcan School* (2006), Rebecca Zurier expands upon the notion of the city as a stage upon which "urban vision, a complex system of visual exchanges, is enacted." Urban vision was not simply the physical act of looking, but also a social and cultural practice adopted in the urban environment. The modern city, she argues, encouraged a "culture of looking," whereby everyone was there to see and be seen, and where the distinction between public and private became blurred; moreover, the proliferation of urban spectacles and visual stimuli worked to enhance this culture.[32] While Zurier excludes Bernstein in her exploration of the Ashcan School, the cultural and historical approach of her scholarship can certainly enhance our understanding of the artist. Bernstein, like the Ashcan painters, also produced many of her finest works within the same cultural milieu and was therefore similarly a practitioner of urban vision, though of a somewhat different strain than Sloan's.

Zurier's analysis of Sloan's urban vision notes that more than any other Ashcan painter, the artist developed a complex idiom that addressed the social concerns of his time. Unlike the other artists who focused on crowds, Sloan was more interested in probing the dynamics of various visual exchanges that occur between urban strangers, as well as between his viewers and the subjects of his works. In etchings such as *Night Windows*, public

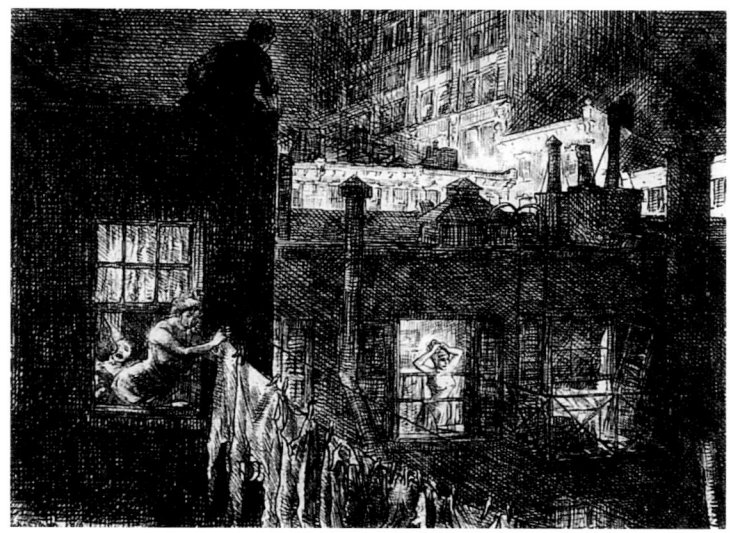

104. John Sloan, *Night Windows*, 1910. Etching, 5¼ x 6¾ inches. Private collection.

and private are conflated, reflecting the notion that in the tightly packed urban environment of New York, privacy is not an option—everything and everyone is on display.[33]

Voyeurism, a theme in Sloan's etching, was very much part of New York's culture of looking at the turn of the century when attempts were made to "normalize" it through film, newspapers, and various other media. At the same time, questions of social class preoccupied Sloan—working-class women in unguarded moments—and reinforced the popular notion of the time that "walls were more permeable in working-class areas" and that the working class were "unconscious exhibitionists," thus justifying the viewer's voyeuristic gaze.[34]

While Sloan made the private public, Bernstein made the public private; her works focus on public spaces yet manage to capture her figures in moments of private introspection. Or as Cohen states, "the figures exist at once in a private world and a public space."[35] In *The Readers* (see fig. 4), for instance, Bernstein depicts a group of people reading books in the New York Public Library. Though the room is filled with people, a sense of privacy is conveyed through the way in which each figure is completely caught up in his or her own activity and is oblivious to the viewer.

Similar observations could be made about Bernstein's *Polish Church: Easter Morning* (see fig. 12), another public scene. Here the large group of figures is engrossed in prayer, reading the Bible, and listening to the sermon, while we, the viewers, observe the individuals in their private moments. There is no suggestion, in either of these works, that our gaze is somehow illicit or voyeuristic, as it is when we view Sloan's *Night Windows*. Nevertheless, as we find out from Bernstein's account of sketching *Polish Church: Easter Morning*, urban vision—even in the most public spaces—could potentially be problematic. In *The Journal*, Bernstein describes the parishioners' incensed reaction as she tried to sketch them in the church—a response suggesting that privacy can be breached even in public spaces, thus raising the question of whether we can implicate Bernstein in the act of voyeurism.[36] Regardless, Bernstein's sketching activities lack the sinister edge we find in Sloan's hobby of gazing into peoples' windows.

Though her "Ashcan period" of the 1910s constituted only a brief moment in the overall scope of her oeuvre, Bernstein never lost her fascination with New York and its crowds, even as she developed a much looser and energetic style in her later years that bears little resemblance to Ashcan painting. The Ashcan artists, on the other hand, increasingly turned away from the streets as their careers progressed. From the 1920s to his death in 1951, for instance, nudes dominated Sloan's oeuvre. In addition, Henri's *Street Scene with Snow* was one of his last works to portray an urban scene; though his teachings influenced numerous artists, his own body of work consisted primarily of portraits done in a style reminiscent of the Old Masters he so admired.[37]

Bernstein's urban vision has a distinct quality to it that operates both within and independently of the Ashcan School. It is only when we challenge her frequent misidentification as an Ashcan painter that we can begin to recognize her as a unique artist in her own right, rather than as a follower of her male contemporaries. Her upbeat depictions of parades, concert halls, libraries, and other public spaces demonstrate an optimism and joy for the energy and crowds of New York City—a quality that is not always present in works by the indoctrinated Ashcan artists, which often contain a critical and even sinister edge. Reconsidering Bernstein's relationship with the Ashcan School not only enriches our understanding of her as an artist, but also opens up new avenues for thinking about the Ashcan artists as the whole.

NOTES

1. Theresa Bernstein, *The Journal* (New York: Cornwall Books, 1991), p. 41. Though *The Journal* is indeed a valuable resource, we must also acknowledge that some of Bernstein's statements are inaccurate. I have yet to locate this quote from *Art News*, which was purportedly written by a critic around 1914, when she exhibited at the MacDowell Club.

2. Marian Wardle, ed., *American Women Modernists: The Legacy of Robert Henri, 1910–1945* (New Brunswick NJ: Brigham Young University Museum of Art in association with Rutgers University Press, 2005).

3. Frederick James Gregg, "Theresa Bernstein a Realist in the Old Sense of the Word," *New York Herald*, November 2, 1919, sec. 3, p. 5.

4. See especially Deborah Fairman, "The Landscape of Display: The Ashcan School, Spectacle, and the Staging of Everyday Life," *Prospects: An Annual of American Cultural Studies* 18 (1993), pp. 205–35; Rebecca Zurier, Robert W. Snyder, and Virginia M. Mecklenburg, *Metropolitan Lives: The Ashcan Artists and Their New York* (New York: W. W. Norton in association with the National Museum of American Art, 1995); Rebecca Zurier, *Picturing the City: Urban Vision and the Ashcan School* (Berkeley: University of California Press, 2006).

5. Bernstein, *The Journal*, pp. 40–41. Bernstein claims in *The Journal* that she met Henri around 1914. The *New York Times* from May 3, 1914, reviews a MacDowell Club exhibition in which Henri and Bernstein both participate, but it makes no mention of *Carnegie Hall and Paderewski*.

6. Girard Jackson, *Theresa Bernstein: Expressions of Cape Ann and New York, 1914–1972* (Stamford CT: Stamford Museum and Nature Center and Smith-Girard, 1989), n.p.

7. Michele Cohen, *Echoes of New York: The Paintings of Theresa Bernstein* (New York: Museum of the City of New York, 1990), n.p.

8. See Cohen, *Echoes of New York*, who writes: "Daingerfield was an academic painter whose moody, suggestive landscapes had a clear stylistic impact on her early atmospheric night scenes" (n.p.).

9. Bernstein, *The Journal*, p. 37.

10. Bernstein, as quoted in Cohen, *Echoes of New York*, n.p.

11. Everett Shinn, "Life on the Press," in "Artists of the Philadelphia Press: William Glackens, George Luks, Everett Shinn, John Sloan; October 14–November 18, 1945," *Philadelphia Museum Bulletin* 207 (November 1945), p. 9.

12. Sylvia L. Yount, "Consuming Drama: Everett Shinn and the Spectacular City," *American Art* 6 (Autumn 1992), p. 89.

13. Cohen, *Echoes of New York*, n.p.

14. "An Art Exhibition without a Jury System of Awards," *New York Times*, May 14, 1911.

15. "At the MacDowell Club," *New York Times*, May 3, 1914, p. 11.

16. This statement is quoted from Girard Jackson, *Theresa Bernstein* (Stamford CT: Smith-Girard, 1985). It is doubtful that this came from Sloan's diaries, as he only kept a dairy from 1906 to 1913, before picking it up again in 1947.

17. "News of New York Exhibitions," *Christian Science Monitor*, May 1, 1915, p. 22. (From Bernstein's scrapbook; see chapter 1, note 112.)

18. Theresa Bernstein Meyerowitz, *William Meyerowitz: The Artist Speaks* (Philadelphia: Art Alliance Press, 1986), p. 47.

19. John Loughery, *John Sloan: Painter and Rebel* (New York: Henry Holt, 1995), p. 343.

20. Bernstein, *William Meyerowitz*, p. 48. Sloan liked to play up the notion that his paintings did not sell until late in his career, but he nonetheless had long been an important figure within the New York art world. In 1948 the Kraushaar Gallery in New York held a retrospective exhibition for the artist, who was by then seventy-seven years old. Bernstein, along with many other artists, was in attendance at the opening to honor the artist's achievements. See Loughery, *John Sloan*, p. 343.

21. Rebecca Zurier, *Art for "The Masses": A Radical Magazine and Its Graphics*, 1911–1917 (Philadelphia: Temple University Press, 1988), p. 32.

22. Speaking to an interviewer in 1940, Sloan stated: "Anyone who thinks I painted my city life pictures with the idea of preaching is mistaken. I reserved such comment for drawings and cartoons made for *The Masses* and *The Call*. . . . While I am a Socialist, I never allowed social propaganda to get into my paintings. I let, wanted social satire in some of them, but not Socialist propaganda." Quoted in Zurier, *Art for the "The Masses"*, p. 56.

23. Cohen, *Echoes of New York*, n.p.

24. Patricia M. Burnham, "Theresa Bernstein," *Woman's Art Journal* 9, no. 2 (Autumn 1988–Winter 1989), p. 23.

25. John Sloan, *John Sloan's New York Scene: From the Diaries, Notes, and Correspondence, 1906–1913*, ed. Bruce St. John (New York: Harper and Row, 1965), p. 155.

26. Robert Henri, "Progress in Our National Art Must Spring from the Development of Individuality of Ideas and Freedom of Expression," *The Craftsman* 15 (January 1909), p. 389.

27. Bernstein, *The Journal*, p. 40.

28. See also Cohen, "Theresa Bernstein in Gloucester: Shaping Artistic Identity," for a discussion of Bernstein's Americanness in relation to Gloucester.

29. Bernstein, *The Journal*, p. 40.

30. Wanda M. Corn, "The New New York," *Art in America* 61, no. 4 (July–August 1973), p. 64.

31. Robert Park, "The City: Suggestions for the Investigation of Human Behavior in the Urban Environment," originally published in *The American Journal of Sociology* 20 (1916), reprinted in Richard Sennett, ed., Classic Essays on the Culture of Cities (Englewood Cliffs NJ: Prentice Hall, 1969), p. 125.

32. Zurier, *Picturing the City*, pp. 45–85.

33. Zurier, *Picturing the City*, pp. 281–84.

34. Zurier, *Picturing the City*, pp. 284–85.

35. Cohen, *Echoes of New York*, n.p.

36. Bernstein, *The Journal*, p. 43.

37. Zurier, *Picturing the City*, p. 125.

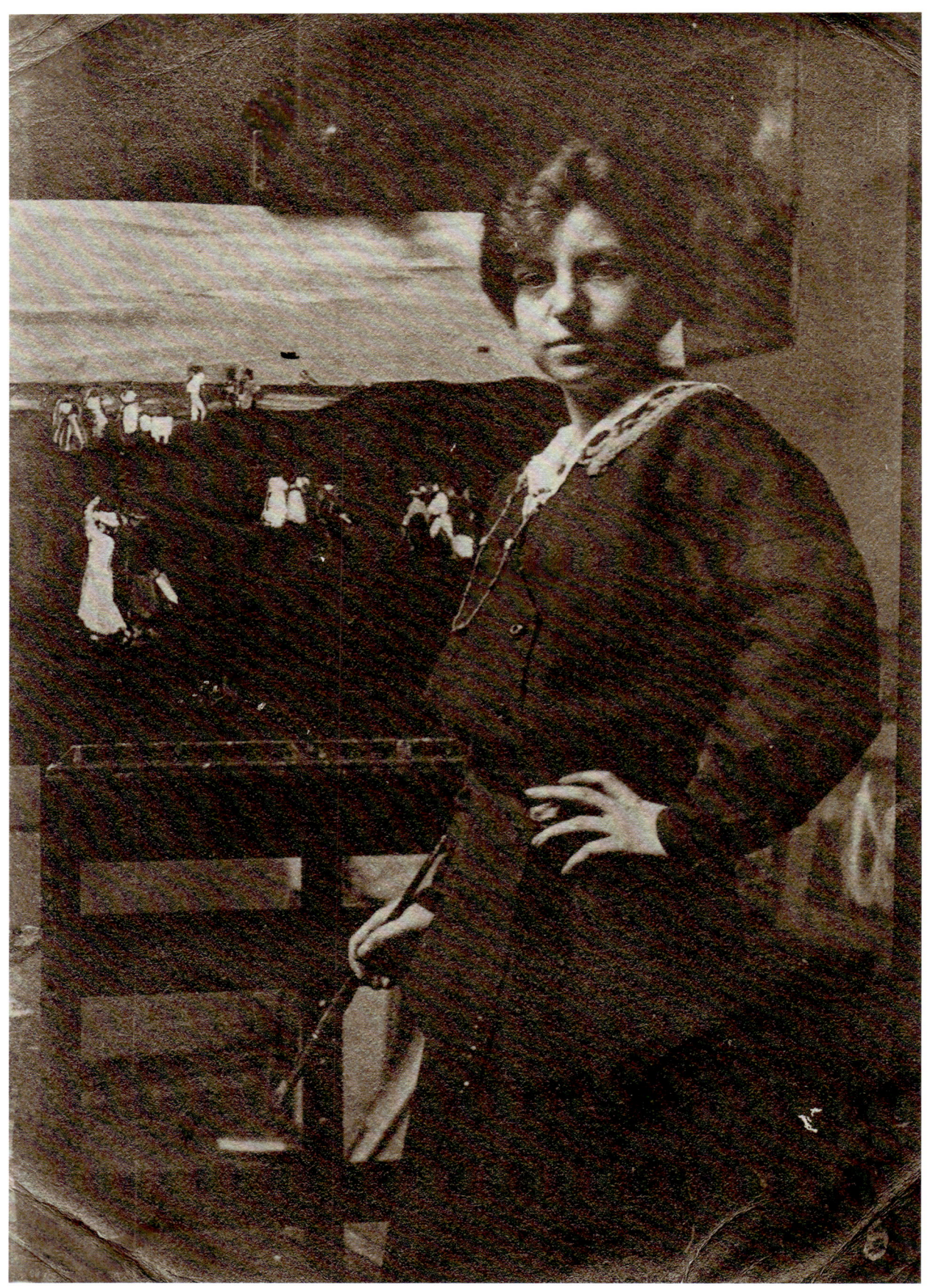

105. Theresa Bernstein in her studio with *The Golf Links* of 1916.

THREE

Theresa Bernstein in Gloucester

SHAPING ARTISTIC IDENTITY

Michele Cohen

*I*n 1972, on the fiftieth anniversary of the North Shore Arts Association, Theresa Bernstein reflected on the group's history and by extension her own enduring connections to Gloucester. For her—born in Cracow, raised and schooled in Philadelphia, then transplanted to New York City—Gloucester offered a "cradle-like serenity."[1] The nation's oldest seaport, it also provided Bernstein with an authentic American past. Nestled along the rocky New England coast of Cape Ann and only twenty-five miles north of Boston, Gloucester was and remains remote yet accessible; its New England pedigree and significant history undoubtedly reinforced its appeal for the patriotic Bernstein. In her introduction to the *Memorial Exhibition of the Third Cape Ann Arts Festival*,[2] she explained the connections between the nation's past and Gloucester's artistic legacy, and by inference, her legacy: "As the Pilgrims discovered New England, so the artists found in the stern and rockbound coast of Cape Ann a message of beauty to be translated into lasting inspiration for those who came after. The combination of hilly and luxurious green close to the mighty ocean exemplifies the simple virtues of our heritage. . . . No region has greater variety of subject matter and natural beauty; and these translations by American artists of the past and the present have brought and will continue to bring many visitors to the shores of Cape Ann."[3]

Gloucester's atmospheric light, spectacular beaches, untamed moors, bustling harbor, rocky outcroppings, and picturesque streets have been immortalized by American painters of all stripes for decades, and Bernstein eagerly joined them in the summer of 1916, shortly before the United States entered World War I. She continued to summer there almost until her death in 2002.

Gloucester also had the distinction of hosting an established artistic community with a significant percentage of women artists. Some came to study, choosing an American city over Rome or Paris, but many were already recognized figures. Among fishermen and "genteel" summer tourists, male and female artists quickly formed their own social networks, cohering into a close-knit circle around East Gloucester's Rocky Neck.[4] In Cape Ann the more liberating summer lifestyle supported an artistic identity that sprung from avocation, not gender, allowing women to assume more equal roles with their male counterparts than they had in urban settings. For Bernstein, Gloucester provided an especially nurturing environment where she could simultaneously sustain her multiple identities as an artist, woman, and partner in an artist couple.[5] Unlike the more restrictive artistic milieus of Boston[6] and New York, in Gloucester women artists were not marginalized in exhibitions, art associations, or critical reviews and they did not form separate groups; there, Bernstein could assume her position as an American artist, unfettered by her sex.

Although Bernstein first came to Gloucester in 1916, on the recommendation of Isabel Vernon Cook, the president of the National Association of Women Painters and Sculptors, it is likely that she had already known about Gloucester through Henry B. Snell, her former teacher at the Philadelphia School of

Design for Women, who had a studio in East Gloucester. Cook knew Bernstein loved beaches with their vibrant patterned umbrellas, dramatic color contrasts, and abundant bathers. In *The Journal*, Bernstein relates that as a young girl, she had vacationed in Atlantic City, recalling the dramatic image of head-to-toe black knitted bathing suits worn by male bathers, "the black accent on the yellow sand that I enjoyed painting. The umbrellas or parasols departed from the somber tones and radiated red or blue designs."[7] When the family relocated to New York City, Bernstein visited local beaches, including Coney Island, Long Beach, Edgemere, and Rockaway Beach.

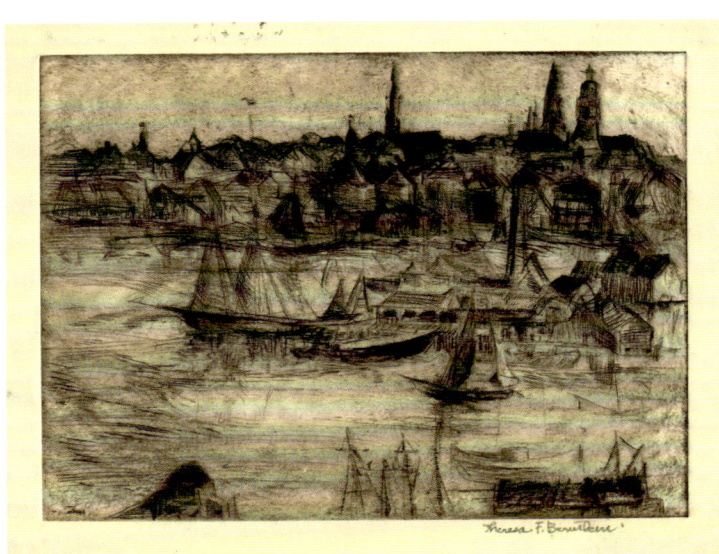

107. *Gloucester Harbor*, 1920s. Etching, 6¼ x 8⅛ inches.
Theresa Bernstein and William Meyerowitz Foundation.

However, upon her arrival in Gloucester, other subjects quickly captivated her: the harbor, fishermen, golf, country fairs, picturesque streets, the rocky coast, and garden parties. Many paintings document recreational activities, social gatherings, or special events like that of the *Grecian Pageant*, staged to raise money for war relief during World War I, or dances at the Hawthorne Inn: reflections of a bygone era. Other paintings provide a bird's-eye perspective on the harbor visible from Bernstein's perch at 44 Mount Pleasant Avenue (the home she and her husband would purchase in 1924) or portray scenes Bernstein encountered on walks nearby, such as golfers up the

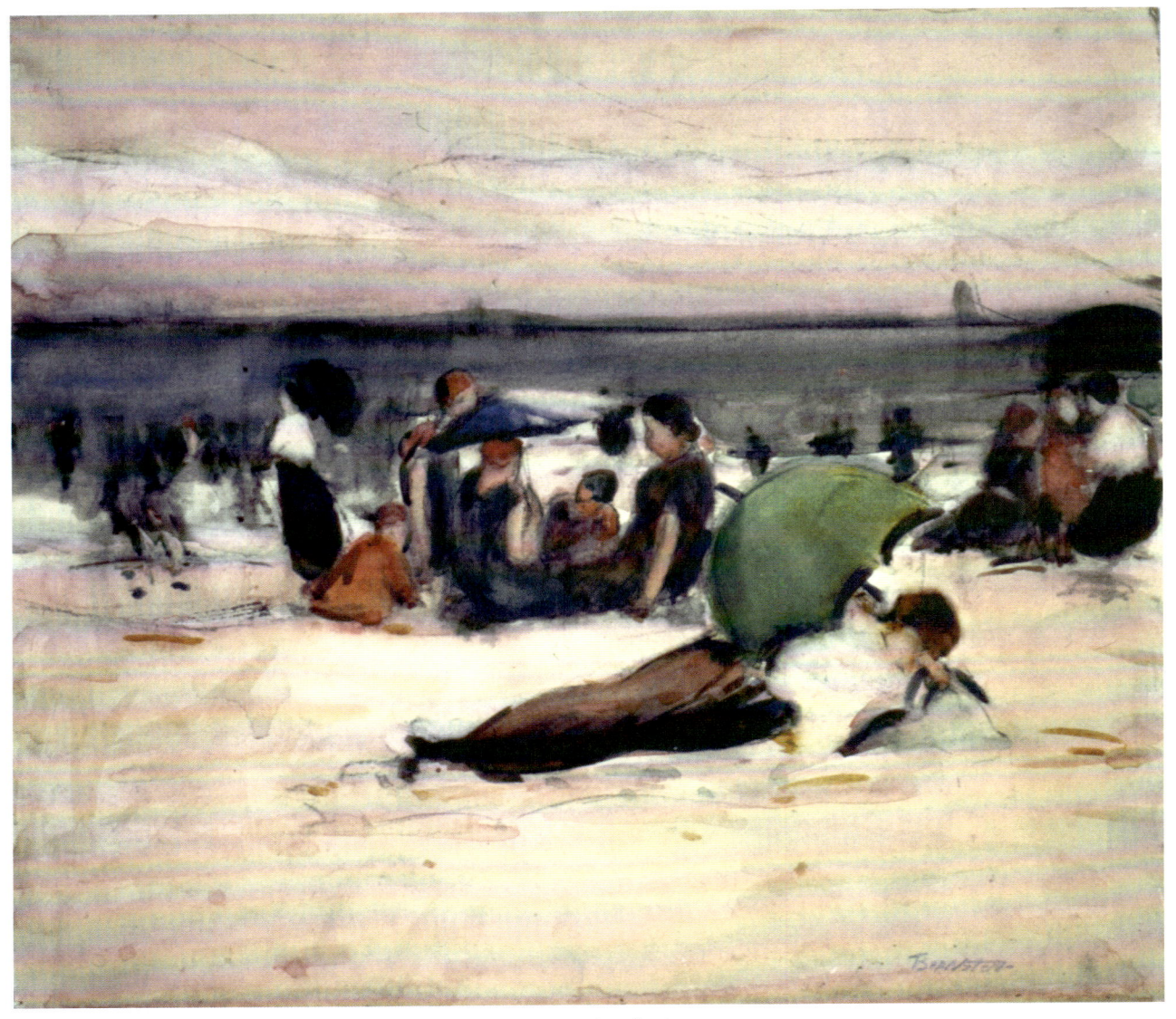

106. *On the Beach*, 1914. Watercolor on paper, 17½ x 19½ inches. Pamlyn Smith Collection.

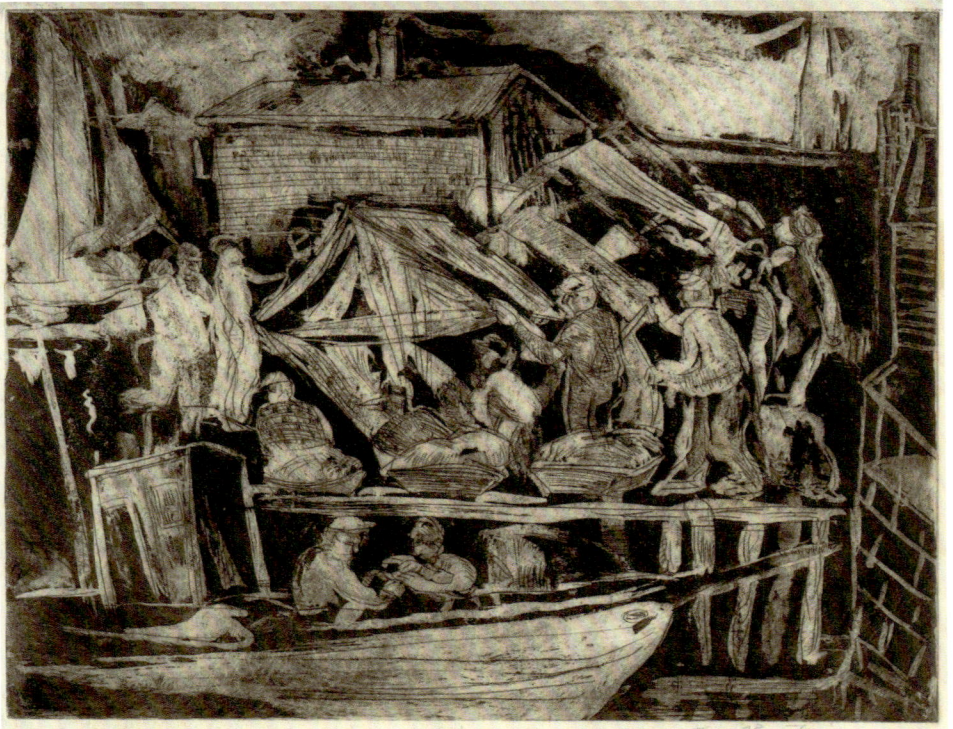

108. *The Net Menders*, ca. 1920. Etching, 7¾ x 9¾ inches. Theresa Bernstein and William Meyerowitz Foundation.

hill. Still others lovingly record their garden, complete with the bench where they often sketched side by side (see fig. 155), while numerous depictions of Good Harbor Beach (see figs. 92 and 179) and other Gloucester landmarks show the arc of Bernstein's style as it evolved over decades. Her Gloucester-inspired paintings constitute an important part of her oeuvre, where the brilliant sun, sparkling sand, rhapsodic sunsets, and lush foliage transform her dark urban palette into washes of color. The paintings also show the very human side of Gloucester and the very visible presence of women, always of interest to this intense observer of social interactions.

In Gloucester, Bernstein would be joining slightly older female colleagues Alice Schille, Jane Peterson, and Martha Walter, who, like Bernstein, were advocates of woman's suffrage and co-exhibitors at the 1915 exhibition held at the MacBeth Gallery. The show raised money for the New York State woman's suffrage campaign.[8] Gloucester and nearby Folly Cove were also the summer retreats for several established older women artists, whom Bernstein no doubt admired.

Cecilia Beaux, also originally from Philadelphia, was the leading female portraitist of her day. She was elected as a full academician of the National Academy of Design in 1902, one of the few women with that honor. Introduced to Gloucester by her friend, Harvard economist A. Piatt Andrew, by 1905 Beaux was a summer regular. She lived on the upscale Eastern Point, just beyond the artist colony on Rocky Neck, a neighbor of the eccentric interior

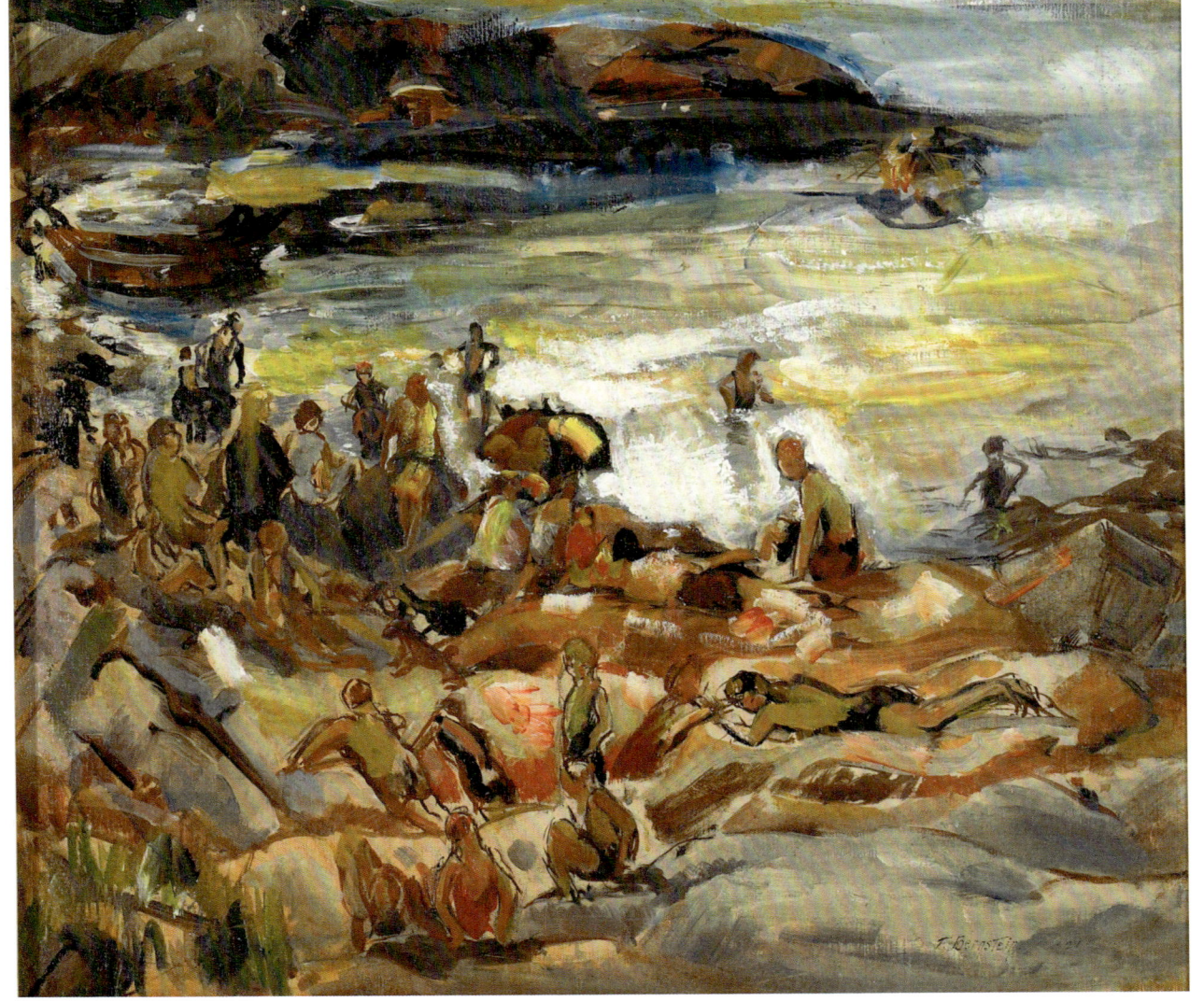

109. *Folly Cove*, 1921. Oil on canvas, 22 x 25 inches. Martin and Edith Stein Collection.

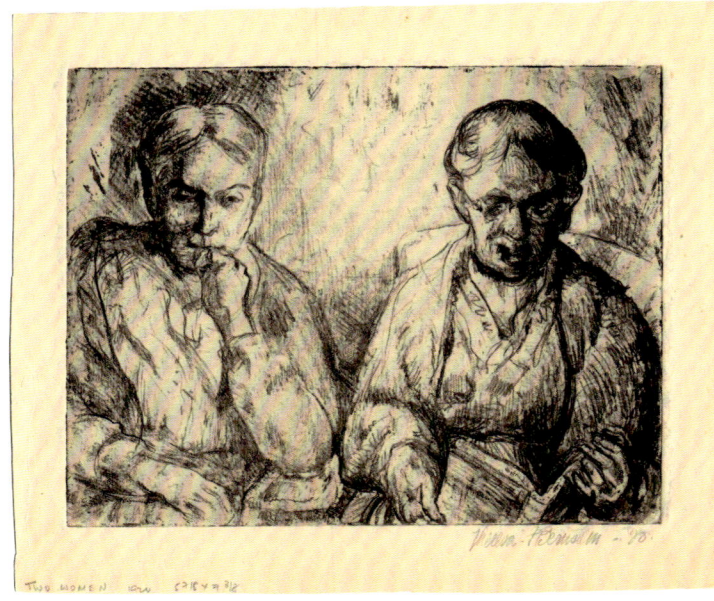

110. *Two Women* (Gabrielle de Veaux Clements and Ellen Day Hale), 1920. Etching, 8 x 9¾ inches. Theresa Bernstein and William Meyerowitz Foundation.

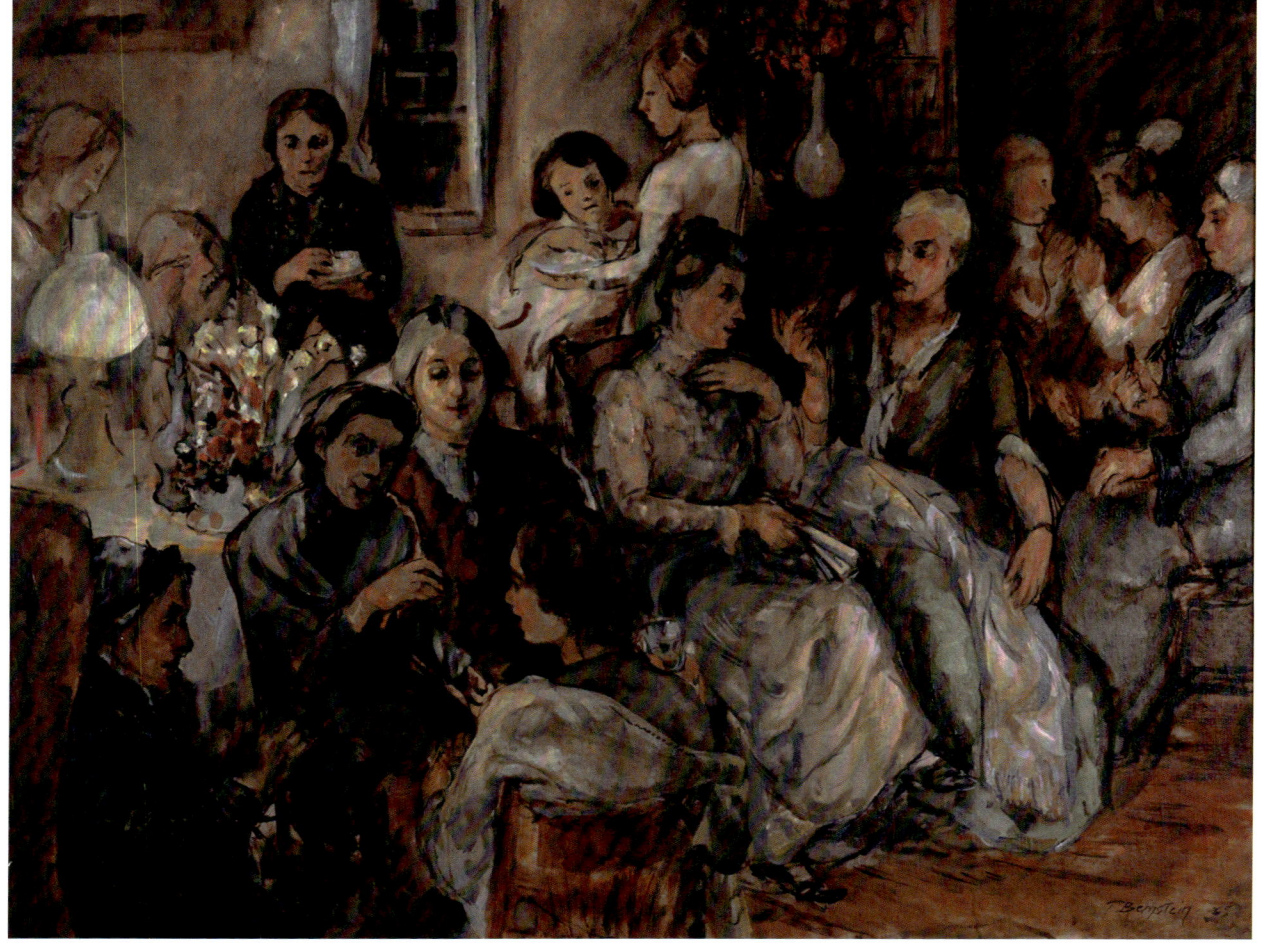

111. *New England Ladies*, 1925. Oil on canvas, 40 x 50 inches. Cape Ann Historical Museum, Gloucester, Massachusetts. Gift of James F. O'Gorman and Jean Baer O'Gorman, 1985.

designer Henry Sleeper. Part of Gloucester's elite social and artistic circles, there she entertained such luminaries as collector and art patron Isabella Stewart Gardner and William James, psychologist, philosopher and brother of writer Henry James.

Agnes Richmond, twenty years Bernstein's senior, was also a presence in Gloucester and a close friend of their mutual friends, the artist couple Charles and Alice Beach Winter, so presumably Richmond was part of Bernstein's and Meyerowitz's social circle as well.[9] Living a more secluded life were artists Ellen Day Hale and her companion Gabrielle de Veaux Clements, who beginning in 1893 were routine visitors to the Hale family vacation home, "The Thickets," in Folly Cove.[10] Hale and Clements would figure prominently in Bernstein's early years in Gloucester, following her marriage to William Meyerowitz in 1919. They appear, too, in Bernstein's portrayal of an elderberry wine party, ironically titled *New England Ladies*.[11]

By coming to Gloucester, Bernstein was following in the footsteps of generations of artists who, since the mid-nineteenth century, had been drawn to various parts of Cape Ann which were made increasingly accessible by public transportation. The railroad came in 1847, followed in the 1890s by the trolley that rolled down East Main Street, coupled with harbor ferries that shuttled vacationers to full-service resorts like the Hawthorne Inn on Wonson's Point. Many of the artists who preceded Bernstein were distinguished American painters noted for their landscapes and seascapes, beginning with native son and luminist Fitz Henry Lane, whose depictions of sea and sky celebrate nature's vastness. Second-generation Hudson River School painters constituted the next wave of artists, among them Sanford Gifford, Worthington Whittredge, Francis A. Silva, and William Trost Richards. Winslow Homer visited Cape Ann and Gloucester in the post–Civil War years, painting light-filled watercolors featuring children posed in reverie or lounging on sun-drenched rocks. From 1877–79 William Morris Hunt spent a brief but memorable two years in Gloucester, producing some of his most celebrated seascapes.[12]

By the 1890s American impressionists flocked to Cape Ann in larger numbers, seeking the atmospheric light and, for some, the artistic camaraderie they had experienced on European sojourns. Gloucester, though not centrally located, was at the crossroads of American art, drawing artists from Boston, New York, Philadelphia, Cincinnati, and even Europe. Frank Duveneck attracted a following of artists who had studied with him in the 1870s in Munich and Ohio, including Joseph DeCamp and John Henry Twachtman. The large artistic presence prompted Karl Baedeker to note in his 1893 guidebook that artists came because "of the picturesqueness of the town itself and . . . the fine scenery of Cape Ann."[13]

No doubt when Bernstein arrived in the summer of 1916, she was eager to join the illustrious list of American painters associated with Cape Ann. Despite her youth, she had already exhibited widely and had attracted numerous positive critical reviews, adding to her growing reputation. In 1916, in one of the earliest mentions of her in Gloucester, Bernstein ranked among the "well known artists who spent the summer here."[14] Photographs portraying Bernstein in her studio during this period depict an assured, self-possessed young woman (see fig. 105).

The previous year, Bernstein had drawn the attention of European collector and publisher John Lane, who purchased her work and wanted her to come to England so that he could promote her paintings. Bernstein declined, asserting her desire to be an American artist, committed to painting quintessentially American subjects. As a Gloucester artist, she would be perceived as an American painter, joining the ranks of notable American painters Fitz Henry Lane and Winslow Homer, whom she celebrated in her 1968 poem, "Gloucester Is the Place to Be":

Gloucester is the place to be

To recall art history.

Here the stalwarts lived and painted,

Lane and Homer

Both the loner.

Here is where Hassam stripped

And the ladies peeked and fainted. (1968)[15]

In another poem, playfully entitled "Artifacts," Bernstein references artists Frank Duveneck and his "buddy" Twachtman, Australian Hayley Lever, Charles Prendergast,

Edward Hopper, Louise Brumback, and John Sloan, many of whom were associates and friends of Bernstein's in both New York and Gloucester.[16]

Arriving in Gloucester as a single, independent, professional woman artist, Bernstein emblemized the New Woman, that novel breed of educated, unmarried, working female freed from the strictures of family life. Bernstein, as historian Laura Prieto has argued, both exemplified this new type of urban woman and simultaneously helped define her in the very images she painted: women in the employment office, women on the train, women on an outing, women attending concerts, women crusading for the vote, women working as teachers or milliners. In most of Bernstein's paintings, whether depicted at work or at leisure, women populate public spaces; they are engaged protagonists.[17] Bernstein's fierce individualism and commitment to an expressive form of painting reinforced this identity, which likely solidified after the loss of her only child in 1920. Because of this personal tragedy, Bernstein never had to balance the obligations of motherhood with those of a professional artist, and as a member of an artist couple, she and William jointly participated in exhibitions, teaching, and socializing with other artists.[18]

Coupled with Bernstein's character and biography, her painting style—combining observation of the real world with a more modernist, emotive sensibility—was well suited to the artistic climate of Gloucester. Bernstein straddled the line between more traditional figurative painters like John Sloan and modernists like Stuart Davis; she favored gestural lines, notational dabs, and startling color combinations, privileging an expressive interpretation over verisimilitude. Possibly attributable to its long landscape tradition, Gloucester was especially welcoming to figurative painters; however, no one style dominated, and artists did not have to choose between figuration and abstraction. Dorothy Grafly, reporter for the *Christian Science Monitor*, recognized the artistic freedom a summer colony offered, observing that "there could be no better atmosphere than that of a summer art colony, a tiny world in which hundreds of artists are themselves experimenting, working out ideas, discarding the impossible, realizing their limitations and their possibilities."[19] In this nonjudgmental artistic atmosphere, Bernstein could flourish as an independent woman artist without having to sacrifice her astute observational powers and abandon the subjects that formed the core of her creative output.[20] Bernstein came of age artistically at that moment of transition when the conventions of nineteenth-century American society and the elitism of traditional art institutions themselves paled in the face of Duchamp's readymades or Elsa von Freytag-Loringhoven's performance art.[21] Gloucester would prove fertile ground in many respects, providing rich subject matter, a relaxed social atmosphere, and an artistic community receptive to both figuration and abstraction where women were equal participants.

As Bernstein recollects, she arrived in Gloucester by train, having accompanied her father on a business trip to Boston. She headed for the Pilgrim House, a popular inn among artists, but with accommodations lacking, she soon found her way to an attic space offered by a fellow art student. One day when she was out painting, art collector and amateur painter William Atwood came by, as he was accustomed to visiting artist studios tucked away throughout town, and spotted a sketch casually wedging open her window. He purchased it, launching Bernstein's association with Gallery-on-the-Moors, which would open in September of 1916.[22]

Conceived and funded by William and Emmeline Atwood, Gallery-on-the-Moors provided a gathering space for painters, sculptors, musicians, writers, and actors.[23] It was a philanthropic gesture that evolved into a prototypical art center and a Gloucester institution. The gallery came about because of the Atwoods' interest in contemporary art and Gloucester's lack of an exhibition space to mount solo and group shows, but even from the beginning it was intended to be a cultural center that defied the notion of conventional galleries. The space included a stage for dramatic and musical performances and a writer's corner, featuring autographed books about Gloucester.[24] Occasionally, hotels like the Hawthorne Inn would sponsor exhibitions, such as the auction of Helen Knowlton's paintings

in 1909, organized by friends as a fundraiser when she was taken ill, or the 1909 group show organized by artists and the art writers Jean Nutting Oliver and Alexander G. Tupper. But there was no dedicated exhibition space with regular showings, and the Atwoods wanted to fill this void. Emmeline Atwood explained, "We felt in this active summer colony there might be many like ourselves who would welcome an opportunity to see what the artists were doing. Here was our chance—beautiful pictures, a leisure public anxious to see them. We would provide the place."[25] When it opened, and for several successive seasons, the Atwoods selected works; the diversity characterizing exhibitions reflected their catholic taste. Eventually, in response to criticism from disgruntled artists, in 1920 they appealed to exhibiting artists to nominate a jury from their midst to plan exhibitions, and then in 1922, the last year the gallery operated, the Atwoods picked a jury of artists to review submissions.

Designed by their friend, the famed architect Ralph Adams Cram, known for his Gothic revival buildings, the gallery was essentially one large room, though cast in the materials and style of a medieval structure. Constructed from simple stucco and hand-hewn timber, with English-style front porch and innovative skylights, it commanded the moors and provided dramatic views of Hesperus Point and the harbor. As Cram elucidated, "The idea aimed at was simplicity without severity and with enough picturesqueness of contour and composition to guarantee the character desired."[26]

The Atwoods had also commissioned Cram to design their summer home, entwined with boulders in the moors nearby. Situated near the artist enclave of Rocky Neck in East Gloucester, yet removed, visitors had to make a pilgrimage to see exhibitions and attend events: the gallery's seclusion and association with Gothic architecture elevated art to a more spiritual plane. Painter Jane Peterson compared the gallery to a beautiful flower "rising . . . from the wild brush and tangle, built on the weather-beaten old rocks and part and parcel of them, for they themselves were quarried to create it . . . this little gem of old Gothic . . . every timber hand hewn, every fixture hand wrought. . . . Reverently should we enter it as a shrine, a pioneer

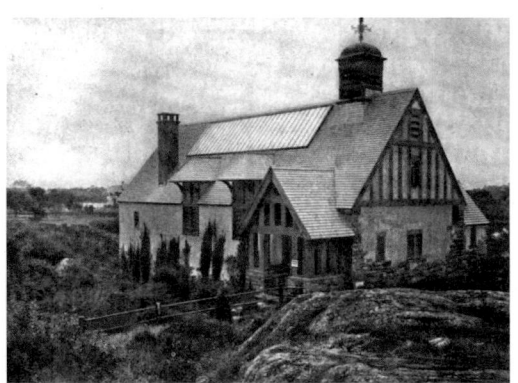
112. Gallery-on-the-Moors, Gloucester, Massachusetts.

gift to art in America."[27] According to Bernstein, Atwood solicited her advice in positioning the gallery's entrance, chosen to maximize views and golden sunset light.[28]

The gallery hosted exhibitions, concerts, plays, and pageants and attracted multitudes. Bernstein recalls that "all society came there to be seen and to look at the paintings, drawings, and etchings," as well as famous musicians, writers, and even playwright Lillian Hellman.[29] From its inception, women participated in all gallery activities, from its founding to having equal representation in shows. They assumed leadership positions as writers, directors, and performers in numerous musical and dramatic productions. The gallery provided a creative outlet for the New Woman, and allowed for the participation of nonprofessionals as well. Heightening its relevancy, the gallery also supported the war effort, mounting exhibitions of war posters, promoting the ambulance corps, and raising funds to aid wounded soldiers. Despite its relatively short life (1916–1922), Gallery-on-the-Moors made a significant impact on Gloucester's cultural life and led to the establishment of the North Shore Arts Association. With its commitment to all art forms, direct engagement of the community, social causes, and egalitarianism among the sexes, Gallery-on-the-Moors carved a new path for the arts in American society, prompting one writer to comment, "The erection of this gallery is tangible evidence of the increasing appreciation not only of art, but of its relation to life in this country."[30] The timing of its opening in 1916 could not have been more fortuitous for Bernstein. She participated in annual exhibitions for the gallery's duration, and because of her affiliation attained entrée to Gloucester's social elite soon after her arrival there, meeting Isabella Stewart Gardner and John Singer Sargent at its inaugural 1916 exhibition. Three years later, when she brought William to Gloucester after their marriage, she introduced him to fellow artists and patrons.[31]

Gallery-on-the-Moors' first exhibition opened on September 2, 1916, and included seventy-three paintings and twenty-two pieces of sculpture. Bernstein showed two works, *The Little Merry-Go-Round* (1913) and *On the Beach*.[32] They hung alongside work of celebrated American artists, including Frank Duveneck (who had the place of honor), Cecilia Beaux, Hayley Lever, Arthur Wesley Dow, Henry B. Snell and Louise Upton Brumback. The first show spanned generations of artists, including the young Stuart Davis, promoted men and women equally, and did not favor a particular style, setting the tone for future exhibitions. The following year conservative critic Frank W. Coburn praised the Atwoods as "devotees of a sort of philosophical anarchism in art."[33]

In the gallery's first season, works by Guy Wiggins, Hayley Lever, Henry Snell, Arthur Dow, Mary Weiss, and Louise Brumback sold.[34] Some critics singled out work by women, as in this review by John Nutting: "Several women painters are to be noted for strong and independent work. Alice Schille for fresh and full colored water colors—'The Old House,' and others; Jane Peterson for decorative studies in water color of Gloucester's varied boats—'Portuguese Fishing Boats,' etc.; Mrs. Brumback capitally expresses the holiday spirit in her 'Gloucester Day'; Miss Richmond shows a fine study of a young woman in bright pink garment, 'Anne,' Theresa Bernstein's polly 'Merry Go-Round' is good, and so are Aline Bernstein's 'Docks and Town' and Ethel Paddock's 'Newburyport.'"[35] The exhibition also included work of five sculptors, three women and two men: Charles Grafly, Albert H. Atkins, Anna Coleman Ladd, Louise Allen Hobbs, and Anna Vaughn Hyatt. Bernstein's *The Little Merry-Go-Round* elicited positive comments by several reviewers, one writer observed how the painting reflects her "racy, modern temper" (see fig. 40).[36] The mosaic of color and subject choice suggest a debt to Maurice Prendergast, whose work Bernstein had seen in New York and who was also a presence in Gloucester.

Over the course of seven summers, Bernstein exhibited a total of eleven paintings and several etchings. Most of the works she contributed portrayed Gloucester scenes, but sometimes Bernstein included works painted elsewhere, like *The Little Merry-Go-Round* (1913) painted three years earlier. Several canvases also appeared in New York exhibitions as part of group exhibitions of The Eclectics or at the National Academy of Design. They encompass a range of subjects, revealing

Bernstein's artistic breadth and enthusiastic embrace of Gloucester—its harbor, tourists, surrounding landscape, and beaches. She received consistently positive reviews.

In the 1919 *International Studio* article featuring Bernstein, author W. H. de B. Nelson, also a painter, astutely commented on the impact Gloucester was having on her work. He wrote, "Gloucester . . . has been seen in a big and spirited way—contours of hill and harbor, dramatic lighting of sky and water, always the dark mass in contrast with a strongly lighted area. Picturesque bits such as rotting piers, quaint wharves, fishing boats and the like, make vain appeal. . . . The result may lack subtlety and beauty of surface but there are certain elements that it will never be deficient in: virile conception, solidity, strong contrasts and fundamental truths banishing anything superficial or trivial."[37] Bernstein never chose subjects because they were fashionable, and one of the great appeals of her paintings today is their originality. They depict scenes and events that might otherwise escape our attention and record aspects of women's lives that would ordinarily be unseen. Bernstein concentrated on her emotional reaction to the scene before her, preferring to make numerous sketches before painting a final composition. In a 1923 interview with Dorothy Grafly, she explained, "When I really feel that I can paint, I go out and do it. If I like what I find, I go back and paint it again and again. Then, when I feel that I have gained sufficient knowledge of my subject, I really paint it."[38] Given her preference for the familiar, Bernstein never tired of Gloucester, a safe haven and a continual source of inspiration. Her depictions of Gloucester were not the conventional seascapes favored by a majority of artists.

In 1917 in the Gallery-on-the-Moors second exhibition, Bernstein showed three paintings: *Sun, Sand, and Sea* (location unknown; reproduced in *International Studio* 1919 feature article) *The Garden Party*, strongly reminiscent of Prendergast, and *Golf, Eastern Point* (location unknown).[39]

This exhibition also included work by Childe Hassam, Stuart Davis, and John Singer Sargent, but Coburn noted that "the eye keeps traveling all the while . . . to Theresa Bernstein's

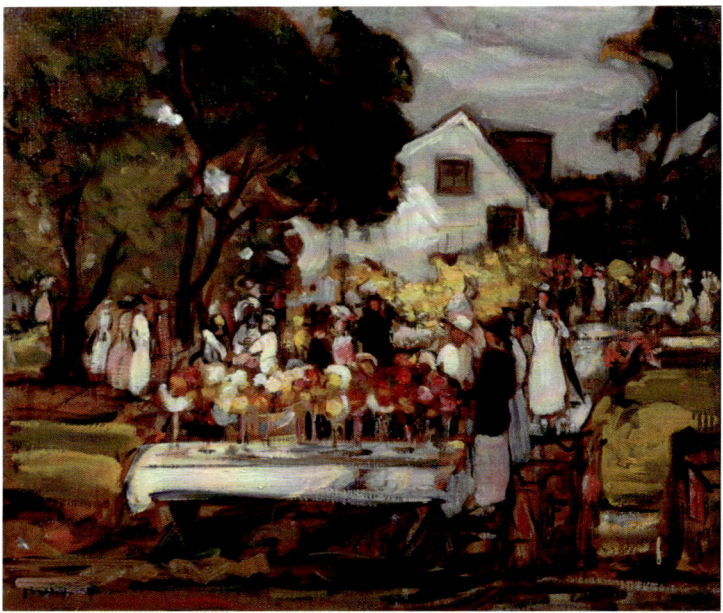

113. *The Garden Party*, ca. 1913. Oil on canvas, 22 x 25 inches. Private collection.

Golf, Eastern Point." It's interesting that Coburn, a Boston critic with a conservative bent, tended to be suspicious of abstract works, but Bernstein's work appealed because it combined an adventurous palette and expressive brushwork with recognizable imagery. The subject, too, reflected the leisure activities enjoyed by mixed company and suggested a more liberated lifestyle. Giving more space to this description than to any other painting in the exhibition, Coburn continued: "Here is the very acme of the doctrine of painting things as one would like to see them. . . . Under no such glassy skies anywhere does green grass grow to every known color but green. Anathema to the observers who expect a picture to be first and foremostly illusory, this work has, nevertheless, that degree of tasteful selection, of stressing of nice combinations of color, that makes it precious in the sight of the more discriminating spectator."[40]

Sun, Sand, and Sea, ca. 1917, is a noteworthy early canvas that captures the mood and motion of bathers with their umbrellas and picnics enjoying the warmth, salt air, and wind of Gloucester's beaches. Recognizing that it was an important painting, Bernstein also exhibited it at the Eclectics show at Boston's Vose Gallery, and it was reproduced in Nelson's 1919 *International Studio* article. A critic for the *Boston Daily Advertiser* commented, "Miss Theresa Bernstein's *Sun, Sand and Sea* and the *Garden Party* are effective works in a low key with rich and handsome color effect. . . . the second work presents in tapestry-like tonality and facture a mass of small figures crowded together in a harmonious jumble of color. Not unlike a large kaleidoscope in low-toned color."[41] In 1918 Bernstein showed another golf subject, *Golf Tournament*, and *Landscape with Figures*,[42] which depicts a group of women in profile promenading around a lake in the foreground, against a background of houses, with red accents and an orange or salmon sky—part landscape, part genre painting.

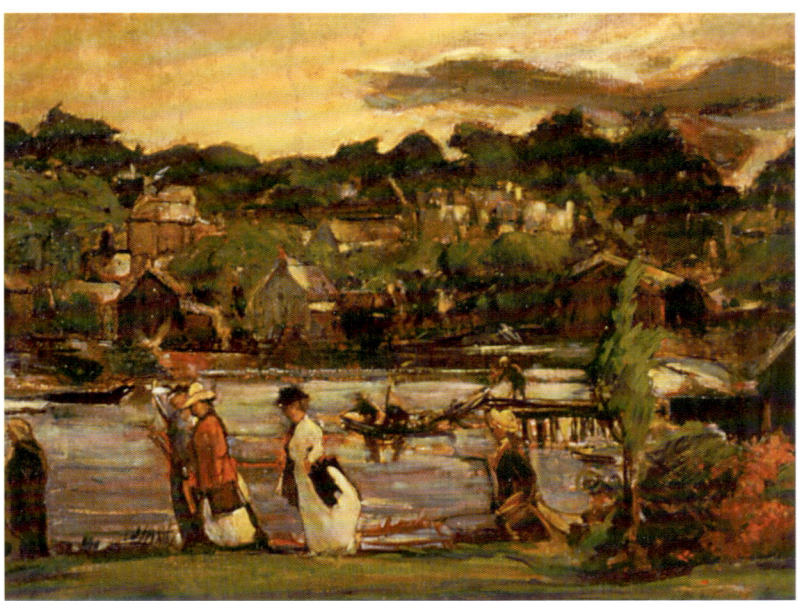

114. *Landscape with Figures*, 1917. Oil on canvas, 27 x 35 inches. Private collection.

Bernstein rarely painted landscapes or seascapes devoid of people.[43] Jean Nutting Oliver praised the painting for its "ripe color harmony and beautiful tonality."[44] Earlier that year, Bernstein had exhibited *Landscape with Figures* at the Ninety-Third Annual Exhibition of the National Academy of Design. Her *Golf Tournament* again drew praise from Coburn, who lauded her "highly personal, expressive and emotional modes of painting," comparing her individuality with El Greco's and noting her "somber tonalities, ecstasies of gloom."[45] Another writer praised Bernstein's simplicity . . . concise brevity . . . and interpretative liberality."[46]

In 1919, during the summer after their wedding, both Bernstein and Meyerowitz exhibited at Gallery-on-the-Moors, he with two etchings, *Houses on the Hill* and *Trees*, and she with one canvas, *Greek Pageant* (also called *Grecian Pageant*) of 1919. Hers was an operatic achievement of landscape elements and complex figure groups depicting an event from the previous summer. This extravagant fund-raiser combined pageantry, politics, and the participation of hundreds; it united artists with nonartists in a display of joie de vivre that challenged social decorum. Women contributed to all aspects of the planning and execution. Proceeds went to aid the French wounded and refugees, the war unit of the Gallery-on-the-Moors, and the American fund for the French wounded. The Community Theatre Association sponsored the pageant.[48] The cast included artists, townspeople, and even Gloucester's society women. Motivated by patriotism and philanthropy, the ladies of Gloucester eagerly traded in their corsets and footwear to dance barefoot on the moors in diaphanous Greek garb à la Isadora Duncan: they were pipers, cymbal players, villagers, standard-bearers, and fruit and flower maidens. The pageant was such a novelty that numerous newspapers featured it with illustrated articles. Bernstein both participated in the planning of the pageant and memorialized it in a painting of that name.

Billed as the largest community "get-to-gether" ever held in Gloucester, it was made possible by the community theater established in 1918 in association with Gallery-on-the-Moors. It involved two hundred men, women, and children and a committee of artists, musicians, dancers, set designers, and even classics scholars, who ensured the authenticity of the open air market preceding the pageant. Conceived as an outdoor performance, it maximized the use of a natural amphitheater ringed by the moors. Boston artist Lucy Conant devised the narrative, built around a harvest thanksgiving combined with preparations for battle. Aided by almost the entire summer art colony, Conant also designed and dyed the costumes. The Greek maidens wore beautiful shades of blue, rose, and yellow, and the warrior maidens wore veils of pale amber and yellow, deepened by the golden light of the setting sun. Jane Peterson and E.

Parker Nordell designed and painted baskets used to bear harvest fruits and the sculptural processional standards.

Several experts provided guidance: the esteemed creative team even included actor and director Margaret Anglin and architect Ralph Adams Cram. Painter Louis Kronberg chaired the executive committee.[49] The caption of one full-spread newspaper summed it up: "North Shore society girls and the art colony have combined to make the Greek Festival at Gloucester in aid of war sufferers the last word in affairs of its kind. Miss Lilias MacLane and Miss Theodora Huntington are shown posing in a Grecian ball movement, which is one of the big features of the festival."[50]

In her journal, Bernstein recalls that she contributed to the set design: "On a hillside adjoining the gallery we produced

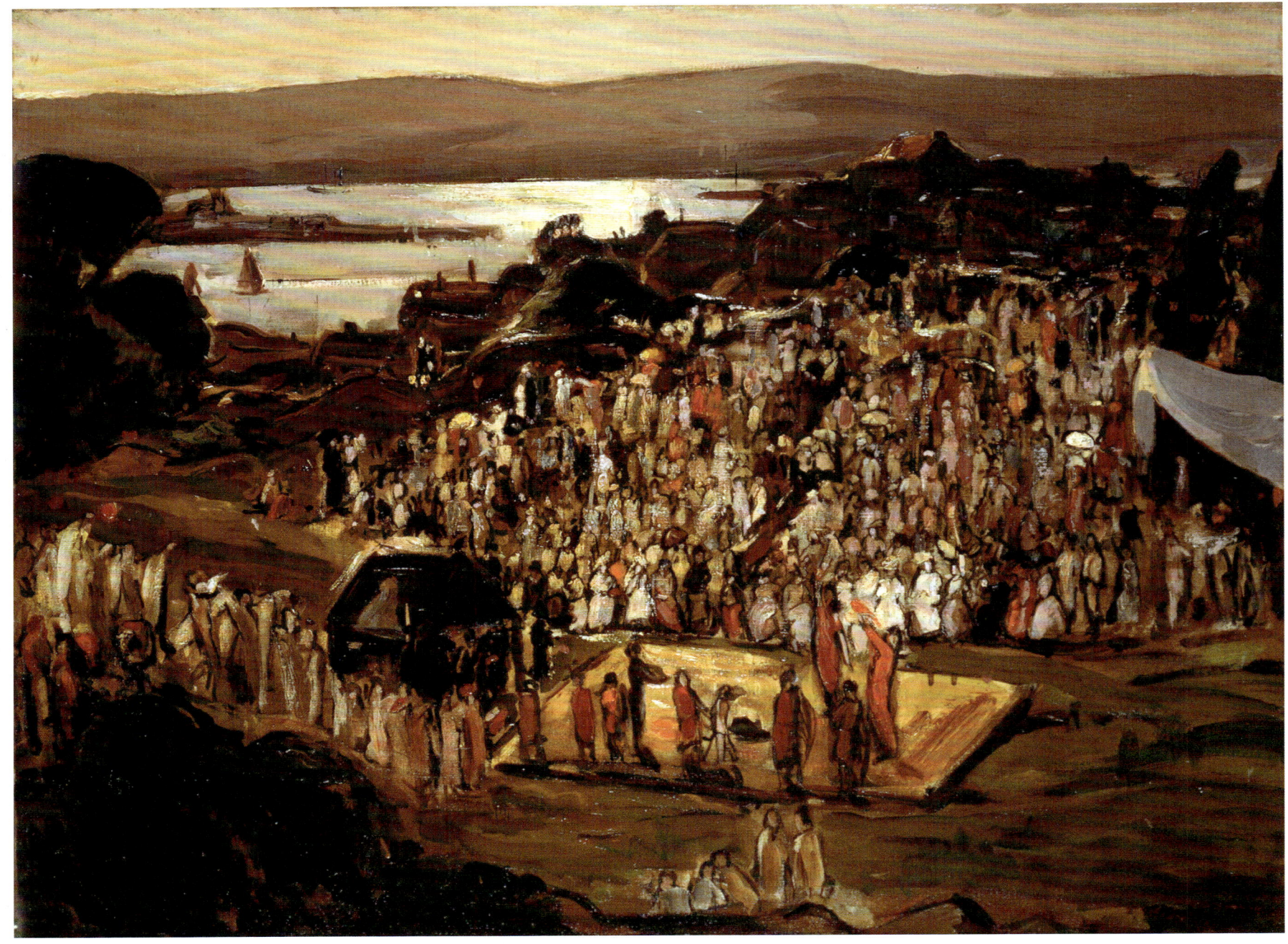

115. *Grecian Pageant*, 1918. Oil on canvas, 29 x 39 inches, National Museum of Women in the Arts, Washington, D.C. Gift of Girard Jackson.

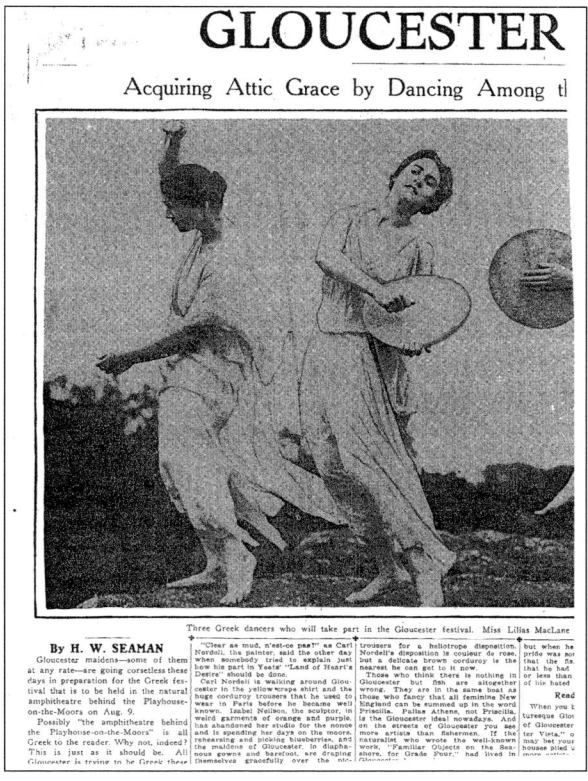

116. Newspaper clipping about Greek Festival in Gloucester, 1918.

a Grecian pageant. I helped make designs out of cheesecloth and sateen, which gave a nice contrast of textures. On the outdoor stage, Mr. Brewster, the young producer [not mentioned in other accounts of the event], directed a set of performances to benefit the wounded soldiers of World War I." Bernstein continues, "The audience sat on folding chairs on the flat ground between the hills. It made a gorgeous spectacle in the bright afternoon sunlight, and I made a number of sketches and a large painting to commemorate it."[51]

Bernstein's oil sketch (*Grecian Pageant*, for the benefit of wounded soldiers, 1918) and the completed painting, provide a bird's-eye perspective on the festivities, capturing the effect of the stage, a processional of dancers, and onlookers tiered on the slope. Bright red accents draw the eye to various parts of the composition. Rather than focus on individual performers or members of the audience, Bernstein sought to capture the mood of this elaborate outdoor spectacle that joined the Gloucester landscape with Gloucester's artists and residents—all for a patriotic cause. Critics commended the completed oil painting,

noting "its lurid sky and rows of dot and dashy little figures floated upon an underlying lake of black pigment. It is one of her most effective."[52] Jean Nutting Oliver called it "An important work, 'big' in feeling."[53]

In the Gallery-on-the-Moors' final three exhibitions, an artist-nominated jury of peers selected work for the 1920 and 1921 seasons, and in the final year a jury nominated by the Atwoods vetted submissions. Bernstein and Meyerowitz exhibited in all three years and received consistently favorable reviews. In 1920 the painting *The Harbor* (also referred to as *Twilight Study*) "by Theresa F. Bernstein," was described as "rich in color and contrasts" by one reviewer and compared to a "painting on glass" by another.[54] The writer for the *Boston Evening Transcript* called *Twilight Study* "gem-like," the harbor glowing "with mellow color, suggesting brown garnets and oldest amber"[55] and called Meyerowitz's *Lilac and Iris* "decidedly original in pattern . . . the motif being a jar of spring flowers as seen in a square window frame, with the town of Gloucester and the harbor beyond." Bernstein would often use a similar composition, combining a still life with a view through the window.

In 1921 Bernstein exhibited *At the Concert* and Meyerowitz showed Still Life and etchings.[56] In 1922, the final exhibition, Bernstein showed *Stormy Sea, Folly Cove* and Meyerowitz showed *The Samovar*, and again, etchings by both artists. Over the course of those two summers, Bernstein and Meyerowitz continued experimenting with etching, using the press in Ellen Day Hale and Gabrielle de Veaux Clements's studio. They made the trip so often that Hale and Clements offered the couple use of their nearby cottage, Gaviotta ("seagull" in Portuguese and the subject of another of her paintings). Bernstein fondly remembered the time she and Meyerowitz shared there.[57]

In 1923 the couple returned to Gloucester after a trip to Europe, but not to Folly Cove. They stayed in a small apartment on the corner of Rocky Neck and Eastern Point Road, which they shared with the artists Peter and Anna Neagoe. Stuart Davis was downstairs with his family.[58] They often climbed the hill of near-by Mount Pleasant Avenue, then just a cow lane. "We relished visiting the friendly hills of East Gloucester. We gazed on the shelf of wharves and the incoming schooners with the furled sails. Soon they would be drying their nets[,] the crews mending them, sitting on the tar stained wharves."[59] The following year they were able to purchase their home, the only home they ever owned, on Mount Pleasant Avenue.[60]

By the time Theresa and William settled on Mount Pleasant Avenue in 1924, they were firmly ensconced in a close-knit artistic circle of a younger generation of artists. Among their closest friends and neighbors were modernist Stuart Davis and the realist painters Charles and Alice Beach Winter, all committed socialists and political activists. It was the Winters, in fact, who had convinced John Sloan to come to Gloucester in 1914. Bernstein and Meyerowitz also counted among their friends Joel and Sarah Glass, Helen Stein, to whom Bernstein taught art, James Britton, Aldro Hibbard, W. Lester Stevens, Robert Henri, Leon Kroll, Jane Peterson, and William Glackens.

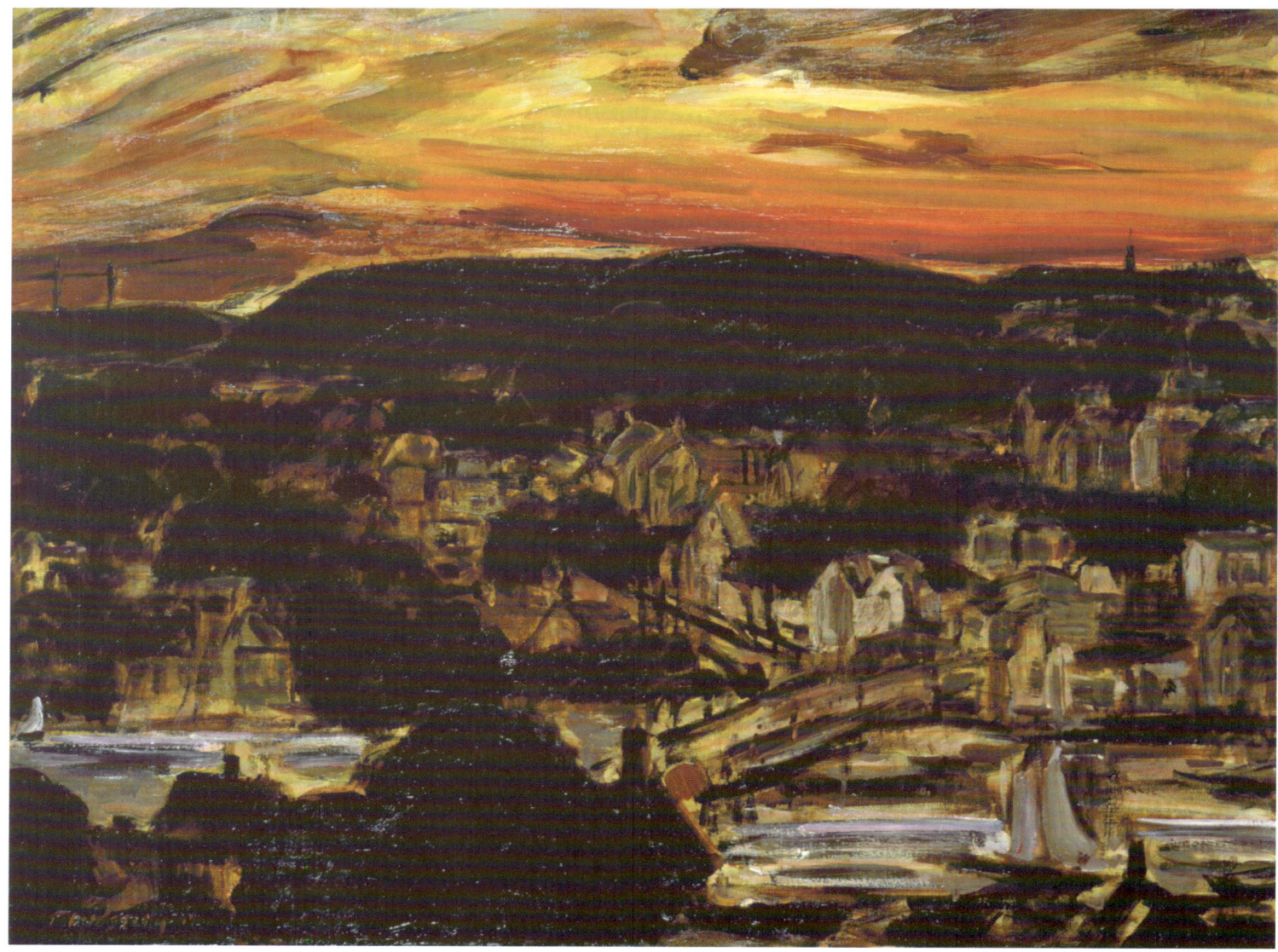

117. *Afterglow–Annisquam*, 1917. Oil on canvas, 27 x 35 inches. Martin and Edith Stein Collection.

Meyerowitz, who met Bernstein through his activities for the People's Art Guild, and the independent Bernstein, a suffragist and avid chronicler of everyday life, fit right in. As a group, they rejected Victorian domestic conventions, juried shows and prizes, and supported leftist political and social causes. Given these views, it is not surprising that in 1925, the year after Bernstein and Meyerowitz moved to 44 Mount Pleasant Avenue, they joined up with Davis, who was a regular summer visitor, to launch the satirical journal, *The Paint Rag* (see fig. 138),[61] prompted partly by the artistic debates ignited by the demise of Gallery-on-the-Moors and the creation of several alternative artist organizations.

The Paint Rag clearly positioned Meyerowitz, Bernstein, and Davis, despite their own stylistic differences, on the side of experimental art versus the conservatism of the academies. While Bernstein came to Gloucester in 1916 already having found her stride, Davis, only two years younger, was still experimenting with color, "problems of composition, paint application, and repeating motifs."[62] Several Gloucester artists in Bernstein's circle were experimenting with the color theories expounded in the Maratta system, but Bernstein distanced herself from any sort of prescribed painting technique. She explained, "I can't work on color theories as do so many of Gloucester's summer colony. Such theories seem cramping."[63]

Davis's paintings from these years bear some resemblance to the subjects and style employed by Bernstein. Compare, for example, his *Gloucester Landscape (Backyard View)* with Bernstein's *Crow Village*, ca. 1920. In both paintings the small clapboard homes and outbuildings of the artists' colony rise up in a tilted plane, with a hint of water along the horizon.

Davis, even more than Bernstein, de-emphasizes illusionistic space. By 1925 Davis had developed his signature style, exploring cerebral spatial concepts in combination with text and graphic imagery found in advertising. Bernstein, so connected to people, was becoming less of a naturalistic painter, but she never embraced the flat colors and pronounced graphic quality of Davis's work. It is tempting, though, to see how especially during the mid-1920s, Davis might have influenced

her in paintings like *Rogers Street*, ca. 1923, where Bernstein was edging toward a looser, linear style, with thinner paint application, a tilted picture plane, and figurative vignettes comprised of dabs of color or black outlines. (Drawn to its harbor views, Bernstein also painted *Rogers Street, 1920s* in a tighter, more controlled style.)

Bernstein and Davis also shared a sense of humor and enjoyed satirizing the social pretentions of all classes, a consistent theme in Bernstein's oeuvre and evident even in Davis's youthful drawings published in the socialist magazine *New Masses*.[64] Wit would continue to be a Davis trademark. Despite their very different approaches to subject matter and painting itself, both Bernstein and Davis embraced Sloan's and Henri's commitment to portraying contemporary life. Both artists viewed themselves as modernists and as youthful challengers to the conservatism of critics like Frank Coburn or art institutions like the National Academy of Design, despite the fact Bernstein still sought validation from the academy and comparable venues and regularly submitted works to these juried shows. Bernstein, however, experienced rejection more often because of her gender than her style. Davis, who in the 1910s and early 1920s turned away from objective naturalism to distill compositions to a balance of lines and flat color planes, sought alternative exhibition venues where his work would be more properly understood. For example, in 1922 Davis joined the Modern Artists of America and exhibited with them at the Joseph Brummer Galleries in New York City, the same year he worked with Bernstein and others to launch the democratic Gloucester Society of Artists. The alliance between Bernstein and Davis reinforces art historian Patricia Hill's observation that artists did not necessarily classify themselves as abstractionists or realists and joined together in a variety of organizations and exhibition venues. Bernstein always rejected the concept of a totally abstract art, and Davis disavowed the use of the term "abstract" in connection to his painting.[65] Bernstein and Davis enjoyed irony and satire and were intolerant of pretentious behavior; they disdained the elitism of juries and conservative

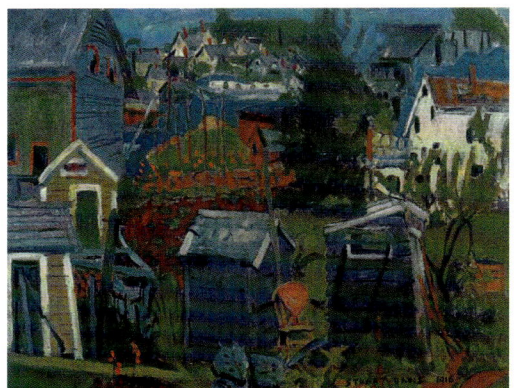

118. Stuart Davis, *Gloucester Landscape (Backyard View)*, 1916. Oil on canvas, 23⅞ x 29⅛ inches. Private collection.

art institutions. For subjects, they both looked to contemporary life, an extension of their mutual admiration for Robert Henri and John Sloan. Both were aware of various Europeanisms, from impressionism to expressionism to cubism, yet each artist consciously asserted an American identity. As Hills elucidates, writing about a 1922 show of the Modern Artists of America exhibiting at the Joseph Brummer Galleries, "A general spirit of 'experimentation,' rather than any one specific 'ism,' best characterized the program of these modern artists."[66]

When it was founded in 1916, Gallery-on-the-Moors provided an essential exhibition space for a variety of artists, but by 1922 it was inadequate for the growing Gloucester art colony. By 1926 Gloucester had close to one thousand artists living and working there.[67] To meet the demand, a group of artists and patrons banded together and purchased an old fish house on the water's edge. On December 2, 1922, they incorporated as the North Shore Arts Association (originally named the Gloucester Art Association).[68] They welcomed emerging and professional artists, residents and patrons, seeking to build a constituency to support visual art on the North Shore.[69] There was also the same spirit of egalitarianism that informed Gallery-on-the-Moors, and an equal number of men and women

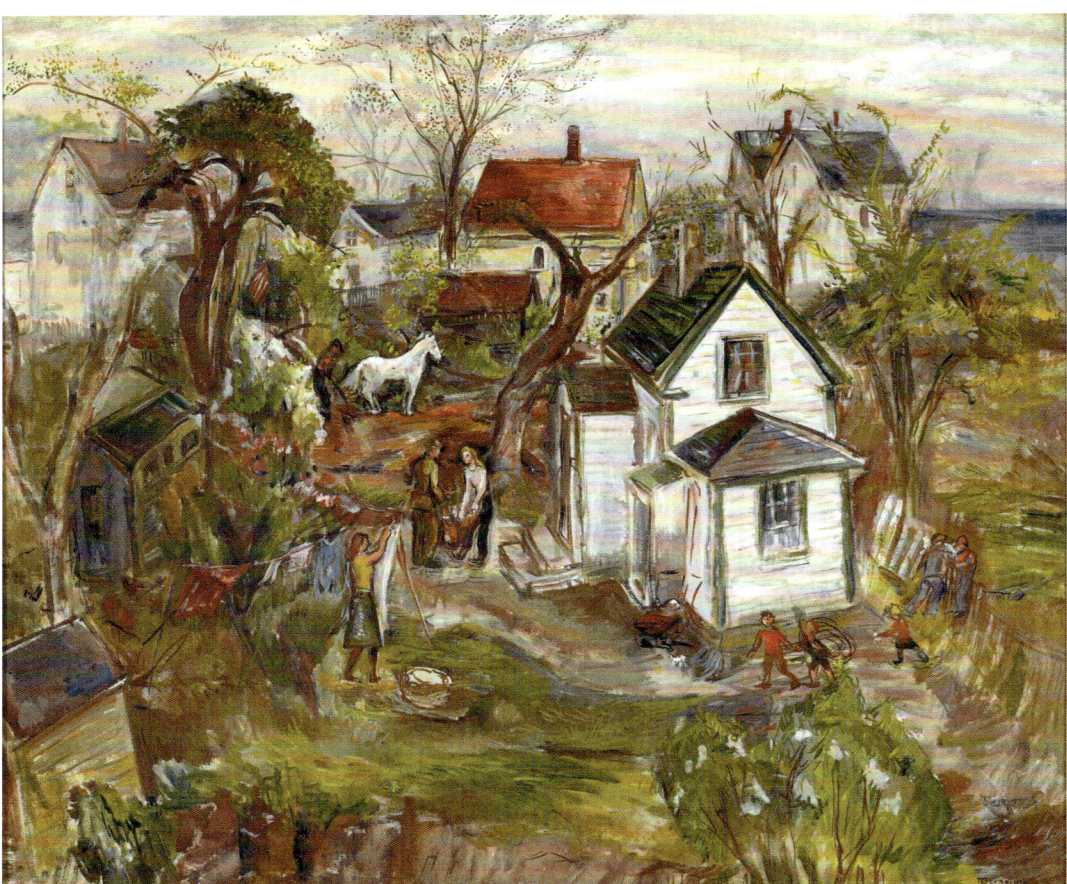

119. *Crow Village*, 1920. Oil on canvas, 29½ x 35½ inches. Martin and Edith Stein Collection.

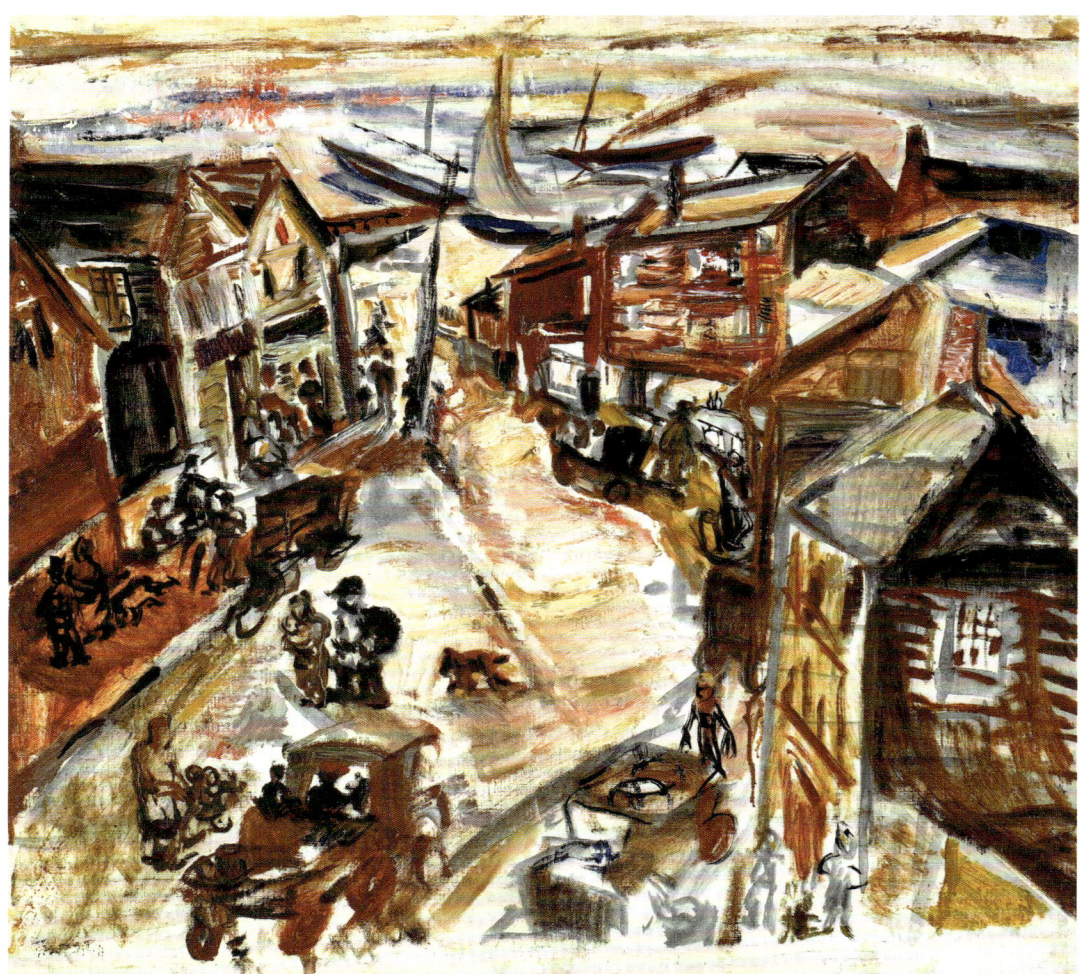

120. *Rogers Street*, ca. 1923. Oil on canvas, 22 x 24 inches. Martin and Edith Stein Collection.

constituted the first board of trustees. In an effort to be viewed as a professional association, the North Shore Art Association adopted a modified jury system, distinguishing between two classes of artists, the artist and associate artist, "embracing both student and professional." Further, to support emerging artists, they permitted them to exhibit one picture in each exhibition exempt from jury review. This was in direct response to the final three seasons of Gallery-on-the-Moors, where juries restricted which painters could be included. Both Bernstein and Meyerowitz exhibited in the inaugural show of the North Shore Arts Association; Bernstein showed *Gloucester* and Meyerowitz showed *Still Life*.[70]

The first North Shore Art Association exhibition opened July 14, 1923, and included many of the same artists who had shown at Gallery-on-the-Moors, including Bernstein

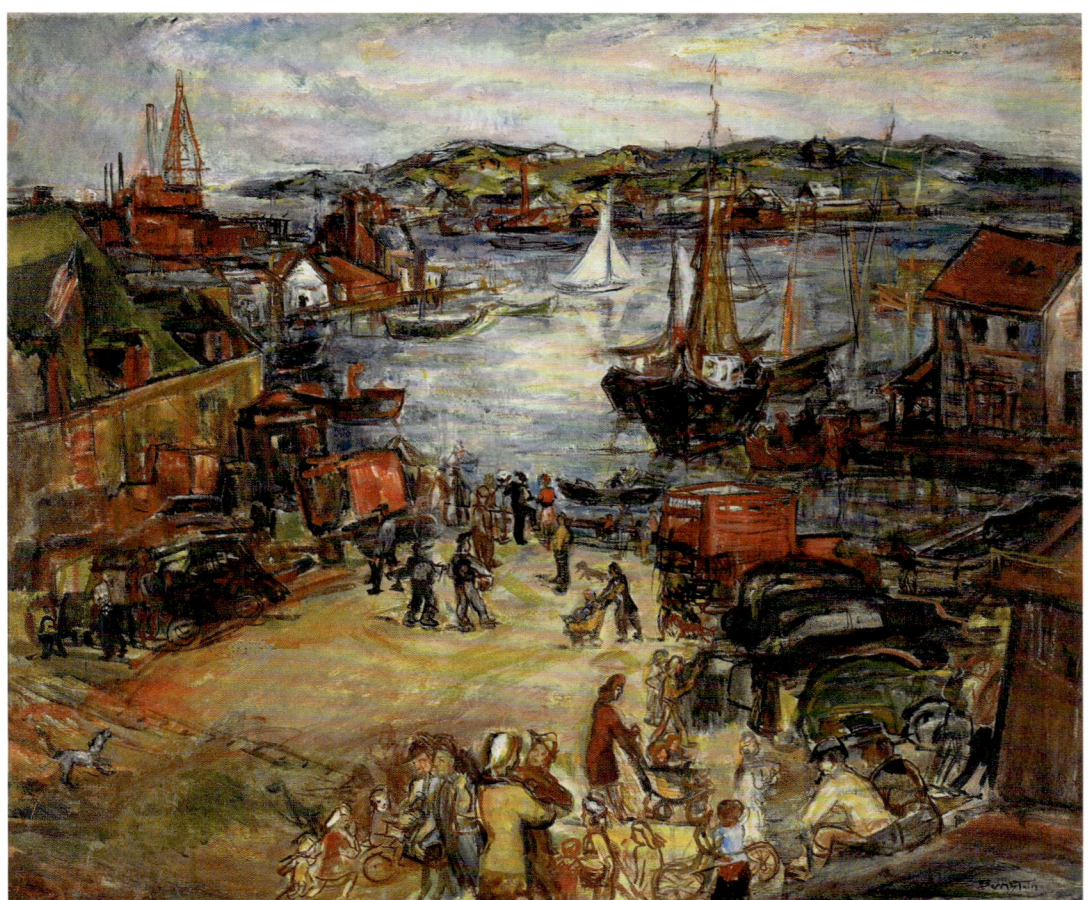

121. *Rogers Street*, 1920s. Oil on canvas, 30 x 36 inches. Martin and Edith Stein Collection.

and Meyerowitz as well as Louis Kronberg, William Atwood, Ellen Day Hale, Aldro Hibbard, Paul Cornoyer, Lester Stevens, Jean Nutting Oliver, George L. Noyes, Frederick Mulhaupt, John Coggeshall, and Hobart Nichols, among others. Simultaneously, led by the iconoclastic Stuart Davis, another artist organization emerged, the Gloucester Society of Artists, with the creed "Open to All and an Equal Chance for All." They disavowed juries completely and elected a female artist, Louise Upton Brumback, as their first president. Bernstein and Meyerowitz were not ideologues, and they did not hesitate to exhibit with this group as well. The inaugural show included a total of 125 paintings, sculptures, and graphics and featured stylistically diverse work, ranging from the abstractions of Milton Avery (Stuart Davis was in New Mexico and did not submit work) to the figurative sculptures of Leonard Craske, known for Gloucester's *Fisherman's Memorial*. In fact, Davis, Bernstein, and Meyerowitz created *The Paint Rag* as a fundraiser for this effort. Bernstein remained an active member of the group for its duration. In 1944 she won the Anne Baker Lewis prize for her *Gloucester Wharves*, praised for catching the "spirit of a fishing town, presenting a welter of types," articulated with a draftsmanship that has a "tang to it."[71] The group disbanded in 1948, when it merged with the Rockport group to become the Cape Ann Society of Modern Artists.[72] Not only did these artist groups further the careers of their members, but they were important social networks and annually sponsored costume balls and carnivals, in which Bernstein and Meyerowitz eagerly participated. Much later in her career, in 1960, Bernstein joined the Rockport Art Association.

Many of Bernstein's Gloucester canvases document places that no longer exist, such as the Hawthorne Inn, which burned down in 1938. The Hawthorne Inn was East Gloucester's only large hotel complex and resort, opened on Wonson's Point in 1891 by hotelier George O. Stacy. It eventually grew to accommodate up to five hundred guests in twenty-four cottages.[73] It catered to women as well as men, offering a separate men's smoking room and women's tea parlor. The new casino, completed in 1912, hosted Sunday morning services, fetes, dances, and galas of all types—just the sort of events Bernstein loved to record.

About *The Hawthorne Casino*, Bernstein recollected that it depicted a dance event on the Fourth of July, when figures swayed to music by Oscar Straus and Victor Herbert. The casino was near Niles Beach, and Bernstein remembers hearing the ocean surf in the background. The casino also hosted events sponsored by the Gloucester Society of Artists.[74] Bernstein was a regular visitor, dining there as a guest of the owner. Eighty years later she recollected details as if events had taken place the previous day:

> The Hawthorne Inn was in its heyday, and
> all society, or those who thought they were
> society, went there with their families for the
> summer. In the evenings there was always
> entertainment—jugglers, dancers, and singers.

In the lobby, the ladies sat. We called them "The Ladies of the Lobby." They had a view of who was coming in and who was going out and who was going out with whom; what romance was flourishing and what marriage was breaking up. Like a jury in a box, with their lap dogs and their knitting, the women sat knitting and needling. Outside, there was a long porch where everybody would sit and watch the tennis players. At the end of the porch was a marvelous view and the far horizon of Eastern Point with Cecelia Beaux' studio and Colonel Andrew's estate.[75]

Bernstein also recollects participating in pageants and charades there, "colorful affairs to benefit World War I veterans. We shoved around big boxes with people arranged on them forming silent poses (tableaux) as a poem was recited by the narrator. They drew inspiration from the *Arabian Nights* or the *Rubaiyat of Omar Khayyam* or the *Rites of Spring*.[76] These entertainments gave Bernstein an opportunity to indulge her dramatic flair.

Throughout the years Bernstein and Meyerowitz summered in Gloucester, they ran an art school. They started teaching as a newly married couple, first focusing on etching and then branching out into drawing and painting. Often they would paint and etch the same subjects, as evidenced in Bernstein's painting and Meyerowitz's etching, both entitled *The Country Fair*. Typical of their stylistic differences, Bernstein's painting capitalizes on the interaction and gestures of figures in the crowd and the movement of the windblown banners strung above the gathering, while Meyerowitz focused more on the spatial relations of the scene's components. Both, however, preferred the spontaneity of working directly from their subject, and Meyerowitz even created etchings on the spot rather than carefully incising plates in the studio.[77]

Photographs document Bernstein and Meyerowitz with

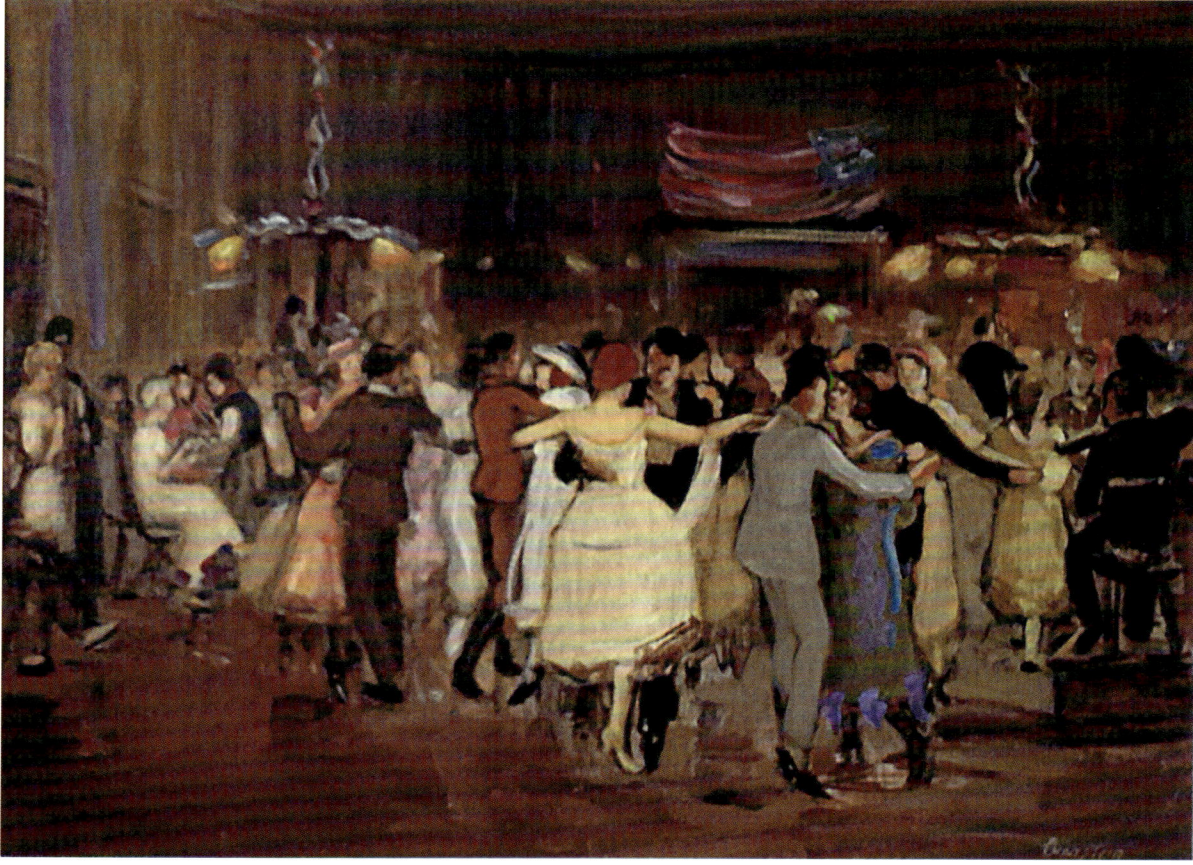

122. *The Hawthorne Casino*, ca. 1920. Oil on canvas, 29 x 39 inches. Private collection.

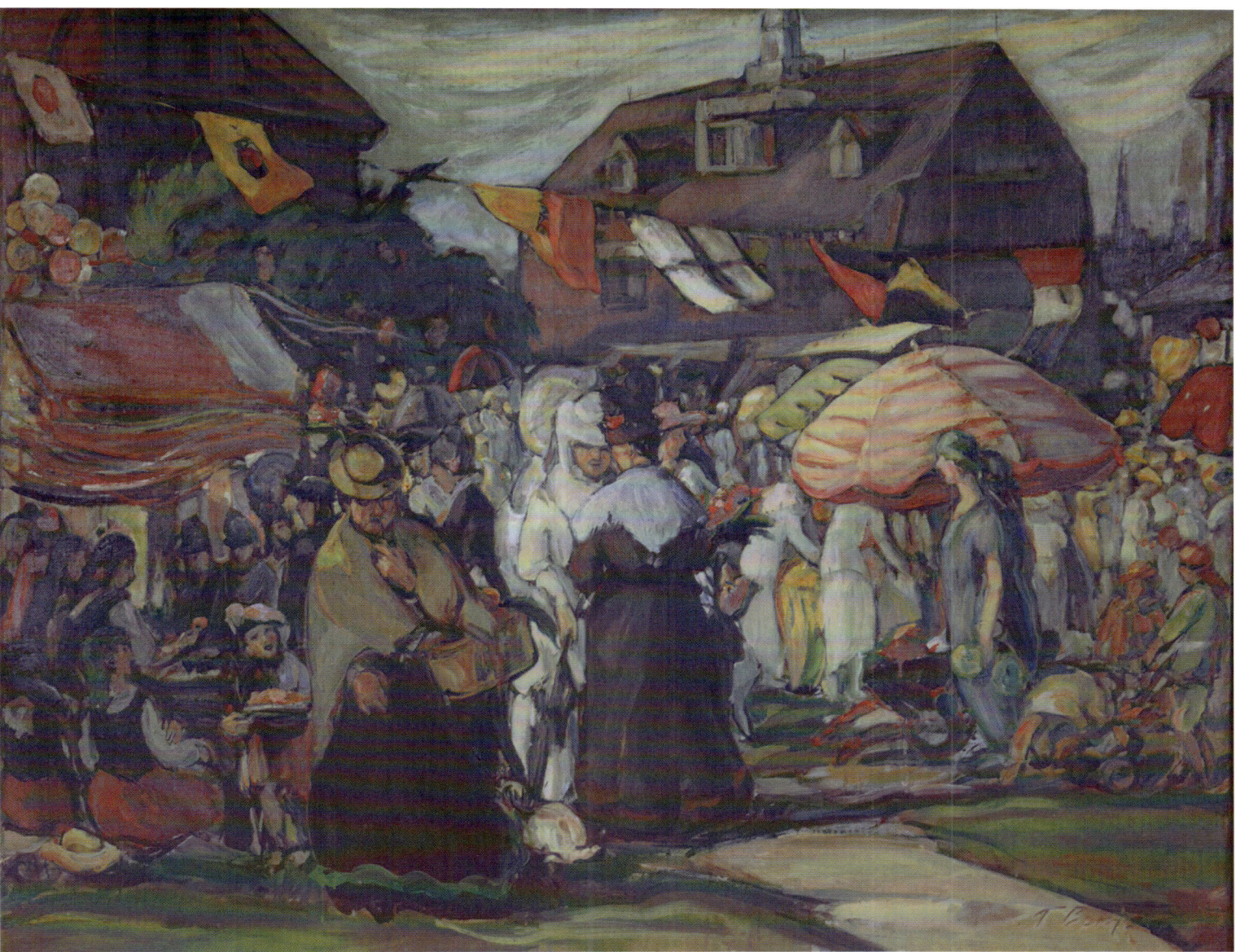

123. *The Country Fair*, 1917. Oil on canvas, 40 x 50 inches. J. J. and Jackie Bell Collection.

students on the wharf and at the beach, where they guided them in making the observations that animated Bernstein's own paintings (see fig. 9). Students ranged from serious adult artists to children and vacationers interested in leisure pursuits. Their home with its remodeled basement provided studio space. They did not impose a style on students but sought to help each person develop his or her creative expression. After all, neither Bernstein nor Meyerowitz dogmatically adhered to realism or abstraction or a particular school of art. Teaching for them was a way to both supplement their income and share what they loved.[78]

For Bernstein, Gloucester was the perfect summer residence: it provided a rich history, spectacular and varied scenery, vacationers and laborers, social gatherings, brilliant light and color, and an established and supportive artistic community in which women were equal participants. Over the seventy years that Bernstein remained connected to this historic town, Gloucester was more than just an escape from the congestion, stress, and constant stimulation of New York City. Beaches might have drawn Bernstein to Gloucester initially, but New England's oldest seaport came to represent far more. It conferred authenticity on American painters, inextricably linking them to past artists, American history, and singular topography. In the early decades of the twentieth century it was a place where artists, especially women, could shirk conventions, paint how and what they wanted, socialize, and even dance barefoot over the moors. That image of Gloucester's shoeless young ladies and matrons cavorting in diaphanous garb, communing with the sweet smell of heather and salt air, best captures the spirit of opportunity that Gloucester represented for Theresa Bernstein—as a modern American painter and a woman.

NOTES

1. Theresa Bernstein, "North Shore Arts Association," 1972, Artist Vertical File, Cape Ann Museum, Gloucester MA.

2. According to historian Mary McCarl, the Cape Ann Arts Festivals began in 1952 with a series of events that focused on different art forms. The Third Cape Ann Arts Festival took place in 1954. Information kindly provided by Stephanie Buck, Librarian and Archivist, Cape Ann Museum, Gloucester MA.

3. Undated but probably written in 1954, Theresa Bernstein's scrapbook.

4. Judith A. Curtis, *Rocky Neck Art Colony, 1850–1950* (Gloucester MA: Rocky Neck Art Colony, Inc., 2008), p. 7.

5. Melissa Dabakis touches on how summer art colonies provided a supportive atmosphere for independent, professional women artists in "Feminist Interventions: Some Thoughts on Recent Scholarship about Women Artists," *American Art* 18, no. 1 (Spring 2004), p. 5. See also Kirsten Swinth, *Painting Professionals: Women Artists and the Development of Modern American Art, 1870–1930* (Chapel Hill: University of North Carolina Press, 2000), pp. 92–93, who writes, "As it had been in Paris, this network [of women artists, not specifically Gloucester] provided emotional support and encouragement as well as vital professional information and assistance." See also Folly Cove Designers, the catalogue for a May 7–October 31, 1996, exhibition at the Cape Ann Historical Museum, Gloucester MA.

6. For an excellent discussion of women artists in Boston, see Erica E. Hirshler, *A Studio of Her Own: Women Artists in Boston, 1870–1940* (Boston: Museum of Fine Arts, 2001).

7. Bernstein, *The Journal*, p. 25.

8. See Mariea Caudill Dennison, "Babies for Suffrage: The Exhibition of Painting and Sculpture by Women Artists for the Benefit of the Woman Suffrage Campaign," *Woman's Art Journal* 24, no. 2 (Autumn 2003–Winter 2004), pp. 24–30.

9. Richmond was part of the artist group that contributed to the *New Masses*. See discussion in Patricia Hills, *Stuart Davis* (New York: Harry N. Abrams, 1996), pp. 29–30, and photo reproduced, p. 39, showing Richmond, the Sloans, Stuart Davis, Alice Beach Winter, and others in front of the Red Cottage.

10. Hirshler, *A Studio of Her Own*, p. 181.

11. This painting sometimes appears under the title *New England Women*. See Bernstein's account in *The Journal*. She writes, "Given at the home of Gertrude Standwood, participants included Ellen Day Hale, Margaret Hoyt and her young son, Bill, Lillian Westcott Hale and her small daughter Nancy, Aunt Porcher and Gabrielle De Vee [sic] Clemens," p. 64. Bernstein also describes this painting in her biography of her husband, *William Meyerowitz*. See Bernstein, *William Meyerowitz*, p. 30.

12. There is an extensive bibliography on Cape Ann artists. See Lisa Peters and Karen Quinn, *Painters of Cape Ann, 1840–1940* (New York: Spanierman Gallery, 1996); and Curtis, *Rocky Neck Art Colony*. See also selected essays in James F. O'Gorman, *This Other Gloucester* (Boston: James F. O'Gorman, 1976).

13. Karl Baedeker, *The United States with an Excursion into Mexico: A Handbook for Travelers* (Leipzig, Germany: Karl Baedeker Publisher, 1893), p. 92, quoted in Peters and Quinn, *Painters of Cape Ann*, p. 5.

14. Unidentified clipping, *American Art News*, September 16, 1916, Gallery-on-the-Moors Scrapbook, 1 of 3, Cape Ann Museum. Other women artists mentioned include Alice Schille, Clara Madera, W. I. Little, H. F. Lohr, Ethel Paddock, and R. D. Wadsworth.

15. "Gloucester Is the Place to Be" (1968), reprinted in Theresa Bernstein Meyerowitz, *The Poetic Canvas* (New York: Cornwall Books, 1989), p. 85. See also "The Artists Who Came to Gloucester" (1968), pp. 28–30.

16. See "Artifacts," in *The Poetic Canvas*, pp. 86–87. Sloan summered in Gloucester between 1914 and 1918, and Hopper, who first visited in 1912, returned in 1923 and several summers thereafter. An unidentified clipping in Bernstein's scrapbook describes a New York exhibition that included works by several Gloucester artists: Louise Upton Brumback's *Apple Tree*, Alice Beach Winter's *The Summer Garden*, Theresa Bernstein's *New England Ladies*, called "a striking example in this well-known painter's distinctive style," and William Meyerowitz's *Status Quo* were all mentioned. Bernstein scrapbook.

17. See Laura Prieto, *At Home in the Studio: The Professionalization of Women Artists in America* (Cambridge MA: Harvard University Press, 2001), p. 146.

18. For a discussion of how this personal loss impacted Bernstein, see the essay by Gillian Pistell in this volume. See also Erika Doss, "Complicating Modernism," in *American Women Modernists: The Legacy of Robert Henri, 1910–1945*, ed. Marian Wardle (New Brunswick NJ: Rutgers University Press, 2005), who explores the relationships between the biographical facts of several of Robert Henri's female students and their professional careers, critical reception, and ultimately their place in the history of American modernism. Doss mistakenly includes Bernstein, who shared stylistic and philosophical affinities with Henri but never studied with him. Note, too, that the reproduction of Bernstein's The Suffrage Meeting, fig. 161, is flipped.

19. Dorothy Grafly, "Gloucester Society of Artists' Fourth Show," *Christian Science Monitor*, September 4, 1923, p. 10.

20. See Swinth, "Modernism and Self-Expression," pp. 163–200, in Wardle, *American Women Modernists*, for a discussion of modernism in relation to American women artists in the first two decades of the twentieth century.

21. See Irene Gammel, *Baroness Elsa: Gender, Dada, and Everyday Modernity—A Cultural Biography* (Cambridge MA: MIT Press, 2002).

22. See Bernstein's account in *The Journal*, pp. 46, 55.

23. O'Gorman, *This Other Gloucester*, provides the most comprehensive account of Gallery-on-the-Moors in "Parnassus on Ledge Road: The Life and Times of East Gloucester's Gallery-on-the-Moors, 1916–1922," pp. 77–96, originally published in *North Shore*, November 16 and 30, December 14 and 25, 1974; revised for republication. Bernstein also provides some colorful descriptions in *William Meyerowitz*, p. 29. See also "An Exhibition of Selected Work from the Museum's Collection by Artists Who Exhibited at Gallery-on-the-Moors, Cape Ann Historical Museum, Aug. 19, 2006, to Jan. 31, 2007," Artist Files: Original Documents, Gallery-on-the-Moors, Cape Ann Museum.

24. See description in "A New Gallery in East Gloucester," *New York Times*, September 10, 1916.

25. "An Exhibition of Selected Work from the Museum's Collection," quoted in Curtis, *Rocky Neck Art Colony*, p. 86.

26. Helen Wright, "The Gallery and Playhouse on the Moors," *Touchstone* 7 (1920), p. 70.

27. Curtis, Rocky Neck Art Colony, p. 86, quoted from O'Gorman, *This Other Gloucester*, p. 80.

28. Bernstein, *The Journal*, p. 55.

29. Bernstein, *William Meyerowitz*, p. 29.

30. Leila Mechen, "The Summer Exhibition," *American Magazine of Art* 12 (October 1921), p. 354.

31. See Bernstein, *The Journal*, p. 55, and Bernstein, in *William Meyerowitz*, p. 29, for Bernstein's description of Gallery-on-the-Moors.

32. The catalogue listed these as #19 *The Little Merry-Go-Round* and #73 *On the Beach*. Gallery-on-the-Moors Scrapbook, 1 of 3, Cape Ann Museum. The latter is likely the watercolor also known as *Beach* (fig. 106), painted before *Gloucester*.

33. Frank W. Coburn, "Gallery-on-the-Moors at Gloucester," *Sunday Boston Herald*, August 26, 1917, Theresa Bernstein Artist File, Cape Ann Museum. See also "Gloucester's Art Show," *Boston Transcript*, September 5, 1916, Theresa Bernstein Artist File, Cape Ann Museum.

34. Curtis, *Rocky Neck Art Colony*, p. 87. See also John Nutting, "Varied Exhibition, 'Gallery on Moors' Showing of 74 Paintings and 22 Pieces of Sculpture from Studios along the North Shore," *Boston Advertiser*, August 30, 1916, Gallery-on-the-Moors Scrapbook, 1 of 3, Cape Ann Museum; and "New Gloucester Art Home Opens Its First Show: "Gallery of the Moors," *Christian Science Monitor*, September 8, 1916, p. 6.

35. Nutting, "Varied Exhibition, 'Gallery on Moors' Showing."

36. "A New Gallery in East Gloucester."

37. W. H. de B. Nelson, "Theresa F. Bernstein," *International Studio* 66, no. 265 (February 1919), p. cii.

38. Grafly, "A Bernstein-Meyerowitz Conversation," *Christian Science Monitor*, September 1, 1923, p. 12.

39. *Sun, Sand, and Sea* was listed as #18; *The Garden Party* as #27; and *Golf, Eastern Point* as #58. Two years later Bernstein sold *Sun, Sand, and Sea* for $650 in her solo show at Milch Gallery in 1919. It was listed as #9. See Bernstein annotated catalogue, referenced in Cohen, unpublished manuscript for "Echoes of New York: The Paintings of Theresa Bernstein," 1990, p. 42.

40. Frank W. Coburn, "The Gallery-on-the-Moors at Gloucester," *Sunday Boston Herald*, August 26, 1917, Theresa Bernstein Artist File, Gallery-on-the-Moors Scrapbook, 1 of 3, Cape Ann Museum.

41. Unidentified clipping, July, 1917, Gallery-on-the-Moors Scrapbook, 1 of 3, Cape Ann Museum.

42. These appeared as #33 *Golf Tournament* and #69 *Landscape with Figures*.

43. See Burnham for a discussion of what she terms Bernstein's "community-scapes." Patricia M. Burnham, *Theresa Bernstein, People and Places: A Retrospective*, Philadelphia Museum of Judaica, 1995, n.p.

44. Jean Nutting Oliver, *Advertiser*, August 18, 1918, Gallery-on-the-Moors Scrapbook, 2 of 3, Cape Ann Museum.

45. Frank W. Coburn, unidentified *Boston Herald* clipping, Bernstein's scrapbook.

46. Review of "The Fine Arts Gloucester Exhibition," *Boston Evening Transcript*, August 22, 1918, Gallery-on-the-Moors Scrapbook, 2 of 3, Cape Ann Museum.

47. Listed as #5 *Greek Pageant*.

48. Unidentified clipping, Gallery-on-the-Moors Scrapbook, 3 of 3, Cape Ann Museum.

49. Other participants included set designers Florence Cunningham and Livingstone Platt, composer Percy Lee Atherton, assisted by Mrs. Frederick Hall and Mrs. George L. Noyes, and choreographers Lileas MacLane and Adeline D. Piper, aided by Ruth Hallock and Cecilia Beaux, who helped the choreographers train dancers throughout the summer. Unidentified clipping, Gallery-on-the-Moors Scrapbook, 3 of 3, Cape Ann Museum.

50. See Jean Nutting Oliver, "Greek Festival at Gallery on Moors," July 29, 1918, Gallery-on-the-Moors Scrapbook, 3 of 3, Cape Ann Museum.

51. Bernstein, *The Journal*, p. 56. Although Bernstein recollects contributing to the creation of the sets and costumes, she is not mentioned in any of the numerous newspaper accounts that document the event.

52. See "A Sombre Greek Pageant," *New York Herald*, August 24, 1919, Gallery-on-the-Moors Scrapbook, 2 of 3, Cape Ann Museum.

53. "Gallery-on-the-Moors Exhibit Sets Record," in *Advertiser*, Boston, n.d., Gallery-on-the-Moors Scrapbook, 2 of 3, Cape Ann Museum.

54. *The Harbor* was listed as #46. Called "rich in color and contrasts" by A. J. Philpott, in "Gloucester Spirit Caught by Artists," unidentified clipping, Gallery-on-the-Moors Scrapbook, 2 of 3, Cape Ann Museum. John Doc, in "Exhibit of High Average at the Gallery-on-the-Moors," *Cape Ann Shore*, August 14, 1920, writes: "Theresa Bernstein, who did the beautiful *Greek Pageant* last summer, is represented by *The Harbor*, in black and brown, which reminds us curiously of a painting on glass." Gallery-on-the-Moors Scrapbook, 2 of 3, Cape Ann Museum.

55. "The Fine Arts: Gallery-on-the-Moors" subtitle: "Fifth Annual Exhibition the Best Showing of Modern American Art Yet Given in East Gloucester," *Boston Evening Transcript*, n.d, Gallery-on-the-Moors Scrapbook, 2 of 3, Cape Ann Museum.

56. Listed as #38 and #37, respectively. In 1922, in the final exhibition, Bernstein showed #63 *Stormy Sea, Folly Cove*.

57. Bernstein, *The Journal*, p. 64.

58. Bernstein, *William Meyerowitz*, p. 39.

59. Bernstein, *The Journal*, p. 71.

60. Bernstein describes this extensively in *William Meyerowitz*. She recollects that Judge Brumback, husband of the painter Louise Upton Brumback, negotiated the purchase for them, as he was a personal friend of Roger Babson, president of the Cape Ann Bank.

61. See Sarah Archino's essay on *The Paint Rag* in this volume.

62. See Hills, *Stuart Davis*, p. 41.

63. Dorothy Grafly "A Bernstein-Meyerowitz Conversation," *Christian Science Monitor*, September 1, 1923, p. 12.

64. See Hills, *Stuart Davis*, pp. 29–35.

65. Hills, *Stuart Davis*, p. 48.

66. Hills, *Stuart Davis*, p. 56.

67. Curtis, *Rocky Neck Art Colony*, p. 62, n. 57, quote from the Cincinnati Enquirer.

68. See Rebecca A. G. Reynolds, "85 Years of the North Shore Arts Association," *American Art Review* 19, no. 5 (2007), pp. 102–11.

69. "The North Shore Arts Association of Gloucester," North Shore Arts Association File, Cape Ann Museum.

70. Unidentified author, handwritten notes, North Shore Arts Association Vertical File, Cape Ann Museum.

71. Dorothy Grafly, "More Than 400 Exhibits Shown by North Shore Association," *Christian Science Monitor*, July 13, 1944, p. 4.

72. See O'Gorman, *This Other Gloucester*, p. 96.

73. See Bryant F. Tolles Jr., *Summer by the Seaside: The Architecture of New England Coastal Resort Hotels, 1820–1950* (Lebanon NH: University Press of New England, 2008), p. 103.

74. Letter from Theresa Bernstein to Murray and Helene Cohen, July 2, 1984.

75. Bernstein, *William Meyerowitz*, p. 28.

76. Bernstein, *The Journal*, p. 55. See also "Artists in Tableaux," unidentified clipping, 1917, Bernstein's scrapbook.

77. Meyerowitz discusses his working method in Grafly, "A Bernstein-Meyerowitz Conversation," p. 12.

78. See discussion of art school in "Our Friends, Students, and Collectors," chap. 8 of Bernstein, *William Meyerowitz*, pp. 53–56.

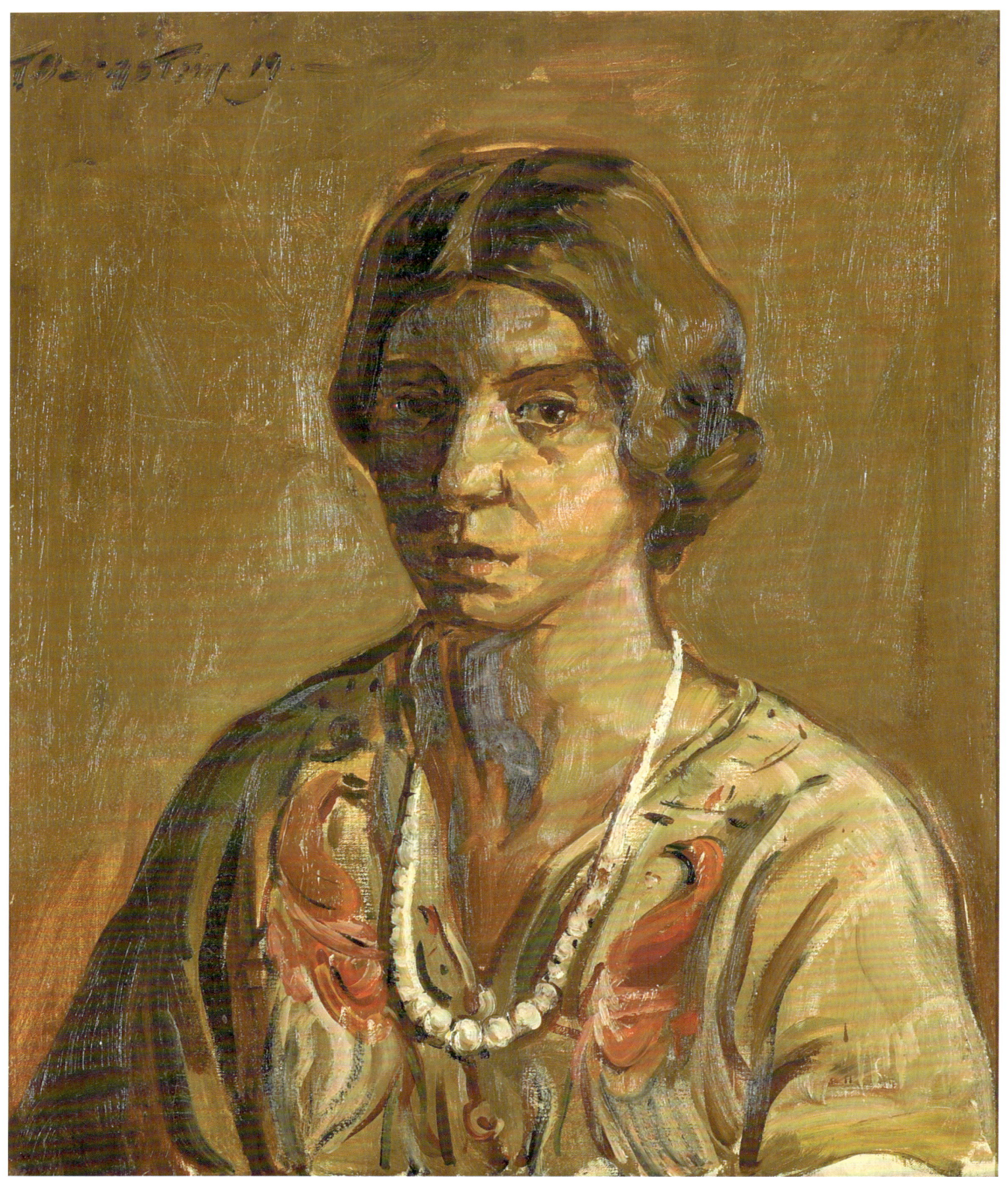

124. *Self-Portrait*, 1919. Oil on canvas, 24 x 20 inches. Martin and Edith Stein Collection.

FOUR # Theresa Bernstein and World War I in New York

Sarah Archino

The impact of World War I on American artists was once overlooked in accounts of early twentieth-century modernism. In his groundbreaking study *American Painting from the Armory Show to the Depression*, Milton Brown wrote that "the direction of American art was not changed by the World War. The events of the war found their way into only a fraction of our art and if those years of crisis had any influence it was through the subsequent effects upon our social and cultural atmosphere. The war years, as far as art was concerned, were merely a hiatus."[1]

The war, however, had a direct impact on a number of artists practicing in New York during these years; although America's direct involvement in World War I did not begin until April of 1917, the effects of wartime culture were felt from the earliest days of the conflict. For an artist such as Theresa Bernstein, who was active in progressive circles and dedicated to observing the streets of New York, the war was nearly inescapable. She also would have been aware of the restrictions of wartime censorship, an increasingly conservative atmosphere that ultimately suppressed publication of the socialist journal *The Masses* and led *The Little Review* to print its April 1917

protest of the war as a blank page, captioned only: "We will probably be suppressed for this."[2]

On a personal level, Bernstein was not untouched by the war. She noted in her book, *The Journal*, that one of her cousins, Vladimir Kahany, whom she had met on a 1912 trip to Europe, was killed on the Russian front in 1915.[3] Closer to home, her future brother-in-law, Nathan, was drafted. Years later, Bernstein would recall that William Meyerowitz, her then fiancé, was called up for the draft during the week the armistice was declared.[4] The reaches of the wartime climate extended to civilians as well, particularly among immigrant communities and the radicals of Greenwich Village, as xenophobia and fears of subversion began to spread. Thus, when the model Baroness Elsa von Freytag-Loringhoven was arrested and incarcerated in New Haven for nearly a month under suspicion of espionage and treason, Bernstein cared for her pet cat.[5]

While Bernstein completed numerous drawings of the parades of Fifth Avenue, she differentiated her work from that of her peers. Unlike artists such as Edward Hopper and George Bellows, who became involved with explicitly political propaganda campaigns, or Childe Hassam, whose flag paintings transformed the bedecked streets of Fifth Avenue into impressionistic vistas of light, movement, and color, the majority of Bernstein's paintings from this period focus on how the war impacted the typical citizen.[6] In addition to the work of aid societies and Red Cross benefits, a number of parades and patriotic events took place in the city streets; their frequency only escalated after the official declaration of war. As early as 1914, parades to support allied troops and aid societies were a common sight, such as the one she captured in the watercolor *Parade 1914*. A bright, colorful scene, Bernstein captures the pomp and celebration of such events, paying special attention to the crowd of women gathered in the foreground. Rather than creating a sense of militarism or tension, the result is one of pure visual interest and excitement, but presented on a deliberately human scale.

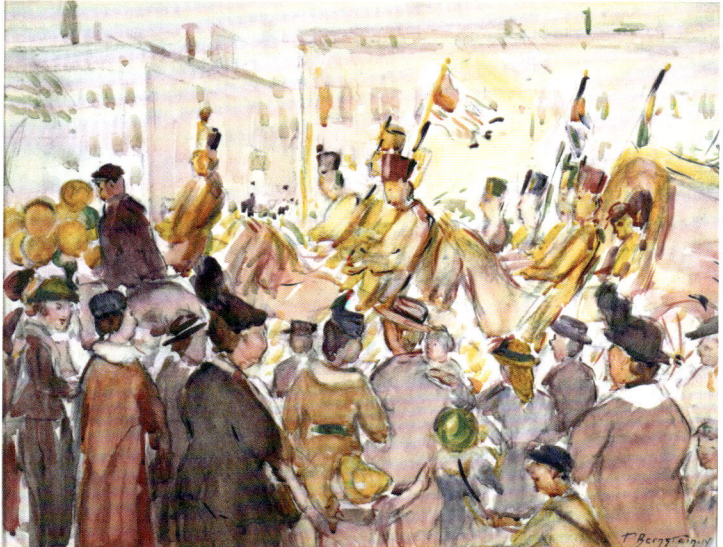

125. *Parade 1914*, 1914. Watercolor on artist's board, 16 x 20 inches. Private collection.

Bernstein's images of the wartime atmosphere presented the full spectrum of the pomp, parades, and military displays. Her commitment to figuration is evident in the manner in which she also captured the throngs of enthusiastic spectators. Bernstein's images of war are neither anonymous crowd scenes nor faceless patriotic displays of might but rather vignettes that highlight the individual and personal effect of the combat upon

her subjects, lending a certain intimacy to her work. As she would later recount, "I was painting scenes in the city. I was interested in the parades; World War I, with its continual activity and patriotic demonstrations, got my complete attention. I painted large canvases of the Veterans' Parade and the demonstrations for new recruits for the army."[7] In contrast to her male counterparts, Bernstein underscored her desire to capture "the faces of the crowds, people congregated at corners greeting the war news, the night scenes, and Columbus Circle."[8]

Even in rapid sketches, such as those done outside the Forty-Second Street branch of the New York Public Library, Bernstein takes pains to enumerate not only the marching soldiers but also the people in the crowd. Bernstein presents an intimate, democratic, and American view of the war. She focuses on the stories and the people, presenting a united front comprised of a broad range of American citizens. In this vein, *Reading the War News* presents a crowd gathered around an illuminated board displaying the latest updates from overseas.

Silhouetted against the bright lights, the eager crowd presses toward the sign as they strain to read news of the war. Painted in 1915, the image reveals how deeply the citizens of New York (many of them recent immigrants) were affected by the conflict, even prior to America's intervention. While the

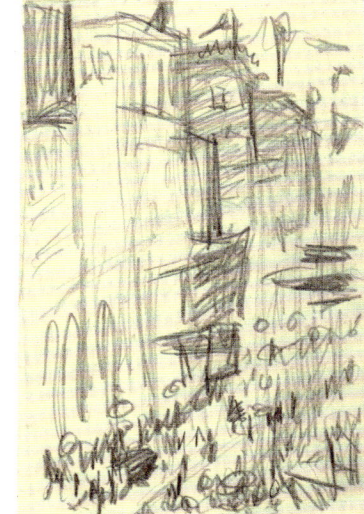

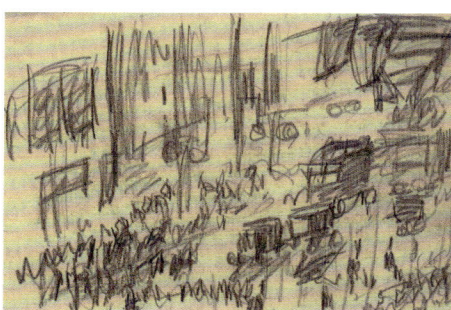

126. *Armistice Day 1*, 1917. Pencil on paper sketch, 5 x 3¼ inches. Theresa Bernstein and William Meyerowitz Foundation.

127. *Armistice Day 2*, 1917. Pencil on paper sketch, 3¼ x 5 inches. Theresa Bernstein and William Meyerowitz Foundation.

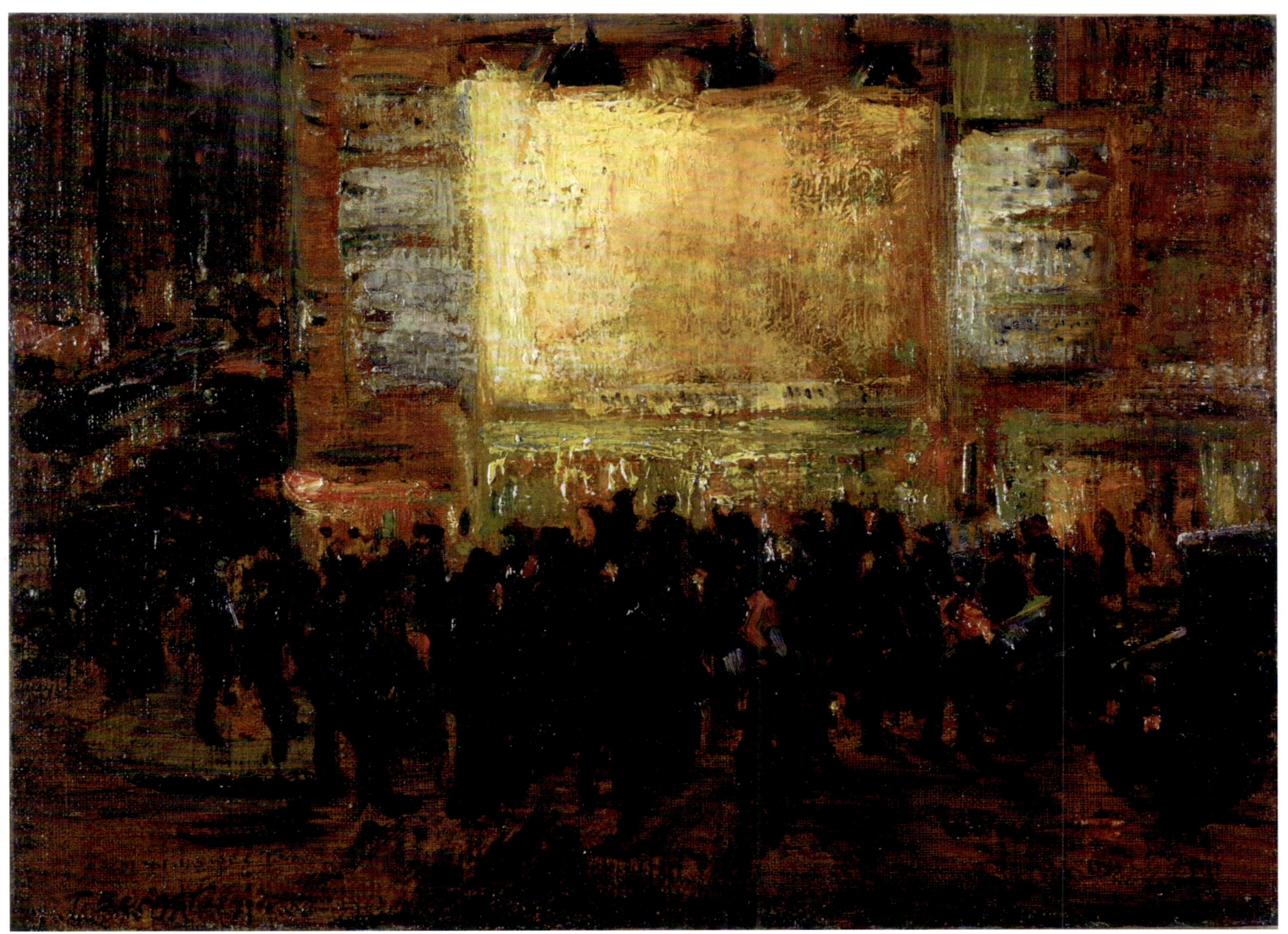

128. *Reading the War News*, 1915. Oil on canvas, 12 x 16 inches. Private collection.

government viewed these immigrant groups with suspicion (and indeed, many of them were of German descent), Bernstein presents them in solidarity, unencumbered by ideological or nationalistic divisions and united in their common concern. Again, Bernstein concentrates her attention on the people gathered in Columbus Circle, although they are simply suggested forms outlined against a brilliant light.[9] Although shadowy, these figures have a sense of individuality as well as movement and transience; they are each frozen for a brief moment before disappearing into the night.

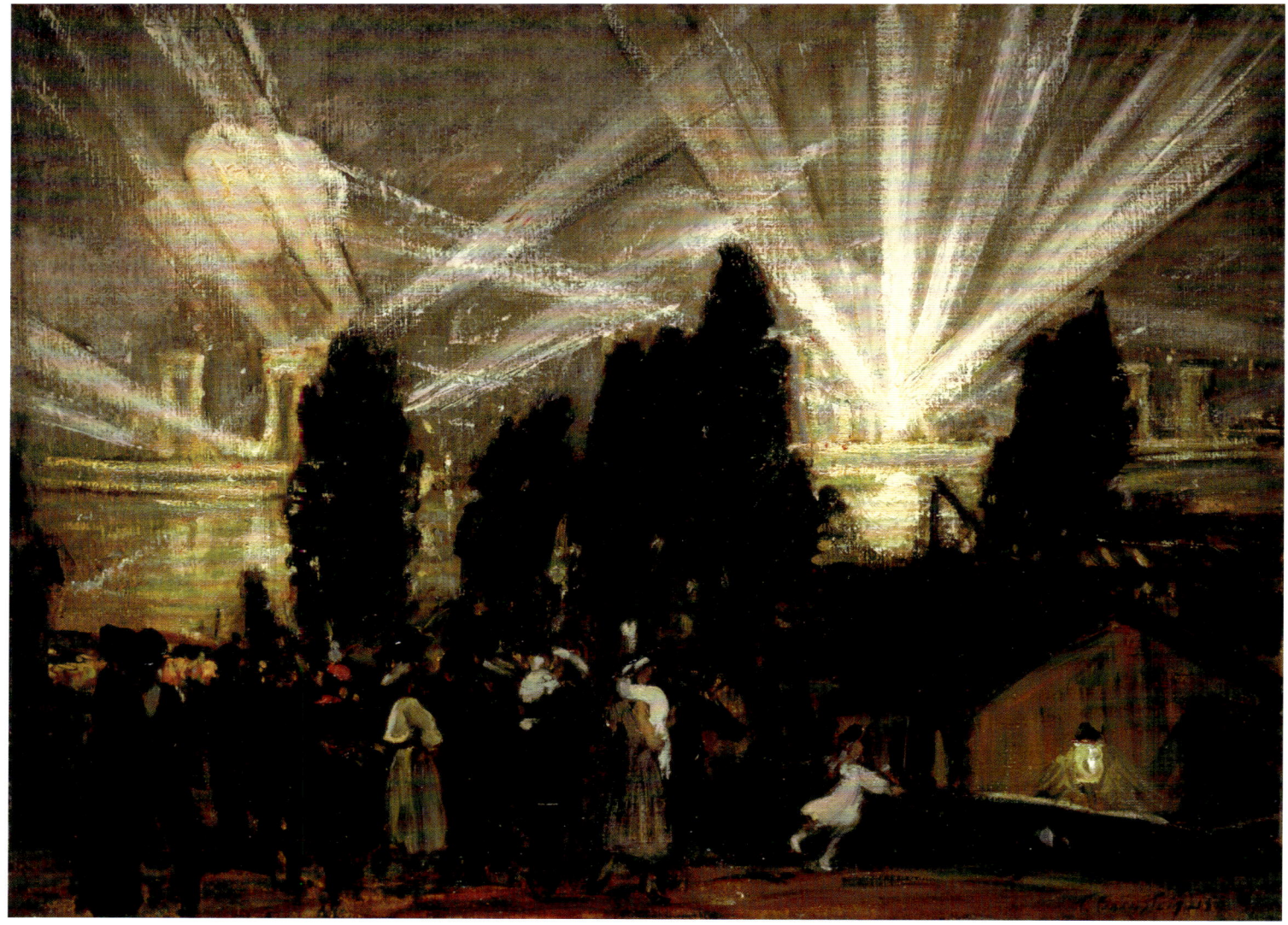

129. *Searchlights on the Hudson*, 1915. Oil on canvas, 27 x 36 inches. Private collection.

Several of Bernstein's wartime images captured the spectacle of nighttime events. Events such as the popular military display of searchlight shows on the Hudson River provided an opportunity to study evening crowds, to capture dramatic plays of light, and to document the war while concentrating on the experience of everyday men and women. She recalled the atmosphere of evenings in the city: "There was always a little cleave of light penetrating the gloom in the twilight scenes of New York. Looking toward the water on West 94th Street, where I lived with my parents because the Holbein studio had no heat or sleeping possibilities, the wet pavement reflected the drab sky. I painted the Hudson from Riverside Drive and from the benches in Central Park."[10] *Searchlights on the Hudson* captures one such gathering of 1915, as the utilitarian lamps were periodically lit for the amusement of local residents.

The searchlights shown were part of the militarization that preceded America's entry into the war; they thrilled the crowds but also warned of the possible danger from the German zeppelins that occasionally threatened the East Coast. A number of searchlights were installed across the Hudson River from New York City, in Bayonne, New Jersey. They illuminated the riverscape, including the visible oil tanks of the Standard, Tide Water, and Vacuum Oil Works.[11] As the American naval fleet moved through New York Harbor, the ships would also operate their searchlights; the resulting light show was a popular attraction.[12] The spectators, pictured at the lower left corner of Bernstein's composition, are a fashionable crowd and include mothers with children, women in fur stoles, and excitable pet dogs.

Such displays were not uncommon and would have certainly been witnessed by Bernstein, who lived with her parents on Manhattan's Upper West Side and frequented the riverside. She later recalled, "the effect was so remarkable I couldn't resist making a painting."[13] As might be expected, the searchlights form the focal point of Bernstein's work, exploding in thickly applied paint that echoes the soaring beams of light, as well as their rippled reflection in the waters below. Although

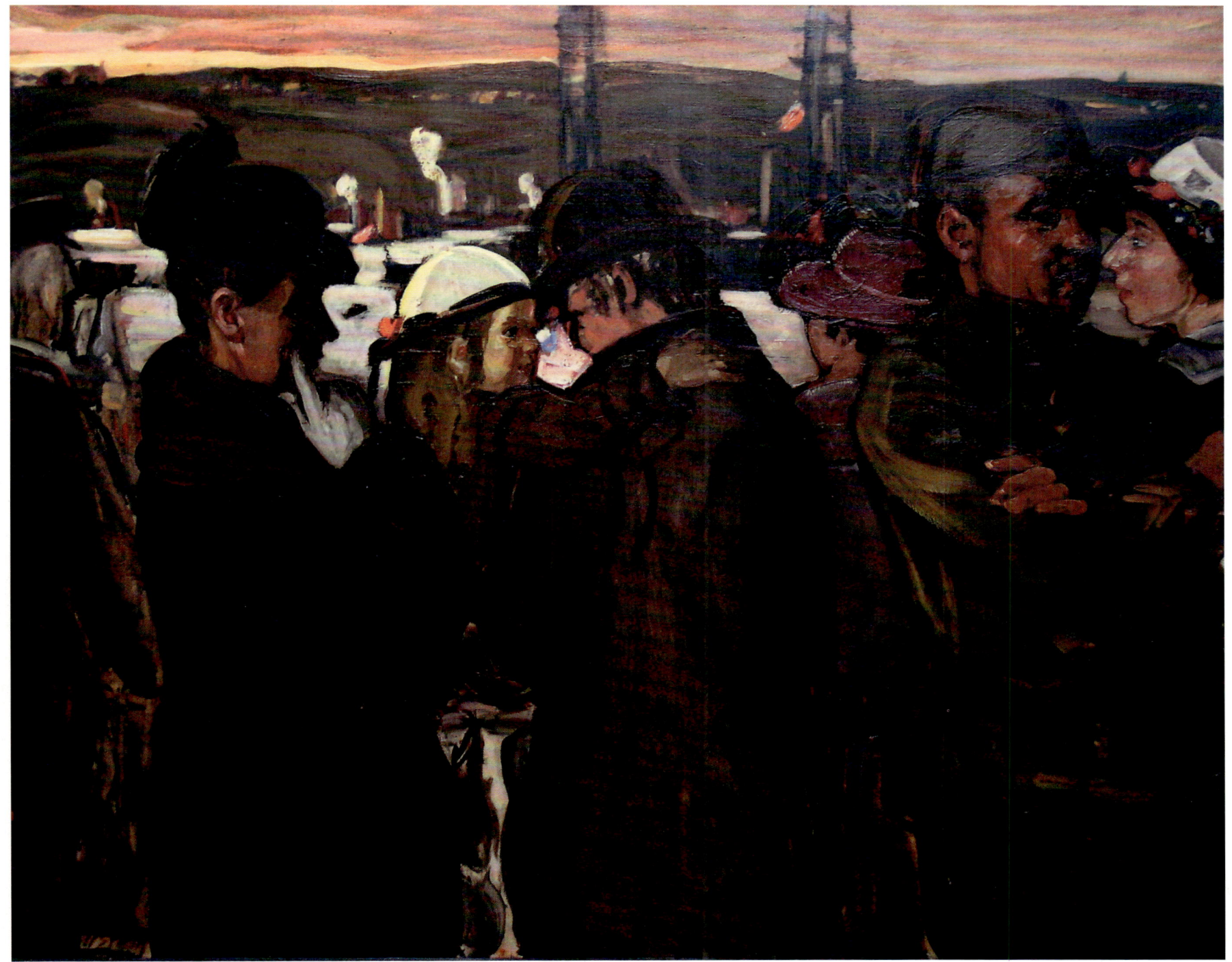

130. *National Holiday*, 1917. Oil on canvas, 40 x 49½ inches. Theresa Bernstein and William Meyerowitz Foundation.

most of the palette is dark, the brilliance of the light is balanced by bright highlights of red and pink, dappled through the crowd gathered below. A popular painting, *Searchlights on the Hudson* was included in an exhibition at Knoedler and Co. in May of 1918. The show, *American Paintings and Sculptures Pertaining to the War*, included works by William Glackens, Robert Henri, John Sloan, Guy Pène du Bois, Mahonri Young, and Jo Davidson, and proceeds were used to invest in liberty bonds.[14]

Bernstein captured another scene on the Hudson riverside in her *National Holiday* of 1917. The billowing smokestacks of passing ships can just be seen beyond the heads of the spectators, who press into the viewer's space. Again, Bernstein captures the wide appeal of these military displays, including the conservatively dressed women in the foreground with a more fashionably hatted woman to the far right. The father, who stands with his charming young daughter in the center of the painting, is contrasted with the uniformed solider.

The gathering most likely depicts the newest national holiday; October 24, 1917, was declared "Liberty Day," closing the New York Stock Exchange as fund-raising drives were held throughout the country.[15] A series of special events, held in cities all over the United States, were intended to raise funds

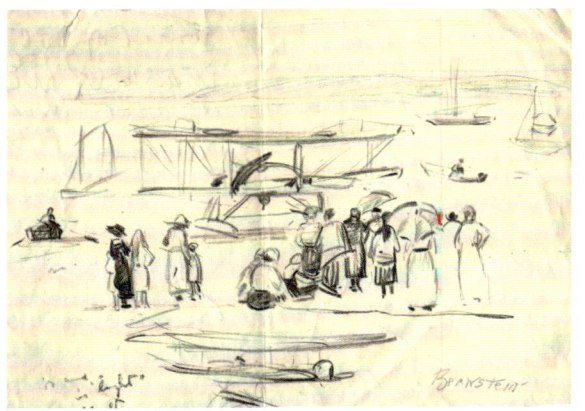

131. *Niles Beach*, 1917. Pencil on paper sketch, 7¼ x 10 inches. Theresa Bernstein and William Meyerowitz Foundation.

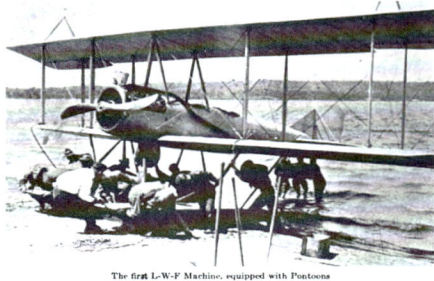

The first L-W-F Machine, equipped with Pontoons

132. L-W-F model with pontoons, 1917. Reproduced in *Aircraft Year Book* (New York: Manufacturers Aircraft Association, Inc., 1919).

through the sale of Liberty bonds. A letter from the secretary of the treasury, W. G. McAdoo, printed on the front page of the *New York Times*, beseeched readers that "this war must become a personal thing to each man, woman, and child of the civilian population, just as it is a personal thing to our soldiers and sailors and their families. . . . When the sun sets on the evening of Liberty Day, ten million

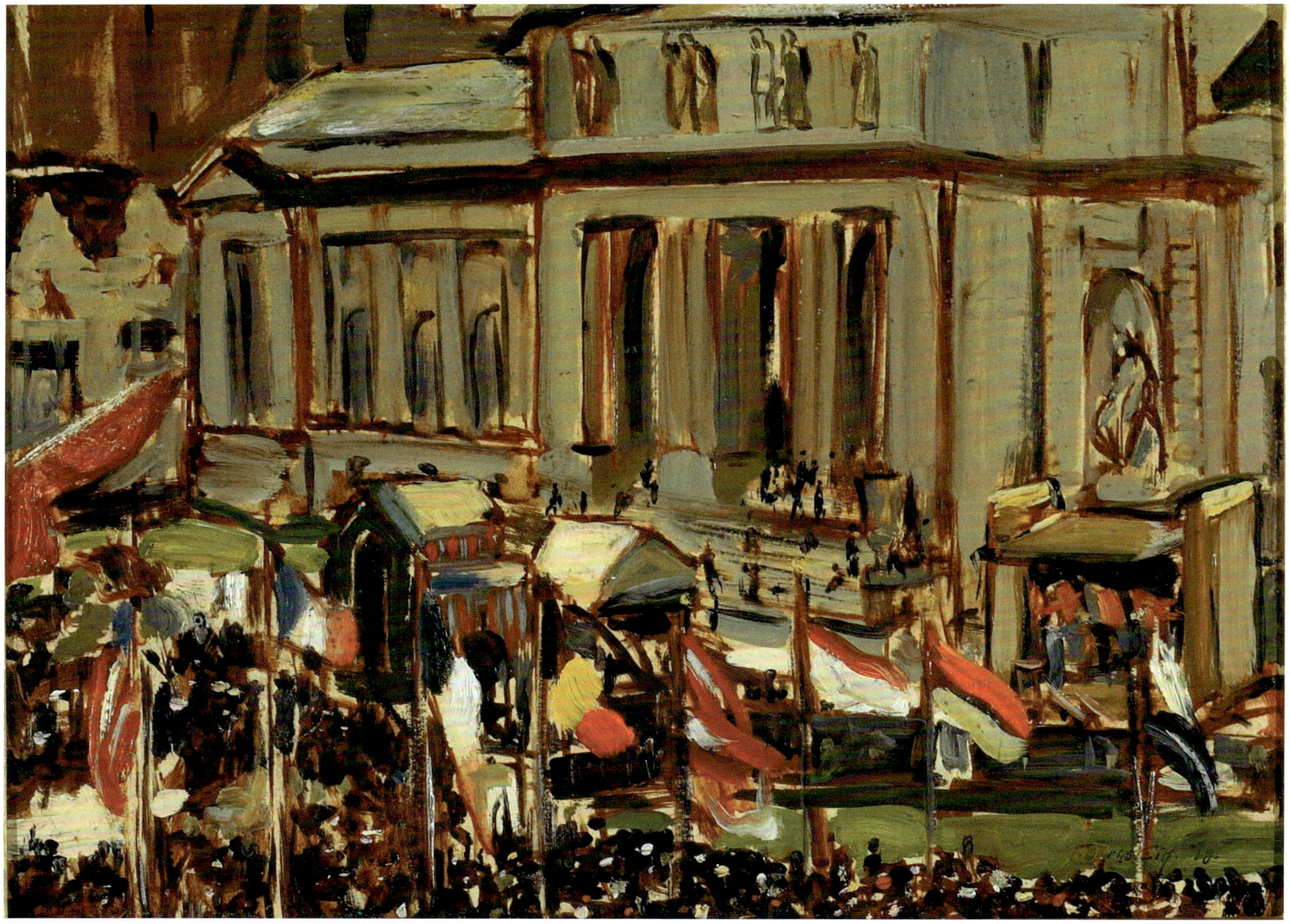

133. *Armistice Day, New York Public Library*, 1918. Oil on canvas, 12 x 16 inches. Martin and Edith Stein Collection.

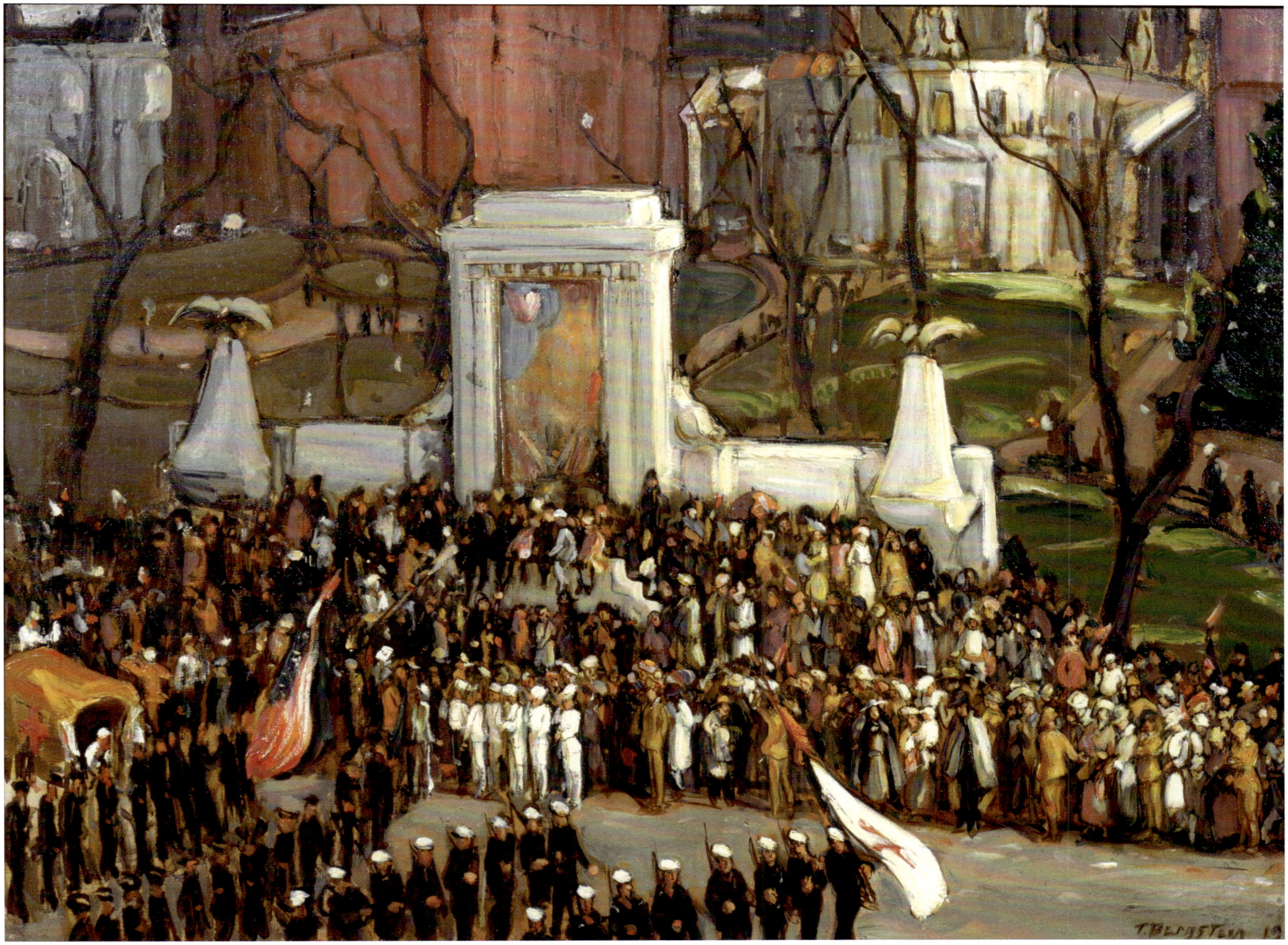

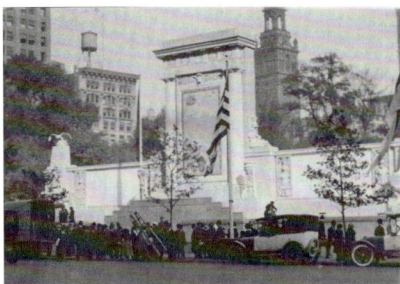

134. *Armistice Day Parade: The Altar of Liberty*, 1918. Oil on canvas, 30 x 40 inches. Private collection.

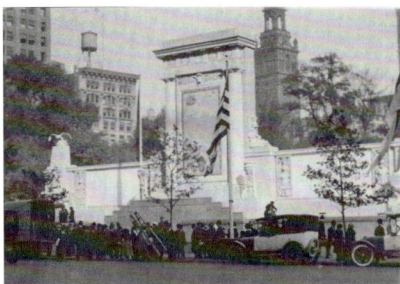

135. Thomas Hasting's Altar of Liberty, 1918. Photograph from private collection.

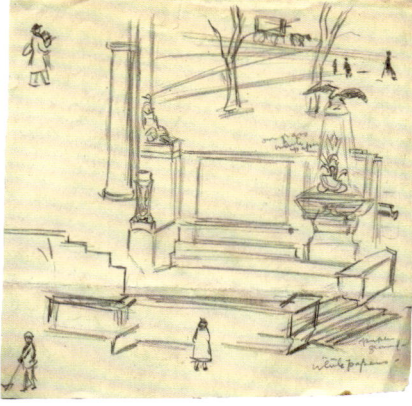

136. Study no. 1 for *Armistice Day Parade: The Altar of Liberty*, 1918. Pencil on paper, 7½ x 7½ inches. Theresa Bernstein and William Meyerowitz Foundation.

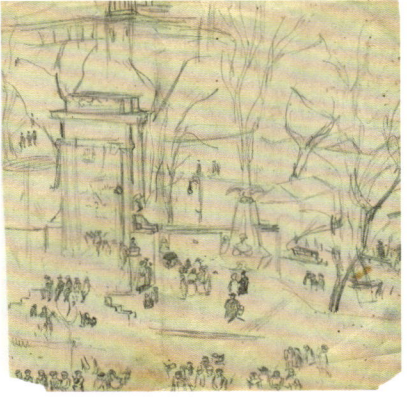

137. Study no. 2 for *Armistice Day Parade: The Altar of Liberty*, 1918. Pencil on paper, 8½ x 8½ inches. Theresa Bernstein and William Meyerowitz Foundation.

Americans should have registered their subscriptions to the second Liberty Loan."[16] Bernstein depicts precisely the sort of democratic crowd who were expected to contribute to the war effort, echoing McAdoo's plea to Americans to support their armed forces overseas.

Bernstein herself contributed an unknown work to the war effort, donating a painting to a government fund-raising exhibition. Among Bernstein's papers, Michele Cohen discovered an April 1919 receipt from the Government Loan Organization of the Treasury Department which read, "We beg to acknowledge receipt of your painting of our subject #A-379 and wish to take this opportunity to again thank you for your splendid contribution."[17]

Even in Gloucester, where Bernstein began visiting in 1916, the wartime climate was evident. Two drawings depict crowds of curious onlookers examining aircraft recently landed on a beach. The inscription on one drawing, "German luft hawk on Niles Beach, Gloucester MA 1917," accompanies an image of a genteel crowd examining two bi-wing planes on the shore. While any newspaper account confirming the existence of a German warplane on American soil has yet to be discovered, it is possible that Bernstein was drawing seaplanes based out of the Chatham Naval Air Station, located across the bay, which opened in 1917 and was in operation until 1922.[18] In particular, there was a model of aircraft, manufactured by the L-W-F Engineering Company, based in College Point, Long Island, which supplied a number of aircraft to East Coast stations during the war.[19] The L-W-F model F was first flown in August of 1917, and when equipped with the optional pontoons, is strikingly similar to the craft sketched by Bernstein. When the end of the war was declared in November 1918, Bernstein also recorded the ceremonies marking the Armistice. In *Armistice Day, New York Public Library*, she captured the parades along Fifth Avenue, which she remembered in *The Journal*: "We celebrated by going to see the Armistice Day parade on 5th Avenue. We watched the parade from the window of an office of a friend on 5th Avenue and 42nd Street, opposite the library. He watched the flags of the nations fluttering in the breeze and a rain of paper from all the windows. People were happy. They hugged each other and said, 'Peace, Peace, It's wonderful.' William etched the parade and I made drawings."[20]

The painting depicts this exact scene, the towering classical public library building fills the background as the crowds gather in the street below. A row of colorful flags flutter in the foreground, but unlike Childe Hassam's paintings of similar parades, Bernstein continues to concentrate on the people beyond.

The coming days would see other jubilant celebrations throughout the city, including parades captured in *Victory Day* (see fig. 55) and *Armistice Day Parade: The Altar of Liberty*. The temporary structures, designed by Thomas Hasting, were located in Madison Square Park; the altar rose four stories above Fifth Avenue at Twenty-Fourth Street, accompanying a triumphal arch at Twenty-Third Street.[21] Again, Bernstein composes the image from above, capturing an overview of the crowds and the architecture, as is visible in one of the two extant sketches that she made on paper. Along with *Armistice Day, New York Public Library*, these paintings have a monumental quality, with a relatively subdued palette and emphasis on classical architecture. She captures the feeling of community that emerged as people gathered around these commemorative structures

In the days and months following the armistice, Bernstein would continue to record fund-raising events, including the *Grecian Pageant* (fig. 115), staged in Gloucester in 1919. One of her last wartime images, the pageant was organized to raise funds for wounded soldiers. Bernstein later recalled that she "helped make designs out of cheesecloth and sateen."[22] The Grecian pageant was viewed from a hillside, where "it made a gorgeous spectacle in the bright afternoon sunlight."[23] In a large painting made to commemorate the event, Bernstein emphasized the gathering crowds and the palpable sense of camaraderie among the residents and visitors to Gloucester as they come together for this occasion.

Throughout the duration of the war, Bernstein's works were politically neutral, capturing the social and cultural aspects of the war and focusing on the mutual support that was generated throughout the city. As she explained in a catalogue of 1960, "for me, a group of people (in action or repose) become a single object in consciousness."[24] In her wartime imagery, Bernstein captured a distinctively American sense of democratic patriotism, this singular consciousness that gathered together the crowds she so loved to paint. As always, she was first and foremost a painter of the people.

NOTES

1. Milton Brown, *American Painting from the Armory Show to the Depression* (Princeton NJ: Princeton University Press, 1955), p. 71.

2. "We Will Probably Be Suppressed for This," *Little Review*, April 1917.

3. Bernstein, *The Journal*, pp. 35–36.

4. Bernstein, *William Meyerowitz*, p. 24.

5. Amelia Jones, *Irrational Modernism: A Neurasthenic History of New York Dada* (Cambridge: MIT Press, 2004), p. 36.

6. Hopper's *Smash the Hun* was awarded first prize by the United States Shipping Board Emergency Fleet Corporation in 1918. This work and the circumstances surrounding its creation are discussed in Gail Levin, *Edward Hopper: An Intimate Biography* (Berkeley: University of California Press, 1995), pp. 116–20. Bellows's *The Germans Arrive* was displayed in a Fifth Avenue storefront. Reproductions were featured in *Collier's* magazine and in bond advertisements, along with the caption "This is Kultur. There is no sharper contrast between German Kultur and the civilization that our forefathers died for, than the difference in the attitude of the two civilizations towards women and children." Support for an interpretation of Hassam's flag series as a formal rather than political exercise dates back to Hassam's time in Paris. In Paris "Hassam was struck by the elegant pattern of the blazing color of flags and the animation of their fluttering against the neutral tone of the brownish-beige buildings," a formal conceit that was echoed in his later paintings of New York, where "the flags appear solid and massive, while the rest of the city and its inhabitants appear to dissolve below," wrote William H. Gerdts, *American Impressionism* (Seattle: Henry Art Gallery Association, 1980), p. 61. Hassam's images of wartime New York almost exclude focus on individual participants.

7. Bernstein, *The Journal*, p. 58.

8. Bernstein, *The Journal*, p. 58.

9. The location is discussed in Michele Cohen's unpublished manuscript, "Echoes of New York: Paintings by Theresa Bernstein," p. 15.

10. Bernstein, *The Journal*, p. 58.

11. "Searchlights on Deadline," *New York Times*, July 23, 1915.

12. "River a Fairyland of Dancing Lights," *New York Times*, April 20, 1919.

13. Quoted in Cohen, "Echoes of New York," p. 15.

14. *New York Tribune*, May, 14, 1918, p. 9.

15. "History of New York Stock Exchange Dates," New York Stock Exchange website, November 2008, http://www.nyse.com/pdfs/closings.pdf.

16. W. G. McAdoo, "Liberty Day," *New York Times*, October 24, 1917.

17. Cohen, "Echoes of New York," p. 39.

18. Joseph D. Buckley, *Wings Over Cape Cod: The Chatham Naval Air Station, 1917–1922* (Orleans MA: Lower Cape Publishing, 2000).

19. Manufacturers Aircraft Association, *Aircraft Year Book* (New York: Manufacturers Aircraft Association, Inc., 1919).

20. Bernstein, *William Meyerowitz*, p. 24.

21. Ilene Susan Fort, *The Flag Paintings of Childe Hassam* (Los Angeles: Los Angeles County Museum of Art, 1988), p. 22.

22. Bernstein, *The Journal*, p. 56. For an extensive discussion of *Grecian Pageant*, see Michele Cohen's essay in this volume.

23. Bernstein, *The Journal*, p. 56.

24. Theresa Bernstein (New York: Cober Gallery, 1960), *William Meyerowitz* and Theresa F. Bernstein Papers, Archives of American Art.

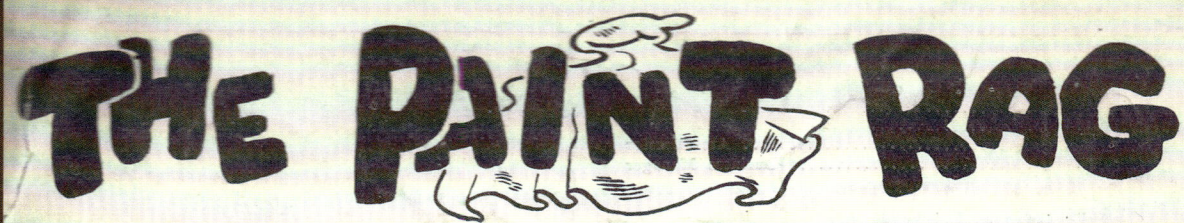

THE PAINT RAG

PUBLISHED BY THE GLOUCESTER SOCIETY OF ARTISTS INC.

GALLERY – EASTERN POINT ROAD — NEAR HAWTHORNE INN CASINO

| NO. 1 | AUGUST 5, 1925 | PRICE 5 CENTS |

Don't miss the
MONTMARTRE
Aug. 13 and 14
From 10 to 6 P. M.
Hawthorne Lane
HAWTHORNE INN

Third Exhibition
and Tea
at the Gallery
Aug. 15th
From 3 to 6

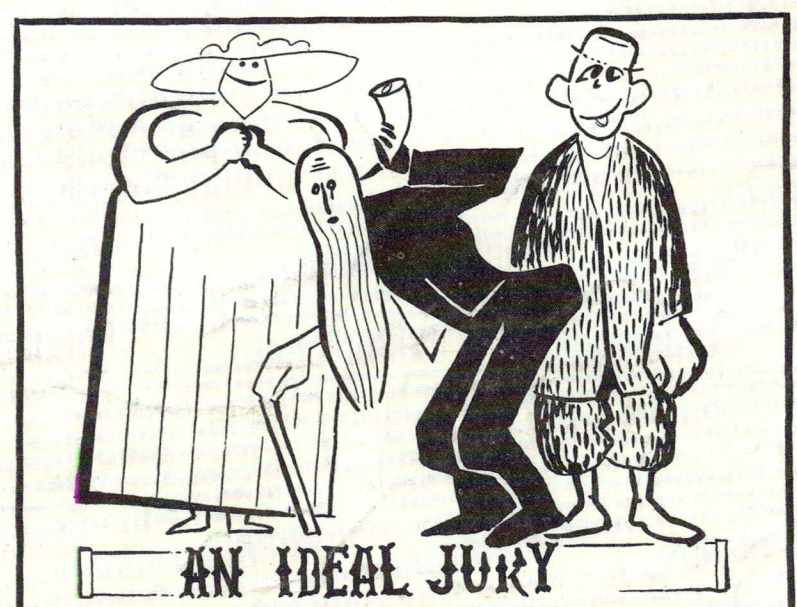

AN IDEAL JURY

EDITORIAL

THE slogan of the Gloucester Society of Artists is—No Jury—No Prizes. It is posted over the gallery at Eastern Point Road—it is on the catalogue—many read it—even club members, yet it seems to convey no meaning of its real significance.

The idea of these so-called Independent Societies which are being formed all over this country, is that the jury and prize system has proved a failure.

The Academy exhibitions are poorly attended and the audience is made up mostly of the ones who are cultured in all branches of art—whether music, literature, painting, or sculpture, and therefore do not care to see again the cut-and-dried efforts that they have seen before, but seek some new venture, some new note that may give them the *something* they are seeking.

Progress makes turncoats of us all. The world would be flat if someone had not said it was round. Monet, Manet, Whistler were all new notes, and were all condemned by the Academy. The Independent exhibitions may not discover a Manet, Whistler, but they will give them a chance just as the Salon Independants gave these great artists in Paris many years ago. Of course everything is a failure in the way of exhibitions, as there are not many geniuses born, but the Gloucester Society of Artists, with many others all over the United States, is trying to find a genius instead of knocking one on the head as they did in the past.

The prize system is absolutely a menace to all exhibitions. Prizes are like kisses—they are given by favor—and as far as it can be discovered, usually the prize winners have a relative on the jury, or are in need of money, or the fellows give it to the artist out of charity—or it is "his" or "her" turn, usually being fixed in a mysterious way like horse racing or stock speculation. In other words, the pie is cut and handed out as best suits that particular jury. "You tickle me and I'll tickle you" is the prize winning motto. Many people do not understand this, and think because a picture has taken a prize it must be good. Politics are in every museum, in the Metropolitan Opera House, and in the drama. The Equity Players insist upon their independent theatre; musicians insist upon their independence in trying out modern music, and no one can stop it now. Everyone might as well ride the wave. It is easier than trying to go through it as the old hats tried to do. They have a one track mind. Let everyone have a chance; it is only the sides of the mountains that are crowded; there is always plenty of room on the top. The people who don't reach the top, carefully slide back to the bottom, so nobody need worry. Good will come in time, and time alone tells the tale. The public must stop and think how much worse the exhibitions of Gloucester might be if it was not for the Gloucester Society of Artists to put a little pep into them. Think it over without prejudice and encourage the Gloucester Society of Artists.

EXTRA — FAKIRS BALL

138. *The Paint Rag* (periodical), no. 1, August 5, 1925. Theresa Bernstein and William Meyerowitz Foundation.

FIVE Dada's Long Shadow

THERESA BERNSTEIN AND *THE PAINT RAG*

Sarah Archino

Although histories of American modernism have tended to isolate the effect of Dada upon American artists, the iconoclastic disruptions of Dadaism cast a shadow far beyond the members of the Arensberg Salon and the European exiles of the World War I period.[1] Such was the case for Theresa Bernstein, who was never associated with Dadaist activities in New York but was doubtlessly aware of them and sympathetic to their dismantling of the institutional structures placed upon modern artists. In 1925 Bernstein contributed to the publication *The Paint Rag*, a work most certainly inspired by the periodicals of New York Dada.

Bernstein was personally connected to two major Dada figures, Marcel Duchamp and the Baroness Elsa von Freytag-Loringhoven, placing her on the periphery of the Dada network. The baroness had modeled for Bernstein on several occasions, and when this eccentric poet and artist was arrested during the war on charges of espionage, Bernstein fed her cat.[2] Her association with Duchamp came through Meyerowitz: "We first met Marcel when he came to one of William's

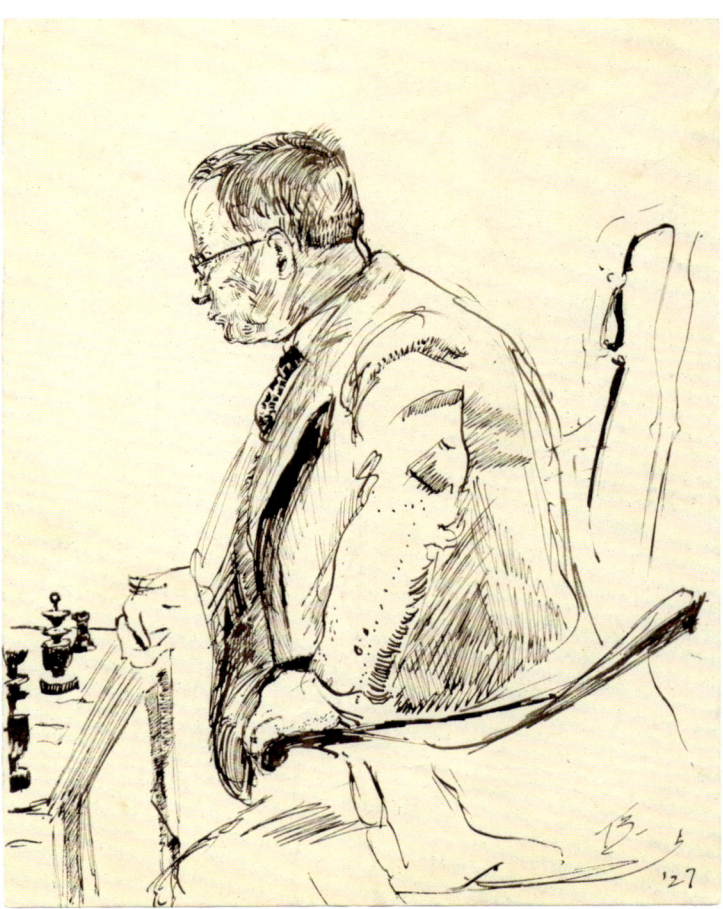

139. *Man Playing Chess*, 1927. Ink on paper, 8 x 6¼ inches. Theresa Bernstein and William Meyerowitz Foundation.

exhibitions. Marcel was an intellectual and a fascinating conversationalist. He would spend a whole day sitting and talking with William. It was too bad that we didn't have a tape recorder in those days. . . . Marcel and William used to play chess together for hours on end."[3]

Aside from these personal connections to Dada, Bernstein's commitment to the proliferation of alternative exhibitions venues, such as the MacDowell Club and the Society of Independent Artists, suggests that she would be sympathetic to Marsden Hartley's American definition of Dada as a method to "reduce the size of the 'A' in art, to meet the size of the rest of the letters in one's speech . . . to deliver art from the clutches of its worshippers and by worshippers I mean the idolaters and commercialists of art. By idolaters I mean those whose reverence for art is beyond their knowledge of it. By the commercialists I mean those who prey upon the ignorance of the unsophisticated, with pictures created by the esthetic habit of, or better to say, through the banality of 'artistic' temperament."[4]

While Bernstein would always remain a painter and create fairly traditional work, her irreverent sense of humor would have allowed her to appreciate the satirical and anti-authoritarian iconoclasm of the Dadaists in America.

Bernstein did not participate in the 1917 Society of Independent Artists exhibition, although she could not have failed to take note of the group; indeed, she loyally participated in their annual shows from 1918 until the organization disbanded in 1944. Historically, the inaugural exhibition has been overshadowed by the controversy of Duchamp's *Fountain*, famously rejected by the purportedly juryless board of directors. Bernstein was most likely aware of the publication of *The Blind Man* (1917), the first issue of which was circulated at the Independents Exhibition and

the second of which defended the *Fountain* against its critics.

The example of *The Blind Man* would become important for Bernstein in 1925, when she collaborated with William Meyerowitz, Stuart Davis, and (most likely) Eben Comins to publish the single issue of *The Paint Rag.*[5] The journal was intended to support the projects of the Gloucester Society of Artists, a group modeled after the Society of Independent Artists. Bernstein was a founding member of the society, which was formed in response to the policy of the local Gallery-on-the-Moors to exhibit only established artists. They

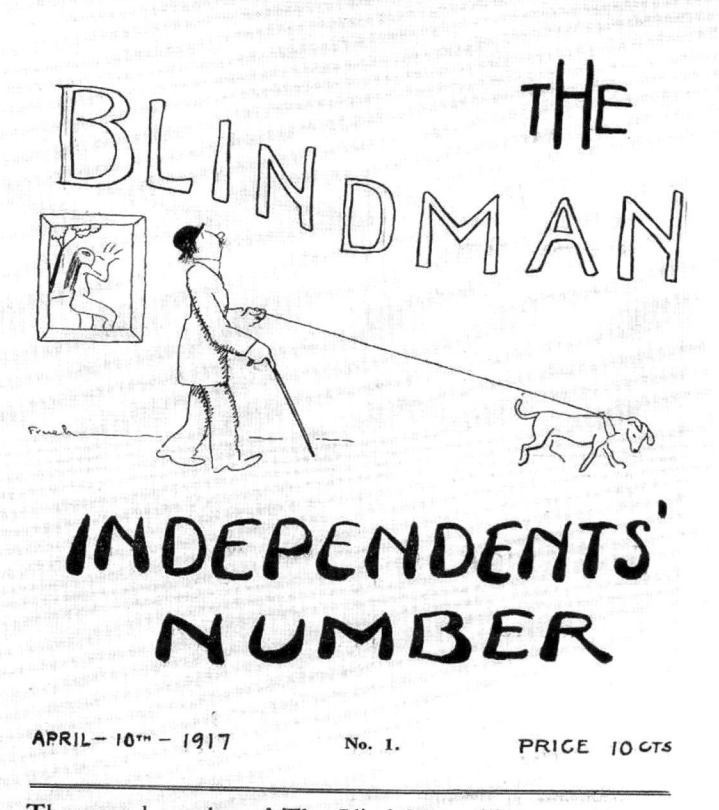

140. *The Blind Man* (periodical), no. 1, April 10, 1917. Private collection.

sponsored nonjuried shows with a membership that included Bernstein, Meyerowitz, Davis, Walter Griffin, Ernest Lawson, Maurice Prendergast, and Nathaniel Dirk, among others.[6] Bernstein later recalled that "our somewhat satirical publication was sold at a masked ball to benefit the society. It cost five cents, and we were only able to pay for one four-page edition."[7] Published on August 5, 1925, the single issue reflects a careful study of the strategies and humor of Dada periodicals in New York. Previously mentioned but unanalyzed in Dada literature, the work demonstrates the influence of the movement on American modernists well into the 1920s.

Like *The Blind Man*, the genesis for *The Paint Rag* was an exhibition; the Gloucester Society of Artists staged a show that echoed the Society of Independent Artists in its mantra, "No Jury–No Prizes."[8] The front page explains the need for such nonjuried shows and decries the academic system of prizes, claiming: "The prize system is absolutely a menace to all exhibitions. Prizes are like kisses—they are given by favor—and as far as it can be discovered, usually the prize winners have a relative on the jury, or are in need of money, or the fellows give it to the artist out of charity—or it is 'his' or 'her' turn, usually being fixed in a mysterious way like horse racing or stock speculation."[9]

The suspicion with which the editorial describes the covert process of selecting prizewinners echoes the language of the Society of Independent Artists and *The Blind Man*. It also reflects Dadaist endeavors to lay bare the commercial processes of art, including such precedents as the People's Art Guild and the Modern Gallery. With connections to Duchamp and Robert Henri, the editors certainly were aware of these sources. In *The Journal* Bernstein recounts a number of episodes in which she and William were jilted by juries and selection committees; as she summarizes, "Titles and awards are really just a bit of sugar coating in relation to life's efforts and successes."[10]

The cover illustration, *An Ideal Jury*, drawn by Davis, recalls the titular blind man, bringing together an assortment of fools who are led by an ancient bearded man. The judges are portrayed as hopelessly incapable of evaluating modern art; instead, they are only able to applaud the mindless repetition of academicism. As Bernstein explained, "Stuart depicted the average art jury as deaf, dumb, and blind, holding their ears and shading their eyes as those who hear no evil, speak no evil, and see no evil."[11]

A second, unsigned essay, "Today and Yesterday," printed on the second page similarly defends the experimental artist. It begins: "In the streets of Ephesus, some two thousand years ago, an itinerant preacher was proclaiming a new gospel which taught that the idols of gold and silver for which Ephesus was famous were not endowed with divine power, but were only a piece of metal made by the artisans of that city and sold for profit."[12] Upon this revelation, the town silversmith (who "had grown rich from the money received by his works") attacked the preacher and led the townspeople in stoning the man. With such strong overtones of Christian persecution, the author extends the scenario to the present day, writing, "If the real artist venture to propose a new method of inspiring beauty, the silversmith still cries from the streetcorner, 'By what right does this pestilential fellow destroy the rule which has brought us so much profit. Tear up his canvases and break his statue into bits.'"

The plight of the struggling American artist, unsupported by a public that preferred to purchase European modernist canvases, was a subject often taken up by artists, critics, and gallerists such as Alfred Stieglitz during the early twentieth century. Few collectors bought the work of emerging

American artists, even fewer paid well; this disparity is the subject of a short script titled, simply, "A Tragedy." In language that closely mirrors the complaints of Stieglitz, the playwright bemoans the reluctance of collectors to support the work of emerging American artists:

Time: Present.

Scene: Private gallery in home of famous collector.

The Actors: Collector; Young Artist

(Young Artist and Collector are seen viewing the collection, many good works, mostly by old fogies.)

Young Artist (after looking about): "Hm! Do you ever buy works of the younger artists?"

Collector: "We-ll-ll, when an artist is brought to my attention by exhibition, invitation to galleries, or newspaper notices, I come to his first one-man show. I find him pretty good (pause), don't misunderstand me, I don't buy him—I watch him! I go to his second exhibition. I find he has improved—again, I don't buy his work. How do I know whether his work is going to live after his death?"

Y.A.: "Don't you depend on your own taste?"

Coll.: "No, I can't. How can I tell—"

Y.A.: "How did you know about the others? What made you believe the others would live?"

Coll.: "Well—hm—you see, all the pictures in my collection are works by N.A.'s or prize winners, and besides, they were recommended to me by the leading Avenue dealers—so you see—with the younger artist, I wait—and then—"

Y.A.: "And then, what?"

Coll.: "I go to his third exhibition—I make up my mind to wait a few years."

Y.A.: "Why don't you encourage the talented young artist? He may be in need, and you—with your vision—could get some of his best work for a small sum—you may be able to wait—but can the artist?"

Coll. (stroking his chin): "I would like to see some more of your work. Can I come to your studio, in a few weeks?"

Y.A.: "With pleasure."

Curtain

EPILOGUE

(Several years elapse)

THEY ARE BOTH WAITING.

Although the artist understands the machinations of the collectors, without a vital alternative, he must continue to play the game according to the rules established by money. The system of private patronage, fueled by dealers and collectors who purchase for prestige, clearly stunts the development of modern art and forces the artist to work without any promise of recognition.

Amid the serious complaints on the inequities of the gallery system, there was also a chatty, humorous quality of *The Paint Rag*. Like its Dada predecessors, *291* (1915–16) and *391* (1917–24), *The Paint Rag* included a society column, although theirs was a parody, penned by "The Lady of the Piazza," offering a selection of observations about Gloucester life and the happenings among the local residents.[13] Bold and droll, the column was yet another arena for institutional critique and anti-academic sentiment. As would befit a woman of her presumed social standing, "The Lady" reviews the exhibition of the Gloucester Society of Artists. While certain artists are praised for works that are "nice and Gloucestery," Stuart Davis and the other editors give themselves scathing reviews that parody the worst criticisms their work had received. For example, "Now take these crazy pictures; those crazy tables, I think his name is Davis. They are atrocious. They are an insult to art, and I ought to know, I studied in art school three months, and I have gotten a diploma." She continues, "I don't see why Theresa Bernstein sent that funny picture of people dancing on the deck of a ship to another exhibition. It ought to have been in the crazy show."

The humorous quality throughout *The Paint Rag* extends to its small asides, not unlike the marginalia found in Robert Coady's Dadaist publication *The Soil* (1916–17). In one instance, a personal notice is printed asking, "Rose Madder— All is forgotten. Write at once," and is signed "Emerald Green." Several limericks and silly poems are published, including:

A Swedish Boy's Essay on a Frog

What a wonderful bird the frog are

When he stand, he sit almost

When he walk, he fly almost

He ain't got no sense hardly

He ain't got no tail hardly neither

And when he sit,

He sit on what he aint [*sic*] got almost.[14]

Written in a vernacular tongue, the poem depends upon its poor grammar and syntax to maintain a semblance of poetic structure; furthermore the subject is mundane, and although the lines pretend to some profundity, the result is ultimately little more than a children's rhyme.

Two other short poems addressed the local art scene of Gloucester, especially its reputation for landscape painting.

Because it is an artist's summer retreat, a number of experimental artists found themselves here alongside traditional painters. The local community often vacillated between sympathetic support and bemused skepticism, as is playfully communicated in "A Gloucester Limerick":

There was an old lady in Gloucester,

Who asked what a picture would cost her.

When they told her the news,

She let out some mews,

And said, "Oh, you naughty imposter."[15]

The "Formula for Landscapes" was structured so as to recall the children's song "Sing a Song of Sixpence," underscoring its condemnation of academic landscape painting with a juvenile quality. It reads:

Sing of song of sunlight,

Palette full of blue,

Add a dash of yellow,

That's the way to do.

Smear around the edges,

With a greenish hue.

They can do it that way,

Surely, so can you.[16]

This singsong was followed by a final editorial that criticized "one of the most over-worked words of the King's English language or Slang's American tongue": atmosphere. Explaining the ineffable quality of this word, "used for everything–painting, writing, playing, acting, walking, dancing, chatting, living," the author demonstrates how both the rural farmhouse and urban alleyway can be meaninglessly grouped as atmospheric.[17]

None of the individual contributions are signed, suggesting that the editors viewed the publication as a completely collaborative effort. Not unlike the playful pseudonyms used by Man Ray in his *Ridgefield Gazook*, page 2 begins with a masthead of invented figures. The staff is composed of an editor-in-chief, "B. B. McPhooff," with assistant editor "L. U. Mullenpop." The art director was "A. N. Giffles" and the business manager, "H. K. Backbone." The officers of the newspaper were merely the components of an office, including "Office Boys, Stenographers, Waste-Baskets, Desks, Telephone, Etc." In her journal, Bernstein reveals that Davis served as the art director and that Meyerowitz was the infamous "B. B. McPhooff."[18] Does this imply that she acted as Meyerowitz's assistant, as "L. U. Mullenpop?"

The Paint Rag featured advertising among its four pages; undoubtedly used to support the publication, it brings together a wide range of artistic and commercial enterprises. Those advertisements purchased for Cape Pond Ice Co.'s "pure ice" were positioned alongside more traditional notices for art supplies and frames. Although typographically uniform, many of the ads employ the hyperbolic language that was becoming synonymous with modern marketing. "1000 Satisfied Customers Dine Each Day at Gorman's Restaurant," one reads. Another entices, "If you want to be beautiful go to Laura Agnes Walker." Even Davis himself uses such practices in advertising his services as an instructor, promising that the "study of Ultra-Modern Painting Method is likely to increase the power of your work. Private instruction by Stuart Davis."

Few copies exist of *The Paint Rag*; its circulation outside Gloucester is unknown. Yet it provides an important example of the continuing influence of Dada into the 1920s, especially the vernacular aspects of the movement and their effect on artists typically excluded from the range of Dadaism. While Davis only briefly experimented with Dadaist collage techniques, and the other editors never attempted a Dadaist aesthetic, the prevalence of skepticism and the irreverence toward the institution were certainly inspired by the activities of Dadaists in the 1910s. These aspects of the movement would continue to impact Bernstein, Meyerowitz and other artists throughout the following decade, in spirit if not directly in style.

NOTES

1. Leah Dickerman's 2005 catalogue, Dada (Washington DC: D.A.P.), places New York among the chief city centers for Dada; however, few Americanists have devoted serious attention to this period as influential to American modernism. I addressed this lack in my PhD dissertation, "Reframing the Narrative of Dada in New York, 1910–1926" (CUNY Graduate Center, 2012).

2. Amelia Jones, *Irrational Modernism: A Neurasthenic History of New York Dada* (Cambridge MA: MIT Press, 2004), p. 36.

3. Bernstein, *William Meyerowitz*, p. 48.

4. Marsden Hartley, "The Importance of Being Dada," in *Adventures in the Arts: Informal Chapters on Painters, Vaudeville, and Poets* (New York: Boni and Liveright, 1921), pp. 247–54.

5. Mentioned in Mark Rutkoski and Earl Davis's chronology in Ani Boyakian and Mark Rutkoski, eds., *Stuart Davis: A Catalogue Raisonné* (New Haven CT: Yale University Press, 2007), p. 130. Only Davis, Bernstein, and Meyerowitz are named as editors. However, Eben Comins not only appears in an advertisement, alongside the aforementioned artists, but he is also lampooned with them in the review, "The Lady of the Piazza." Given that four pseudonyms are listed in the masthead, it is likely that he was involved in the production of this issue.

6. Bernstein, *The Journal*, p. 84.

7. Bernstein, *The Journal*, p. 84.

8. Editorial in *The Paint Rag*, August 5, 1925, n.p.

9. Editorial in *The Paint Rag*, August 5, 1925, n.p.

10. Bernstein, *The Journal*, p. 44.

11. Bernstein, *The Journal*, pp. 84–85.

12. "Today and Yesterday," *The Paint Rag*, August 5, 1925, n.p.

13. "The Lady of the Piazza," *The Paint Rag*, August 5, 1925, n.p.

14. "A Swedish Boy's Essay on a Frog," *The Paint Rag*, August 5, 1925, n.p.

15. "A Gloucester Limerick," *The Paint Rag*, August 5, 1925, n.p.

16. "Formula for Landscapes," *The Paint Rag*, August 5, 1925, n.p.

17. "An Over-Worked Word," *The Paint Rag*, August 5, 1925, n.p.

18. Bernstein, *The Journal*, pp. 84–85.

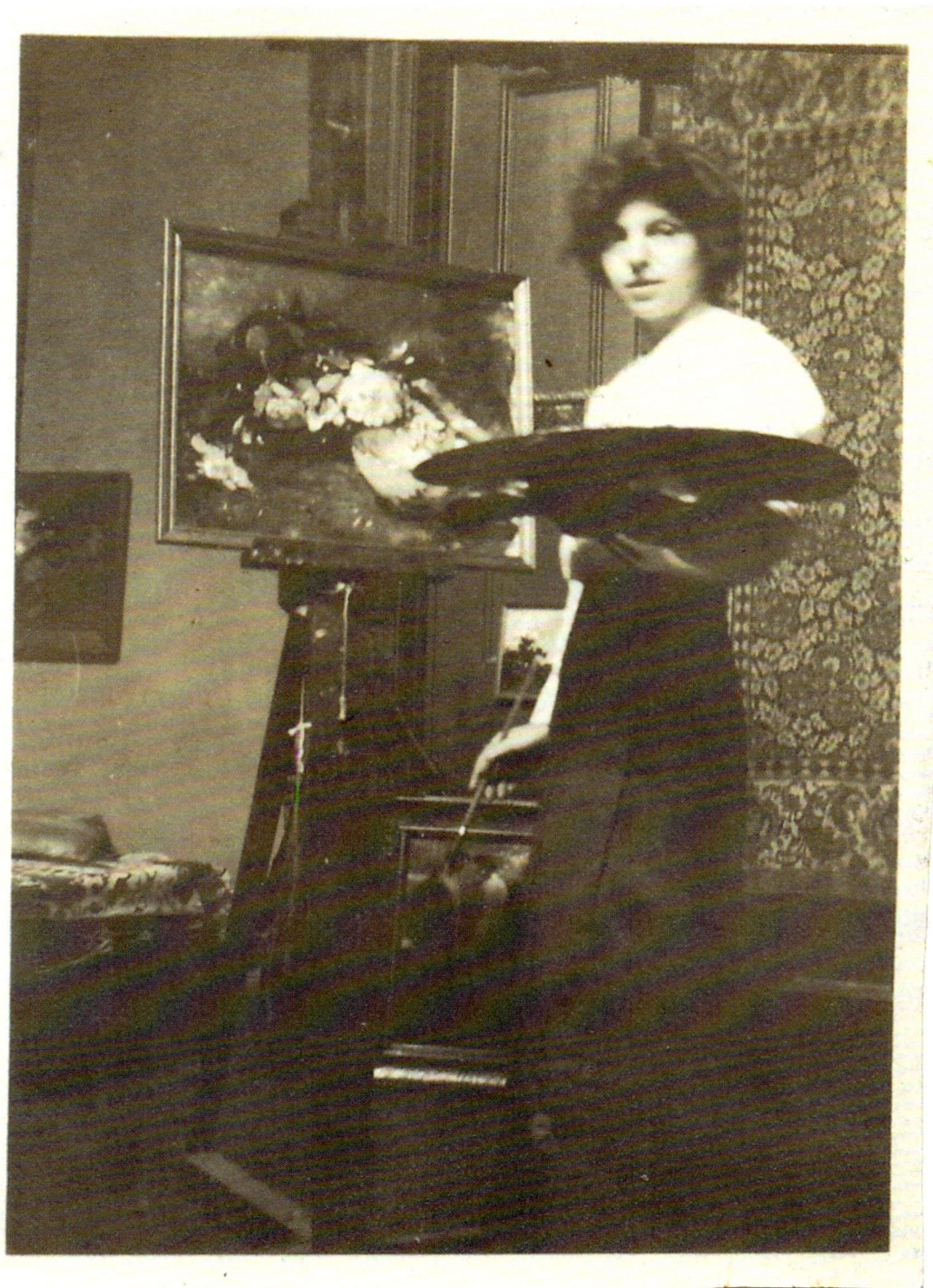

141. Theresa Bernstein at her easel, January 1914.

SIX

Theresa Bernstein's World in Still Life

Patricia M. Burnham

*F*rom girlhood to within two years of the end of her very long life, Theresa Bernstein created art. Almost all her copious output depicted recognizable subjects such as portraits and typical moments from contemporary life, beach scenes, or events from the world of music or both World Wars. And then there were the scapes: of land (only a few), of community, and of town.

Still lifes Bernstein particularly favored, in apparent contrast with the people and events she painted with such zest. A contrast might be supposed between the remarkable activity of her brushstrokes and her calm representation of inanimate objects (such as plants, flowers, fruit, and ornaments). But such was not the case. Many of her still lifes do not stand very still, especially her flower pieces in which blossoms dominate the picture. Some shared space with other objects, and often she incorporated flowers and/or fruit into larger settings. Another category, clearly of signal importance to her, was a term she coined, "Symbolic Documentaries." They were profoundly referential, philosophical—and rather subdued. Bernstein's still lifes may have been comparatively few in number, but they seem to have played a contrapuntal role in her artistic expression. She painted them throughout her life and continued to do so until she could paint no more.

She began her artistic studies at the Philadelphia School of Design for Women (1907–11), which provided a traditional curriculum tempered by the progressive representational styles of teachers like Henry B. Snell, Elliott Daingerfield, and Daniel Garber. Still lifes were a routine assignment. Bernstein and fellow student Elizabeth Schwartz "worked on a still life of a fish a la William Chase," she later enthused at length in one of her autobiographical publications, *The Journal*. Unlike some of her classmates who protested the smell of the fish, she and her friend were more interested in the aesthetic aspects of the assignment: "We said, 'Look at the beautiful silver coloring and scales.'" On another occasion, she "delighted in doing feathery wild flowers of the glow of brass. . . . A beautiful silver bowl with a hammered out nude figure was one of my earliest objects for still lifes."[1]

Although William Merritt Chase (1849–1916) did not teach at the school, it appears that his style of still life was encouraged there. Indeed, he boasted about his fish pieces in a 1908 essay published by *The Delineator*.[2] Chase, in teaching,

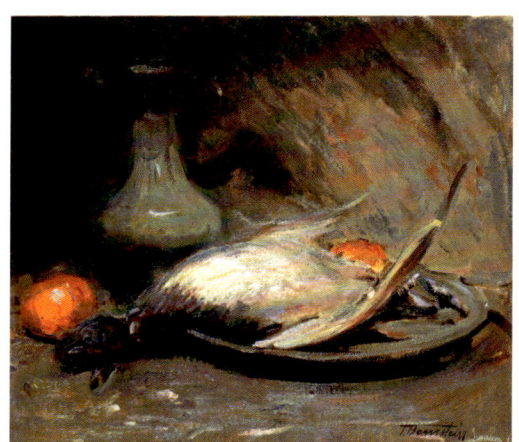

142. *Still Life after Harnett*, 1911. Oil on canvas, 17 x 19 inches. Private collection.

recommended still lifes as a necessary exercise, although he himself is best known for his quasi-impressionist Long Island seascapes, urban cityscapes, and "aesthetic" portraits. He taught for the longest stretch at the Art Students League in New York (1878–96, 1907–12), where Bernstein studied with him after moving with her parents to New York in 1911.[3]

Still Life after Harnett, ca. 1911, is one of her earlier still lifes. Although it bears no date itself, if the date that has accompanied it, 1911, is accurate, she might have painted the canvas late in her last year at art school in Philadelphia. The title is somewhat odd because William Michael Harnett specialized in *trompe l'oeil* realism, the opposite of Chase's style. Yet *Still Life after Harnett* does imitate Chase (for example, Chase's *An English Cod*, 1904, Corcoran Gallery of Art), although with a looser touch and lighter palette. Two years later, Bernstein painted *Still Life after Whistler*, ca. 1913, reaching back to James McNeill Whistler (1834–1903), whose reputation in the United States remained high.

Bernstein in fact mentions Whistler several times in *The Journal*, admiring his *Nocturne in Blue and Gold:*

Old Battersea Bridge (ca. 1872–73) and his literary accomplishments.[4] In contrast to the robust *Still Life after Harnett*, Bernstein's *Still Life after Whistler* offers an evocative study in tonality.

When Bernstein painted *Self-Portrait*, 1914, she

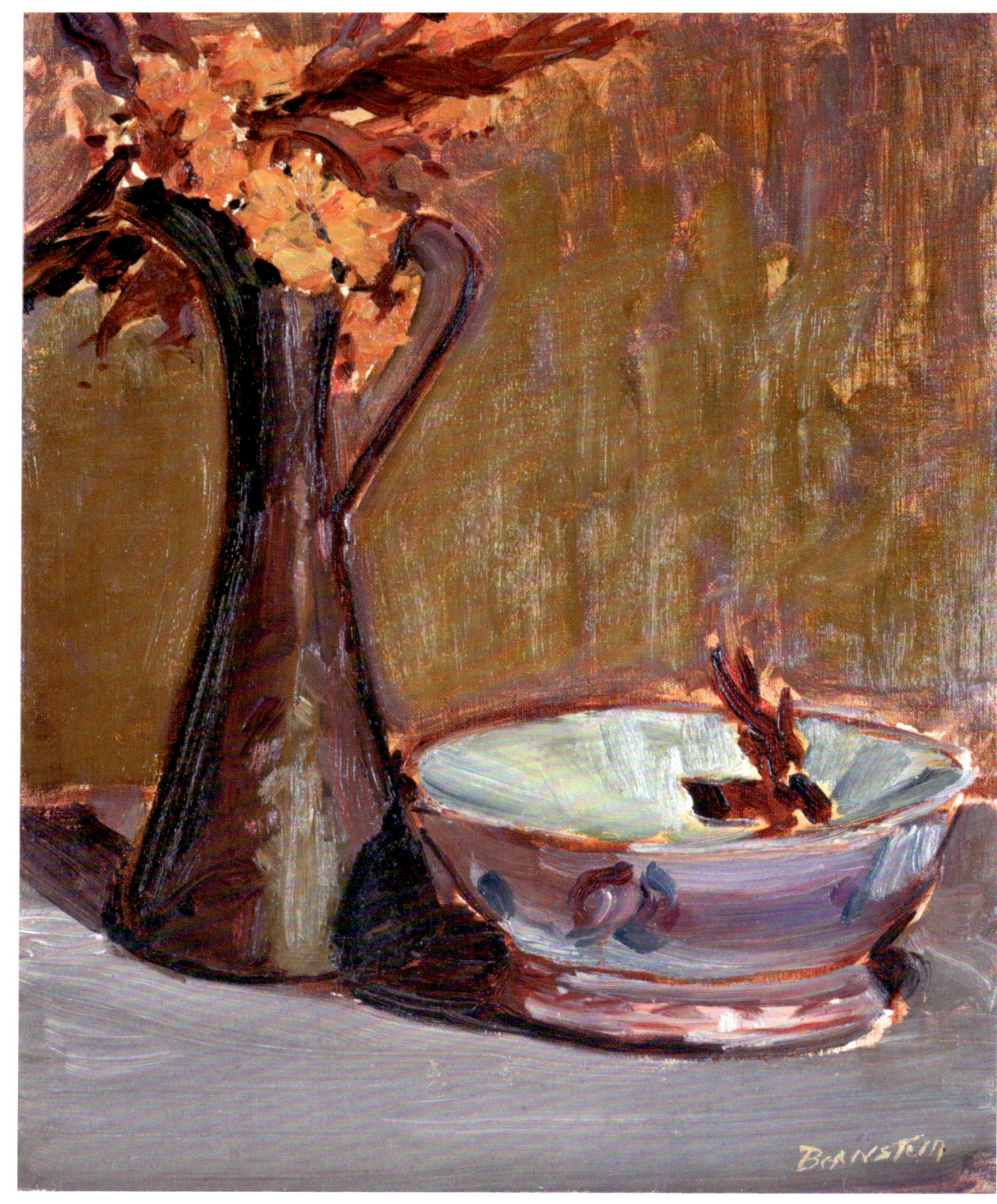

143. *Still Life after Whistler*, ca. 1913. Oil on canvas, 20 x 18 inches. The Graduate Center, CUNY. Gift of Girard Jackson.

introduced aspects of still life into the composition. She deftly incorporated bright yellow flowers and multicolor leaves that radiate from behind her head. The lively reds, green, and browns stand in for her sense of who she was at that particular moment. Indeed, Bernstein's expert use of the flower motif helped her characterize herself as young, vital, bold, and energetic. Bernstein frequently painted herself but more often her husband, artist William Meyerowitz, after their marriage in 1919. She usually presented herself as a demure, quiet woman who wore simple, elegant clothing and expensive pearls (perhaps

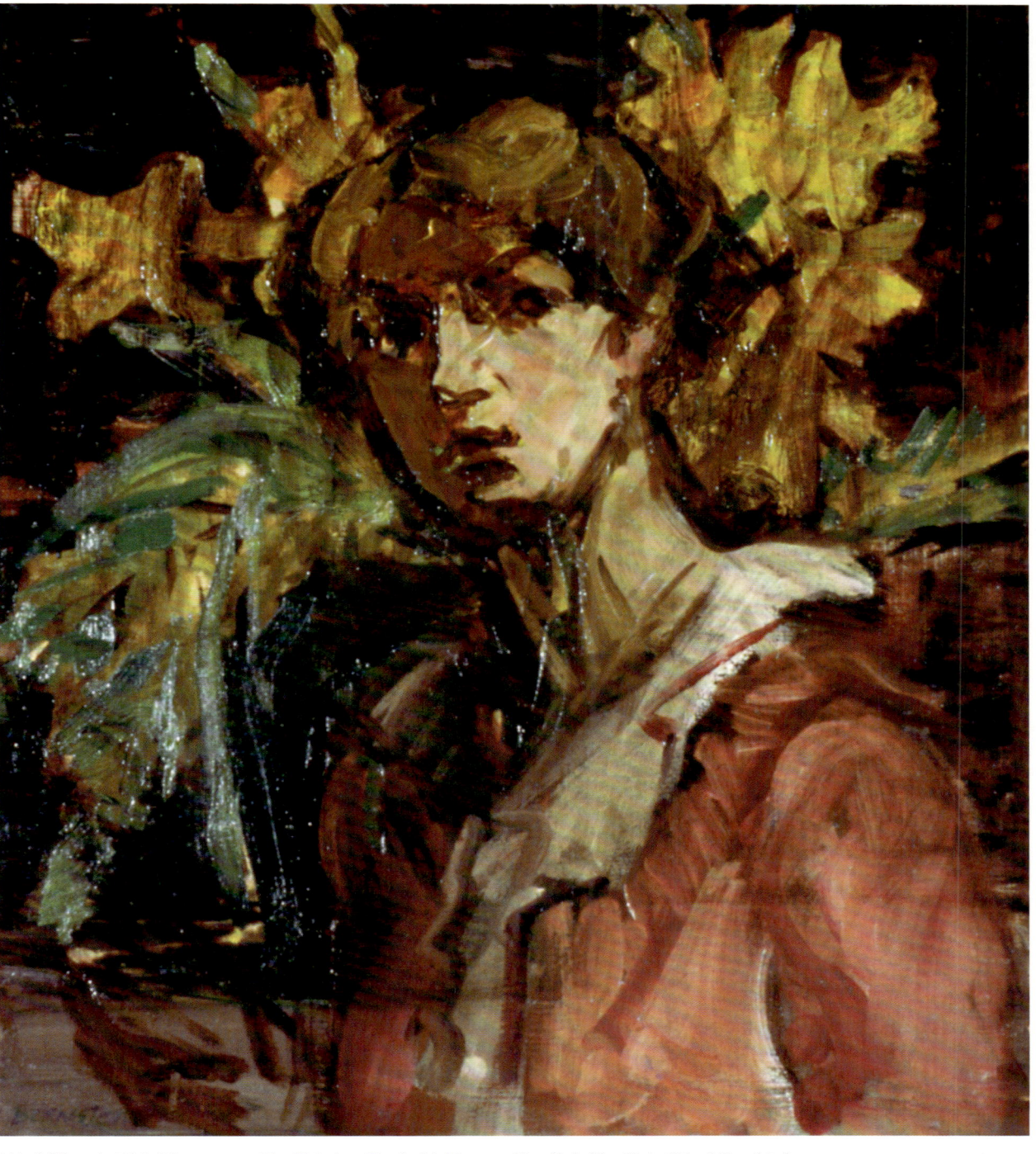

144. *Self-Portrait*, 1914. Oil on canvas, 25 x 22 inches. The Jewish Museum, New York, New York. Gift of Girard Jackson.

a reflection of her bourgeois upbringing in Philadelphia). Later, she showed herself as a working artist, sporting practical outfits and a sunhat. So did her husband, although he sometimes portrayed her as a serious woman wearing fine but unobtrusive clothes—and the pearls. The 1914 *Self-Portrait*, however, is not only dramatic but also the most original of her self-portraits, and is indeed one of her best early paintings.

Gloucester Sunset (Tulips), 1919, is an example of one of Bernstein's outstanding still lifes. Although the tulips dominate the space, they also combine with a crumpled tablecloth and, intriguingly, in the upper part of the canvas, a picture of a Gloucester sunset—her copy of a recent etching by her husband. By this time, the couple liked Gloucester so much that they decided to spend their summers there for the rest of their lives. The painting and its title can be thought of as a way of not only honoring her husband's work but also acknowledging their attachment to Gloucester. There she discovered an alternate to her beloved New York world that would generate a kind of imaginative polarity or dialectic in her life.[5] *Gloucester Sunset* lacks the formality that often defines still lifes. These tulips are abundant, huge, and scattered (although surprisingly triangulated), partly obscuring Meyerowitz's etching. What appears to be a tablecloth carelessly positioned on the table also makes a subtle reference to Cézanne's still lifes. The colors range from bright, especially the reds, to small touches of pastel. Above all, the painting bustles with movement. The generous dimensions command attention; to be sure, Bernstein had painted "big" from early on, but her earlier still lifes had been smaller. It is as if *Gloucester Sunset* was meant to achieve seriousness and monumentality not only by facture and design but by its expanded size.

Only five years later, *Paul Revere Bowl and Silver Moon*, 1924, offers a different sensibility. The fruit, the bowl, the pitcher, and the wildflowers seem to be equal in importance. Spatial context is not emphasized; brush marks are visible but undramatic. The painting somewhat resembles some of the quieter work done by her husband. Throughout their lives, they borrowed from each other, although never giving up their own individuality. Paul Revere bowls had shown up often in her still lifes. This one, however, is a later glass copy rather than the traditional and highly esteemed silver fashioned by the famed

145. *Gloucester Sunset (Tulips)*, 1919. Oil on canvas, 40 x 30 inches. Private collection.

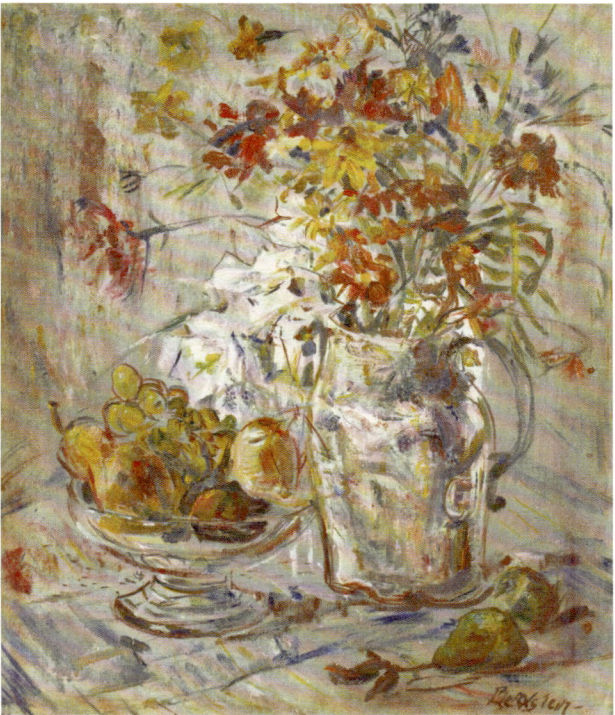

146. *Paul Revere Bowl and Silver Moon*, 1924.
Oil on canvas, 24¼ x 20¼ inches. Martin and Edith Stein Collection.

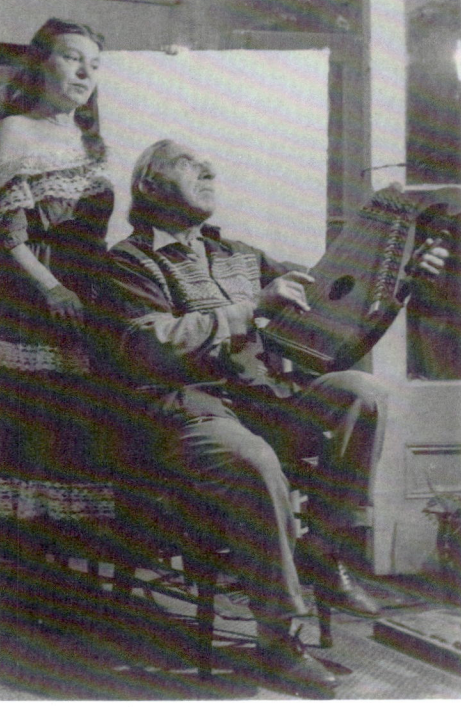

148. Theresa Bernstein and William Meyerowitz with his zither.

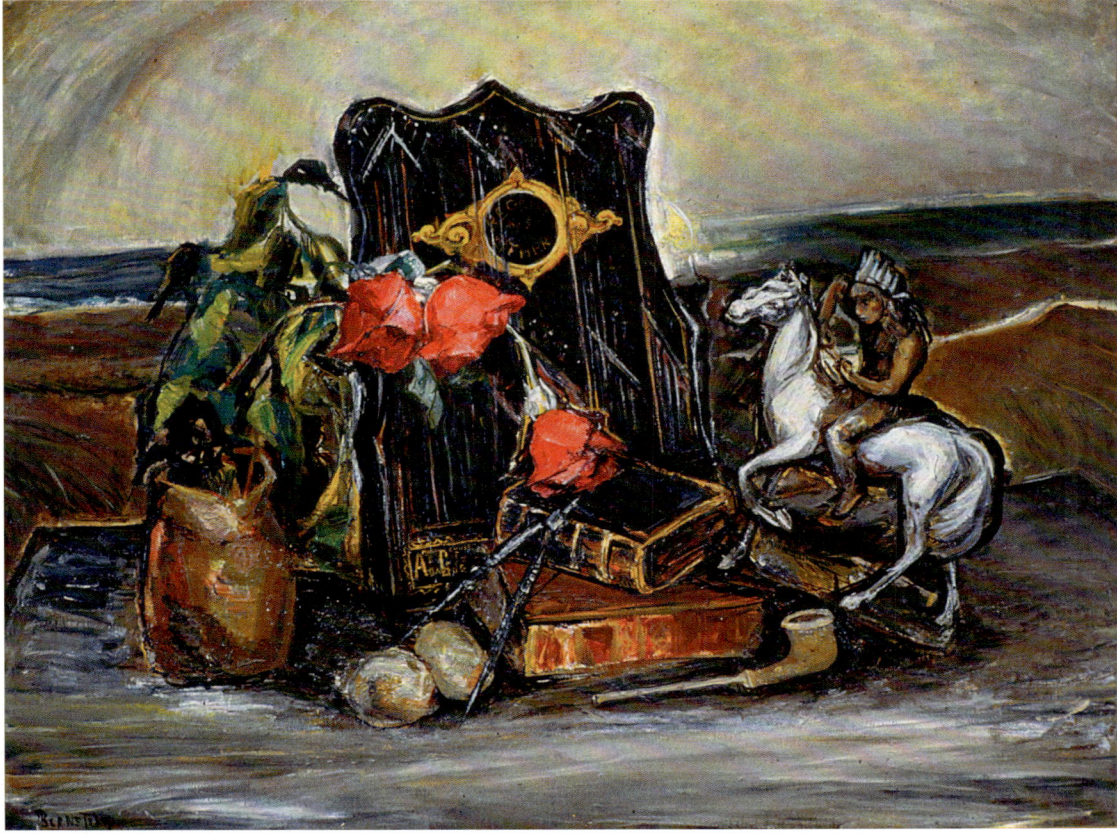

147. *Music on the Shore*, 1919–22. Oil on canvas, 27 x 35 inches. Private collection.

eighteenth-century Boston silversmith. The reference to Revere may be meant to affirm her claim to American identity, since Revere had come to symbolize patriotism.

In the meantime, Bernstein had produced her first Symbolic Documentary–*Music on the Shore*, 1919–22–with a tight collection of objects that she considered meaningful. She painted the objects in careful detail (her husband's zither, three American Beauty roses, a figurine of a Native American on horseback, books by Francis Parkman, the venerable historian of the Western movement, a compass, a peace pipe, and two potatoes), but what meaning did they portend?[6] As with her *Paul Revere Bowl and Silver Moon*, she evokes American history beyond conventional narrative or genre by offering specific "documents" of American life. Meyerowitz's zither is the largest object, a musical instrument placed on the shore. His father, Gershon, who was a cantor, taught his son the songs he sang at the synagogue. William's voice was such "a fine baritone" that he earned money as a member of the chorus at the Metropolitan Opera during the era of Enrico Caruso, who sang *La Juive* and other roles.[7] Later, William sang at the soirees that the couple often held in their living room, either accompanying himself on the zither or accompanied by a friend on the piano. The symbolic attraction of the zither for Meyerowitz might have been that the instrument appeared in the book of Daniel.[8]

Her choice of objects for this painting also documents her lifelong devotion to reading American history and her patriotism, expressed in her written commentary, private conversations, and many paintings. The objects here are "American" but also personal–flowers, a positive attitude toward the American Indian, a great regard for Parkman, and admiration for the high level of agriculture in the United States. The play between historical and individual perspectives increases the depth of meaning–a practice that would continue in further Symbolic Documentaries.

Although Bernstein and Meyerowitz were not considered avant-garde, they knew and consorted with such modernists as Marcel Duchamp, with whom Meyerowitz played chess; Stuart Davis, their close friend and Gloucester neighbor; and Theodore Stamos, the abstract painter, whom they knew from summers on Cape Ann.[5] Bernstein was certainly aware of such movements as symbolism, surrealism, abstract expressionism, and the other flavors of modernism, but she limited herself to borrowing bits and pieces of what she observed, making sure that they complied with the main direction she wished to follow in her art.[10] The result was the distinctive state of mind and pattern of thought evident in the Symbolic Documentaries, especially *Music on the Shore*.

The 1930s were difficult for the entire nation, no less for artists like Bernstein and Meyerowitz. One still life in particular may capture something of the complexities of the time: *Marblehead*, 1932. Marblehead had been one of the grandest harbor areas in Massachusetts, boasting great regattas

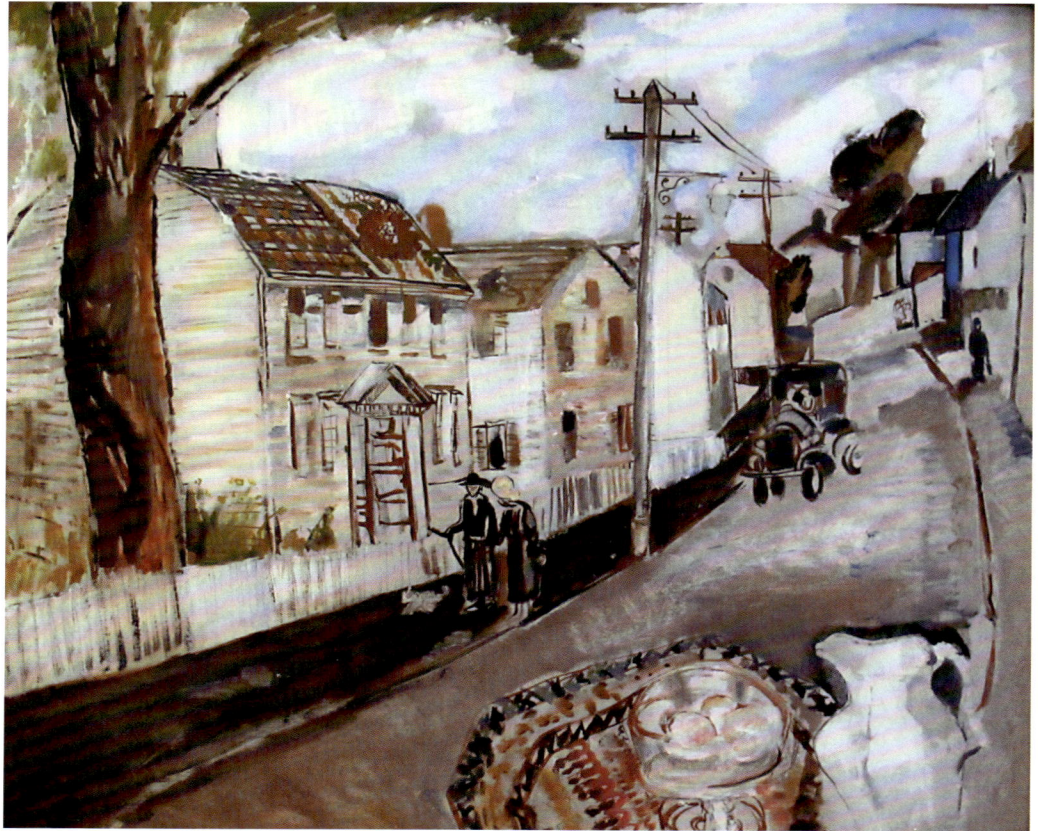

149. *Marblehead*, 1932. Oil on canvas, 25 x 30 inches. Private collection.

and a stock of spectators, sailboats, and yachts. That aspect of the place had drawn Bernstein's eye, but here she draws the viewer into the old town, leaving behind maritime panache. Her curved road draws the eye from the lower left-hand corner along a white picket fence and dark ribbon of sidewalk diagonally up and across the canvas. The curve is anchored by a looming tree in a yard behind the fence and is interrupted by the figures of two women wearing hats, who stand with a small dog in front of a house that looks like "olde towne" fallen on hard times, its door framed by a Palladian pediment and slightly skewed columns, while up the street stands a ramshackle jalopy and modern electric poles gawking against the sky.

This particular glimpse of Marblehead (which was first settled in 1629) mingles an elegiac air of decline with the marks of modernity in the awkward poles and the vehicle (although that, too, looks run-down). The limited palette is applied thinly. In earlier years, Bernstein's ordinary practice had been to plumb the rich, dark depths of Ashcan colors, or their opposite—light, sassy hues. Here, however, she economized with a subdued palette, using little more than browns, grays, beige, and touches of black.

Yet before the eye absorbs the sweep from the lower left to the far background, a palpable still life confronts us at the lower right: a table covered by a figured cloth and set in the street holds a white pitcher and a Victorian glass fruit-stand with three lemons. The presence of the lemonade stand surprises. Though staying within the monochromatic palette, the objects seem suspended as the eye moves without pause from their more intimate domestic space to the space at once exterior and public delineated by the peopled sidewalks and the houses. Bernstein teases the viewer to read the still life as located in the street rather than on a windowsill through which a viewer might peer out. Playing with ambiguity, she introduces symbolic reference: the survival of Victorian manners (Sandwich pressed-glass compote, white China pitcher) along with the signs of decadence that mingle with innovation on this old street in this old town.

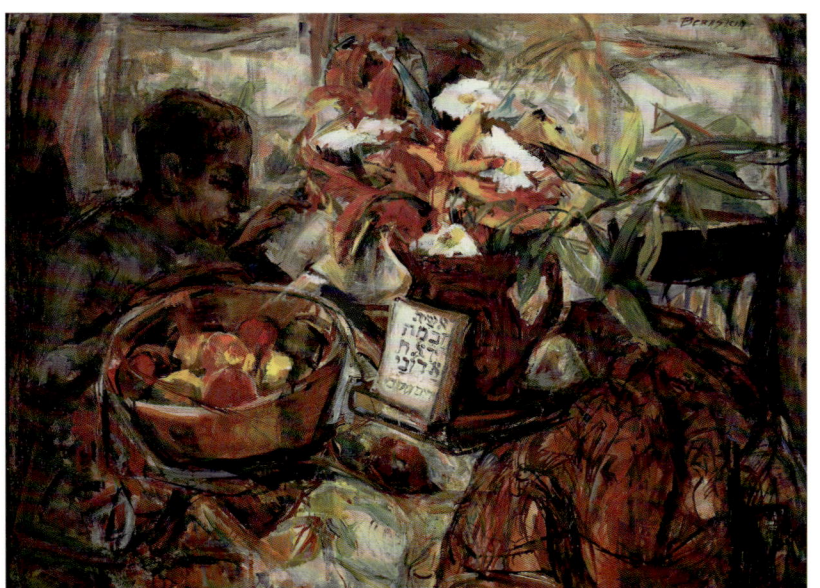

150. *The Student*, 1945. Oil on canvas, 30 x 40 inches. Martin and Edith Stein Collection.

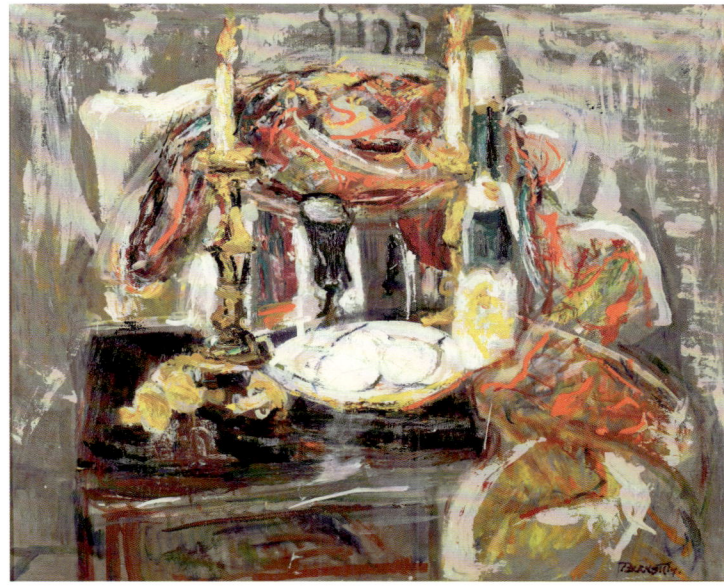

151. *The Seder*, 1940. Oil on canvas, 23 x 29 inches. Martin and Edith Stein Collection.

Are those women in (old-fashioned?) hats potential customers for lemonade? *Marblehead* may not be exactly a Symbolic Documentary, but it prompts reflection, measured in its control of color, and original in its manipulation of space and things that make the old town street a significant place.

Among Bernstein's significant compositions in the 1940s were her Symbolic Documentaries, several of which treat Jewish themes. *The Student*, 1945, portrays a serious, scholarly young person immersed in books written in Hebrew, surrounded by flowers and fruit. In fact, the flowers, fruit, and other objects are placed in the foreground, almost hiding the student. Their role is to emphasize the importance of solitude and Bernstein's own personal passion for learning. (After all, she who loved books so much painted a remarkable work, *The Readers*, as early as 1914, although in a more secular context; see fig. 4.) The gender of the student is not clear, but the art historian Samantha Baskind has surmised that the student is a woman, based on the translation of the Hebrew words on the cover of the book pictured–"A wise woman knows God."[11]

The Seder, 1940, pays homage to the meal that inaugurates the feast of Passover, commemorating the exodus of the Jews from ancient Egypt. Bernstein's artistic temperament was such that she did not make a complete inventory of all the sacred vessels and ritual foods of Passover, each redolent with meaning– but what she does include is sufficient and significant. The two brightly lit candles (Observance and Remembrance) announce the beginning of the ceremonies. The cup of wine between the candles honors the prophet Elijah as a symbolic remembrance; the door is then opened so that Elijah can come in and join the Seder. Boiled eggs sitting on a plate centered on the Seder table

are said to have multiple meanings, one of which is mourning because of the destruction of the Temple.[12] Bernstein does not itemize the bitter herbs, but perhaps the yellow-colored food at the left is "charoset," the combination of fruits and nuts meant to recall the clay with which the Israelites made adobe bricks when they were slaves in Egypt, as recounted in the *Haggadah*. (The subtitle of a reproduction of her painting *The Seder*, published in her book *Israeli Journal*, is "Celebrating the feast of freedom.")[13] The words of blessing (kiddush) are hinted at in the very top of the canvas. There is an uncompleted human form at the right who is probably about to serve food. In some ways, *The Seder* is one of her more "modern" paintings. The assertive brushwork and large, freestanding strokes express emotion, energy, and spontaneity that speak of joyous celebration, but it is the symbolic "documents" that are the sober reminder of a long and harrowing history.

Her painting *The Menorah* of 1948 celebrates the birth of the state of Israel that year–much longed-for by Bernstein and Meyerowitz, who were both early and passionate Zionists. The new state adopted the menorah as its primary emblem.[14] It is the "document" that Bernstein decided upon for her painting, since

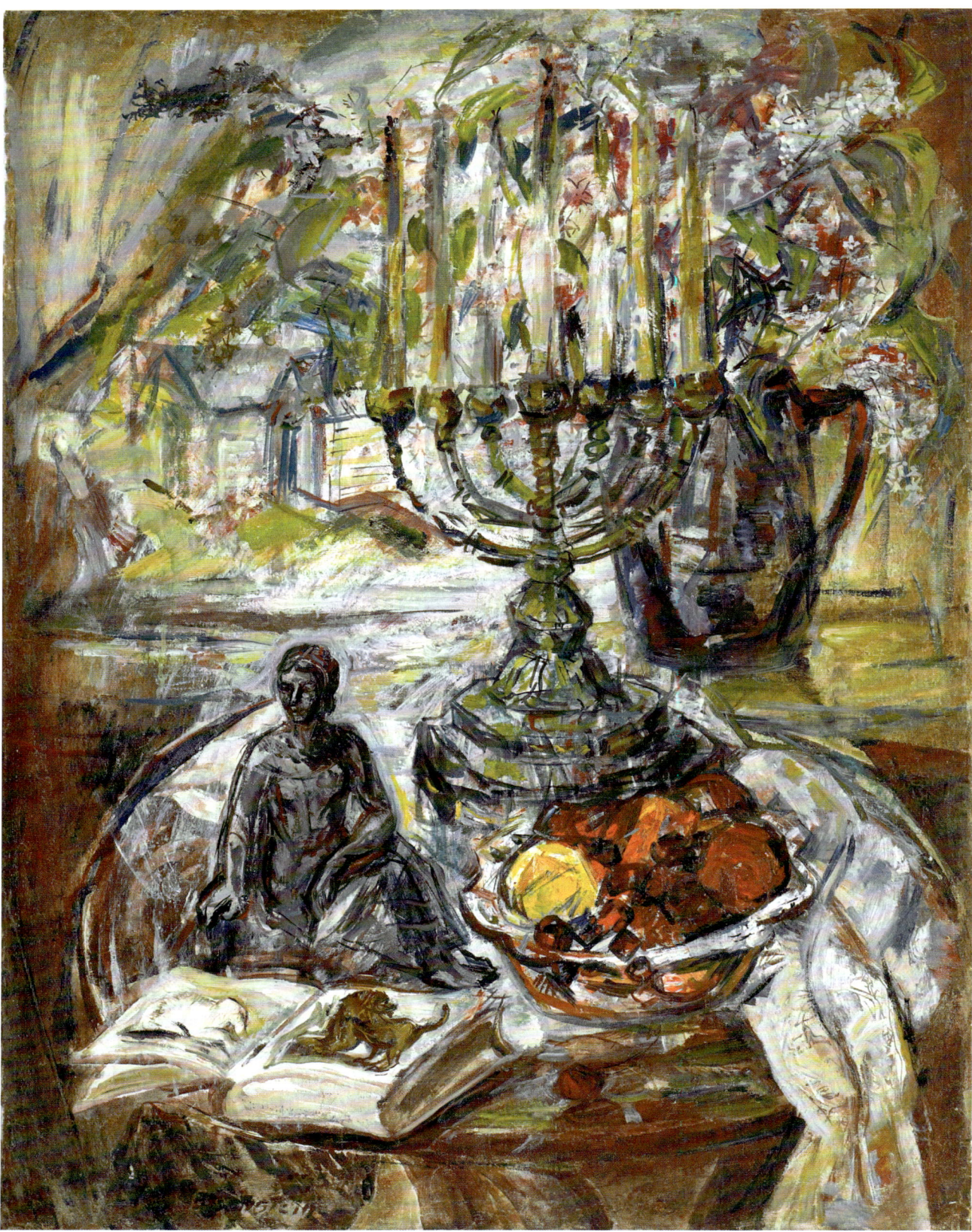

152. *The Menorah*, 1948. Oil on canvas, 35¼ x 27 inches. Martin and Edith Stein Collection.

Jewish tradition linked the seven-branched candelabrum to the time of Moses and to the later temples in Jerusalem. In the painting, at the lower left sits a small statue of a woman pointing at an open book with an image of a lion at the right, and perhaps a lamb or a kid on the left. Bernstein might have been thinking of the utopian vision of peace (Isaiah 11:6) that a wolf would be "a guest of the lamb. . . . The calf and the young lion shall browse together." A passage in Genesis 49:9–10 offers a different description of a lion, perhaps having more similarity with Bernstein's lion: "Judah, like a lion's whelp . . . couches like a lion recumbent, the King of beasts. . . . The scepter shall never depart from Judah, or the mace from between his legs." The Jerusalem municipal flag (adopted in 1949) features the city's coat of arms, a shield blazoned with a lion rampant, flanked by olive branches–thereby reconciling war and peace. The painting's background looks out on a rustic backyard (which may indicate Gloucester as its place of production). The bowl of fruit in the foreground may refer to the fruitfulness of the new state. A few years later, Bernstein and Meyerowitz made the first of thirteen visits to Israel and painted the lively variety that they saw: synagogues (one that was very old), weddings, street scenes, a kibbutz, an orange grove, and much more. As a complement to the documentary enthusiasm of these works, the Symbolic Documentary, *The Menorah*, conveys with extraordinary depth and grandeur Bernstein's admiration and pride in the establishment of the new state.

Bernstein again in the 1960s experimented with Symbolic Documentaries, two of which reflect life in New England (past and present). *Boston Tea*, ca. 1960, presents an aspect of New England social life but also conjures up a historical era. Surprisingly, a large bouquet of beautiful, varied, bright flowers overwhelming their pitcher takes center stage in the painting. Three Bostonian women in long dresses have come together to sip their tea as they converse. Bernstein shows them seated in an enormous cup that puckishly

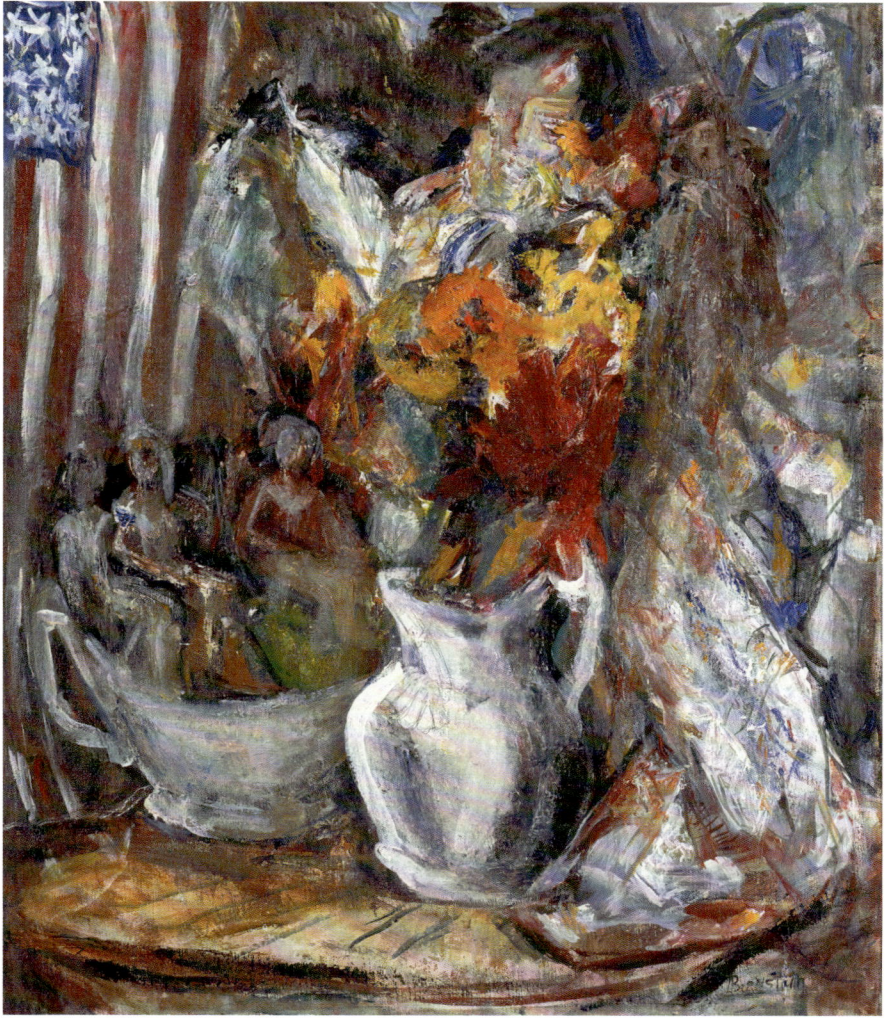

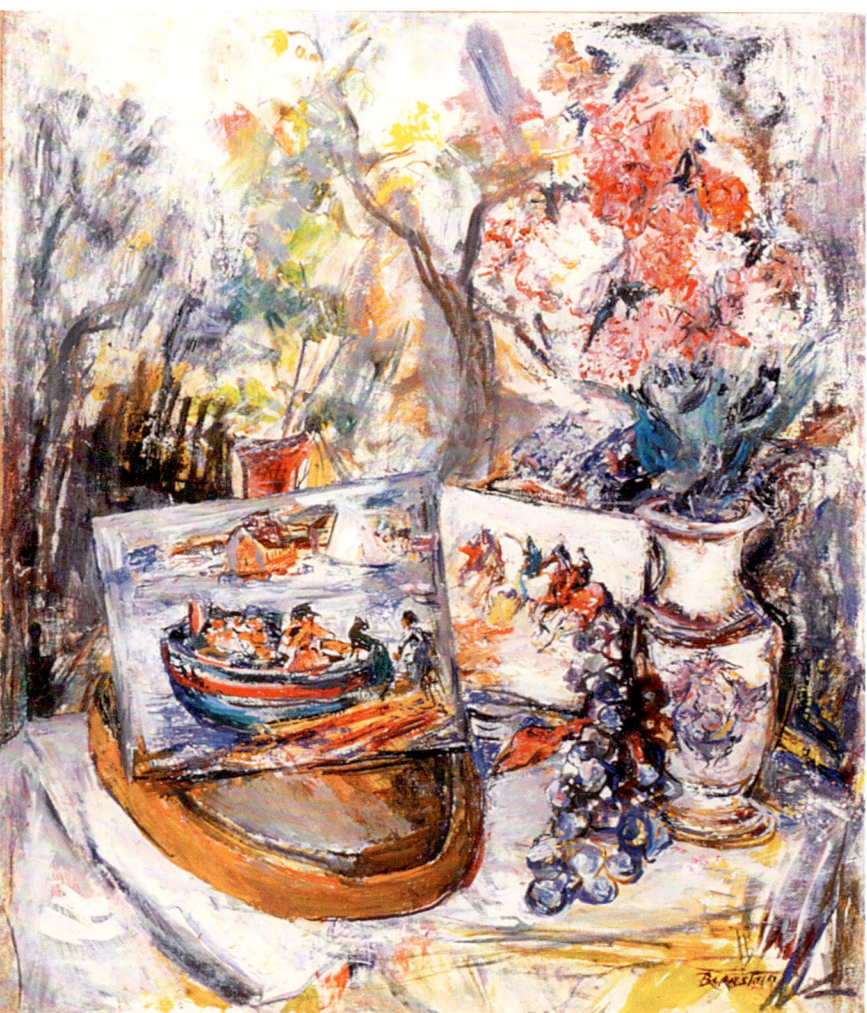

153. *Boston Tea*, ca. 1960. Oil on canvas, 30 x 25 inches. Private collection.

154. *Sailor's Honeysuckle Still*, ca. 1960. Oil on canvas, 30 x 25 inches. Private collection.

references the importance of tea to social life. She ends up reminding us of the earlier role of tea in our national history. In *New England Ladies*, painted in 1925, Bernstein depicted a large group of Bostonian women talking animatedly while sipping tea and elderberry wine (see fig. 111). These are portraits of real people, who had a Gloucester connection and whom she had come to know. That earlier experience may have prompted her to consider a playful but serious painting about tea and Boston, resulting in this complex Symbolic Documentary.

Behind the three women is a large American flag that reaches from the top of the canvas almost to the bottom. Rapidly sketched in above the flowers is a wraithlike man wrapped in an American flag, looking intently to his right; at the upper right of the flowers is a ghostlike figure who appears to be wearing a tricolor hat with bayonets behind him, alluding to the American Revolution. The standard drapery at the right reiterates the red, white, and blue colors of the nation's flag. The original tea party, of course, was the Sons of Liberty's

Boston Tea Party of 1773. Her way of conflating the two senses of "tea party" is witty but also fiercely intelligent.

Sailor's Honeysuckle Still, ca. 1960, reflects a different kind of subject matter of interest to Gloucesterites—the water, the fishermen, the sailors. It is about sailors and their lore, subjects that Bernstein employed to honor her husband's work. Once again, she inserts a copy of one of his horse paintings, and next to it, one of his fisherman paintings, showing a person who is perhaps just coming in with his catch.[15] Her title has to do with a local saying—the sailors knew they were near shore when they could smell the honeysuckle. Color, especially blues and purples, is used with abandon—the grapes, the design on the vase containing the flowers, the water around the boat, and above all, in fresh brushwork throughout the rest of the painting. The use of color to unify the composition recalls *Still Life after Whistler*, but the intensity of tone here, and the freer and stronger strokes of paint speak of a different era. There is a seemingly joyous freedom in Bernstein's work in this decade;

the Symbolic Documentaries benefited from it.

It is well known that Bernstein and Meyerowitz frequently painted each other and for each other.[16] Two examples illustrate how she transformed her relationship with him into art. *In the Garden*, ca. 1950, depicts "objects" in a ladder-like verticality starting at the bottom with drapery, grapes, and pears. At the center is a copy of a picture of Theresa painting outside in the garden, legs crossed, with a yellow hat protecting her from the sun (presumably a copy of a portrait of Theresa by William). She borrowed one of his white horses, however, and shows him invading the garden, full of romantic ardor. Although Bernstein could be very serious, she could also be humorous. A painted portrait bust of William tops the ladder.

Documentary Still, 1972, is the culmination of Bernstein's documentaries and, of course, the many paintings of her husband (see fig. 157). The context in which it was displayed in the Gloucester house also adds to its meaningfulness. When I first visited Theresa for the first time in Gloucester in the summer of 1987, the first major piece of art that I saw in the living room was this painting, where I could immediately read the close bond between them. The little painting-within-the-painting of both of them, cheek to cheek from younger years, was centered so that one saw them together immediately. As usual, she inserted one of William's horse paintings above. The canvas lacks the raucous color she often indulged in (although a few free strokes appear here and there), but the harmonies produced a special kind of serenity. She includes the standard vase with a few flowers but only one palette, though both were artists. Of course they did not use the same palette in life, but here the sole palette can express the "oneness" of art as a bond between them.

For the greater part of her last decade (1992–2002), Bernstein was still professionally active. When I made one of my summer visits to her in Gloucester in 1992, I had to come to terms with the fact that she was over one hundred years old. Her hearing was perhaps a little worse, but she was still sharp as a tack and making art vigorously. She had been a widow for eleven years. By

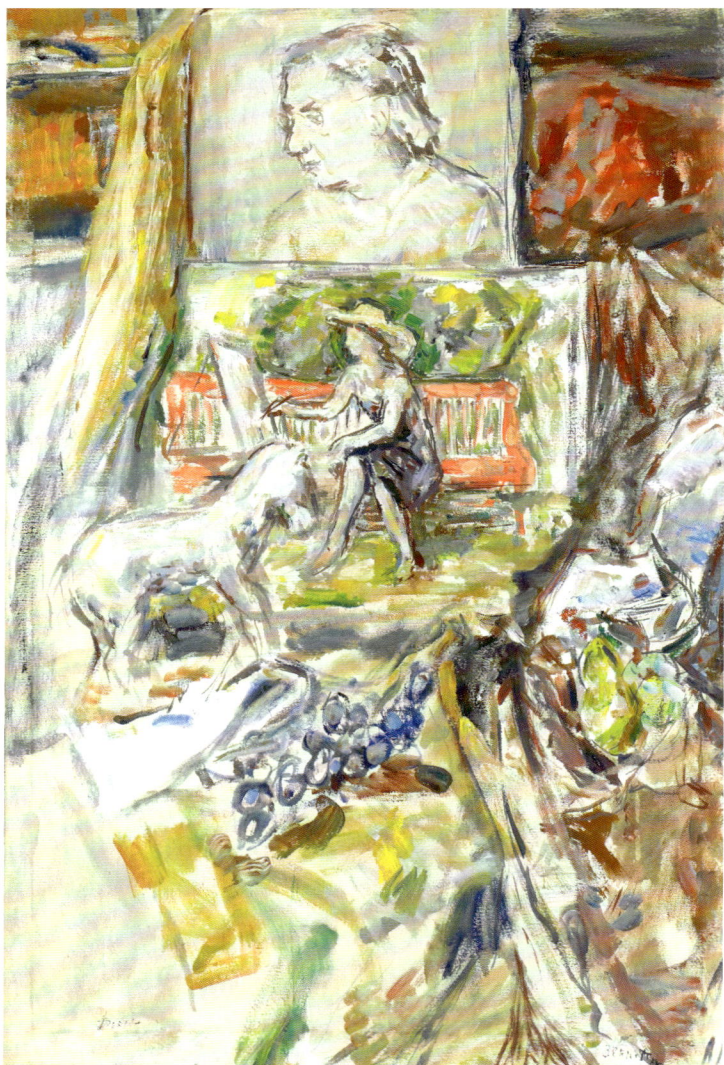

155. *In the Garden*, ca. 1950. Oil on canvas, 30 x 19½ inches. Martin and Edith Stein Collection.

this time, when she wasn't giving talks locally or being interviewed by media folk or otherwise participating in art events, she had to figure out how to resist ageism by fashioning new ways of making art. Still lifes, especially flower pieces, worked best for her in those final years. She would ask her many visitors to bring flowers to her and put them in a vase. Then she would draw or paint the bouquets (or mix both) with pencil, ballpoint pen, and/or actual paint on thick paper. Sometimes the guest would stay until it was done; usually, she would ask the guest to come the following day. When the guest returned, he or she was either given the work of art or asked to purchase it. I was a purchaser that summer. I dutifully showed up at the house with flowers and picked up the finished painting the following day. The flowers are so energized that they look like whirling dervishes. When I first saw it, I laughed with gratitude and great joy. I could not help but notice the strong swipe of blue shaping the left side of the glass vase, and I realized that Theresa Bernstein was still capable of firm control over her hand at the age of 102.

Bernstein thrived on diversity, from townscapes, cityscapes, communityscapes, landscapes, beachscapes (in abundance), to portraits, people en masse, genre, musical events, theater, and even murals, not to mention the still lifes, which played a lively counterpoint to all the rest. Into the flower pieces Bernstein threw her heart, but she saved her prodigious mental faculties for the Symbolic Documentaries.

NOTES

1. Theresa Bernstein Meyerowitz, *The Journal* (New York: Cornwall Books, 1991), pp. 23–24.
2. William Merritt Chase, "How I Painted My Greatest Picture," *Delineator* 72 (December 1908), pp. 967–68.
3. The records at the Art Students League state that Theresa Bernstein took two courses there between August and October 1911, one of which was with Chase. Georgia O'Keeffe, who studied with Chase at the Art Students League between 1907 and 1908, but only later came to know Bernstein, was also a fan of his still life course.
4. Bernstein, *The Journal*, pp. 9, 23, 39.
5. See Michele Cohen's essay, "Theresa Bernstein in Gloucester: Shaping Artistic Identity," in this volume.
6. Based on conversations he had with Bernstein, Girard Jackson has published an interpretation of the symbolism in his *Theresa Bernstein: Expressions of Cape Ann and New York, 1914–1972* (Stamford CT: Stamford Museum and Nature Center and Smith-Girard, 1990): The roses "represent the country's natural beauty," "[the] compass acknowledges the contribution of Christopher Columbus, a peace pipe appears alongside," and "the potatoes affirm the 'produce of the American soil'" (n.p.).
7. See Bernstein, *William Meyerowitz*, pp. 14, 19–20.
8. Daniel 3:5: "that whenever you hear the sound of the horn, flute, zither, lyre, harp, pipe, and all kinds of music, you fall down and worship the golden image that Nebuchadnezzar the king has set up." Bernstein, *The Journal*, pp. 117–19.
9. For Bernstein and Meyerowitz's friendship with Man Ray, see Gail Levin's essay in this volume.
10. For example, in her publication *The Poetic Canvas* (New York: Cornwall Books, 1989), Bernstein dedicated an entire chapter to surrealism, but does not make much of symbolism. Two lines in the opening poem, "Surrealism (Salvador Dali)," show off her wry wit: "You stand there and puzzle / Your mind's in a muzzle" (p. 97).
11. Samantha Baskind, *Encyclopedia of Jewish American Artists: Artists of the American Mosaic* (Westport CT: Greenwood Press, 2006), p. 50. Baskind comments that Bernstein "slightly misspelled" the wording on the cover of the book.
12. Usually in the Seder meal, there is only one egg per plate, but perhaps this plate with two eggs represents both Theresa and William.
13. Theresa Bernstein Meyerowitz, *Israeli Journal* (New York: Cornwall Books, 1994), p. 23.
14. The emblem on the flag of the state of Israel is the star of David; the president's flag, however, has the menorah as its emblem.
15. Bernstein reminisced in *The Journal*, p. 63, about William's interest in fishermen: "I always felt the fishermen were a sort of brotherhood linked to William's own efforts to find the meaning of art and its relation to life, whereas the fishermen were seeking to sustain life itself."
16. See Gillian Pistell's essay, "Documentary Still: Portrait of a Relationship," in this volume.

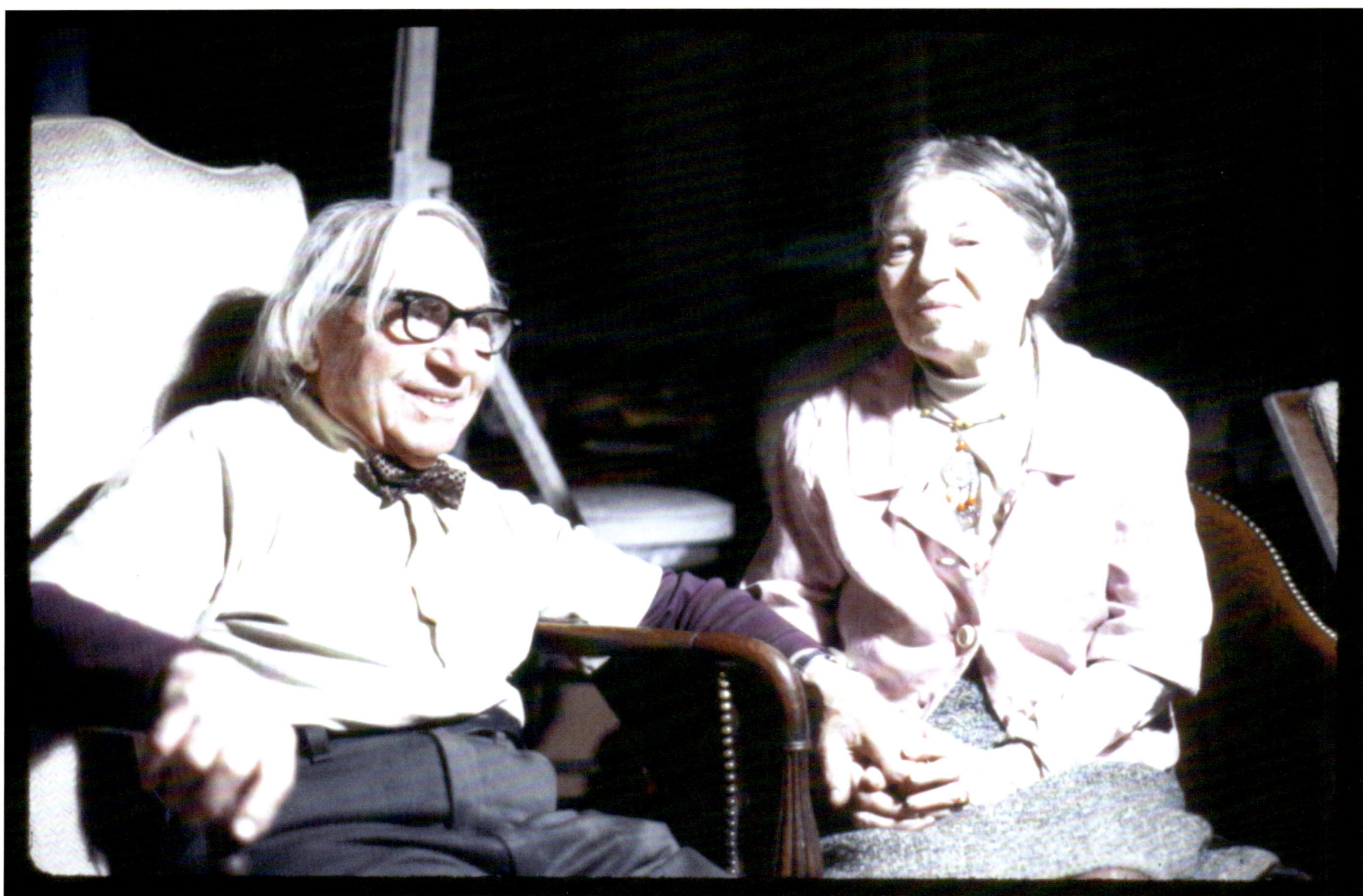

156. Theresa Bernstein and William Meyerowitz in their New York studio, 1978.

SEVEN

Theresa Bernstein's *Documentary Still*

PORTRAIT OF A RELATIONSHIP

Gillian Pistell

*I*n 1972, after fifty-three years of marriage, Theresa Bernstein sat down to paint a still life, adding one more picture to her already large and impressive oeuvre. She did not title this particular still life in the same descriptive fashion as she had done for many of her other still lifes. She called this picture *Documentary Still*, a title that is not descriptive of its superficial content but instead describes the picture's latent subject: her relationship with her husband, William Meyerowitz, and their existence as an artist couple.

What does it mean to be an artist couple? Unless the product of such collaboration is a single work, art historians tend to, or even strive to, separate the individuals that comprise the artist couple. This situation oftentimes results artificially in a superior member of the partnership overshadowing a perceived inferior member, a division that is usually split by sex: the superior member is male and the inferior is female. Take for example Jackson Pollock and Lee Krasner, two artists of arguably equal talent with similar, although not identical, training who were married to each other. In spite of this, only Pollock achieved critical renown that carried on beyond his death in

1956, as he became an American cultural symbol. Krasner, on the other hand, has only recently been given serious critical consideration. Even after Pollock's death, Krasner's fame seemed to stem more from being his widow than for her own work.[1] One might expect to find a similar situation with Bernstein and Meyerowitz. A closer look at these artists' work and careers, however, suggests that the case of Theresa Bernstein and William Meyerowitz stands as a counterexample. Their relationship was not negative, but rather symbiotic, and may have inspired them to each explore new and important artistic territory. Bernstein's *Documentary Still* is evidence of this fact, and can be used as a lens through which we can explore the subtle nuances of the artists' relationship.

A white cloth, reminiscent of an artist's drop cloth, dominates the center of *Documentary Still*. It is draped from a tall table and cascades onto the top of another, upon which several objects are assembled. A palette and small brush sit upon a sketchbook, placed next to a round platter, on which stands a painting of two people and a vase holding wispy, wilted flowers. The flowers rise vertically in the near-center of the picture and

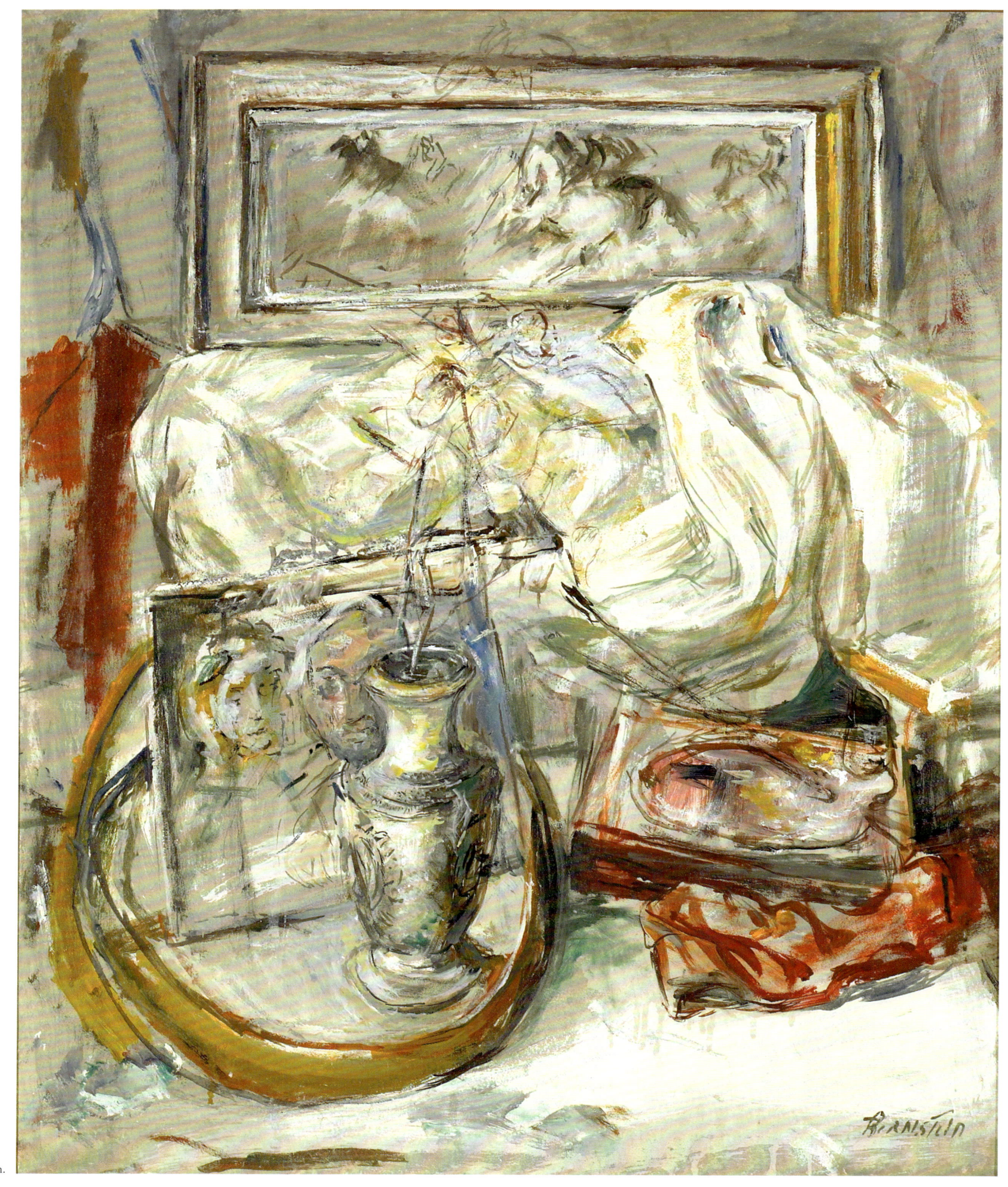

157. *Documentary Still*, 1972.
Oil on canvas, 30 x 25 inches.
Martin and Edith Stein Collection.

disappear into the object on the taller table behind them: a painting of several black and white horses with their riders. The composition is very tight—all the objects are drawn toward the others by directional lines, such as the paintbrush toward the wilted flowers, and the flowers toward the painting of the horses, as well as by Bernstein's own loose and dynamic brushwork, in an overall cool range of colors that swirls the entire composition. Every object depicted in the work holds specific symbolic value; indeed, Bernstein once stated that she considered such still lifes as "documentaries" because they tell a story.[2] *Documentary Still* tells the story of Bill and Theresa.

The most poignant object in *Documentary Still* is the double portrait that sits on the lower table. The couple depicted is in fact Meyerowitz and Bernstein, which can be deduced from both Bernstein's description of the work, as well as through comparisons with other portraits the two artists painted of themselves and of each other. This particular painting is very similar to an etching Meyerowitz executed in 1921. In both images, the artists are close and embracing each other, contemplating their audience as if they are a single individual rather than two separate people. The double portrait shown in *Documentary Still*, however, appears to be contemporary with when Bernstein painted it, 1972. The two look older, especially Meyerowitz, who is shown in front of Bernstein. Despite the loose brushwork, we can see clearly his unkempt white hair and glasses, looking very similar to a portrait Bernstein painted of him in 1964. The double portrait, combined with the picture's title of *Documentary Still*, indicate that it is indeed a document of Bernstein's and Meyerowitz's life together as both artists and a devoted couple.

In arranging her still life, Bernstein placed the most important object in the painting closest to the double portrait of herself and her husband. This object is the vase that holds the wilted flowers that accompany the portrait on the round platter. Meyerowitz and Bernstein are connected in that they are husband and wife—a family—so it follows that the flowers can be

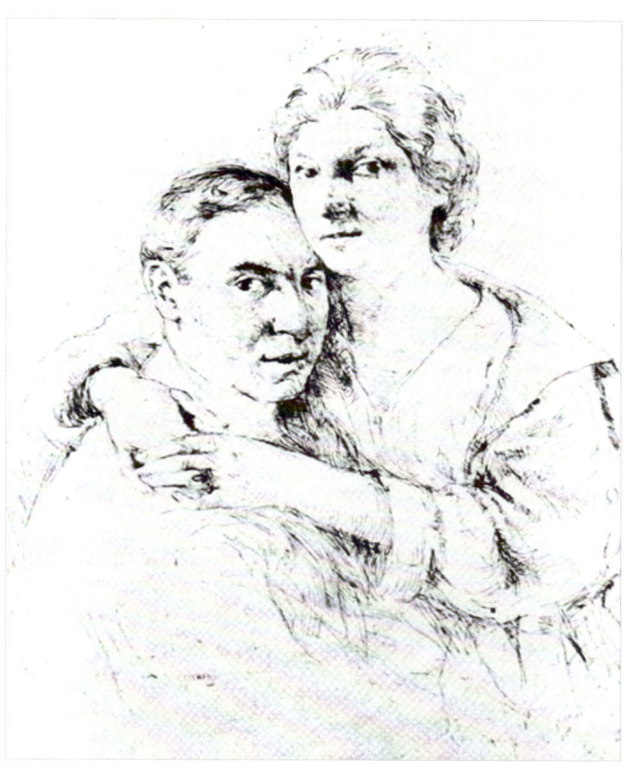

158. William Meyerowitz, *William and Theresa*, 1921. Etching, 8 x 10 inches. Helen and Edward Ezrick Collection.

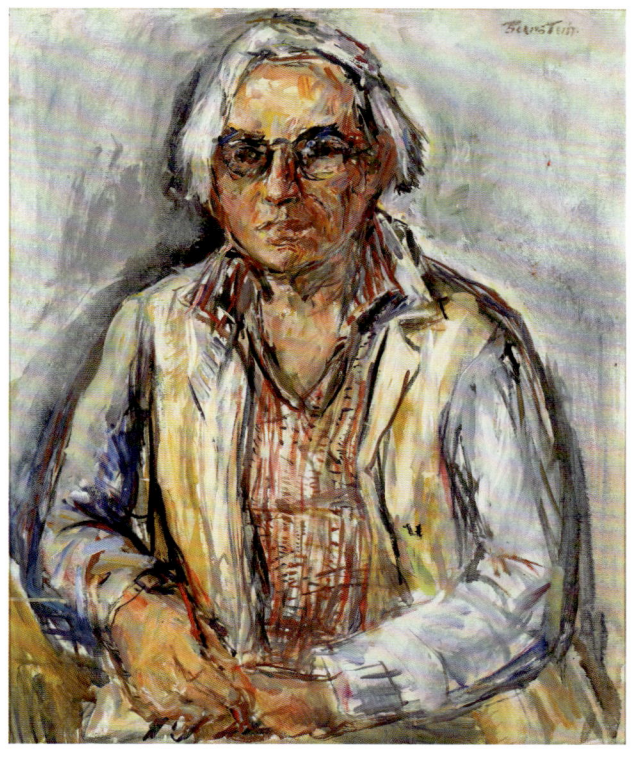

159. *Portrait of William Meyerowitz*, 1964. Oil on canvas, 30 x 25 inches. Martin and Edith Stein Collection.

seen as an extension of their family, but one that has wilted from their lives, one that is dead. On May 11, 1920, Bernstein and Meyerowitz lost their infant daughter to pneumonia. Both Bernstein and Meyerowitz were emotionally broken from this loss, and for reasons unknown, she would never have another child.[3] But it is important to ask what the significance of the death of their child was for their relationship and art. There has, in fact, been a great amount of psychological research in this area, much of which is pertinent to Bernstein's and Meyerowitz's situation.

she executed shortly after the death of her daughter. The first is *Joy of Life*, painted in 1920 (see fig. 63), a picture that, like that of Matisse before her, is an homage to life itself, with children playing and couples relaxing on a waterfront. In fact, art historian Patricia Burnham has identified the couple lounging in the lower left corner of the picture as Bernstein and Meyerowitz themselves, but with a poignant addition: they are shown interacting with their child, a sad reminder of what is missing

As shown by records from support groups, parents who lose a child relive their child's death over and over again and are continually plagued with a sense of incompleteness.[4] As a response to this feeling, many parents, especially the women, attempt to fill this sense of incompleteness with something else, usually their work. According to a long-term study published in 1996, the essential nature of women's work after the death of their child changes. They become more devoted to their profession or some other project, which usually takes on an almost nurturing and personal quality, whether it is in the actual product of their labor or in the relationships associated with that work.[5]

We can see a change in the content of Bernstein's work, specifically in three pictures that

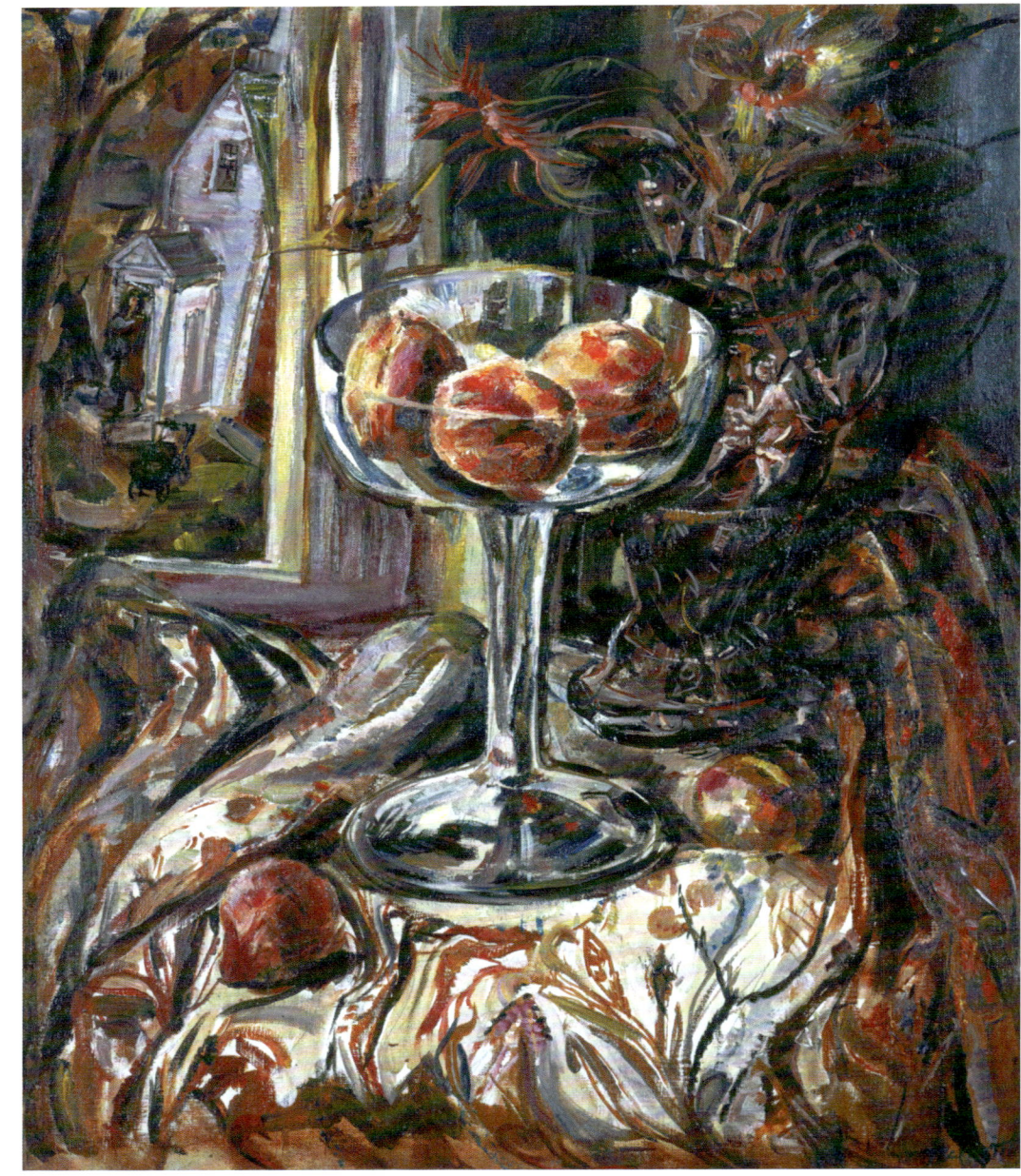

160. *Loss*, 1920. Oil on canvas, 27 x 30 inches. Rowena Young and Buddy Steves Collection.

from their lives. Indeed, this painting is tinged with sadness and uncertainty despite the carnivalesque feeling that permeates most of the canvas. In the lower right corner, a grim reaper wields his scythe as he approaches Bernstein, Meyerowitz, and their child—a tragic reminder of the artist's reality.

The second picture is even more heart-wrenching when one knows the context in which it was created. It is Bernstein's *Mother and Child*, also painted in 1920 (see fig. 62). This picture shows a woman gazing down caringly at her child whom she is holding in her arms. The two figures are painted with bold, loose brushstrokes that give them a tangible, solid quality communicating a very powerful sense of motherhood, especially considering Bernstein's own time as a mother was so fleeting.[6] The very physicality of this work suggests that Bernstein was attempting to capture and preserve on canvas what she had lost in reality.

The third picture, titled *Loss*, is a still life composed of swirling dark reds, greens, grays, and blacks that form a table upon which sits a large glass cup and a picture, of which we can see only a corner. The cup holds three pieces of fruit that appear to be peaches, with two more lying on opposite sides of its base. The picture, along with a vase of dark-colored flowers, sits behind the glass. In the framed image in the upper left of *Loss*, we can see a mother watching over her baby in its carriage. There is a sinister element to this otherwise bucolic scene. A dark figure, another grim reaper like that in *Joy of Life*, approaches the mother and child. This whole canvas is saturated with sadness, from its dark palette and dying flowers to the ominous image in the background. It is almost as if, through these three pictures, Bernstein was working through her grief.

Turning once again to 1972's *Documentary Still*, all the objects represent Bernstein's family, both present and past. Indeed, the death of her child would haunt Bernstein for the rest of her life, and she returned numerous times to vases and flowers as representations of this loss, not only in her art but also in her poetry. In 1982 Bernstein composed the short poem "The Vase":

They sit in circles on the beach
Like figures on a vase
They are the peoples of the earth
And the earth is their vase
Each one is a special entity
Each one an isolated me
They sit in circles on the sand
Or bathe within the strand
The mother and the babe
The child with curiosity
The youth with world to see
The maid awaiting what will be
Figures on the rim
Of vase earth's fertility[7]

This poem uses the object of the vase as a representation of motherhood and fertility. The figures on the vase—the mother and child—are forever perched on the rim and cannot progress into the future. Instead, they are trapped on the brink of their possible life, or the rim of the vase, just as Bernstein was frozen in motherhood and would never experience life as the mother of a growing and developing child, a child who will always remain a baby in her memory.

The flowers in *Documentary Still*, however, also point toward another important facet of Bernstein's life, one that also contained a nurturing element to it and one that occupied so much of her time and attention that it could be considered another profession in and of itself. The flowers are directly pointing upward toward a painting of black and white mounted horses. This painting is a reference to her husband's work; horses fascinated Meyerowitz since his youth, and after his exposure to contemporary art in Europe in 1922, he became increasingly intrigued by the futurists' and other European avant-garde movements' explorations of motion. Indeed, he would repeatedly combine these two interests in his own work.[8]

In *Documentary Still*, Meyerowitz's horses hold a place of prominence at the top center of the canvas. This promotion of Meyerowitz's work in the picture mirrors Bernstein's encouragement of his work in real life. It is possible that there was a financial reason behind this situation. Men's work did sell for more than women's, generally speaking, for most of the twentieth century.[9] A letter Bernstein wrote to Homer St. Gaudens, organizer of the Carnegie International Exhibitions, chastises him for not including either her or Meyerowitz's work in the show,[10] and demonstrates that money was indeed on Bernstein's mind: "Another year has passed and again—you have left the names of such artists as both my husband W M Meyerowitz and myself out of your roster for the coming exhibition. . . . In addition grave financial problems of the artist—even makes the question of a rental fee a timely one."[11] But there could also have been an underlying need to nurture something that drove what would become almost an obsessive compulsion for Bernstein to promote and sell her husband's work. Indeed, Bernstein's friend and dealer Jerry Jackson wrote: "She purposely took a back seat to her husband and enjoys promoting his work. She's an expert at selling so if you let the conversation drift, she'll sell you a Meyerowitz before you know what hit you."[12] Indeed, Bernstein continued to promote her husband's work decades after his death, working diligently on such projects as an exhibition of Meyerowitz's etchings at the Library of Congress in Washington D.C. in 1987. According to Bernstein, this show took three years of "concentration, letters, at least 10 letters, telephone calls, projections, suggestions, applications, producing inspirations," but was worth it when "finally the giant of libraries woke up from its historic snooze and decided, 'Yes, it would be great to have a little shine of a memory of an artist, an immigrant boy that came to the United States with a portfolio of his paintings done in Ukraine, no money, with a father who was a cantor . . . with a mother and five sisters and brothers who were waiting to be brought to the New World . . . with burning desire to seek knowledge of the art of art, with no patronage.'"[13] The death of her daughter affected Bernstein greatly; it left a void in her life that she needed to fill,

and her husband's career was what she used to accomplish this. The fact that she continued to do so after Meyerowitz died, when he would no longer have any personal gain from such promotion, indicates that it had taken on a personal quality for Bernstein, that it was something she needed to do for herself.

While Meyerowitz's work at the top of *Documentary Still* does hold some prominence in the picture, it is not the only reference to art depicted. On the bottom right of the canvas is a paintbrush and an artist's palette smeared with the same colors used to create *Documentary Still*, as if it is a representation of Bernstein's own palette for this picture. These two artist's tools are references to Bernstein's own work—painting was the medium in which she excelled as opposed to etching, which was Meyerowitz's primary talent. In fact, Meyerowitz was known for his pioneering experiments in color etching, but there is no indication of that in *Documentary Still*.[14] This omission suggests that while Bernstein was very much involved in the promotion of her husband's work, she did not ignore and neglect her own. Although they were sometimes considered as an inseparable pair, more often they were presented as two artists from New York City. They were usually listed as "William Meyerowitz" and "Theresa Bernstein," only very rarely as "William Meyerowitz and his wife, Theresa Bernstein" and never "Theresa Bernstein-Meyerowitz."[15] Furthermore, Bernstein showed several times without Meyerowitz, especially in exhibitions featuring the New York Society of Women Artists.[16] From these shows, we can see that Bernstein was also very concerned with promoting her own career. The letter to Homer St. Gaudens quoted above chastises the museum director for including neither Meyerowitz nor herself, because she wanted her career to prosper as well. If she did not, she would not have shown without Meyerowitz or perhaps she would not have shown at all. Indeed, several scholars have suggested that Bernstein's relationship with Meyerowitz in fact improved his reputation by association with his wife because she was the superior artist of the two.

While they did paint similar subjects such as scenes

from daily life in both New York City and Gloucester, Massachusetts, they approached these subjects in very distinct ways, especially when they worked in their different preferred media, Bernstein in painting and Meyerowitz in etching.[17] Indeed, the two artists managed to remain true to their own styles and methods throughout their long relationship. A comparison between a still life of Meyerowitz's to Bernstein's *Documentary Still* illustrates this fact. Meyerowitz's *Still Life with*

vases and flowers—the two artists approached their subjects in disparate ways, rooted in their distinct choices of media but also in their personal artistic method and language.

Throughout the course of his career Meyerowitz experimented in various media and with different styles, most notably cubism and futurism. Bernstein acknowledged this interest of her husband's in the horse painting in *Documentary Still*. Compare it, for example, to Umberto Boccioni's *Dynamism*

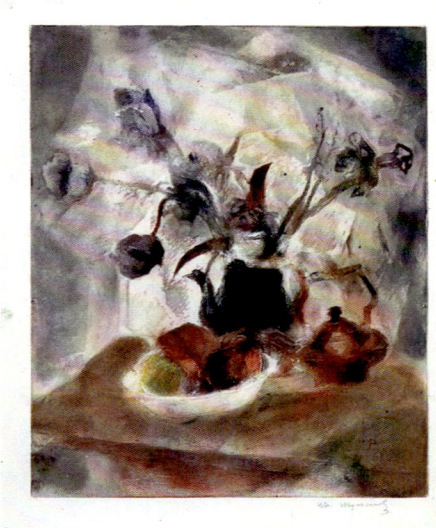

161. William Meyerowitz, *Still Life with Iris*, late 1930s. Etching and aquatint, colored *à la poupée*, 9⅞ x 7¹⁵⁄₁₆ inches. Private collection.

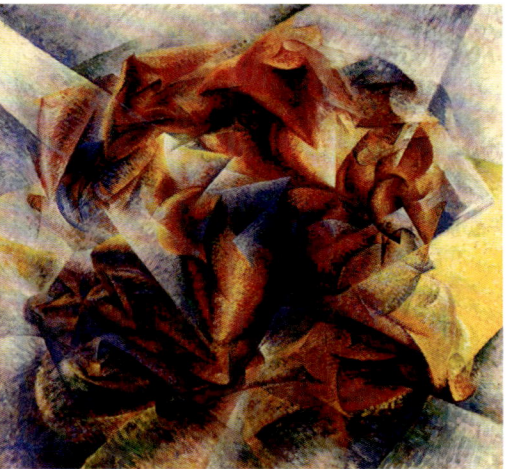

162. Umberto Boccioni, *Dynamism of a Soccer Player*, 1913. Oil on canvas, 6 feet 4⅛ inches x 6 feet 7⅛ inches. Sidney and Harriet Janis Collection, Museum of Modern Art, New York, New York.

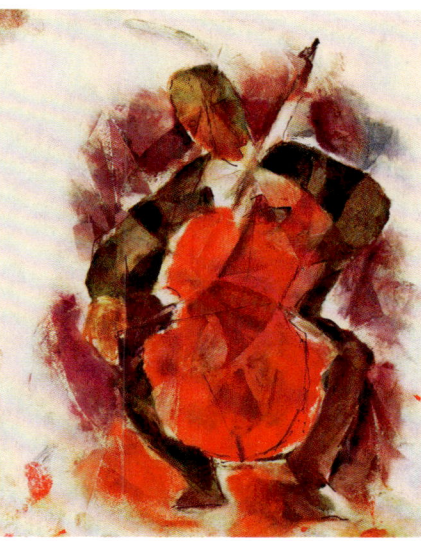

163. William Meyerowitz, *The Cellist*, mid-1930s. Aquatint, colored *à la poupée* with pen and black ink, 10⅝ x 8 inches. Private collection.

Iris is an etching and aquatint colored *à la poupée* from the late 1930s that depicts a table upon which sits a large teapot filled with several irises, with a bowl of fruit on its left and a smaller teapot on its right. The picture's palette is generally cool with soft blues, greens, and purples, with the occasional splash of red and yellow. In fact, the only thing that really jumps out from the composition are the bold etching marks, particularly those that define the fruit and the spout of the teapot. The entirety of the composition is broken up into fragmented sections of color that are reminiscent of cubism, a style with which Meyerowitz experimented. However, one can see that Meyerowitz's *Still Life with Iris* is quite different from Bernstein's *Documentary Still*. While similar in content—both show typical still life objects like

of a Soccer Player. While devoid of Boccioni's brilliant color scheme, Meyerowitz's horses demonstrate a similar interest in forms in motion. Within an indistinct swirl of a background, riders and their mounts blur into one another in a massive futurist-like depiction of collective movement. We can see this interest played out even more in his etchings depicting musicians and musical performances. Take his aquatint *The Cellist* from the mid-1930s, for example. The cellist and his instrument are situated amid a fragmented swirl of purple planes. The figure and objects are treated in the same manner but in black and red, respectively. The cellist's face and hands are rendered without any sort of defining characteristics, indicating that this picture is not about the cellist for which it was titled, but is instead about the music and energy that he is creating. The vibrant colors and swirling pattern of the planes of the picture make the cellist's music almost audible.

Like her husband, Bernstein also made several pictures of musicians and musical performances during her career, but as with the still lifes, she approached the subject in a different manner. While she also captured the energy and expressivity of these performances, she did so in a markedly different way, namely in a more realist manner that she favored, and in oil painting, the medium in which she most frequently worked. Let us look at her picture *Lil Hardin and Louis Armstrong* from ca. 1927 (see fig. 77). In this canvas, the two musicians are center stage, their band surrounding them, with Hardin belting out a song to Armstrong's accompaniment. Nothing in this picture is abstracted as it is in Meyerowitz's picture, but Bernstein's use of very loose and gestural brushstrokes, the opposite of her husband's hard line, reflects just as successfully the moment's energy and dynamism. The difference in technique and style demonstrated by these two works is essential in understanding the relationship between Bernstein and Meyerowitz, especially in their art-making processes. The two artists lived together and worked side by side for a little over sixty years, mostly in a tiny studio apartment that served both as their living quarters and their workspace. Contrary to what one may assume, however, Bernstein's and Meyerowitz's art remained individualized. While it is true that in some of their pictures, small elements do seem to draw from the other's work—cubistic architectural elements in some of Bernstein's Gloucester and New York landscapes, for example, are reminiscent of Meyerowitz's fragmented planes in his more abstract works—the two artists' styles remained for the most part true to their own personal inclinations, as we can see in the two respective pictures of musicians described above.

Bernstein stayed true not only to her artistic instincts when continuously confronted with her husband's work but also to her own style despite the numerous movements that were popular throughout her long lifetime. The fact that she was able to do this was a source of great pride for Bernstein. She even addressed this in her statement for an exhibition of her work at the Cober Gallery in 1960. The following so perfectly and concisely articulates Bernstein's thoughts on this subject and how she personally approached her practice that it must be quoted in full:

My approach to painting is direct. I try to keep my expressions in touch with life and to enlarge upon these works with a technique that will best express the motive. The confusion in art today has had an influence on many people so that they do not trust their own judgment. It is like steering a boat loaded with one's ideas through a turbulent sea. But one must have an anchor; an ideal plus a goal. Otherwise, one is scampering about the immense in search of Venus, Mars, or the moon. Art is the magnet that keeps man from facing a too scientific future—the rocket which does not return to earth is not a success.

The idea of a world of people is a heartwarming one, and I like people. If I see and hear a group of musicians (classical or jazz) their actions and the interplay of the music will have a definite sway over my interpretation.

Rhythms—quick or long and slow—will find echo in my painting. The single object or figure is easy for the child's eye to grasp; but for me, a group of people (in action or repose) become a single object in consciousness.

The idea is an intensification of the theme. In my Night Club scenes, some of the excitement of the performances is woven into the choice of color. But I am also interested in the interplay of motions; I try to catch the unconscious movements and crystallize them so that they appear as vital attitudes.

Thus, life about me is my book and mentor. I try to understand and to communicate to others the same joy that I have experienced and to open for them a door to the world in which we live.[18]

Another quotation, this one in reference to the work she showed in an exhibition at the Uptown Gallery in New York City in 1937, also demonstrates her negative feelings about the avant-garde art pervading many of the galleries in the city: "You have been visiting galleries where fur-lined tea cups and melted watches were on view. You have been battling your way through crowds to see French titles and old masters. You have followed the critics in applauding the stand-patters—the species that never changes, painting one picture on various canvases all their lives—the current-event illustrators and the dime novel, moving picture wall-washers. In this exhibition your experience will be your own and you will be convinced that classic simplicity pervades all lasting art."[19] This statement, along with others where she says that she "couldn't warm up to those cubes and triangles—they didn't have enough life force," indicate that she not only strove to remain true to her realist roots, but she actively tried to stay away from the artistic styles that were continuously developing around her.[20]

Perhaps Bernstein was able to remain true to her own vision despite the continuous presence of Meyerowitz and contemporary artistic developments because by the time the two met, Bernstein's artistic practice had already solidified. Indeed, when Bernstein and Meyerowitz married in 1919, Bernstein was almost thirty years old and had already produced many of her major works like *In the Elevated*, which she painted in 1916 (see fig. 43). This picture depicts several people sitting in New York City's elevated train. The insight into the mentality of these passengers betrays the fact that Bernstein was much more perceptive than one would expect from a young woman of only twenty-six years. The passengers sit in their train car, either reading, staring out in front of them, or idly looking out the window as the modern world flies by, an energy made all the more tangible by the rushing lines of bright color along the aisle and ceiling, as well as in those that jump out at the eye in the seats and that punctuate the passengers' clothing. This picture is the work of a mature artist sure in her eye and in her ability to translate what she sees onto her canvas, not an amateur artist who is susceptible to outside influence. Instead, she could adopt Meyerowitz into her life as simply another element that enriched her practice but did not mold it. Indeed, she addressed this situation in one of her many poems entitled "We Used to Think":

We used to think that painting was
A thing to give you joy
But no they say, it is not so
A painting should annoy
We used to think that sculpture was
A thing just for a lark
But no they say, it is not so
It's danger in the dark
We used to think that he and she
Could dance just holding hands
But no they say, it is not so
They contort to the bands
We used to think those in the pink
Had fever for a pill
But no they say, it is not so
They have it in the till
We used to think that clothes were such
She wore a dress and he wore pants
But no they say, it is not so
The clothes are simply those
We used to think that hair was hair
His would be short and hers quite long

But no according to our song
The hair is simply there
We used to think that marriage was
A thing that death do part
But no they say, it is not so
The reverse is the chart.[21]

This poem demonstrates that Bernstein considered painting and her marriage to be equal parts of her life and that gender expectations could be inverted; one did not overshadow the other in either importance or prominence and would continue forever, beyond the supposed finality of death.

Perhaps even more importantly, however, is that Meyerowitz encouraged Bernstein to stay her own course and to not let other people's disparaging words, whether about her work or her existence as a female artist, discourage her.

Unfortunately, Meyerowitz could not protect his wife from harsh comments in the press. Take for example this review of a show in 1949 at Boston's Doll and Richards Gallery that featured both Bernstein's and Meyerowitz's work: "At Doll & Richards, William Meyerowitz and his wife, Theresa Bernstein, have opened a large show of pieces not exhibited in New York. Here the male artist reveals again his harmonic mastery of color, his ability to fuse the abstract and the beautiful, his characteristic sense of rhythm surely linked to his informal concerts and love of music as demonstrated summers at Gloucester. Miss Bernstein, on the other hand, goes in more for genre, does not penetrate so deeply as her husband, stresses line more than form. Yet she has an electric style that tells what she wants to say and, as in a large scene of Gloucester Harbor, fine assembly of detail."[22] While not particularly scathing, the critic held Meyerowitz's art in higher regard than that of his wife, whom he placed within the stereotypical mold of a female artist with pedestrian style and content. The very language of this review betrays this critic's preexisting assumptions and serves to embed his beliefs into the minds of his readers; he labels Meyerowitz as "male," and he calls Bernstein "Miss Bernstein" in the same sentence in which he identifies her as the "male artist's" wife. It is clear from these words that this critic would have had the same opinion of Bernstein's work no matter what she showed.

In the face of such criticism, Meyerowitz encouraged and supported his wife, both emotionally and professionally. Indeed, Meyerowitz's last words to his wife were, "You must go on—I love you."[23] He knew she would be able to do so because, while she was a devoted wife, she was also feisty and independent. He knew she could make it on her own and urged her to do so without guilt. Bernstein was not just an artist—she was a devoted wife. These two roles remained virtually inseparable throughout the majority of her life, and so, as art historian Francis Naumann, who met Bernstein, asked, "Would there have been a Theresa without a William?" The poignant iconography of Bernstein's and Meyerowitz's life together that is laden in *Documentary Still* suggests that no, there would not have been a Theresa without a William, or at least not the Theresa that we can come to know through the art she left behind—hundreds of pictures that record both a century of history and love.

NOTES

1. Anne M. Wagner, "Fictions: Krasner's Presence, Pollock's Absence," in *Significant Others: Creativity and Partnership*, ed. Whitney Chadwick and Isabelle de Courtivron (London: Thames and Hudson, 1993), *passim*; Gail Levin, *Lee Krasner: A Biography* (New York: William Morris, 2011).

2. Charles Movalli, "Conversation with William Meyerowitz and Theresa Bernstein," *American Artist* 44 (January 1980), pp. 67, 90.

3. Joan Whalen, "Theresa Bernstein: American Modernist," *American Art Review* 18, no. 3 (2006), p. 114.

4. R. Wayne Willis, "Some Concerns of Bereaved Parents," *Journal of Religion and Health* 20, no. 2 (1981), p. 134.

5. Elizabeth B. Farnsworth and Katherine R. Allen, "Mothers' Bereavement: Experiences of Marginalization, Stories of Change,"
Family Relations 45, no. 4 (1996), p. 365.

6. Whalen, "Theresa Bernstein," pp. 113–14.

7. The poem "The Vase" can be found in the Moore College of Art and Design Archives' files on Theresa Bernstein.

8. Jonathan Bober, ed., *The Etchings of William Meyerowitz*, March 22–May 19, 1996 (Austin TX: Archer M. Huntington Art Gallery, 1996), pp. 3, 5.

9. Gail Levin, "Art World Power and Women's Incognito Work: The Case of Edward and Jo Hopper," in *Gender, Sexuality, and Museums*,
ed. Amy K. Levin (New York: Routledge, 2010), *passim*.

10. "Pittsburgh International," *Time*, May 5, 1924.

11. Theresa Bernstein to Homer St. Gaudens, undated letter, William and Theresa Meyerowitz Foundation, New York.

12. Jerry Jackson to Debbie Alterman, letter, 1982, Moore College of Art Archives.

13. Theresa Bernstein, audio file 14, Theresa Bernstein CUNY website.

14. Bober, *The Etchings of William Meyerowitz*, p. 8.

15. There are numerous examples of this labeling, but for a specific example, see Howard Devree, "Brief Comment on Some of the New Group and One-Man Shows in the Galleries," *New York Times*, June 15, 1941. See some exceptions cited by Gail Levin in her essay in this volume.

16. For an example of a review of one of these shows, see "New Exhibitions of Art at Fair," *New York Times*, September 24, 1940.

17. Dorothy Mayhall, ed., *Theresa Bernstein: Expressions of Cape Ann and New York, 1914–1972, A Centennial Exhibition* (Boston: Simmons College, 1989), *passim*. See also the discussion of their different versions of *Country Fair* in the essay by Michele Cohen in this volume.

18. Theresa Bernstein, "Statement," in *Theresa Bernstein* (New York: Cober Gallery, 1960). This statement was found in a catalogue currently preserved in the Moore College of Art and Design Archives' files on Theresa Bernstein.

19. "Needed: A Few Mellons," *Art Digest*, February 15, 1937.

20. Joan Whalen, ed., *Theresa Bernstein (1890–): A Seventy-Year Retrospective* (New York: Joan Whalen Fine Art, 1998), p. 8.

21. Theresa Bernstein, "We Used to Think," in *The Poetic Canvas* (London: Cornwall Books, 1989).

22. Lawrence Dame, "Regarding Boston," *Art Digest*, April 15, 1949, p. 18.

23. Girard Jackson, "Theresa Bernstein: Expressions of Cape Ann and New York, 1914–1972," in *Theresa Bernstein: Expressions of Cape Ann and New York, 1914–1972, A Centennial Exhibition*, ed. Dorothy Mayhall (Boston: Simmons College, 1989), p. 37.

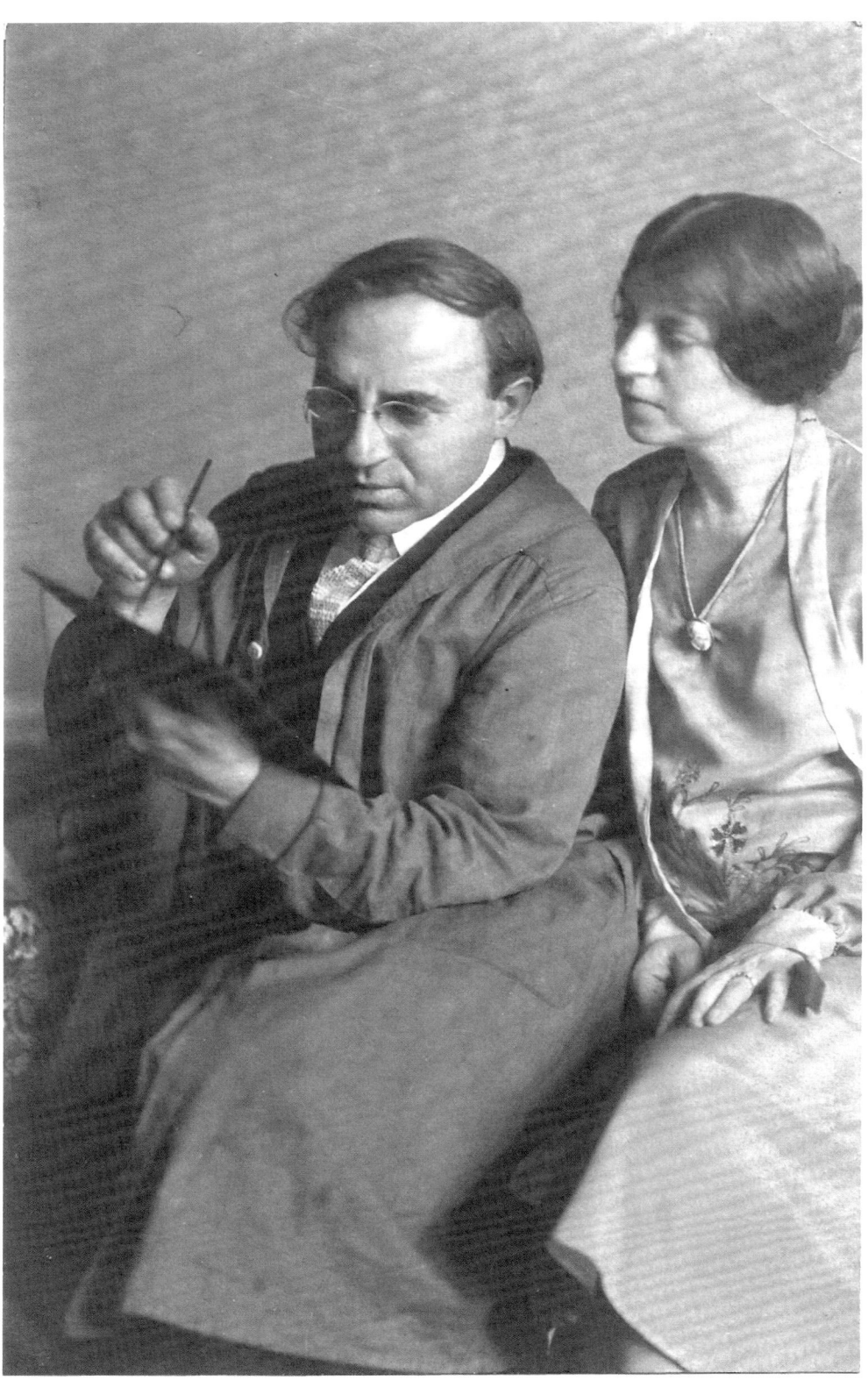

164. William Meyerowitz demonstrating etching as Theresa Bernstein looks on, ca. 1925.

EIGHT

Impressions

THERESA BERNSTEIN AS PRINTMAKER

Stephanie Hackett

Theresa Bernstein, in her autobiographical account, *The Journal*, explains that she always had a feeling for "visual impressions."[1] Although the artist favored oil paints as her medium of choice, a study of her print impressions, especially the etchings and monotypes that she created during her lengthy and illustrious career, serves to develop a deeper understanding of the artist both on a personal level and as a member of the greater American art community. The etching revival in America, which involved the resurgence of the creation of prints in all mediums and the rise of the numbers of collectors of these works, began in the late nineteenth century, peaked in the early 1930s, and experienced yet another wave of renewal beginning in the 1980s.[2] Therefore, studying Theresa Bernstein's print career, which spanned nearly the entirety of this revival, places the artist into a particularly important and specific movement in American art history and leads to a better understanding of her artistic ideals, style, and personality as a whole.

This essay will discuss Bernstein's etchings as seen through the lens of her relationship with her husband, the painter and printmaker William Meyerowitz (1887–1981). Although Bernstein's role as promoter of Meyerowitz's work can be interpreted as stifling to her own career, it was actually this role that gave her an entry into the popular world of printmaking in the first place. Thus she gained confidence to create etchings of her own, even as she explored other channels such as teaching and writing, which took her beyond painting. In addition, Bernstein's work in monotype can be linked to the history of the emergence and rise in popularity of the medium and can be juxtaposed to the work of high-profile artists such as Maurice Prendergast, John Sloan, Robert Henri and George Luks. Such a comparison reveals Bernstein to have been respectful of her artistic predecessors and forward thinking in the modern and rapidly changing times in which she lived and worked.

THE ETCHING REVIVAL IN AMERICA

The process of etching involves a few simple tools: a printer's metal plate, a waxy ground that is resistant to acid, an etching needle, also known as a burin, a bath of acid, paper, and a printing press.[3] The artist first covers the plate with the waxy ground, and then, using the etching needle, scratches his or her design into the ground, exposing the metal of the plate beneath.[4] Afterward, the plate is dipped into the acid bath, which eats away at the areas of exposed metal; these etched lines can then be inked and the plate is ready for the printing press.[5] Unlike the process of engraving, used most frequently by the old masters of the Renaissance and which, because of its difficult technique involving carving directly into hard metal, resulted in linear, highly planned artworks, etching offers a "freer, sketchier style and [a] more personally expressive and spontaneous mood."[6]

The excitement engendered by the stylistic possibilities that the novel medium of etching provided, combined with the influences of European artists who were already in the midst of their own print revival, ushered the etching revival into America.[7] The European artists were inspired by the etchings of Rembrandt and of their contemporary colleague James Abbott McNeill Whistler (1834–1903). In 1877 the New York Etching Club formed, signaling "the start of . . . an intense American involvement with the medium of etching."[8] The production and purchasing of prints and related print material would be an American fixation until the start of the Great Depression in 1929. It was not until the 1980s that the prints created during this time and the artists who created them would be reevaluated and viewed with renewed interest by art historians and collectors.[9]

The American etching revival of the late nineteenth century and of the first decades of the twentieth century is recognized as a "democratic" event, both for artists and for collectors, in the history of American art.[10] The process of etching, though clearly requiring a certain level of skill, was one that could be learned through experimentation and did not require training in a prestigious art academy.[11] Therefore, etching was a medium available to any artist who desired to try it. In addition, artists were encouraged to be involved in the creative process from the beginning, the application of the ground upon the plate, through to the end, the transfer of ink from the plate to the sheet. For the collectors, the creation of reproducible images provided them with products that, while being less expensive than paintings, were still considered original works of art. Larger numbers of artists were able to make more prints for a growing group of consumers, who considered their collections to be their own "medium of expression."[12] For a time, prints and printmaking pervaded American culture, and the artists who created these works were treated with the utmost respect both within the art community and the more general American community.

WILLIAM MEYEROWITZ AND THERESA BERNSTEIN: A PAIR OF PRINTMAKERS

Printmaking in America was so important to American culture during the early decades of the twentieth century that Bernstein would have been aware of this movement in the art community even if she had not met and married a printmaker. However, it was their relationship and partnership in the studio, as well as her role promoting her husband's work, that gave Bernstein such insight to this specific niche of printmaking. This interest and activity helped to broaden her career and to strengthen her overall skill as an artist.

In an undated handwritten document explaining her perspective on prints, printmaking, and printmakers, Bernstein praised her husband as one of the finest artists of his day, who experimented with and obtained a level of mastery over the medium of etching and, in particular, etching in color. Of her own participation in etching, Bernstein downplayed her talents and modestly wrote, "I have been an interested spectator and sometimes an active ally."[13] Although Bernstein's role in the world of printmaking eventually became more involved, it was only natural at the beginning of their married and working life together, for Meyerowitz, who had already reached a certain level of acclaim as a printmaker, to act as teacher and Bernstein as student.

William Meyerowitz was a true representation of the

ideal etching revival printmaker. As a youth, he emigrated from Ukraine and moved to New York with his family. He acquired a printing press that had originally been in the service of the U.S. Treasury. For the remainder of his career he remained a devotee of the print world, working on the press that he had acquired as a young man and brewing his own combination of chemicals to create the acid baths necessary to the process.[14] Bernstein explains that "for William, to etch was as personal as to compose a letter in his own handwriting. He communicated his emotions, ideas, and artistic decisions" through the medium.[15] He depicted subjects that were meaningful to him and his wife. Bernstein's delicately rendered etchings in black and white, *Central Park (Figures on Horseback)*, ca. 1920s (a subject of particular importance to Meyerowitz), and *The Inner Harbor*, 1922, suggest Meyerowitz's influence on technique and subject matter. Also evident are Bernstein's own technical skill and her interest in scenes of daily life that the couple shared.

Girard Jackson, in the catalogue for the 1989 exhibition, *Theresa Bernstein: Expressions of Cape Ann and New York, 1914–1972, A Centennial Exhibition*, sets up an interesting comparison between two very early works, of the same subject and nearly identical size, by William Meyerowitz and Theresa

Bernstein: *Armistice Day*, 1918.[16] Both images depict a crowded street scene filled with people and flags; heavily inked, crosshatched lines create a feeling of dynamism and vivacity. However, Bernstein, despite being Meyerowitz's student, demonstrates her own artistic and stylistic point of view. While Meyerowitz sets the vantage point of the scene from a bird's-eye view, isolated from and elevated far above the action in the streets, Bernstein places the viewer directly into the hub of excitement, among the people, and as part of the action in the street. In the end, Bernstein achieves a level of intimacy and energy in her work that differs from that of her husband.

Bernstein was clearly a skilled printmaker and independent thinker, and therefore, it seems to have been an active decision on her part to participate in the world of etching from the sidelines, in the role of public member of that community, whose opinion and authority on the medium were well respected, rather than as a frequent exhibitor, a role that she more often left to her husband. Bernstein acted as teacher alongside Meyerowitz in their Summer Art Course at their home in Gloucester, Massachusetts; among the variety of techniques taught was printmaking.[17] In 1933 Bernstein acted as writer and scholar in her publication, the first of its kind, on the history of

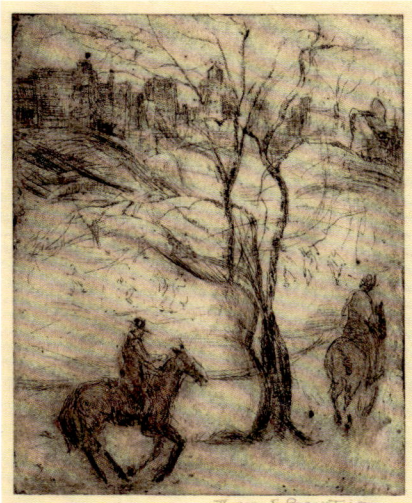

165. *Central Park (Figures on Horseback)*, ca. 1920s. Etching, 7⅛ x 5⅛ inches. Theresa Bernstein and William Meyerowitz Foundation.

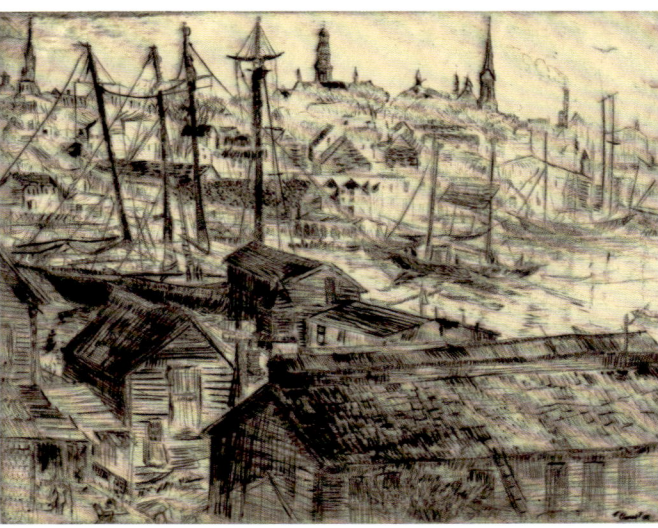

166. *The Inner Harbor*, 1922. Etching, 5.88 x 7.88 inches. Theresa Bernstein and William Meyerowitz Foundation.

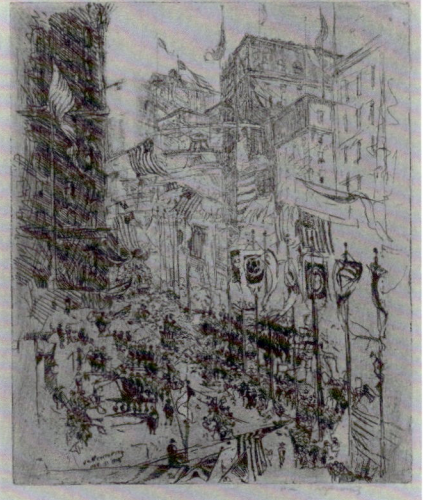

167. William Meyerowitz, *Armistice Day*, 1918. Etching, 9¾ x 8 inches. Private collection.

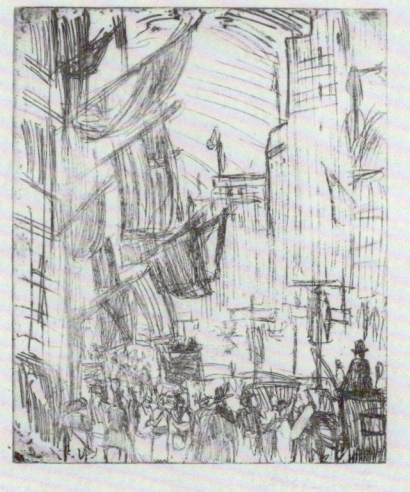

168. *Armistice Day*, 1918. Etching, 10 x 8 inches. J. J. and Jackie Bell Collection.

color in graphic arts for the first Society of American Graphic Artists Exhibition at the Brooklyn Museum.[18] She and Meyerowitz were members of this group, which was later known as the Society of American Etchers. Throughout her career and in addition to her own painting, Bernstein skillfully acted as promoter, happily shaping the successful direction of her husband's print career.[19] In due time, the world of printmaking became Bernstein's life too.

THE ETCHINGS OF THERESA BERNSTEIN

Elizabeth Helsinger in "The 'Writing' of Modern Life," which includes an exploration into the etching revival in the United States, explains that despite the fact etching had a long history in Europe prior to its introduction in America, it was nevertheless viewed by artists as novel and exciting.[20] Printmaking existed as an alternative method of communication seemingly uncomplicated by "expectations" in style and subject matter from other artists and the viewing public.[21] As a result, etching, while still requiring a certain level of technical skill, also allowed artists to explore abstraction, the self, and the world about them in new ways; the technique, combined with the products' smaller physical size, allowed artists a heightened level of introspection and the possibility of sharing their personal "experience" with the world.[22] For Theresa Bernstein, as we have seen, the wider world of printmaking and her highly public and active role within it served to strengthen her own career. Many of her etchings themselves (which may number more than a hundred), however, demonstrate this desire to use the medium to understand the self more deeply and to express her personality in the most effective way possible. Her etchings are certainly worthy of study.[23]

The cataloguing of Bernstein's prints is largely incomplete. Though more studied, the prints of Meyerowitz also need a definitive catalogue. The locations of many of the works are unknown. The William Meyerowitz and Theresa F. Bernstein Foundation probably represents the most organized view of the

artist couple's bodies of work. Therefore an analysis of Bernstein's prints in this collection is particularly helpful in establishing an understanding of her techniques and goals. It is especially significant to note that within the relatively small collection of Bernstein's graphic works housed at the foundation are a relatively large number of self-portraits. The following four works, one from 1918, two from the 1920s, and one from 1930, demonstrate the artist's understanding of the medium as one that is simultaneously dynamic and quietly introspective. Throughout her career, it was a medium that offered her an opportunity for self-reflection and a way to depict her "vital enthusiasm for life."[24]

The four self-portraits vary in style and technique, demonstrating Bernstein's skill level and her desire to experiment within the medium of etching. For example, in one *Self-Portrait*, 1920, in which she depicts herself as a printmaker (a theme repeated often by the artist in her etchings) holding a printer's plate and the etching tool, the burin, the figure of Bernstein, both detailed and realistic, reveals a particular talent for draftsmanship. Additionally, Bernstein experimented with soft ground etching, which results in the atmospheric, tonal quality on the printed surface.[25] And finally, in each of the works, Bernstein clearly shows an interest, to different degrees, in minimizing her use of line to create simple and sometimes abstracted, though complete, affective figures.

What is most compelling about these four images is that despite their differences in style and technique, Bernstein's intent to reveal herself through her work is powerfully and fully realized in each one in similar ways. In each impression, Bernstein is placed close to the viewer and stares out with an unflinching, quiet, questioning, and intense gaze. There is nothing in the background to distract the viewer from the figure of Bernstein, and even in the many prints in which she is depicted with her printer's tools, these objects are placed low in the composition and remain secondary to her expressive facial features.

Meyerowitz's etching *Self-Portrait*, ca. 1930, acts as an

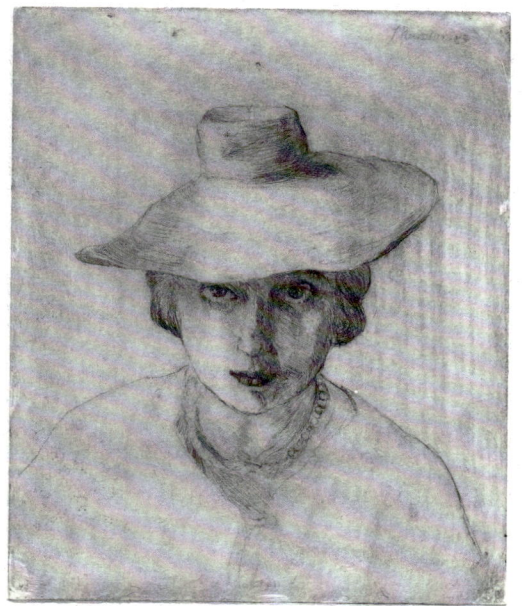

169. *Self-Portrait in Hat*, 1920. Etching, 6 x 8 inches.
Theresa Bernstein and William Meyerowitz Foundation.

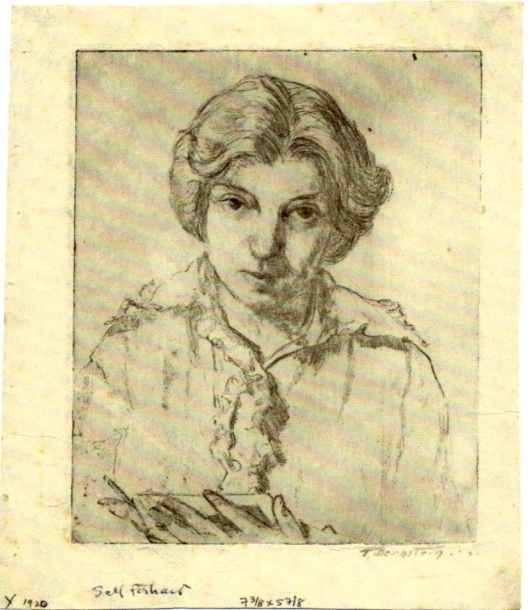

170. *Self-Portrait*, 1920. Etching, 7⅛ x 5⅞ inches.
Theresa Bernstein and William Meyerowitz Foundation.

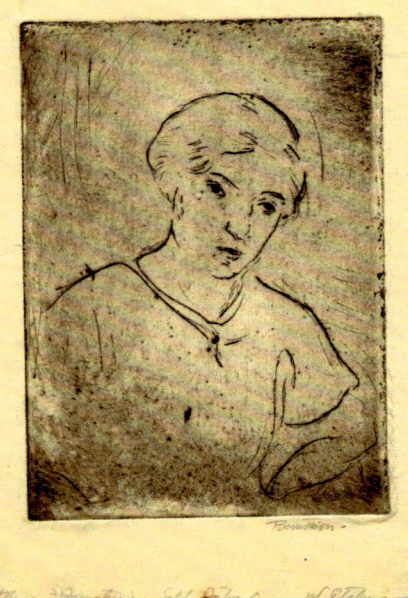

171. *Self-Portrait*, 1918. Etching, 7.6 x 6.6 inches.
Theresa Bernstein and William Meyerowitz
Foundation.

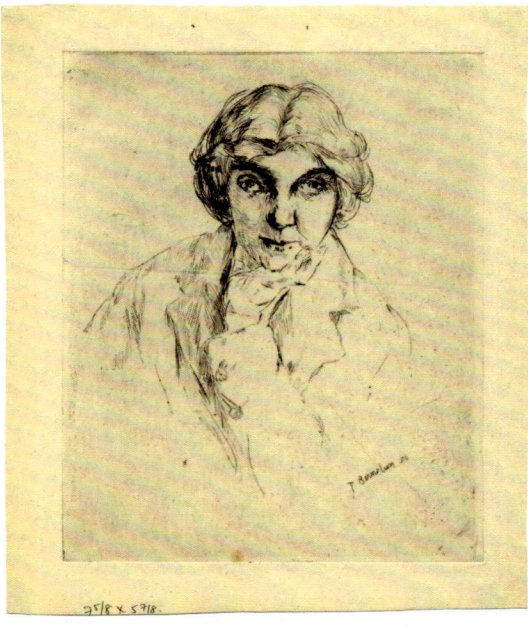

172. *Self-Portrait*, 1930. Etching, 7.36 x 5.88 inches.
Theresa Bernstein and William Meyerowitz Foundation.

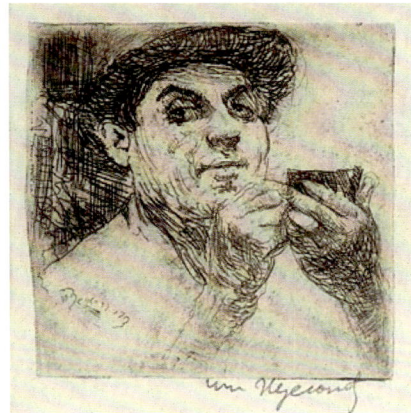

173. William Meyerowitz, *Self-Portrait*, ca. 1930.
Etching, 3 x 3 inches. Private collection.

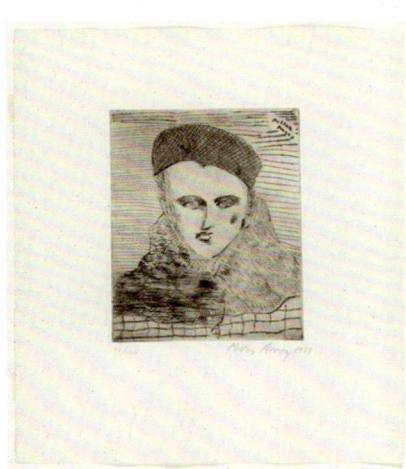

174. Milton Avery, *Sally with Beret*, 1939.
Drypoint, 8 x 6 inches. Private collection.

interesting counterpoint to the etched self-portraits of his wife. While the work reveals the stylistic similarities and technique they shared as partners in the studio, it also brings attention to their differences. These distinctions are crucial in that they are responsible for creating the individual and independent senses of personality and spirit that the prints evoke. Like his wife, Meyerowitz places himself in the forefront of the image, directly into the viewer's space; his gaze is equally intense and unflinching. However, the purpose of Meyerowitz's print, composed of boldly dynamic, heavy, and powerful lines, seems to be to show himself in the role of skillful printmaker rather than as just a man exposed to the viewer. He holds his printing tools close to his chest and is clearly in the process of creating. Suddenly, the viewer of this print is no longer just an objective viewer, but in fact becomes the subject of Meyerowitz's artwork within the artwork. With one arch of an eyebrow, Meyerowitz's scrutiny becomes appraising and somewhat confrontational as opposed to Bernstein's glimpses of herself, which are ultimately probing and unguarded.

Theresa Bernstein desired to portray her real self, as opposed to a caricature of herself. Her ability to do so with great skill is emphasized by a comparison of her *Self-Portrait*, ca. 1920, in which the artist is shown peering up at the viewer from underneath a wide-brimmed hat, and of Milton Avery's (1885–1965) drypoint *Sally with Beret*, 1939. Avery was a frequent visitor to the Bernstein and Meyerowitz summer home in Gloucester, Massachusetts, and often played chess with Meyerowitz.[26] In addition, he was a colleague in the arts to both Bernstein and Meyerowitz and was himself one-half of a successful artist couple. Compared to Bernstein and Meyerowitz, he entered onto the printmaking scene late. He first ventured into intaglio printmaking in 1933 with a depiction of his daughter March, in *Baby Avery*, and he pulled his first monotype, again an image of his daughter, *Artist's Child*, in 1950. Like Meyerowitz and Bernstein, Avery was similarly drawn to the fact that printmaking was an inexpensive process, and he used it to capture the intimate and familiar subjects of his family and landscapes dear to him.[27] In *Sally with Beret*, Avery depicts his wife, Sally Michel (1902–2003), in a way that initially appears very similar to Bernstein's *Self-Portrait*. Hat upon her head, and with only her face and shoulders included in the compositional space, Sally Michel also gazes up and out at the viewer before her. However, unlike Bernstein's work, Avery uses a series of lines and repeating patterns to build up the figure of his wife, and his focus, unlike Bernstein's, lies in increased abstraction and design elements to capture her essence.

These examples make it clear that although Bernstein, Meyerowitz, and Avery manipulated the medium of etching in different ways, they each used it as a means to capture elements of personality, whether their own or another's. It was this ability and its variations that drew them to the medium in the first place. In a way, the print, in etching form, became a signature of the artist and a story of the self in graphic form.[28] "The main function of a print is its intimacy," Bernstein once explained in the aforementioned undated, handwritten document explaining her perspective on prints, printmaking, and printmakers. In this document she reveals her belief that "the greatest printmakers are those who can conquer the physical means" of their media and use it to emotionally impact their viewing audience.[29] Bernstein would continue these explorations through her work in monotype.

THE MONOTYPE—A BACK STORY

The monotype, within the world of printmaking, is known as the "painter's medium."[30] The process of creating a monotype, in its simplest form, involves the artist "drawing" upon the surface of a printing plate or other flat surface with printer's ink or oil paint.[31] The artist is then able to manipulate the image, specifically the balance of light and dark contained within the composition, by wiping away certain amounts of ink or paint in the desired areas.[32] Finally, the rendering is transferred through the pressure of a press or other device onto a sheet of paper.[33] The result, once described by American printmaker Joseph Pennell as a "squashed painting," is at once controlled and completely spontaneous.[34] Although the artist is responsible for creating the initial image, he or she cannot control what will occur during the moment the image is transferred. As the name monotype implies, this particular printing process results in one, original impression. If an additional impression is produced, it is generally much lighter and is therefore known as the "ghost."[35]

Although the first monotypes were produced in Europe as early as the seventeenth century, they were not introduced to the United States until the last decades of the nineteenth century as part of the previously discussed etching revival.[36] A few key players, many of whom were directly or indirectly quite significant in regards to the progression of Bernstein's artistic career, were involved in experimenting with this "new" medium. This group included William Merritt Chase (1849–1916), Bernstein's teacher for a brief time in 1911 at the Art Students League in New York City, and Maurice Prendergast (1858–1924), a member of The Eight, with whom Bernstein is often linked because of her subject matter and stylistic sensibilities. In addition, Prendergast was Bernstein's artistic predecessor in the North Shore Massachusetts communities. In the early years of the twentieth century, other members of The Eight, including Robert Henri (1865–1929), George Luks (1867–1933), and John Sloan (1871–1951), also embraced the novelty of monotype and its painterly and sketch-like qualities.

However, while these artists were involved in the resurgence of monotype, their collective attitude toward it also contributed to its general decline into obscurity. Although Maurice Prendergast actively and consistently included monotype in his repertoire, William Merritt Chase primarily viewed monotype as a teaching tool, while other members of The Eight, for example Henri and Sloan, who in Sloan's journal are reported as having "a little monotype fun with the etching press," believed monotype to be the less serious of printmaking mediums.[37] In addition, there was "no market for monotype"; print collectors viewed the works as paintings and painting collectors viewed them as prints.[38] Many print shows, the forum in the twentieth century for artists to have their work become known, refused to accept monotypes as part of the exhibition, claiming: "all print mediums are accepted, except monotype."[39]

Artists' attitudes toward monotype and viewers' responses to them combined with the overall decline of print collecting by the 1940s, led to the monotype becoming a largely overlooked medium and one whose importance was highly misunderstood throughout history. It was not until the 1970s and 1980s, with the second wave of the etching revival, that art historians found a renewed interest in reinterpreting those works in monotype by Chase, Prendergast, and the remaining Ashcan artists, among others. They also began to acknowledge and study the significant number of other artists, including Bernstein, who had been experimenting with the medium themselves.[40]

Joann Moser's *Singular Impressions: The Monotype in America* is the "first comprehensive [and most recent] survey" of this medium, misunderstood and unappreciated by artists, art historians, and general lovers of art throughout time.[41] It should be noted that Theresa Bernstein is included in the text as an example of the few forward-thinking and significant artists who experimented with monotype during the 1920s, '30s, and '40s and, in fact, contributed to its rise in popularity as a medium through the remainder of the twentieth century. According to Moser, on one level the process of creating a monotype, as well as the occasional monotype over etching, offered Bernstein the opportunity to experiment and to reach a level of spontaneity that painting, even with the artist's use of highly active and expressionistic brushstrokes, would not be able to achieve.[42] And on another level, Moser claims, monotype was Bernstein's "painterly contribution" or answer to her husband William Meyerowitz's own experimentations in perfecting the complicated art of color etching beginning in the early 1920s.[43] The medium of monotype, one that required little time to learn and an equal amount of technical skill and "special equipment," allowed Bernstein to continue working alongside her husband as printmaker. Monotype provided her with a sense of freedom and individuality, in that this medium, although in many ways technically similar to the process of color etching, was hers alone to master. As a result, monotype became a natural extension of her work in oil on canvas.[44]

THE MONOTYPES OF THERESA BERNSTEIN

The William Meyerowitz and Theresa F. Bernstein Papers, 1915–1978, which are housed at the Archives of American Art, and which include exhibition records, reviews, and catalogs for the artist couple throughout their careers, reveal that Theresa Bernstein exhibited her monotypes infrequently. However, the quality of shows in which she was invited to exhibit reflects the art community's and the viewing public's respect for her work in a medium that itself continued to remain largely unappreciated. In addition, it demonstrates Bernstein's accomplishment in reaching a high level of skill in a medium that she did not consider her primary mode of self-expression and in which she was entirely self-taught.

Nineteen forty-eight, in particular, was a banner year for the artist. From March 12 to 31, Bernstein's *Children of Gloucester*, a work executed in the mediums of drypoint and color monotype, hung in the Ninth Annual Exhibition of the American Color Print Society at the Print Club of Philadelphia, and was offered for sale at the price of fifty dollars.[45] From April 26 to May 24, Bernstein had a solo show at the Smithsonian Institution in Washington DC, in which thirty-six etchings and monotypes in color, from the 1920s through the 1940s, were displayed.[46] Finally, from October 25 to November 11, Bernstein exhibited an untitled *Monotype in Color* in the Twenty-Fourth Annual Exhibition of the New York Society of Women Artists, an organization in which she held a directorial position. It appears that later, Bernstein also showed her monotypes in September 1976 when seven of her most recent prints were exhibited alongside a much larger selection of her husband's paintings and color etchings at Smith-Girard Art Brokers in Stamford, Connecticut.[47]

The main reason for the relative infrequency of Bernstein's exhibiting her works can most likely be related directly to the belief that monotypes were a secondary and/or invalid medium and were therefore generally not included in print exhibitions, rather than a demonstration of disinterest on the artist's part. In fact, exhibition records, as well as the extant works themselves, show that Bernstein began creating monotypes as early as 1918 (an example of which is the not completely successful and slightly muddy *Boys Gathering Firewood*, 9¾ x 8 inches) and consistently continued to develop her skill and to produce works of an increasingly elevated quality through the 1970s. In her monotypes, Bernstein focuses on the same subjects that she depicted in her paintings throughout her life; these subjects are eclectic and include scenes of basketball players, musicians, Gloucester beachgoers, New York streets, portraits, and faraway locales. However, unlike Bernstein's paintings, the monotypes are small, intimate, and sketch-like. The works are pervaded with a sense that the creative process itself was a deeply personal and introspective one. In fact, Bernstein takes advantage of the spontaneous, sketch-like quality of the medium to depict scenes, situations, and events that recapture and bring back to life significant moments that were at one time immediate and very real to her. Nowhere is this most clearly viewed than in her monotype *Venice*, 1922–1955 (see fig. 88). Currently in the collection of the Metropolitan Museum of Art, *Venice* was a gift of the Society of American Graphic Artists, Dorothy Noyes and John Taylor Arms Collection, in 1955. John Taylor Arms himself was a key player in the American etching revival and president of the Society of American Graphic Artists, which, although its name changed several times throughout the twentieth century, was originally founded in 1915 as the Brooklyn Society of Etchers.[48] Additionally, Arms was a friend and confidant to Bernstein and Meyerowitz, with whom he shared a mutual respect.[49]

Bernstein's monotype *Venice* depicts the scene mentioned in her memoir of a trip she took to Europe with her husband in 1922. Although its composition matches that of its twin painting (only in reverse), the effect upon the viewer is quite different. The image is relatively small at 8½ x 12⅝ inches, but the viewer is positioned in such a way, with a bird's-eye view, that the magnificent city appears to stretch on for miles. A delicately curving line beginning in the center foreground of the composition serves to separate the canal filled with the lily-like gondolas from the regal Venetian architecture, and as it arcs to the upper left background of the scene, moves the eye throughout the composition. The depiction of the city in only a few rich colors– gold, red, and brown–is not only typical of a monotype but also shows the entire city of Venice to be unified by color and saturated with the rich sunlight that had originally dazzled the artist. The intent of the print was not to create a realistic portrayal of the grandeur of the city. Rather, Bernstein attempted to present and recapture a vivid impression of a very specific, fleeting, inspiring, intimate moment, and more important, the emotions she experienced at that time. This point is emphasized by the fact that, arguably, the monotype was not created as the study for a painting but as a meditation of the event *after the fact* of the creation of the original painting (see fig. 89).

The concept of the creation of a print, not as a prior study for a painting but as a separate work created at some point later in time, makes sense within the larger context of Bernstein's story of spontaneously capturing Venice on canvas, in which it seems there was little time for previous study or lengthy premeditation. In addition, this practice of creating prints after the painting, was not unusual but was utilized by other artists, including Milton Avery, who often used drypoint in order to explore the same imagery he had previously worked through on his canvases and to experiment with the different effects that could be achieved through printmaking.[50]

It is also unclear as to whether other monotypes, including *Music Lovers*, 1932–33, and *Prayer Meeting*, 1938, for whom accompanying paintings exist, were created as studies to a painting or as a response to that painting. Nevertheless, they deserve to be appreciated as individual artworks in their own right, separate from the paintings to which they are related. They, and Bernstein's monotypes in general, also reflect the artist's desire to capture a specific moment in time. *Music Lovers* portrays an audience listening, the specific moment when a note is heard and appreciated. Likewise, *Prayer Meeting*, conveys the moment of prayer, the moment when words leave a person's mouth and travel to God's ear.

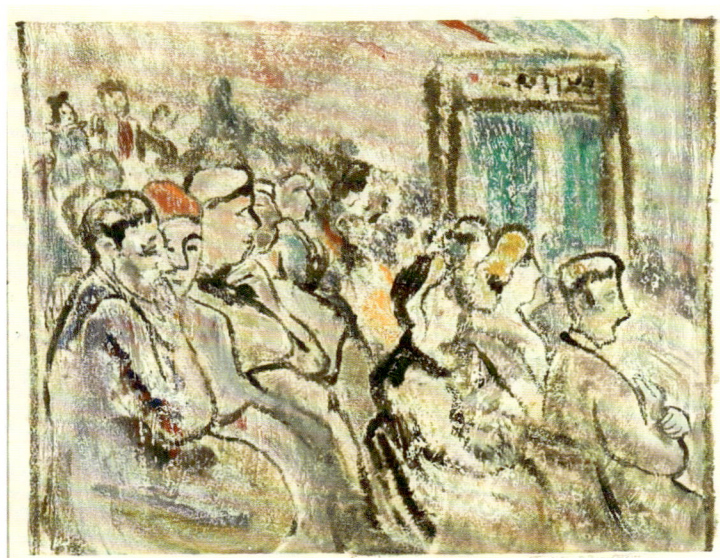

175. *Music Lovers*, 1932–33. Monotype, 7¼ x 8¼ inches.
Martin and Edith Stein Collection.

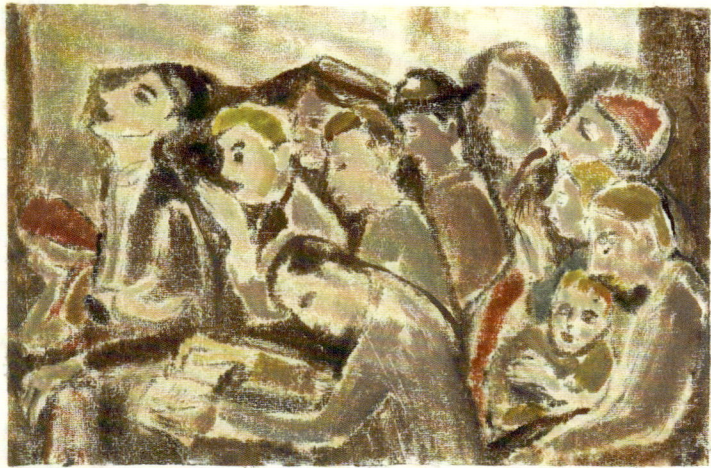

176. *Prayer Meeting*, 1938. Monotype, 11 x 16¼ inches.
Martin and Edith Stein Collection.

INFLUENCES ON BERNSTEIN'S MONOTYPES

Stylistic similarities and subject matter in the work of both earlier and contemporaneous artists can be observed in the monotypes of Bernstein. Throughout her career, she remained acutely aware of the changes in the evolving art world and her shifting position within it. As always, Meyerowitz would remain her great partner and influence, and especially in printmaking, he would act as her greatest teacher. However, if in fact monotypes were Bernstein's

"painterly contribution" or response to Meyerowitz's color etchings, then a stylistic analysis, demonstrated here through a comparison of Bernstein's *Venice* and Meyerowitz's *The Drying Wharf*, 1925, reveals that Bernstein's answer was one of divergence and that she had successfully represented her own individual personality through the genre of color printmaking.[51]

Jonathan Bober in *The Etchings of William Meyerowitz* states that by the mid-1920s, William Meyerowitz's color etchings had reached "their highest level of sheer painterliness and technical refinement."[52] *The Drying Wharf*, 1925, echoes elements found in Bernstein's monotype, including a vast sense of space contained within a physically small image, a curving line to draw the viewer's eye throughout the composition, and the use of only a few colors to unify all aspects of the scene and create an emotive, atmospheric quality. However, Meyerowitz's technique, a laborious process involving etching and the application of layers of color upon a plate, results in an image that is ultimately grounded in and based on line, and appears ordered and structured in a way that Bernstein's monotypes are not.[53]

Bernstein's greatest, though indirect, influence and ally in the medium of monotype may have been American artist Maurice Prendergast, who, like Bernstein but unlike many of his fellow artists experimenting in the medium at the time, saturated his compositions with vibrant and unusual color and increasing abstraction.[54] Bernstein's *Venice*, ca. 1922–1955, may itself be a knowing homage to Prendergast, who in 1898–99 traveled to Italy, where he, again like Bernstein, sought to recapture the experiences from his trip through the medium of monotype and to imbue his monotypes with a sense of timelessness: an impression of a momentary event that would now last forever.[55]

While Bernstein's view of Venice is grand and sweeping, Prendergast's depictions of Italy are mostly more intimate portrayals of women; however, a comparison between Prendergast's work of a few years later, *Figures by the Shore*, 1900–1902, and Bernstein's *Good Harbor Beach*, 1933, clearly shows the artistic commonalities and lineage that they shared.

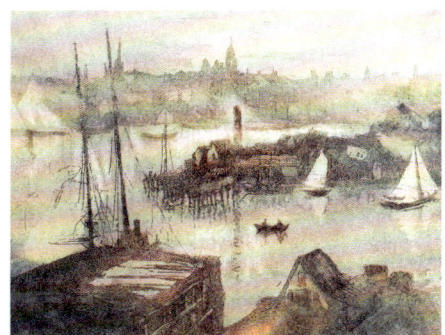

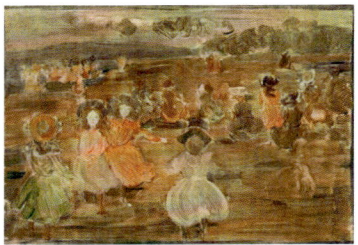

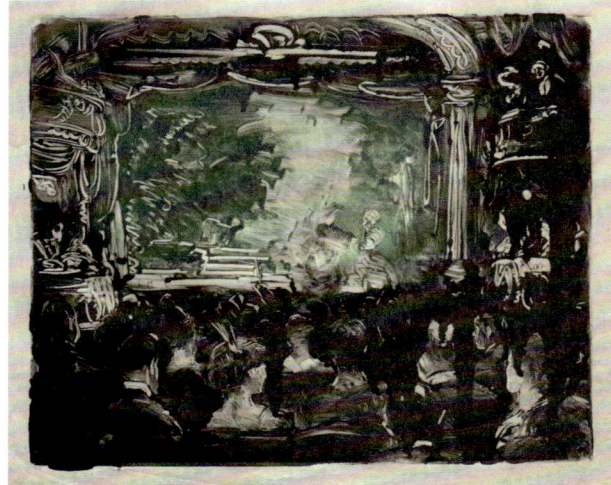

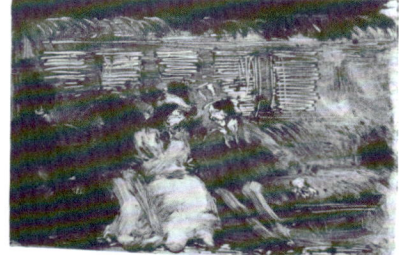

The two monotypes, both of which most likely present a depiction of North Shore Massachusetts beachgoers, rely upon a composition in which the figures, above all, are of central importance. In both works, the beach, with the figures upon it, takes up the majority of the composition, with an unnaturally colored sky as the remainder; in Bernstein's work, there is evidence of water in the background, but it is mostly obscured by standing figures and by a jutting stretch of land with a large structure upon it. The figures are heavily abstracted, and in Bernstein's case appear more as outlined forms of color. And again, in both works it is this vibrant sense of color, yellow in Bernstein's work and orange in Prendergast's, which, applied with a heavy "brushstroke", that unites the compositional space. The end result is an image that is active, vibrant, unified, and energetic, and like a sketch, it seems to exist within the moment.

It is this sketch-like quality, intrinsic to the process of creating a monotype and its end result, that attracted Ashcan artists like Robert Henri, John Sloan, and George Luks to the medium in the first place.[56] Despite their limited interest in this specific artistic outlet, they were drawn to its ability to create a sense of movement, vitality, and spontaneity. These qualities also exist, in different ways and to different degrees, in the actual sketching process: one that these artists used frequently to capture the immediacy of daily and city life around them. Therefore, it is then easy to see why they were drawn to the medium and why they, like Bernstein, began to use the monotype as an alternate form of a sketch to depict events about town, as evidenced in John Sloan's *The Theater*, 1909, Robert Henri's *Couple in a Streetcar*, ca. 1907, or George Luks's *Cake Walk*, 1907.

The similarities between a work like George Luks's *Cake Walk*, 1907, and Theresa Bernstein's later work *Hot Times*, ca.

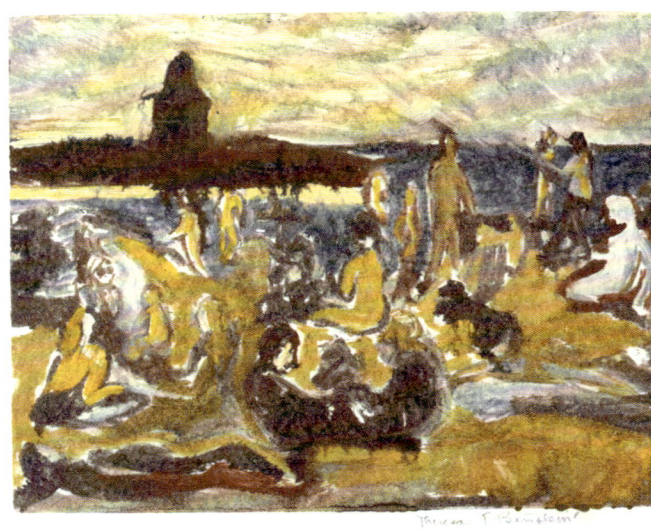

1950s, are striking and therefore deserving of mention. Luks's image in black and white depicts an African American couple, dressed in finery and performing the *Cake Walk*, a popular dance routine that originated in the slave culture of nineteenth century America.[57] The focus is on this couple, who are placed against an empty backdrop and who appear ready to leap right off the page. Luks manipulated the medium of monotype by wiping the ink on the plate, thereby creating lines reminiscent of a brushstroke, lines that are highly active and dynamic and that create the feeling of constant movement.[58] Bernstein's image is more ordered in that her figures are placed within the center of the compositional space. Yet she too wiped ink and layered color to create highly abstracted figures, placed against a similarly blank background, that appear as whirling masses of form, color, and energy. In fact, they appear to be almost levitating off the ground. In both works, Luks and Bernstein successfully captured and relayed the feeling of immediacy in the performances they had witnessed, making the viewer feel he or she is also witnessing the event firsthand.

Gladys Engel Lang and Kurt Lang, in their sociological study "Recognition and Renown: The Survival of Artistic

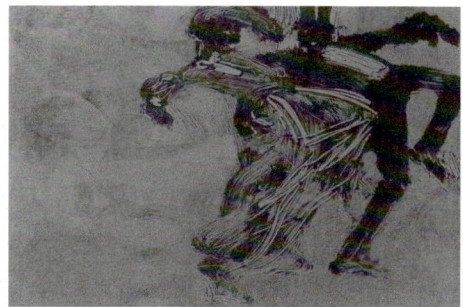

182. George Luks, *Cake Walk*, ca. 1907. Monotype, 8½ x 11 inches. Delaware Art Museum, Wilmington.

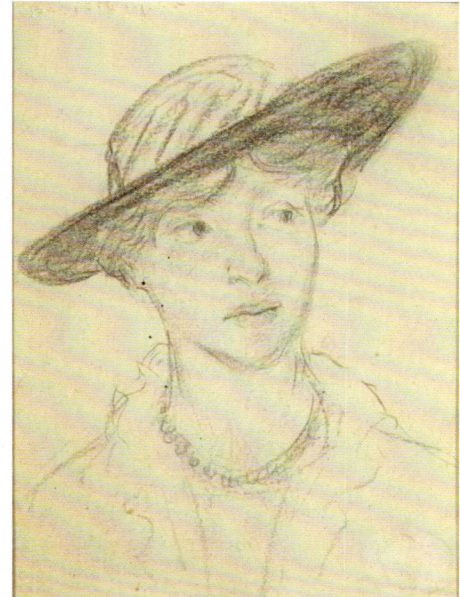

184. *Self-Portrait*, ca. 1918. Etching, 11 x 8½ inches. Martin and Edith Stein Collection.

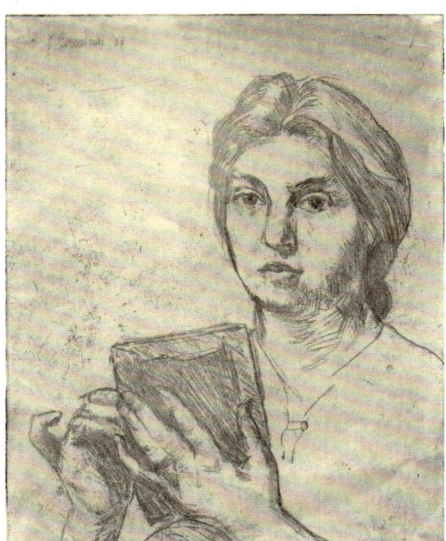

185. *Portrait of the Artist*, 1920. Etching, 7.4 x 5.88 inches. Theresa Bernstein and William Meyerowitz Foundation.

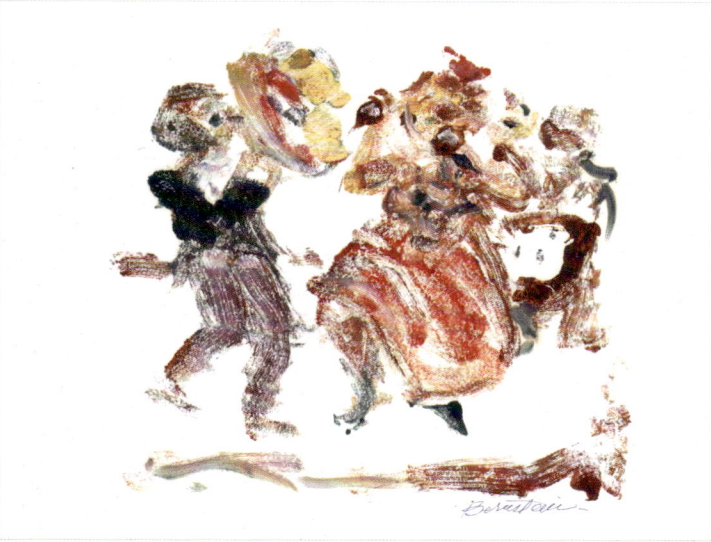

183. *Hot Times*, ca. 1950s. Monotype, 8½ x 10¼ inches. Girard Jackson Collection.

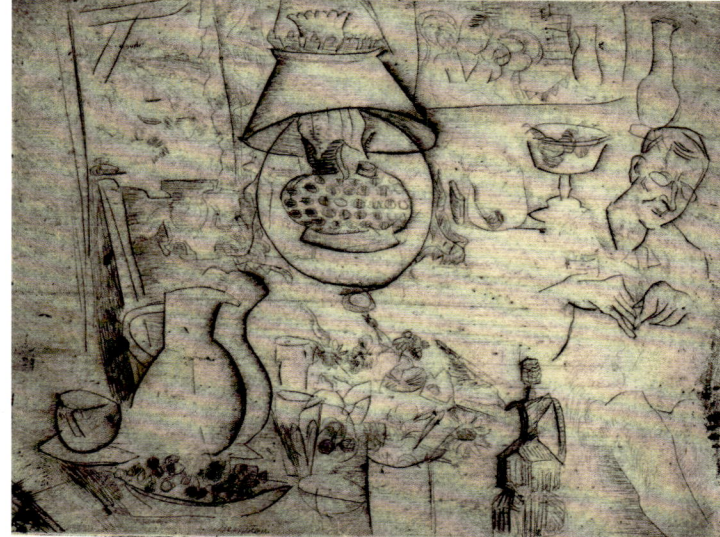

186. *New England Home*, 1925. Etching, 5.88 x 7.26 inches. Theresa Bernstein and William Meyerowitz Foundation.

Reputation," investigate the reasons why an artist either achieves longevity during or after his or her career or sinks into eventual obscurity. Focusing on the multitude of artists who created prints during the American etching revival, the Langs reveal that despite many of these artists' high level of talent, they and their works have been largely forgotten in time. The Langs explain that a major factor in this collective forgetfulness is that the artists' "reputations change as styles go out of fashion."[59] The wave of the etching revival ebbed, and as the popularity of etchings declined, so did the popularity of the artists who made them.

It becomes a more complicated discussion for an artist like Theresa Bernstein, who in the first place did not base her entire career on the creation of etchings or monotypes but appears to have produced a smaller number of works both for exhibition and for personal study and experimentation. Therefore, it is possible to overlook her body of print work, both within the wider context of the etching revival and within her individual career. However, it also soon becomes clear that Bernstein's prints deserve a thorough investigation. An understanding of these works places her among some of the most accomplished artists of her day, and more importantly, leads to a wider, richer, and more complete appreciation of the diversity of her achievements.

NOTES

1. Bernstein, *The Journal*, p. 9.

2. Gladys Engel Lang and Kurt Lang, "Recognition and Renown: The Survival of Artistic Reputation," *American Journal of Sociology* 94 (1988), p. 82.

3. Bamber Gascoigne, *How to Identify Prints: A Complete Guide to Manual and Mechanical Processes from Woodcut to Inkjet* (New York: Thames and Hudson, 2004), p. 10.

4. Gascoigne, *How to Identify Prints*, p. 10.

5. Gascoigne, *How to Identify Prints*, p. 10.

6. Rona Schneider, "The American Etching Revival: Its French Sources and Early Years," *American Art Journal* 14, no. 4 (1982), p. 40.

7. Eugenia Parry Janis, "Setting the Tone—The Revival of Etching, the Importance of Ink," in *The Painterly Print: Monotypes from the Seventeenth to the Twentieth Century*, ed. Sue Welsh Reed (New York: Metropolitan Museum of Art, 1980), p. 9.

8. Schneider, "The American Etching Revival," p. 40.

9. Lang and Lang, "Recognition and Renown," p. 82.

10. Joann Moser, *Singular Impressions: The Monotype in America* (Washington DC: Published for the National Museum of American Art by Smithsonian Institution Press, 1997), p. 85.

11. Elizabeth Helsinger, "The 'Writing' of Modern Life," in *The "Writing" of Modern Life: The Etching Revival in France, Britain, and the U.S., 1850–1940* (Chicago: Smart Museum of Art, University of Chicago, 2008), p. 2.

12. Helsinger, "The 'Writing' of Modern Life," p. 3.

13. Theresa Bernstein, "Theresa B. Meyerowitz—Art Statements & Articles," William Meyerowitz and Theresa F. Bernstein Papers, 1915–1978, Archives of American Art, Smithsonian Institution.

14. Bernstein, *William Meyerowitz*, p. 80.

15. Bernstein, *William Meyerowitz*, p. 79.

16. Girard Jackson and Dorothy Mayhall, *Theresa Bernstein: Expressions of Cape Ann and New York, 1914–1972, A Centennial Exhibition* (Stamford CT: Stamford Museum and Nature Center and Smith-Girard, 1989), n.p.

17. Theresa Bernstein, "Exhibition Catalogues," William Meyerowitz and Theresa F. Bernstein Papers, 1915–1978, Archives of American Art, Smithsonian Institution.

18. Bernstein, *The Journal*, p. 87.

19. Theresa Bernstein, "Correspondence, 1944–1966," William Meyerowitz and Theresa F. Bernstein Papers, 1915–1978, Archives of American Art, Smithsonian Institution.

20. Helsinger, "The 'Writing' of Modern Life," p. 1.

21. Helsinger, "The 'Writing' of Modern Life," p. 1.

22. Helsinger, "The 'Writing' of Modern Life," p. 1.

23. Jackson and Mayhall, *Theresa Bernstein: Expressions of Cape Ann and New York*, n.p.

24. Marian Wardle, ed., *American Women Modernists: The Legacy of Robert Henri, 1910–1945* (New Brunswick NJ: Brigham Young University Museum of Art in association with Rutgers University Press, 2005), p. 88.

25. Wardle, *American Women Modernists*, p. 88.

26. Patricia M. Burnham, "Theresa Bernstein," *Woman's Art Journal* 9, no. 2 (Autumn 1988–Winter 1989), p. 25.

27. Una E. Johnson, introduction to *Milton Avery: Prints and Drawings, 1930–1964* (Brooklyn: Distributed by Shorewood Publishers, 2008), p. 10.

28. Helsinger, "The 'Writing' of Modern Life," p. 1.

29. Bernstein, "Theresa B. Meyerowitz—Art Statements & Articles," Archives of American Art.

30. Michael Mazur, "Monotype: An Artist's View," in *The Painterly Print*, p. 55.

31. Mazur, "Monotype," p. 55.

32. Mazur, "Monotype," p. 56.

33. Mazur, "Monotype," p. 55.

34. Gascoigne, *How to Identify Prints*, p. 46.

35. Joann Moser, *Singular Impressions: The Monotype in America* (Washington DC: Published for the National Museum of American Art by Smithsonian Institution Press, 1997), p. 3.

36. David W. Kiehl, "Monotypes in America in the Nineteenth and Early Twentieth Centuries," in *The Painterly Print*, p. 40.

37. Moser, *Singular Impressions*, p. 65.

38. Moser, *Singular Impressions*, p. 135.

39. Colta Ives, David W. Kiehl, Sue Welsh Reed, and Barbara Stern Shapiro, preface and acknowledgments to *The Painterly Print*, p. ix.

40. Ives, Kiehl, Reed, and Shapiro, preface and acknowledgments to *The Painterly Print*, p. ix.

41. Table of contents in Moser, *Singular Impressions*.

42. Moser, *Singular Impressions*, p. 132.

43. Moser, *Singular Impressions*, p. 132.

44. Moser, *Singular Impressions*, p. 131.

45. American Color Print Society, *Ninth Annual Exhibition*, March 12–31, 1948 (Philadelphia: Print Club of Philadelphia, 1948.)

46. *Exhibition of Etchings and Monotypes in Color by Theresa F. Bernstein*, April 26–May 24, 1948 (Washington DC: Smithsonian Institution, 1948).

47. *The Russian-Born American Artist William Meyerowitz: An Exhibition of Paintings and Etchings for the Benefit of the Greenwich Philharmonia Orchestra of Greenwich, Connecticut*, September 18, 19, 25, 26, 1976 (Greenwich: Smith-Girard Art Brokers, 1976.)

48. Ben L. Bassham, *John Taylor Arms: American Etcher* (Madison: University of Wisconsin, 1975), p. 4.

49. Theresa Bernstein, "Correspondence (1926–1967)," William Meyerowitz and Theresa F. Bernstein Papers, 1915–1978, Archives of American Art, Smithsonian Institution.

50. Johnson, introduction to *Milton Avery*, p. 10.

51. Moser, *Singular Impressions*, p. 132.

52. Bober, *The Etchings of William Meyerowitz*, p. 6.

53. Bober, *The Etchings of William Meyerowitz*, p. 5.

54. Nancy Mowll Mathews and Elizabeth Kennedy, *Prendergast in Italy* (London: Merrell, 2009), p. 99.

55. Mathews and Kennedy, *Prendergast in Italy*, p. 111.

56. Moser, *Singular Impressions*, p. 60.

57. David W. Kiehl, "Nineteenth- and Early Twentieth-Century American Monotypes," in *The Painterly Print*, p. 180.

58. Kiehl, "Nineteenth- and Early Twentieth-Century American Monotypes," p. 180.

59. Lang and Lang, "Recognition and Renown," p. 80.

Appendix 1

SELECTION OF WRITINGS BY THERESA BERNSTEIN

1933   "American Color Print Exhibition." *Brooklyn Museum Quarterly* 20, no. 2 (April), pp. 24–29.

1933   "The Artist and the Community." *Gloucester Daily Times*, August 18.

1941   "New England Harbor: A Colored Etching by William Meyerowitz." *Christian Science Monitor*, [no byline; month and day unknown].

ca. 1941 "Lighthouse off Cape Ann, Massachusetts: A Color Etching by William Meyerowitz," *Christian Science Monitor*, [no byline; month and day unknown].

1954   "Memorial Show Offers Lessons." *Cape Ann Summer Sun*, August 6.

1960   "Artist's Statement." Exhibition catalogue, Cober Gallery, New York.

1964   "Reflections on the Art Status." Unpublished draft of an article written in 1964. William Meyerowitz and Theresa F. Bernstein Papers, 1915–1978, Archives of American Art, Smithsonian Institution, Washington DC [Reel D285].

1973   "The 350th Anniversary of Gloucester, 1623–1973." Gloucester, MA [broadsheet].

1984   "William Merritt Chase (1849–1916)" in *Etchings and Paintings: William Meyerowitz/Theresa Bernstein*, June 10, 1984–October 20, 1984. Paterson Public Library, Paterson NJ, n.p. [pamphlet].

1984   "Concerning the Process of Etching," August 24, 1984. Unpublished MS.

1985   "How I Wrote the Book, 'William Meyerowitz, the Artist Speaks,'" July. Unpublished MS.

1986   *The Artist Speaks*. New York: Cornwall Books.

1989   *The Poetic Canvas*. New York: Cornwall Books.

1991   *The Journal*. New York: Cornwall Books.

1992   *The Sketchbook*. Woburn MA: Published privately with the assistance of her friends.

1994   *Israeli Journal*. Cranbury NJ: Cornwall Books.

1996   "The Review," June 4. Unpublished MS, private collection.

2000   *Rabbitville*. Lunenburg VT: Sinehour Press, published by her friends with her drawings and stories.

Appendix 2

PUBLIC COLLECTIONS OF THERESA BERNSTEIN'S WORKS

IN THE UNITED STATES

Art Institute of Chicago, Chicago, Illinois

Boca Raton Museum of Art, Boca Raton, Florida

Boston Public Library, Boston, Massachusetts

Brigham Young University Museum of Art, Provo, Utah

Brooklyn Museum, Brooklyn, New York

Butler Institute of American Art, Youngstown, Ohio

Cape Ann Museum, Gloucester, Massachusetts

Corcoran Gallery of Art, Washington DC

Dallas Museum of Art, Dallas, Texas

Harvard University Art Museums, Cambridge, Massachusetts

Howard University Gallery of Art, Washington DC

Huntsville Museum of Art, Huntsville, Alabama

Jack S. Blanton Museum of Art, Austin, Texas

Jewish Museum, New York, New York

Library of Congress, Washington DC

Metropolitan Museum of Art, New York, New York

Montclair Art Museum, Montclair, New Jersey

Moore College of Art, Philadelphia, Pennsylvania

Museum of the City of New York, New York, New York

Museum of Fine Arts, Boston, Massachusetts

National Museum of American Art, Smithsonian Institution, Washington DC

National Museum of Women in the Arts, Washington DC

New-York Historical Society, New York, New York

New York Public Library, New York, New York

Ogunquit Museum of American Art, Ogunquit, Maine

Philadelphia Museum of Art, Philadelphia, Pennsylvania

Phillips Collection, Washington DC

Princeton University Art Museum, Princeton, New Jersey

Rockport Art Association, Rockport, Massachusetts

Seattle Art Museum, Seattle, Washington

Toledo Museum of Art, Toledo, Ohio

Trustman Art Gallery, Simmons College, Boston, Massachusetts

Washington County Museum of Fine Arts, Hagerstown, Maryland

Weatherspoon Art Gallery, Greensboro, North Carolina

Zimmerli Art Museum, Rutgers University, New Brunswick, New Jersey

OUTSIDE THE UNITED STATES

Museum of Art, Ein Harod, Israel

Musee d'Art et d'Histoire du Judaïsme, Paris, France

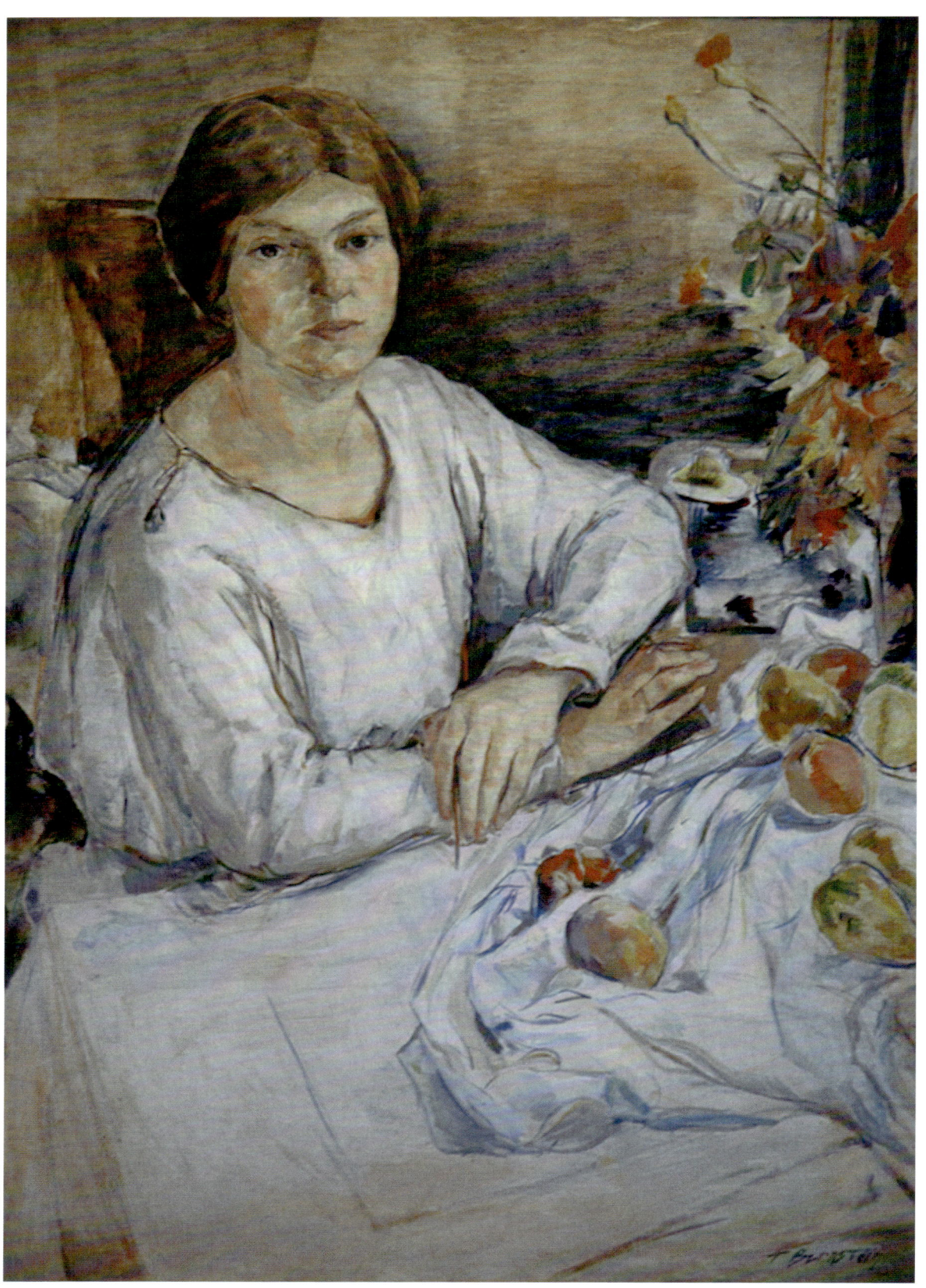

187. *Self portrait*, ca. 1931, Oil on canvas, 30 x 40 inches. Private collection.

Chronology of Theresa Bernstein's Life

1890

March 1: Born in Cracow, the only child of Anna Ferber and Isadore Bernstein. Family immigrates to the United States and settles in Philadelphia when she is just a year old.

1903

Enters William D. Kelley High School in Philadelphia; lives with her parents at 1631 North 29th Street.

1905

Summer: Travels with her mother and family friends to Berlin, Vienna, Munich, Zurich, Paris, and other European cities.

1907

May 19: Participates in confirmation exercises at the Jewish Reform Congregation Keneseth Israel in Philadelphia.

June 24: Graduates from William D. Kelley School. Wins Board of Education Scholarship, Philadelphia School of Design for Women (now Moore College of Art and Design) for the year 1907–8.

Attends lectures at the Pennsylvania Academy of Fine Arts.

1909

Wins prize for oil painting, *White Roses* (#33), in *Sixth Annual Competitive Exhibit of Art Students* at Wanamaker's, the Philadelphia department store. Also shows *Roses* (#26), *Fruits and Flowers* (#27), *Study of a Girl* (#28), *Still Life* (#29), *Katie* (#30), *Picnic* (#31), *Roses* (#32), and *Still Life* (#34).

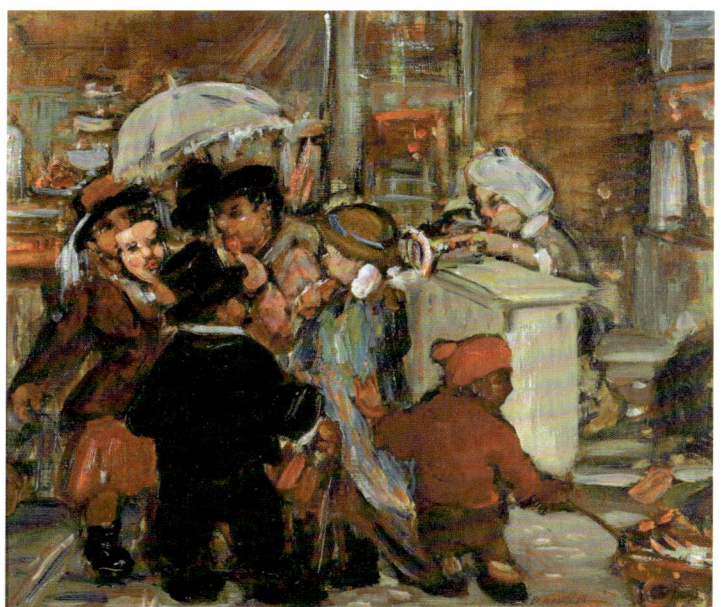

188. *Halloween*, ca. 1912. Oil on canvas, 26 x 30 inches. Martin and Edith Stein Collection.

189. *Kindergarten Class*, 1914. Oil on artist's board, 9 x 12 inches. Martin and Edith Stein Collection.

1910

Wins prizes of $10 for a watercolor and for an oil painting in the School of Design's annual competitive show of student work.

Travels to Lumberville, Pennsylvania, to paint outdoors with her teacher Daniel Garber. Visits William Lathrop's studio in New Hope during this trip.

1911

Graduates from Philadelphia School of Design for Women, having completed four-year Normal Art course in teacher training and won the John Sartain Prize.

Moves with parents to New York City, staying at their apartment at 122 West 94th Street in Manhattan. She rents a small studio at 145 West 55th Street, but continues to live at home with her parents.

Takes second trip to Europe with her mother. Travels to Berlin and Munich. Discovers the work of Edvard Munch, Vasily Kandinsky, and Franz Marc.

Summer: Takes trip to study in Blowing Rock, North Carolina, with Elliott Daingerfield.

August 23–September 23: Studies at the Arts Students League program in Woodstock, New York.

October–December: Studies with William Merritt Chase in his last year at the Art Students League, New York City.

1912

November: Shows sketches at the William H. Powell Art Gallery, 983 Sixth Avenue, between 55th and 56th Streets.

1913

Visits the *International Exhibition of Modern Art* (the Armory Show) at the Sixty-Ninth Regiment Armory and Alfred Stieglitz's gallery at "291" on Fifth Avenue.

National Academy of Design chooses her *Open-Air Show* (1912–13) for its annual Winter Exhibition (December 20–January 18, 1914). The exhibition travels to the Carnegie Institute in Pittsburgh and the Art Institute of Chicago, where John Lane, an English collector and publisher of *International Studio*, purchases it.

1914

April: Shows *The Concert*, *Basket of Flowers*, and four other works in the sixteenth MacDowell Club group exhibition.

May 2–17: Participates in a group exhibition at the MacDowell Club with K. R. Chamberlain, Stuart Davis, Henry Glintenkamp, C. Bertram Hartman, Robert Henri, Ruth Jacobi, Adelaide Husted Long, Frank Montegue Moore, Marjorie Organ, Josephine Paddock, Alethea Hill Platt, Henry Reuterdahl, Gertrude Lundborg Richards, John Sloan, Clara Tice, Hilda Ward, and Arthur Young.

May 7–June 7: Shows watercolor *Full-Blown Roses* (#13) in *Twenty-Sixth Annual Exhibition of Water-colors, Pastels, and Miniatures by American Artists* at the Art Institute of Chicago. Shows watercolor *On the Beach* at Philadelphia Water

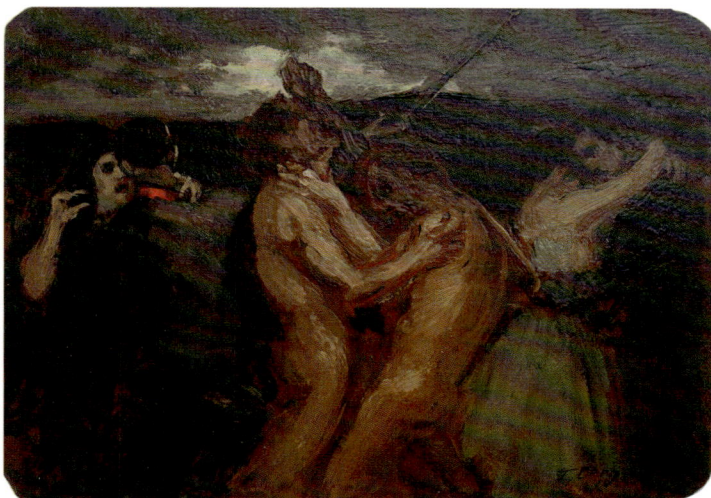

190. *War: Brother against Brother*, 1914. Oil on board, 9 x 12 inches. Theresa Bernstein and William Meyerowitz Foundation.

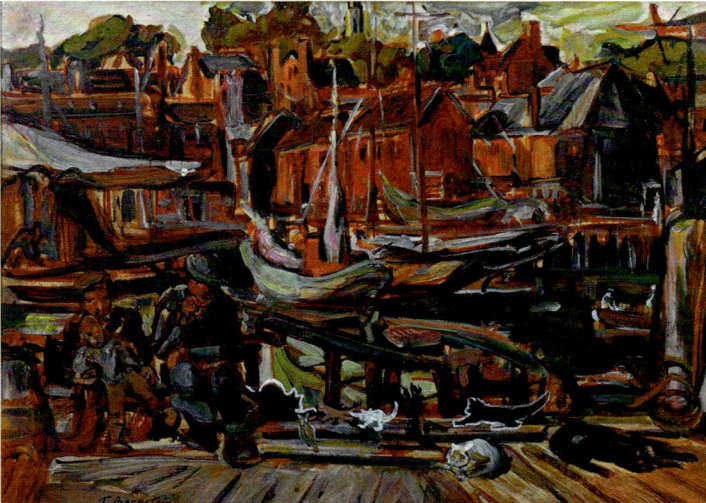

191. *On the Docks, Gloucester*, ca. 1916. Oil on board, 14¼ x 19⅞ inches. James B. Hand Fine Art.

Color Club, Pennsylvania Society of Miniature Painters.

November 3–December 6: Shows *Open-Air Show* (#25) in Twenty-Seventh Annual Exhibition of American Oil Paintings and Sculpture at the Art Institute of Chicago.

December 19–January 17: Shows *Opera Night* and *The Suffrage Meeting* at National Academy of Design Winter Exhibition.

1915

Wins Shillard Gold Medal at the Plastic Club, Philadelphia, for *Outing on the Hudson*.

February: Shows *Open-Air Show* in the Panama-Pacific Exhibition in San Francisco.

March 20–April 25: Shows *The Music Lovers* at Ninetieth Annual Exhibition of the National Academy of Design.

April: Shows *Outing on the Hudson* in an exhibition of women's art at Anderson Galleries.

May: Shows set of drawings for the poems of Rabindranath Tagore in the group show *Drawings at MacDowell Club*.

May 13–June 13: Shows *Watching the Bathers* (#39) in *Twenty-Seventh Annual Exhibition of Water-colors, Pastels, and Miniatures by American Artists* at the Art Institute of Chicago.

May 20: Invited guest at a gathering of the former students of Elliott Daingerfield, organized by Emily Sartain, principal of the Philadelphia School of Design for Women.

June: Shows at 8 West Eighth Street as one of 217 works and wins one of ten special prizes of $25 awarded by Mrs. Harry Payne (Gertrude Vanderbilt) Whitney under the auspices of the Society of Young Artists. Founding member of "The Eclectics" and participates in their first group show at the Folsom Galleries, 396 Fifth Avenue.

September 27–October 16: Participates in *Exhibition of Painting and Sculpture by Women Artists for the Benefit of the Woman Suffrage Campaign* at the Macbeth Gallery, 450 Fifth Avenue. Donates one painting with half the proceeds going to the cause.

November 16–January 2, 1916: Shows *The Opera Lobby* (#29) in *Twenty-Eighth Annual Exhibition of American Oil Paintings and Sculpture* at the Art Institute of Chicago.

November 20–December 24: Shows *Afternoon on Riverside*; *Summer Day, Coney Island*; *Bathers at Brighton*; and *The Gossips* in *Exhibition of Small Pictures and Sculptures*, Association of Women Painters and Sculptors, Arlington Art Galleries, 274 Madison Avenue.

December 18–January 16, 1916: Shows *The Little Merry-Go-Round* and *The Fleet on the Hudson* at National Academy of Design Winter Exhibition.

1916

January: Shows *Sunset on the Hudson*, *Opera Night*, *Fantasy*, *Little Cafe*, and *Caprice* in an exhibition of *The Eclectics* at Folsom Galleries.

February 1–March 1: Shows *Central Park* (#45), *Sunset on the Hudson* (#60), and *The Suffrage Meeting* (#63) in *A Collection of Paintings by American Artists* at the Syracuse Museum of Fine Arts.

Winter: Meets artist William Meyerowitz for the first time. He visits her at her studio on West 55th Street. Shows

The Fleet on the Hudson at the Pennsylvania Academy of the Fine Arts Annual Exhibition.

February 1–March 1: Shows *Central Park*, *Sunset on the Hudson*, and *The Suffrage Meeting* in exhibition *A Collection of Paintings by American Artists*, Syracuse Museum. Among others in the show are J. Alden Weir, Frederick C. Frieseke, Gifford Beal, Guy Pène du Bois, and D. Putnam Brinley.

February: Wins National Arts Club Prize of $100, given by John Agar, for her oil painting *In the Elevated* in *Twenty-Fifth Annual Exhibition of the National Association of Women Painters and Sculptors*.

March 16–26: Shows *Summer Resort*, *The Suffrage Parade*, *High School Girls*, and *Decorative Portrait* in *Exhibition of Painting and Sculpture* at the MacDowell Club.

May: Exhibits at the Catharine Lorillard Wolfe Art Club, 802 Broadway, and wins mural prize for *Lilies of the Field*.

May 20: Participates in group show of forty artists at the Braus Galleries, 2122 Broadway.

Summer: Goes to Gloucester for the first time.

September: Participates in opening show at Gallery-on-the-Moors, East Gloucester, Massachusetts, and shows *The Little Merry-Go-Round* (#19) and *On the Beach* (#73).

November 2–December 7: Shows *The Suffrage Parade* (#21) and *The Beach* (#22) in *Twenty-Ninth Annual Exhibition of American Oil Paintings and Sculpture* at the Art Institute of Chicago.

December: Shows *Beach Group* in *Annual Exhibition of Small Pictures and Sculpture* by the National Association of Women Painters and Sculptors at Arlington Galleries.

December–January 2, 1917: Shows *In the Elevated*, *Open-Air Show*, *The Beach*, *Shakespeare Masque*, and *The Mountains* at the MacDowell Club.

December 16–January 14, 1917: Shows *The Golf Links* and *The Preparedness Parade* at National Academy of Design Winter Exhibition.

1917

Paints with William Meyerowitz in Ridgefield, New Jersey.

February 4–March 25: Shows two oil paintings, *The Golf Links* and *The Preparedness Parade*, in the *112th Annual Exhibition of Painting and Sculpture* of the Pennsylvania Academy of the Fine Arts, Philadelphia.

February: Shows at the National Association of Women Painters and Sculptors exhibition. Participates in *The Philadelphia Ten*, first group show of eleven artists held at the Art Club of Philadelphia.

March: Shows a portrait in the Seventh Annual Exhibition at Connecticut Academy, Hartford, Connecticut.

March 17–April 22: Shows *Polish Church: Easter Morning* at Ninety-Second Annual Exhibition of the National Academy of Design.

April 2–16: Shows with the Society of Friends of Young Artists along with Benjamin Kopman, Agnes Pelton, Marguerite Zorach, and William Zorach at Knoedler Galleries, 556 Fifth Avenue.

April 16–28: Participates in second annual exhibition of The Eclectics.

May: Shows at Vose Galleries in Boston. Participates in People's Art Guild exhibition at the Jewish Daily Forward Building on East Broadway with Stella, Walkowitz, Stieglitz, Maurer, Hartley, Marin, Halpert, Brodzky, Sloan, Henri, Bellows, and William Meyerowitz, among others.

August: Shows *Sun, Sand, and Sea* (#18) (location unknown; reproduced in *International Studio* 1919 feature article);

The Garden Party (#27) (location unknown), and Golf, Eastern Point (#58) (location unknown) in Gallery-on-the-Moors.

November 8–January 2: Shows Polish Church: Easter Morning (#10) and The Garden Party (#11) in Thirtieth Annual Exhibition of American Oil Paintings and Sculpture at the Art Institute of Chicago.

December 15–January 13: Shows The 18th Regiment at National Academy of Design Winter Exhibition.

Appears in Lorinda Bryant's book American Pictures and Their Painters, which reproduces The Opera Lobby.

1918

Wins Whitney Prize, Friends of Young Artists, and C. L. Wolfe Club Landscape Prize.

Shows Western Massachusetts at the Vose Gallery. This painting, which depicts the hills near Stockbridge, is sold to a Mrs. Longyear, resident of Stockbridge and a leader of the Christian Science Church. Mrs. Longyear donates the painting to a museum in her home state of Michigan. (Painting now lost.)

Shows Polish Church: Easter Morning at the Pennsylvania Academy of the Fine Arts Annual Exhibition.

January: Shows The Balcony, The Socialist's Wife, The Golf Links, and Sunset Glow at the MacDowell Club.

February: Shows Portrait of a Lady in the third exhibition of The Eclectics at the Folsom Galleries.

March 13–April 21: Shows Landscape with Figures in Ninety-Third Annual Exhibition of the National Academy of Design.

April 20–May 12: Shows Smoldering Day and Intelligence Bureau at the Society of Independent Artists.

May: Shows Searchlights on the Hudson in the exhibition American Paintings and Sculptures Pertaining to the War at M. Knoedler and Co. Proceeds from the exhibition are invested in liberty bonds. Participates in Exhibition of Water-colors, Pastels, and Drawings, at the MacDowell Club.

August: Shows Golf Tournament (#33) and Landscape with Figures (#69) at Gallery-on-the-Moors.

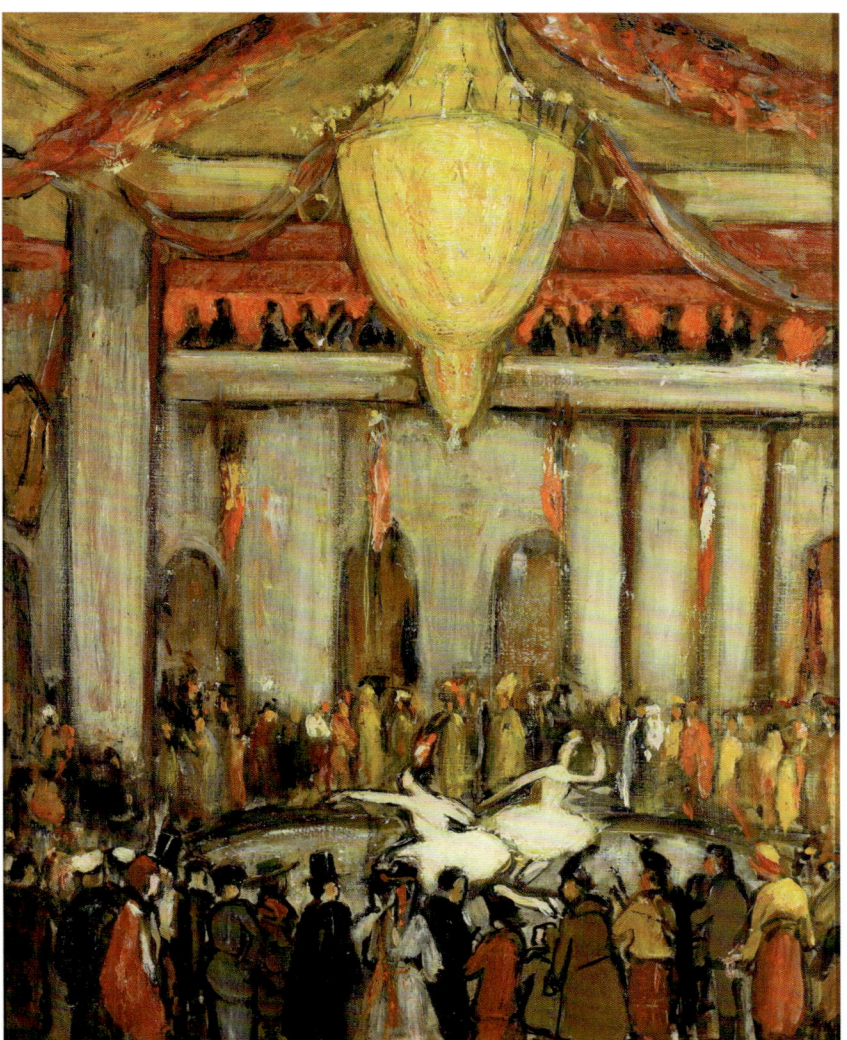

192. Figure Skaters at the New York Hippodrome, 1918. Oil on canvas, 35 x 27 inches. Martin and Edith Stein Collection.

Childe Hassam, Henry Snell, and John Sloan are also included in the exhibition.

November 7–19: Participates in exhibition with Frederick K. Detwiller, George Pearse Ennis, Alice Judson, Oscar H. Julius, Victor A. Seydel, H. Vance Swope, and James Wieland at the MacDowell Club.

November 11: Views Armistice Day Parade on Fifth Avenue. This event inspired several paintings.

November–December: Participates in an exhibition of etchings by Manhattan Painter-Gravers' Club at the Mussman Gallery, 144 West 57th Street. William Meyerowitz, John Sloan, and Mahonri Young are also included.

December: Participates in Fourth Annual Exhibition of The Eclectics at the Babcock Galleries.

December 17–29: Participates in exhibition with George Bellows, Robert Henri, John Sloan, and others at the MacDowell Club.

December 11–January 12, 1919: Shows Patriotic Parade at National Academy of Design Winter Exhibition.

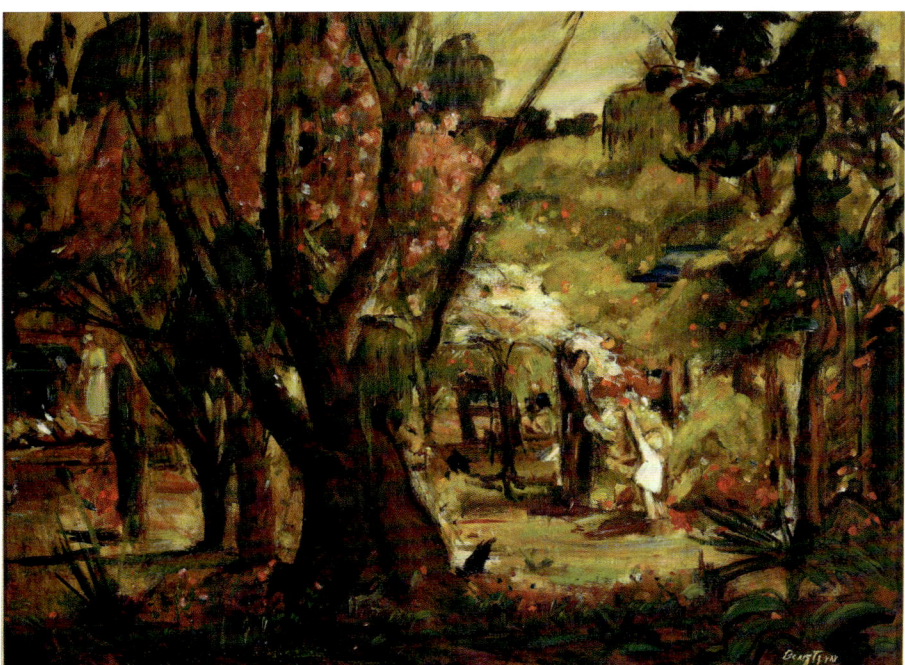

193. *Sheep Meadow, Central Park*, 1919. Oil on canvas, 30 x 40 inches. Martin and Edith Stein Collection.

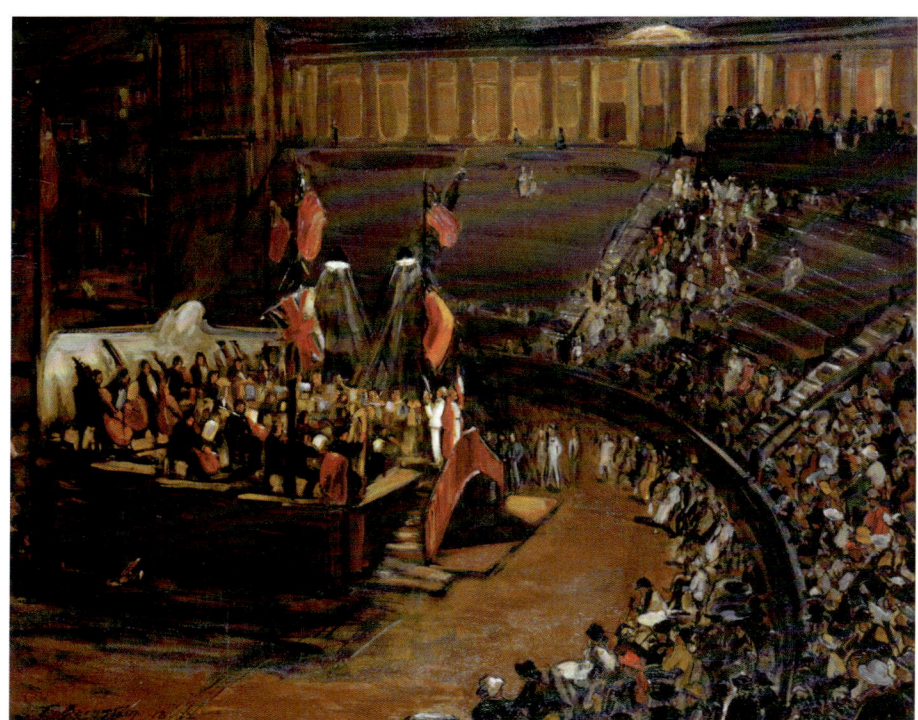

194. *Lewisohn Stadium*, 1919–22. Oil on canvas, 40 x 50 inches. Martin and Edith Stein Collection.

1919

February 9: Marries William Meyerowitz (born July 15, 1887, in Kozeletz, Russia). The couple take a honeymoon trip to Florida, where Bernstein paints. Return to live at 39 West 67th Street.

February: Participates in the *Twenty-Eighth Annual Exhibition of the National Association of Women Painters and Sculptors* held in the Fine Arts Building. Shows *Fourth of July* at the Pennsylvania Academy of Fine Arts Annual Exhibition.

March 28–April 14: Shows *Garden Party* and *Portuguese Synagogue* at the Society of Independent Artists, Waldorf Astoria Hotel.

May: Participates in the last group exhibition held at the MacDowell Club, which featured forty-two artists including John Sloan, Edward Hopper, Walter Tittle, and Randall Davey.

Summer: Shows *Greek Pageant* (#5) in Gallery-on-the-Moors.

November 1–15: Has solo show at Milch Gallery, 108 West 57th Street, New York; ten paintings sell on the opening day of the show.

December 2–31: Participates in *Exhibition of Paintings by Louis Kronberg, Theresa F. Bernstein, and Arthur C. Goodwin* at Detroit Institute of the Arts. Shows *Polish Church*, *Grecian Pageant*, *Portrait of a Lady*, *Big Trees*, *In the Elevated*, *Golf Links*, *Landscape with Figures*, *Election Parade*, *Lilies of the Field*, *18th Regiment*, *Promenade*, and *Florida Sky*.

1920

January 29, 1920: Gives birth to daughter and only child, Isadora G. R. Meyerowitz, in Manhattan.

February: Has *Exhibition of Oil Paintings by Theresa F. Bernstein and Etchings by William Meyerowitz* at Syracuse Museum of Fine Arts, Syracuse University, Syracuse, New York.

February 8–March 28: Shows *The Little Houses* and *Patriotic Parade* in the 115th Annual Exhibition of Paintings at the Pennsylvania Academy of the Fine Arts. Jury chaired by Daniel Garber and includes Arthur B. Carles and Robert Henri, among others.

March 11–April 1: Shows *Portrait*, *Robert J. Cole*, and *Summer Time* at the Society of Independent Artists. One painting (title not given) sells to C. J. Burns for $100.

April: Participates in exhibition of paintings by Robert Henri, Charles Bittinger, Theresa Bernstein, and etchings by William Meyerowitz at the Memorial Art Gallery, Rochester, New York.

April 6–May 9: Shows *The Altar of Liberty* and *The Bohemian* at Ninety-Fifth Annual Exhibition of the National Academy of Design.

May 11: Daughter dies of pneumonia at the age of three months and twelve days.

Summer: Spends season at Folly Cove, Gloucester. Meyerowitz develops color etching. Shows *The Harbor* (also referred to as *Twilight Study*) at Gallery-on-the-Moors. Teaches Louise Nevelson in New York studio.

December 1–25: Participates in *Annual Holiday Exhibition of Selected Paintings of Limited Size* at Milch Galleries.

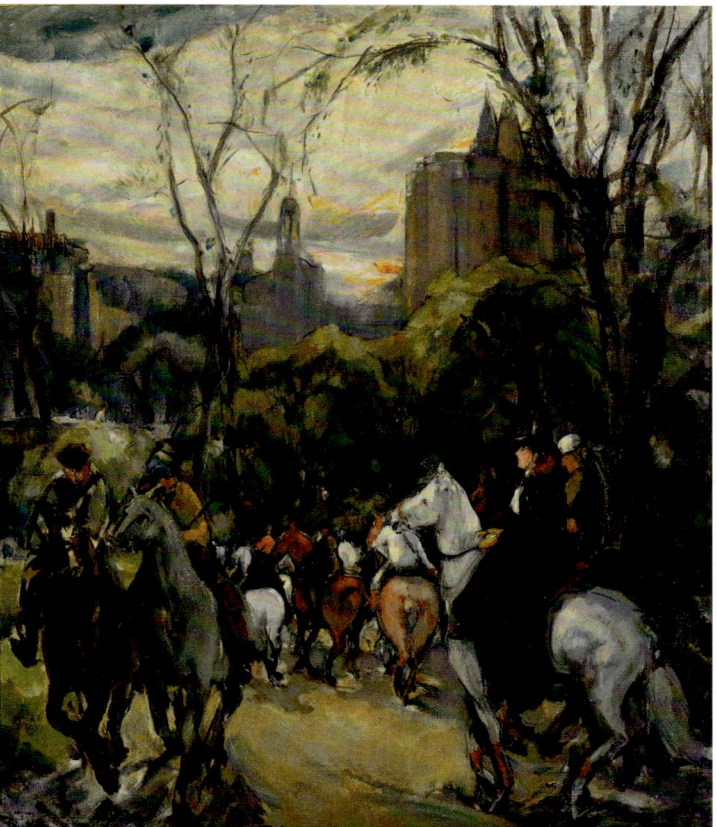

195. *Riders in Central Park*, 1921. Oil on canvas, 24 x 20 inches.
Martin and Edith Stein Collection.

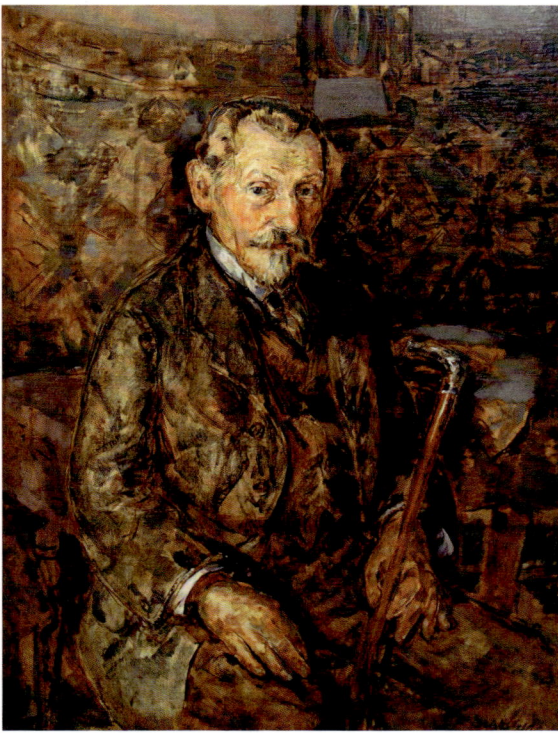

196. *Portrait of Grandfather*, 1922. Oil on canvas, 39¼ x 29¼ inches.
Theresa Bernstein and William Meyerowitz Foundation.

1921

Shows *Grecian Pageant* at the Pennsylvania Academy of the Fine Arts Annual Exhibition.

February 26–March 24: Shows *Figure Composition* and *Portrait* at the Society of Independent Artists.

March 5–April 3: Shows *The Cove* at Ninety-Sixth Annual Exhibition of the National Academy of Design.

Spring: Invited with Meyerowitz to make portraits of Albert Einstein at the first Zionist meeting in America, held in New York. This was Einstein's first trip to America. Meyerowitz is asked to be a jury member for the group that became the Rockport Art Association. The Gloucester Society of Artists was also established at about the same time. William and Theresa are involved.

Summer: Shows *At the Concert* (#38) in Gallery-on-the-Moors.

November 3–December 11: Shows *The Village* (#20 in Thirty-Fourth Annual Exhibition of American Oil Paintings and Sculpture at the Art Institute of Chicago.

November 19–December 18: Shows *Girlhood* at National Academy of Design Winter Exhibition.

December 17–January 22, 1922: Exhibits *Polish Church* (#53) in *Eighth Biennial of Oil Paintings by Contemporary Artists* at the Corcoran Gallery of Art, Washington DC.

December: Exhibits at Syracuse Museum of Fine Arts. Etchings by Meyerowitz are also shown. Participates in exhibition at Albright-Knox Gallery in Buffalo.

1922

January 26–February 28: Shows *Central Park* and *New England Ladies* in *An Exhibition of Etchings, Chicago Society of Etchings*, at the Art Institute of Chicago; priced at $15 each.

March 10–12: Participates in two benefit shows, one held at the Architectural League of New York, preceding auction on March 15, and another for the National Association of Women Painters and Sculptors. Shows *Girlhood* and *The Village* at the Pennsylvania Academy of the Fine Arts Annual Exhibition.

March 11–April 2: Shows *Figure Composition* and *Late Afternoon* at the Society of Independent Artists.

March 25–April 23: Shows *The Concert* and *Still Life* at Ninety-Seventh Annual Exhibition of the National Academy of Design.

April: Participates in *Thirty-First Annual Exhibition of the National Association of Women Painters and Sculptors* at Anderson Galleries. Participates with Meyerowitz in exhibition of prints by contemporary artists at the American Academy of Arts and Letters in New York; both are listed in the *New York Times* review.

May: Participates in the Seventh Annual Exhibition of The Eclectics at the Dudensing Galleries 45 West 44th Street.

Participates in Street Fair for the Benefit of the Association for the Aid of Crippled Children.

Participates with Meyerowitz in the first semiannual exhibition in the People's House (7 East 15th Street). Also included are Walter Pach, Leon Kroll, Stuart Davis, George Bellows, Robert Henri, John Sloan, Gaston Lachaise, and William and Marguerite Zorach.

July 1–22: Participates in the National Association of Women Painters and Sculptors exhibition held at the Parish Art Museum, Southampton, Long Island.

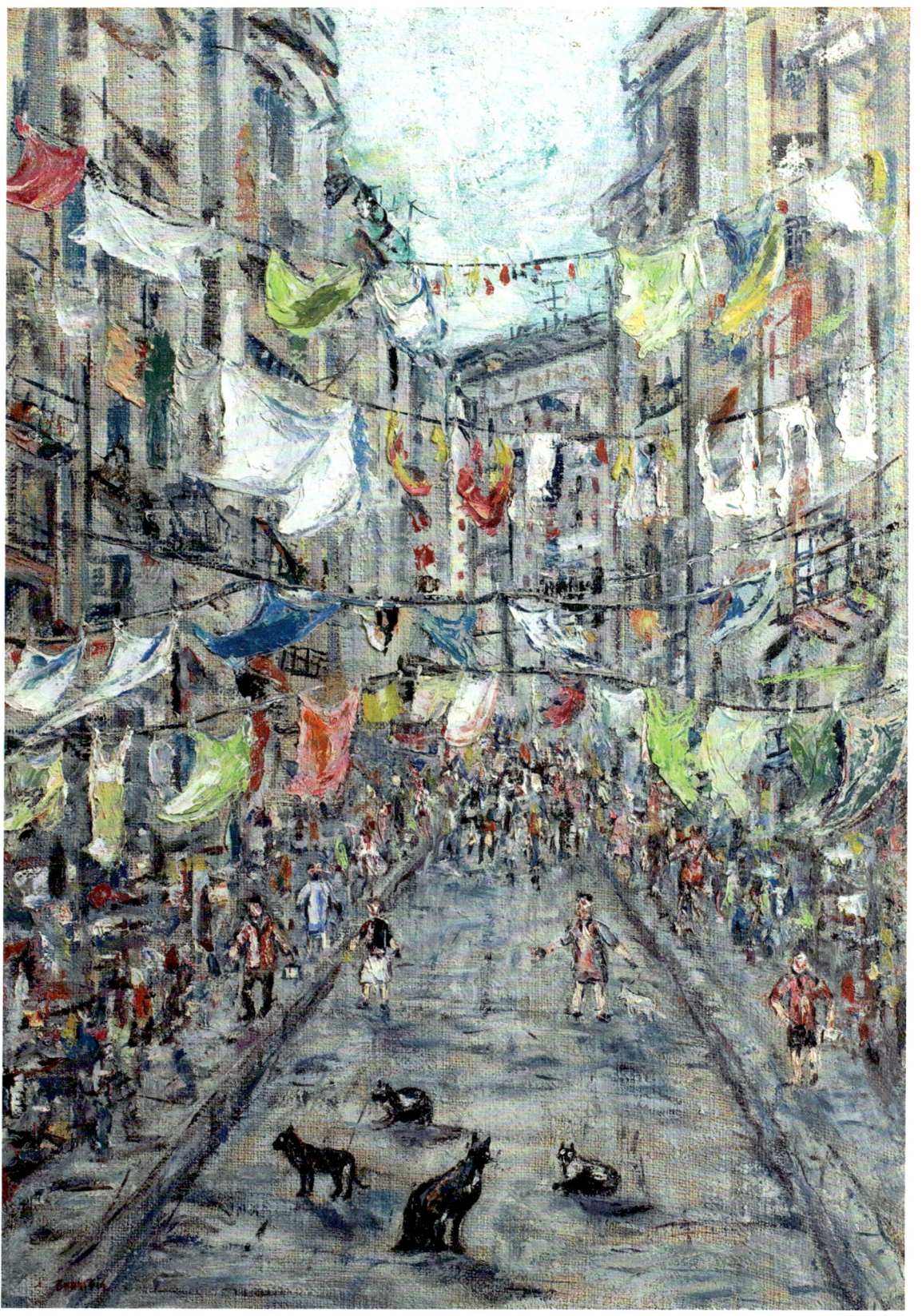

197. *Five Points Laundry Day*, ca. 1922–24. Oil on canvas mounted on board, 34 x 23 inches. Girard Jackson Collection.

Summer: Shows *Stormy Sea, Folly Cove* (#63) at Gallery-on-the-Moors. Becomes founding member of North Shore Arts Association, Gloucester. Embarks on five-month trip to Europe with William Meyerowitz, visiting London, Holland, Berlin, Poland, Vienna, Venice, Florence, Rome, and Paris. Exhibits works at the Victoria and Albert Museum in London.

1923

Shows *The Cove, European Summer Resort*, and *Children's Pageant* at the Pennsylvania Academy of the Fine Arts Annual Exhibition.

January–February 10: Participates in first annual show of a new group of painters called "The Cosmopolitans" at Babcock Galleries. The Cosmopolitans (Frederick Detwiller, Jerry Farnesworth, Jane Peterson, and Helen Sawyer, among others) announce that they have organized "for the purpose of increasing art interest in America by giving people of good taste and moderate means an opportunity to secure at prices commensurate with their incomes. . . . The members have agreed to cut their prices for the present exhibition to $50, $75 and $100. They have agreed to select from their output each year two or three of their best examples which they will sell at these rates."

February 24–March 18: Shows *The Stadium* and *Self-Portrait* at the Society of Independent Artists.

March 24–April 14: Shows Gloucester studies and figure compositions at the Art Club of Philadelphia in an exhibition of ten women painters.

May 21–June 9: Shows *Opera Orchestra* at the *Salons of America*, Anderson Galleries.

Summer: Resides with Meyerowitz in Gloucester. Lives in a small apartment on the corner of Rocky Neck and Eastern Point Road with artists Peter and Anna Neagoe. Shows *Gloucester* at the first exhibition of the North Shore Arts Association.

September: Shows etchings in Gloucester Society Fourth Show, Gloucester, Massachusetts.

October: Shows *The Milliners* at the exhibition of the National Association of Women Painters and Sculptors (including European artists). Her painting wins the $100 John Clerici Prize. Shows *Central Park* in Concord Annual Autumnal Exhibition, Concord Art Association, Massachusetts.

November 1–December 9: Shows *The Music Lovers* (#19) in *Thirty-Sixth Annual Exhibition of Paintings by American Artists* at the Art Institute of Chicago.

December: Participates in the National Association of Women Painters and Sculptors exhibition at the Ferargil Galleries (607 Fifth Avenue). Receives

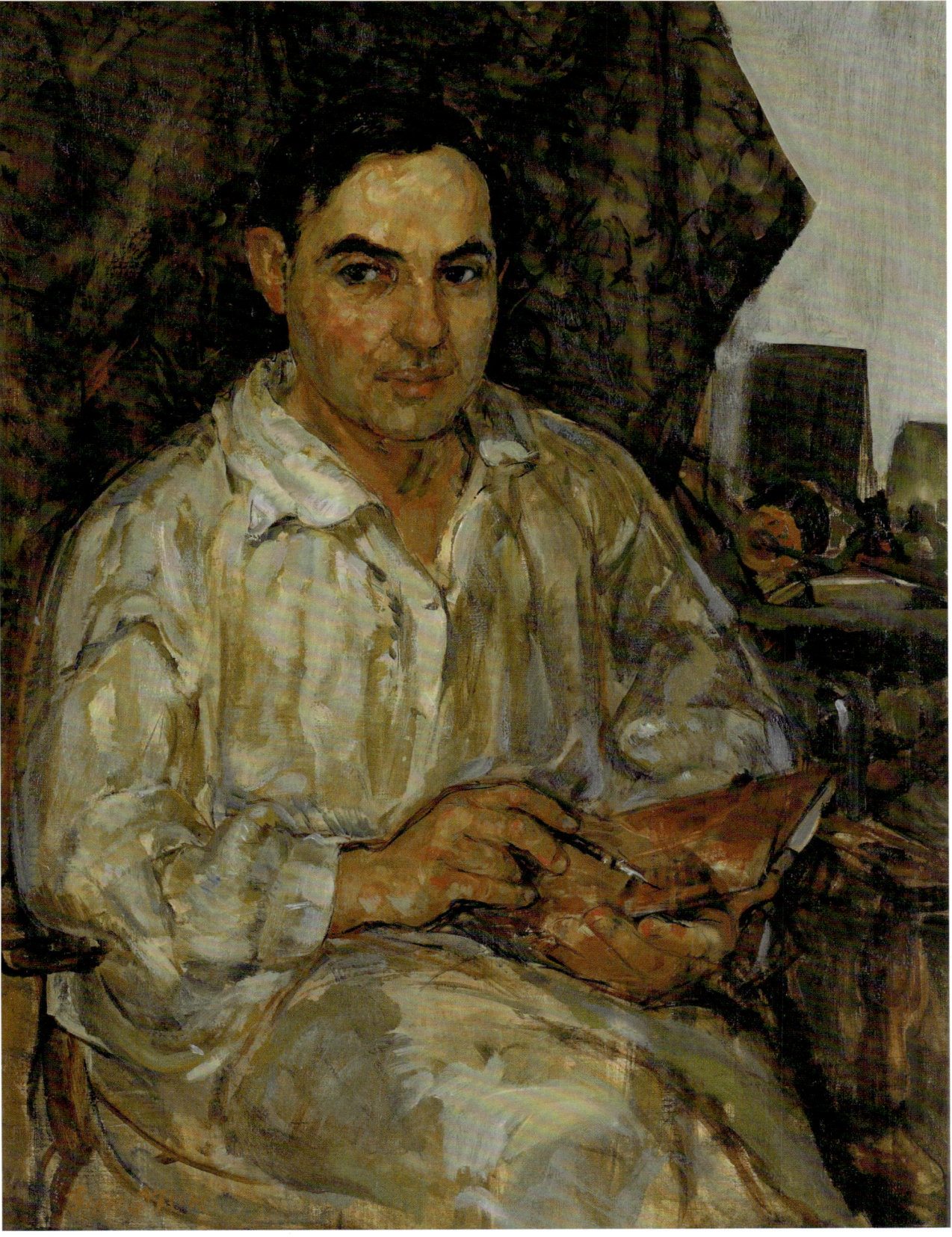

198. *Portrait of William*, 1923. Oil on canvas, 37 x 25 inches. Martin and Edith Stein Collection.

second honorable mention for *Ostende*.

Shows *The Lace Shawl* at the Brooklyn Society of Etchers.

Shows *Girlhood* (#30) in Ninth Biennial Exhibition of U.S. paintings at the Corcoran Gallery of Art, Washington DC.

Teaches painting at the Hawthorne House. Ellen Day Hale invites Meyerowitz and Bernstein to use her etching press in Folly Cove, and Meyerowitz becomes famous for colored etchings.

1924

Purchases house with Meyerowitz at 44 Mount Pleasant Avenue in Rocky Neck, East Gloucester.

February: Shows *The Country Fair* at the Pennsylvania Academy of the Fine Arts Annual Exhibition.

February 4: The Phillips Memorial Gallery (later The Phillips Collection), Washington DC, purchases *Girlhood*, 1921, for its permanent collection, paying $800.

March 7–30: Shows *The Colored Church* and *Sketch* at the Society of Independent Artists.

March 22–April 20: Shows *Late Afternoon* at Ninety-Ninth Annual Exhibition of the National Academy of Design.

May: Shows *The Immigrants* at the Pittsburgh International Exhibition at the Carnegie Institute. Participates in *School of Design Alumnae Exhibit* at the Philadelphia School of Design for Women.

May 20–31: Shows *Paisley Shawl* at *Salons of America*, Anderson Galleries. Shows *The Immigrants* (#20) and *View of Gloucester* (#21) in *Thirty-Seventh Annual Exhibition of American Oil Paintings and Sculpture* at the Art Institute of Chicago.

November 6–30: *Exhibition of Paintings by American Artists* includes *Girlhood*, lent by the Phillips Memorial Gallery, Baltimore Museum of Art. Meyerowitz's *Fruit and Flowers* is also included along with works by artists such as Bellows, Henri, Sloan, and Marjorie Phillips.

November 15–December 7: Shows *New England* at National Academy of Design Winter Exhibition.

December: Participates in *Exhibition of Small Paintings, Sculptures, and Miniatures* of the National Association of Women Painters and Sculptors. Wins the John Clerici Prize of $50 for the best painting: *Sunset Hour*.

1925

Shows *Orchestra and Chorus*, *Early Morning: Gloucester*, and *The Milliners* at the Pennsylvania Academy of the Fine Arts Annual Exhibition, Philadelphia.

William Meyerowitz is featured etcher in the Fox Film Company's *The Magic Needle*. This follows his 1923 solo show at the Smithsonian Institution's U.S. National Museum.

March: Participates in *Ten Philadelphia Painters* at the Arts Club Philadelphia.

March 6–29: Shows *Figure Painting* and *Landscape in Massachusetts* at the Society of Independent Artists.

April 1–24: Shows *The Cove* at One Hundredth Annual Exhibition of the National Academy of Design.

April 28–May 16: Shows *Mother and Child* at *Salons of America*, Anderson Galleries.

May: Shows *Mrs. Whitney's Reception* in the Tenth Annual Whitney Studio Club Exhibition at Anderson Galleries. Exhibits at National Academy of Design.

July: Shows *The Immigrants* in North Shore Arts Association Annual Exhibition.

October 29–December 13: Shows *The Milliners* (#21) in *Thirty-Eighth Annual Exhibition of American Oil Paintings and Sculpture* at the Art Institute of Chicago; price for the unsold painting was $3,000.

December: Shows a drawing in oil at the National Association of Women Painters and Sculptors exhibition. To help finance the Gloucester Society, Bernstein, Meyerowitz, and Stuart Davis created a journal called *The Paint Rag* (one issue).

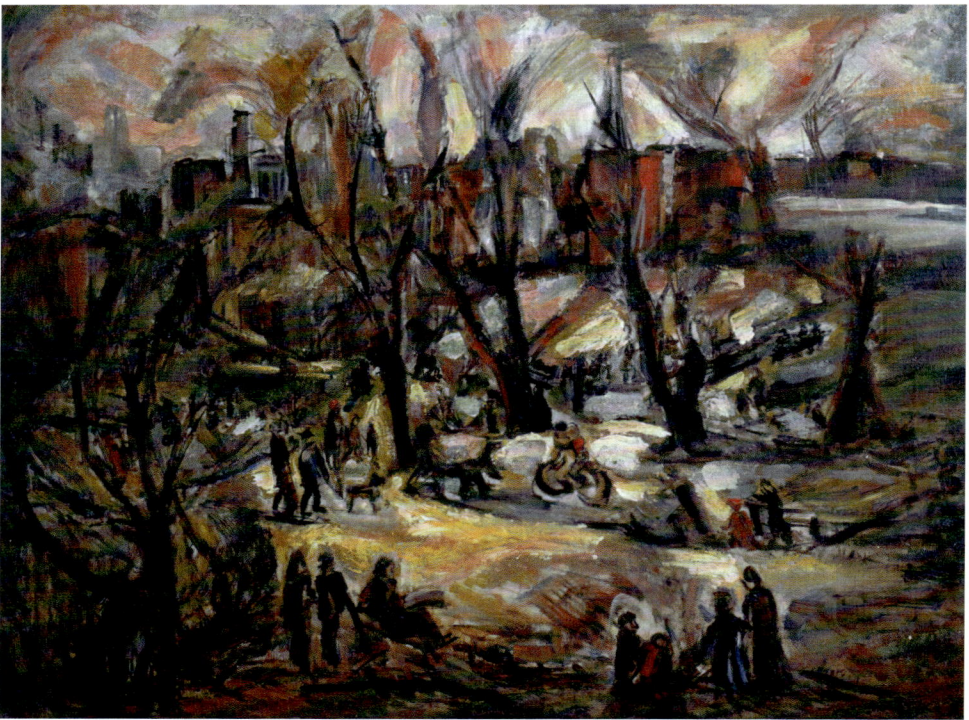

199. *Central Park*, ca. 1926. Oil on canvas, 27 x 35 inches. Joan Whalen Fine Art.

1926

Gets first piano (with help from her mother).

February 27–March 15: Shows twenty paintings in solo *Exhibition of Paintings by Theresa F. Bernstein* at the Civic Club, 14 West 12th Street.

March: Participates with Meyerowitz in the annual exhibition of the Whitney Studio Club.

March 5–28: Shows *Figure Composition* and *Beach Folly Cove* at the Society of Independent Artists.

April 4–May 16: Participates in exhibition *Contemporary American Oil Paintings* at the Corcoran Gallery of Art, Washington DC.

May 18–June 5: Shows *New England Harbor* at *Salons of America*, Anderson Galleries. Paints *The Chess Players*, depicting William Meyerowitz playing chess with the Massachusetts champion Stuart Davis watching.

October 28–December 12: Shows *New York Snow Scene* (#26 at $500) and *Tatania* (#27 at $800) in *Thirty-Ninth Annual Exhibition of American Painting and Sculpture* at the Art Institute of Chicago.

1927

Shows *Harbor Scene* at the Pennsylvania Academy of the Fine Arts Annual Exhibition.

February 16–March 5: Shows *Landscape* (#19) in *Twelfth Annual Exhibition of Paintings and*

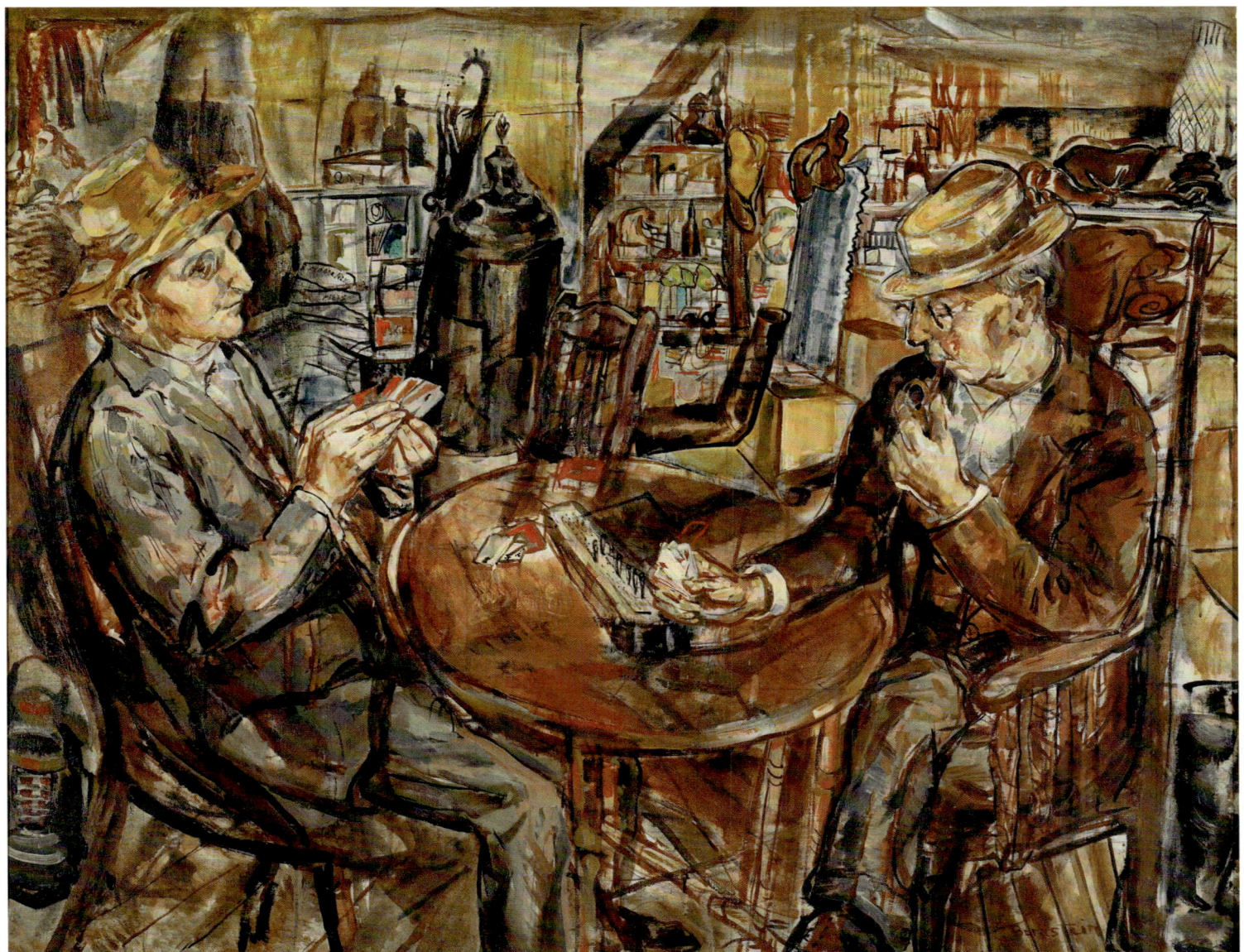

200. *Cribbage Players*, 1927. Oil on canvas, 50 x 40 inches. Martin and Edith Stein Collection.

Sculpture by the Members of the Club, Whitney Studio Club; includes Meyerowitz's *Portrait Arrangement* (#138).

March: Shows *Fishing Port* and *Tansy Hill* in the Second Annual Exhibition of the New York Society of Women Artists at Anderson Galleries.

March 11–April 3: Shows *Beach Group* and *Autumn Landscape* at the Society of Independent Artists.

October 27–December 14: Shows *New England Ladies* (#18) in *Fortieth Annual Exhibition of American Painting and Sculpture* at the Art Institute of Chicago.

November: Duncan Phillips acquires *Garnersville* for his museum. Eight of Bernstein's paintings published in the *Menorah Journal*.

November 29–December 18: Shows *Beach Scene* at National Academy of Design Winter Exhibition.

1928

Shows *New York Snow Scene* at the Pennsylvania Academy of the Fine Arts Annual Exhibition.

February 9–March 21: Exhibits *Gloucester* (#21) in *Exhibition of Etchings* under the management of the Chicago Society of Etchers at the Art Institute of Chicago.

February 27–March 10: Participates with Meyerowitz in group exhibition of watercolors and small sculptures at the Sherwood Studio Building. Shows *Minna* (#75 for $500) and *Classic Still Life* (#76 for $400) in the annual show of the Society of Independent Artists. William Meyerowitz also shows two works.

March–April: Shows watercolors at the Studio Bookshop, along with sculptural repoussé by Paul Lobell, and gold and silverwork by S. M. Abrahams.

March 21–April 8: Shows *Harbor View* in 103rd Annual Exhibition of the National Academy of Design.

April: Wins Joan of Arc Silver Medal for *Tatania* at the National Association of Women Painters and Sculptors annual exhibition at the Brooklyn Museum.

May: Participates with Meyerowitz in the seventh annual spring exhibition of *Salons of America*, Anderson Galleries. Other artists include William Zorach, Max Weber, and Yasuo Kuniyoshi, among others.

May 8–26: Shows *New York Snow Scene* at *Salons of America*, Anderson Galleries.

July: Shows *Gloucester Harbor* in the North Shore Arts Association exhibition.

1929

January: Shows twenty-six canvases at Arnold Constable, a department store at Fifth Avenue and 40th Street.

February 7–March 10: Shows *New England Ladies* in *An Exhibition of Etchings*, Chicago Society of Etchers, Art Institute of Chicago.

March: Participates with Meyerowitz in show at the National Academy of Design.

April: Shows *Polish Church* in the *Hundred Important Paintings by Living American Artists* at Grand Central Palace, an exhibition organized by the Arts Council.

May 2–June 2: Shows *Gloucester Fisherman* (#20) in *International Watercolor Exhibition*, Art Institute of Chicago.

July: Shows *Gloucester Fisherman* in Society of Gloucester Artists exhibition. Also includes Meyerowitz's *Arrangement*.

October 24–December 8: Shows *View of Gloucester* (#23) in *Forty-Second Annual Exhibition of American Paintings and Sculpture* at the Art Institute of Chicago.

Mother dies; father loses his business.

1930

Commissioned with Meyerowitz by the Jefferson Foundation to etch and paint the home of James Monroe, designed by Thomas Jefferson. Her painting is placed in the James Monroe High School in the Bronx. Current location unknown.

Shows *Beach Scene* at the Pennsylvania Academy of the Fine Arts Annual Exhibition.

March 8–30: Shows two paintings at the Society of Independent Artists.

April 22–May 8: Shows *Sunset Ave* and *Nude* at *Salons of America*, Anderson Galleries. Has solo show, Grand Central Galleries, New York. Is photographed by Peter A. Juley and Son, New York. Meyerowitz has show at the Corcoran Gallery, Washington DC, and meets Oliver Wendell Holmes, who became a patron and a subject for later work.

October 13–December 14: Shows *Tatania* (#15) in *Forty-Third Annual Exhibition of Paintings and Sculpture* at the Art Institute of Chicago; Meyerowitz shows *The White Horse* (#118).

December 1–January 12, 1931: Has solo exhibition at the Baltimore Museum of Art. Checklist of eighteen paintings, including *Madonna*, is reproduced on the cover of brochure. William Meyerowitz is given a show at the same time.

December–January: Exhibits *Polish Church* in Corcoran Biennial.

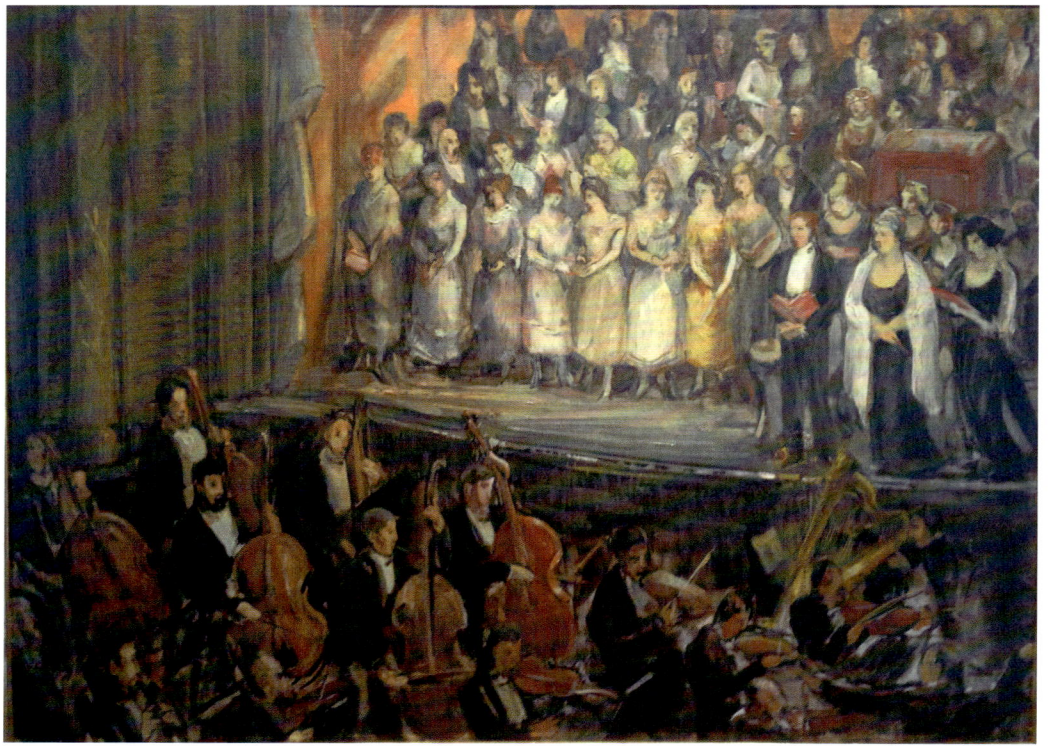

201. *Verdi's Requiem*, 1930. Oil on canvas, 30 x 40 inches. Private collection.

1931

Moves with Meyerowitz to 54 West 74th Street, a raw space that Meyerowitz renovated into a studio sleeping loft. Distributes brochure announcing the opening of the tenth annual summer painting and etching course with Meyerowitz in Gloucester, Massachusetts. Shows *Little Harbor* at the Pennsylvania Academy of the Fine Arts Annual Exhibition.

February: Has joint exhibition with William Meyerowitz at Central Synagogue.

March 7–30: Shows *Prima Donna* and *Beach Scene* at the Society of Independent Artists.

April 20–May 9: Shows *Dancer Resting* at *Salons of America*, Anderson Galleries.

June: Participates in Annual Summer Exhibition at the Brooklyn Museum. Included are Meyerowitz, David Burliuk, Eugene Dunkel, George Dunkel, Aaron J. Goodelman, Minna Harkavy, and others.

October 15–December 6: Participates in Thirtieth International Exhibition at the Carnegie Institute in Pittsburgh.

October 29–December 13: Shows *The Harbor* (#16) in *Forty-Fourth Annual Exhibition of American Oil Paintings and Sculpture* at the Art Institute of Chicago; Meyerowitz shows *Still Life* (129).

1932

January–February: Participates in New York Society of Women Artists exhibition in Squibb Building. Opening exhibition also includes work by Adelaide Lawson, Anne Goldthwaite, Marjorie Phillips, Dorothy Varian, Mildred Crooks, Marjorie Organ, Mary Tannahill, Doris Rosenthal, and Lucy l'Engle.

March 31–May 30: Shows *Gloucester Harbor* (#213) in *International Watercolor Exhibition: Twelfth Year* at the Art Institute of Chicago.

October: Exhibits with Meyerowitz at Cronyn and Lowndes Galleries, along with Charles Demuth, Yasuo Kuniyoshi, Max Weber, and others.

Commissioned to paint a portrait of Harvard professor Harry Austryn Wolfson by his cousin, Dr. Harry Savitz.

Father dies. In the months before his death, Bernstein lives in Brookline with Jean Ross while her father is at Beth Israel Hospital in Boston.

1933

Receives a commission to paint a portrait of David Gordon Lyon, emeritus professor at Harvard University and founder of Harvard's Semitic Museum.

Shows *New England Town* at the Pennsylvania Academy of the Fine Arts Annual Exhibition.

April: Participates in the 1933 International at Rockefeller Center.

April 7–30: Shows *American Figure Composition* and *Still Life, Technocracy* at the Society of Independent Artists.

June: Shows at the Academy of Allied Arts, 349 West 86th Street.

June 1–November 1: Shows *View of Gloucester*, 1929 (#507), in *A Century of Progress: Exhibition of Paintings and Sculpture* at the Art Institute of Chicago. William Meyerowitz also shows one painting.

July: Shows, with William Meyerowitz, in their studio, where they also conduct summer classes.

August: Participates in joint retrospective with Meyerowitz at North Shore Arts Association, Gloucester. Both show work for the first time at the Brooklyn Museum as members of the Society of American Graphic Artists. Is asked to write the first article on the history of color in graphic arts for the *Brooklyn Museum Bulletin*.

September 18–October 7: Shows *Gloucester Landscape* in *Paintings and Sculptures by Wives of Painters and Sculptors*, Contemporary Arts, 41 West 54th Street, with artists such as Sally Michel Avery, Edith Dimock Glackens, and Marguerite Zorach.

1934

February: Shows with New York Society of Women Artists. Shows *Marblehead* at the Pennsylvania Academy of the Fine Arts Annual Exhibition.

March 14–April 15: Shows *Marblehead* at 109th Annual Exhibition of the National Academy of Design.

March 29–April 29: Shows *Bass Rocks* (#192) at *Annual International Water Color Exhibition, Thirteenth Year*, Art Institute of Chicago.

April 9–May 6: Shows *Beach Scene*, *Violetta*, and *Harbor Scene* at *Salons of America*, Forum Gallery, RCA Building, Rockefeller Center.

April 13–May 6: Shows *Harbor of Gloucester* and *N.Y. Girl* at the Society of Independent Artists. Shows *Gloucester Harbor* in *A Century of Progress: Exhibition of Paintings and Sculpture*, Art Institute of Chicago.

April: Shows at Uptown Gallery along with Meyerowitz, Paul Meltsner, Anne Neagoe, Ruth Sanders, Nat Eastman, Herman Kay, Nathan Dolinsky, and John Soble.

December: Is in group show *Americans and Mexicans* at Uptown Gallery.

1935

January: Shows with Meyerowitz, Philip Evergood, Charles Harsanyi, and Stewart Klonis, among others, in group show at Uptown Gallery.

March 13–April 9: Shows *Beach Scene* at 110th Annual Exhibition of the National Academy of Design.

April: Shows *Columbus Avenue* in New York Society of Women Artists at Argent Galleries. Shows portrait in group show at Uptown Gallery.

April 6–28: Shows *Figure Composition* and *Portrait* at the Society of Independent Artists.

May 7–25: Shows *Landscape with Figure* at *Salons of America*, Anderson Galleries.

October: Participates in group show at Uptown Gallery. Signs "Call to Artists" for a congress to be held in New York.

October 24–December 8: Shows *New England Wharves* (#17) in *Forty-Sixth Annual Exhibition of American Paintings and Sculpture* at the Art Institute of Chicago.

November: Participates in Print Sale to Aid American Artists' Congress, ACA Galleries, New York City.

December: Landscapes in group show at Uptown Gallery. Travels to Washington to paint a large work of the American Artists' Congress.

1936

On committee to ask U.S. Congress not to cut off funding for the WPA; sent to hearing in Washington DC as representative of the New York Society of Women Artists.

January: New York Society of Women group show, Squibb Building. With Meyerowitz in group show at Uptown Gallery, along with Theodore Roszak, George Rickey, and others.

February: Shows with William Meyerowitz at Uptown Gallery.

February–March: On committee with N. Cikovsy, Stuart Davis, D. Dorenz, Minna Harkavy, Eugene Higgins, Frank C. Kirk,

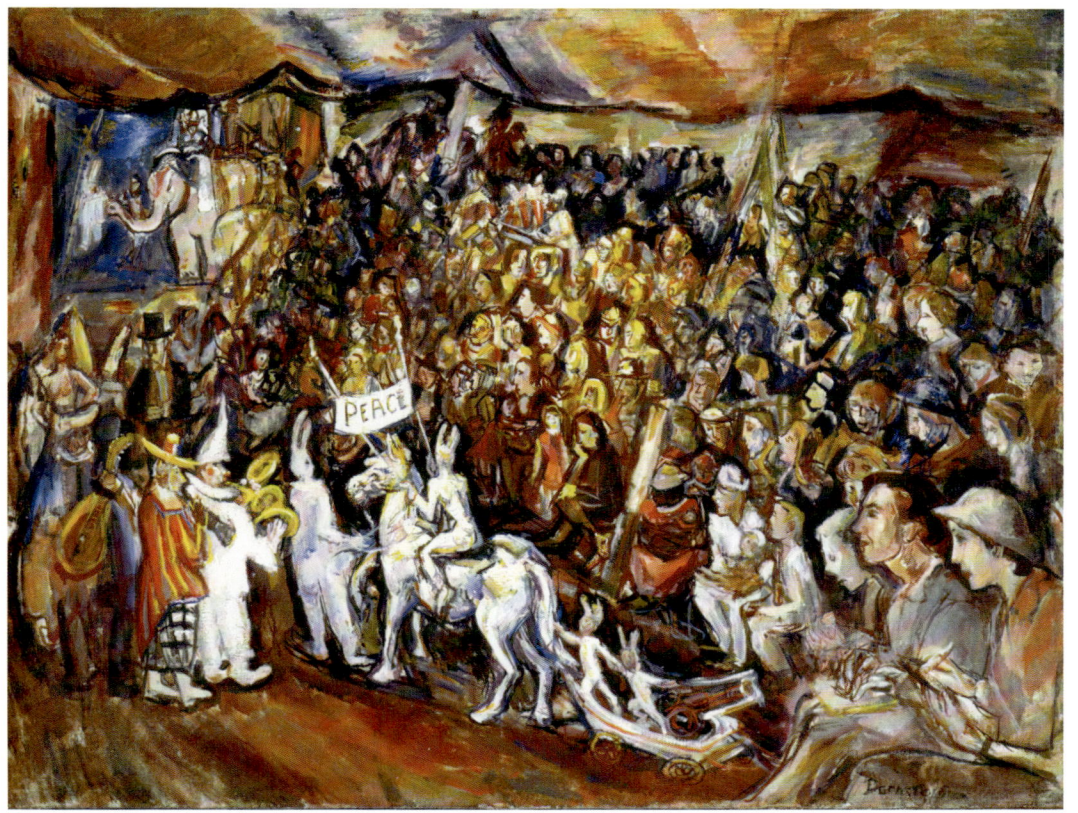

202. *The Circus*, 1936. Oil on canvas, 28 x 35½ inches. Girard Jackson Collection.

P. Sol Wilson, and Adolf Wolff to collect donated art for a new museum in Birobidzhan, the Soviet autonomous Jewish region. Works donated by one hundred artists in New York are shown.

April 24–May 17: Shows *Choral Society* and *American Landscape* at the Society of Independent Artists. Shows *The Beach* in *Forty-Seventh Annual Exhibition of American Oil Paintings and Sculpture* at the Art Institute of Chicago.

April: Shows at Uptown Gallery.

May: Participates in exhibition of art arranged as benefit for Little Red School House, Bleecker Street, along with William Zorach, Chaim Gross, Max Weber, Arshile Gorky, Yasuo Kuniyoshi, and others. Shows *Still Life* in Municipal Art Committee group show at 62 West 53rd Street.

June 21–August 20: In Fifth Invited Exhibition, Goose Rocks Beach, Maine, along with artists William Meyerowitz, John Steuart Curry, Anne Goldthwaite, Rockwell Kent, and Millard Sheets.

December: Dayton Art Institute purchases her painting *Girl in Old-Fashioned Bonnet* for its permanent collection. Price paid is $300.

1937

February 15–March 12: Has show *Paintings by Theresa Bernstein*, Uptown Gallery.

March: Has two paintings, including a portrait, in group show at Uptown Gallery.

March 28–May 9: Shows *New England* (#165) in the Fifteenth Biennial Exhibition of Contemporary American Oil Paintings, Corcoran Gallery of Art, Washington DC. William Meyerowitz also in this show, which toured museums.

April 2–25: Shows *Figure Composition* and *Carpenter's House* at the Society of Independent Artists.

November 18–January 16, 1938: Shows *New England* (#23) in *Forty-Eighth Annual Exhibition of American Oil Paintings and Sculpture* at the Art Institute of Chicago; Meyerowitz shows *Gloucester Fishermen* (#149).

1938

Paints mural, *The First Orchestra in America*, in U.S. Postal Office in Manheim, Pennsylvania, for the Treasury Department.

Completes two other mural studies for the Treasury Department: *Women of America* and *The Elevated Station*.

January: Shows *Holiday Beach Scene* in 133rd Annual Exhibition of the Pennsylvania Academy of the Fine Arts, Philadelphia; William Meyerowitz is also in the show.

February: Shows with New York Society of Women Artists at Grant Studios.

February 4–27: Shows twenty-one paintings in *Exhibition of Oil Paintings by Theresa F. Bernstein* at Arnot Art Gallery, Elmira, New York.

March: Shows as one of forty-nine women artists at Municipal Art Galleries, 3 East 67th Street.

April: Exhibits with Saul Berman, Stuart Davis, Moses Soyer, and others in *Roofs for 40,000,000* by An American Group, Inc., at the Maison Francaise in Rockefeller Center.

April 27–May 18: Shows *Holiday Beach* and *Country Children* at the Society of Independent Artists.

April 28–May 30: Shows *Central Park* (#160) and *Gloucester Harbor* (#161) at *International Watercolor Exhibition, Seventeenth Year*, at the Art Institute of Chicago.

May: Donates painting to the Joint Distribution Committee in New York for its art exhibition and sale to benefit its operations aimed at rescuing Jews at risk in Europe.

October 2–30: Shows *Gloucester Fisherman, Morning* at Exhibition of American Watercolors, Toledo Museum of Art, Toledo, Ohio.

December: Participates in Christmas show, Uptown Gallery. Travels to Boston to paint a portrait of the biblical scholar Professor Robert H. Pfeiffer of Harvard on a commission from one of his former students.

1939

January: Participates in group show at Albany Institute of History and Art, Albany, New York.

March 19–April 19: Shows *Symphony Orchestra* and *Study* at the Society of Independent Artists.

March 23–May 14: Shows *Gloucester Fishermen, Morning* (#165) and *Gloucester Fishermen, Afternoon* (#166) in *International Watercolor Exhibition, Eighteenth Year*, at the Art Institute of Chicago. Meyerowitz shows *The Equestrians* (#406). Grant Wood is one of three jurors.

April: Participates in group show with the New York Society of Women Artists at the Riverside Museum and in group show of prints with Meyerowitz, Wanda Gag, Peggy Bacon, Jack Markow, Will Barnet, Minna Citron, Yasuo Kuniyoshi, and others at Wanamaker's.

March 26–May 7: Shows *Dancer Resting* (#241) in the *Sixteenth Biennial Exhibition of Contemporary American Oil Paintings* at the Corcoran Gallery of Art, Washington DC. Travels to Washington DC to paint the portrait of Madame Bistra Radoff, wife of the Bulgarian ambassador.

1940

Exhibit with Meyerowitz at the Ogunquit Art Association.

February: Shows with New York Society of Women Artists at Grant Studios.

March 15–April 11: Participates in 114th Annual Exhibition at the National Academy of Design.

April: Shows *Gloucester Fisherman, Afternoon*, *Old Houses*, and *Marblehead* in *Nineteenth Annual International Exhibition of Water Colors* at the Art Institute of Chicago.

April 19–May 12: Participates with Meyerowitz in group show at the Society of Independent Artists. Shows *Gloucester Sisters* and *Still Life*.

May: Contributes work for an art auction at the American Artists School on 131 West 4th Street to benefit a scholarship fund. Bernstein and Meyerowitz are interviewed by Michael M. Engel, chair of the Professional Artists Group, Washington Heights Art Center, at final meeting of the season.

September: Shows in the American Art Today Building at the New York World's Fair with the New York Society of Women Artists.

November: Shows artwork with Meyerowitz and several other artists at the gallery of the American Artists School. Bernstein and Meyerowitz in group show at the gallery of the AWA Clubhouse.

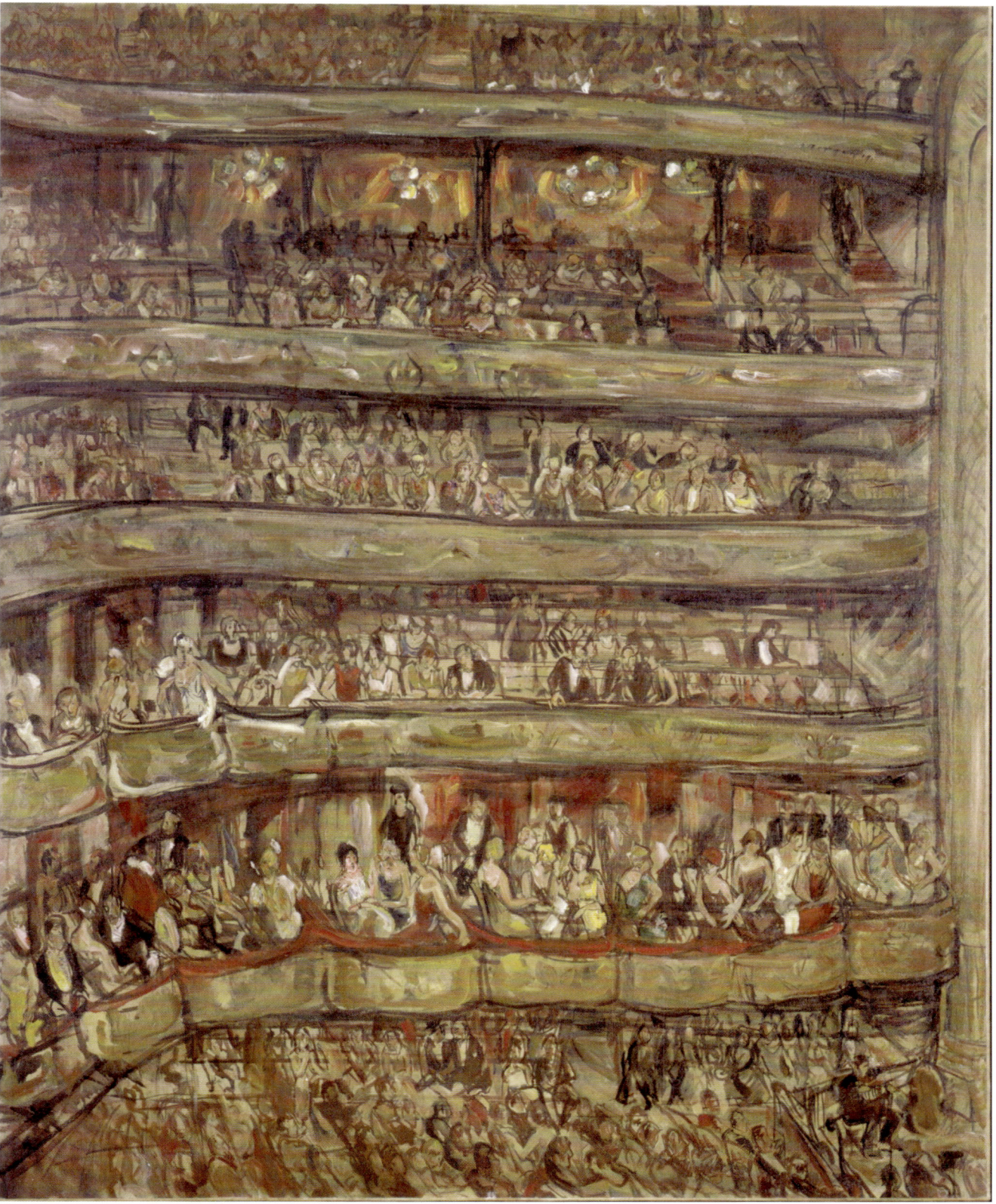

203. *Metropolitan Opera House*, 1939. Oil on canvas, 55 x 45 inches. Private collection.

1941

March: Shows with the New York Society of Women Artists at 460 Park Avenue Galleries.

March 23–May 4: Shows *Bass Violins* (#16) in the *Seventeenth Biennial Exhibition of Contemporary American Oil Paintings* at the Corcoran Gallery of Art, Washington DC.

April: Participates in a group show at the Vendome Art Galleries with Meyerowitz and approximately sixty other artists.

April 17–May 7: Shows *American Girl* at the Society of Independent Artists.

September: Shows with the New York Society of Women Artists at the Riverside Museum.

1942

January: Gives pastel demonstration and a lecture on modern art for the Professional Artists Group of the Washington Heights Art Center.

March: Shows with the New York Society of Women Artists at the American British Art Center.

April 8–28: Shows *Beach Scene* and *Water Front Street* at the Society of Independent Artists.

April 8–May 16: Shows *Boat Landing*, which sells for $450, at 116th Annual Exhibition of the National Academy of Design.

June: Contributes work to *Happier Days* exhibition at the Parke-Bernet Galleries. Sales benefit the American Red Cross.

December: Attends a dinner with Meyerowitz for distinguished American public figures in support of the Committee for a Jewish Army of Stateless and Palestinian Jews.

1943

March: Shows with the New York Society of Women Artists at the American British Art Center.

April: Serves as juror, along with William Meyerowitz and Edward Hopper, for an exhibition of paintings by members of Local 19, International Ladies' Garment Workers Union. The exhibition is a benefit for the British War Relief Society.

April–May: Shows *Rivington Street* in group show at Children's Art Center of University Settlement House, 184 Eldridge Street, with William Meyerowitz, Jo Davidson, Arthur B. Davies, Jacob Epstein, Bernard Gussow, William Auerbach-Levy, Jerome Meyers, and Abbo Ostrowsky.

April: Comes in second in a contest for the most popular vote by visitors to the annual exhibition of the National Association of Women Artists at the American Fine Arts Galleries.

May 5–19: Shows *Street Scene* and *Harvest Scene* at the Society of Independent Artists.

May: Shows with Meyerowitz in a large group show of American, British, and Mexican artists at the American British Art Center.

November: Shows with the New York Society of Women Artists at the Riverside Museum. William Meyerowitz is made an academician of the National Academy, an organization that had not accepted Bernstein as a member.

1944

May 8–28: Shows *The Visiting Hour* and *Harlequin Still Life* at the Society of Independent Artists.

July: Wins the Mary Baker Lewis Prize of $100 for *Gloucester Wharves*, the best painting at the North Shore Arts Association exhibition.

October: Shows in the exhibition *Tribute to President Roosevelt*, sponsored by the Independent Voters Committee of the Arts and Sciences in the American Fine Arts Society Building.

1945

March 14–April 3: Shows *Gloucester Harbor*, which sells for $450, at 119th Annual Exhibition of the National Academy of Design.

July: Shows with Meyerowitz in annual summer salon at the American British Art Center and in the Twenty-Third Annual Exhibition of the North Shore Arts Association. Has solo show at Dayton Art Institute, Ohio.

October: Shows with the New York Society of Women Artists at the Riverside Museum.

December 4–21: Sells *Sunset Avenue* for $500 at 120th Annual Exhibition of the National Academy of Design. Shows at Eastman School of Music, Scranton Museum (Pennsylvania), and Elmira, New York.

1946

May: Shows with the New York Society of Women Artists at the National Academy of Design. Shows with twenty-five artists in a group show *The Jew in Art* held at the Sara Delano Roosevelt Memorial House and sponsored by the B'nai B'rith Hillel Foundation.

July: Shows *Spring-Crow Village* in North Shore Arts Association Annual Exhibition.

1947

January 4–22: Shows *Good Morning*, which sells for $600, at 121st Annual Exhibition of the National Academy Design.

February 3–15: Shows thirteen paintings and receives a catalogue introduction by Edward Alden Jewell in *Exhibition of Paintings* at Doll and Richards Gallery, Boston.

July: Participates in Rockport Summer Artists Group show at Redmen's Hall, Rockport, Massachusetts.

August 25: Contributes work to Spanish Fiesta to benefit the Spanish Refugee Appeal, sponsored by its Boston chapter. Shows at Gloucester Society of Artists.

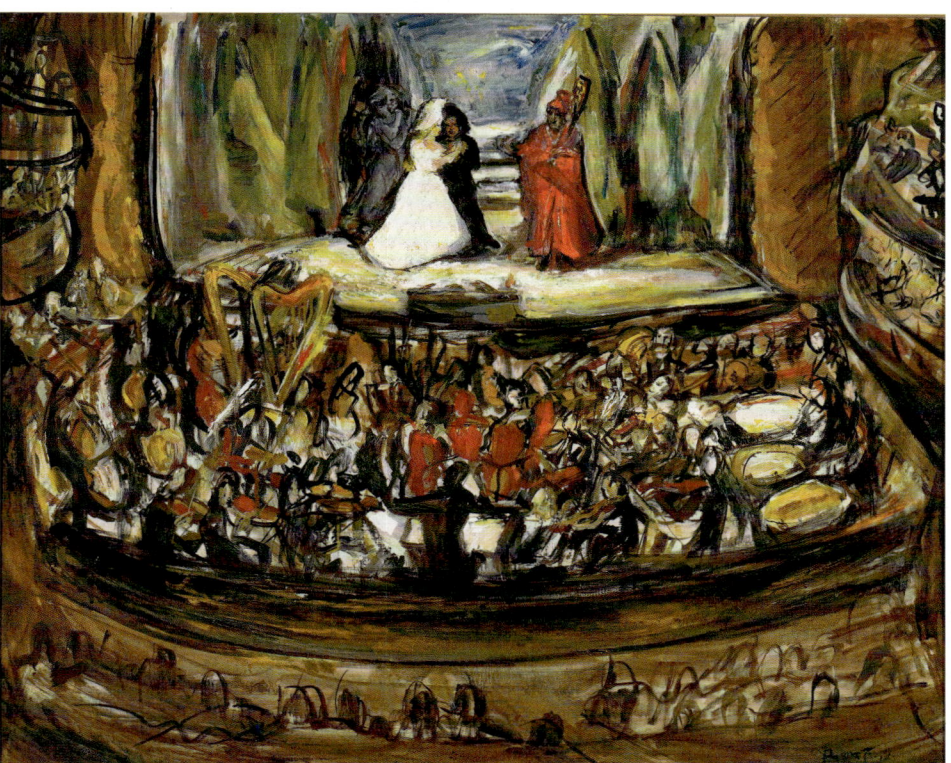

204. *Opera "Don Carlos"*, 1948. Oil on canvas, 36 x 30¼ inches. Martin and Edith Stein Collection.

1948

April 26–May 24: Has solo exhibition of etchings and monotypes in color, Smithsonian Institution, U.S. National Museum.

July–August: Invited to join the Cape Ann Society of Modern Artists; participates in show at Hawthorne Inn Gallery, East Gloucester, Massachusetts.

December: Contributes a work for exhibition at the Jewish Museum through the American Artists for Israel Committee, sponsored by the American Fund for Palestinian Institutions.

1949

March 10–23: Shows *Medallion Flowers* (watercolor), which sells for $150, at 123rd Annual Exhibition of the National Academy of Design.

April: Has joint show with Meyerowitz at Doll and Richards Gallery, Boston.

August: Shows at the Cape Ann Society of Modern Artists.

1950

March 10–April 9: Shows *Harbor Scene*, which sells for $450, at 125th Anniversary Exhibition of the National Academy of Design.

August: Has solo show at Bass Rocks Theatre, Gloucester, Massachusetts. Participates in *Exhibition of American Painting*, Metropolitan Museum of Art.

1951

With Meyerowitz, travels to Israel for the first time.

April 26–May 13: Participates in Annual Exhibition of the National Association of Women Artists, National Academy of Design. Wins Margaret Cooper Prize for Painting for her portrait *Sarah*. Receives purchase award from the Library of Congress for *Fisherman's Wharf*.

1952

October–November 1: Shows nineteen works at Ballroom Gallery, Public House Inn, Sturbridge, Massachusetts.

1953

April 6–18: Shows twelve paintings in *Theresa Bernstein Paintings*, joint show with Meyerowitz at Doll and Richards, Boston.

1954

Shows in thirty-eighth annual exhibition of the Society of American Graphic Artists at Kennedy Gallery. Receives honorable mention for *Venice*, 1945.

1955

Society of American Graphic Artists donates *Venice* to the Metropolitan Museum of Art.

1956

Participates in exhibition of the Knickerbocker Artists at the National Arts Club, 15 Gramercy Park. Receives honorable mention. William Meyerowitz is a member of the jury.

Visits Ralph and Minna Troop in North Carolina. Witnesses segregation on a bus.

Shows *The Jazz Players* in Art USA exhibition in Madison Square Garden. Meyerowitz shows an abstract canvas of horses.

1959

Shows *Gladioli* in Thirty-Seventh Annual Exhibition of the North Shore Arts Association, Gloucester, Massachusetts.

1960

Takes trip to Spain.

William Meyerowitz becomes director of the Audubon Society of Artists until 1967.

1961

Travels from Andalusia to the Rock of Gibraltar, Granada, and the Alhambra.

William Meyerowitz suffers a heart attack.

1963

Takes trip to Bar Harbor, Maine. Shows at Joan Purcell Gallery.

November 22–December 8: Shows oil painting *Green Pears* in *Exhibition of Paintings Eligible for Purchase under the Childe Hassam Fund*, American Academy of Arts and Letters.

1967

Receives Maria Canterella Prize for *Still Life*, National Association of Women Artists.

Travels with Meyerowitz to Israel.

November 12–December 24: Has solo exhibition *Paintings by Theresa Bernstein*, Columbus Museum of Arts and Crafts, Columbus, Georgia.

1968

Exhibits designs for WPA murals at the Midtown Gallery.

1969

November: Exhibits in *Paintings by Theresa Bernstein and William Meyerowitz*, Waterbury Jewish Community Center, Waterbury, Connecticut.

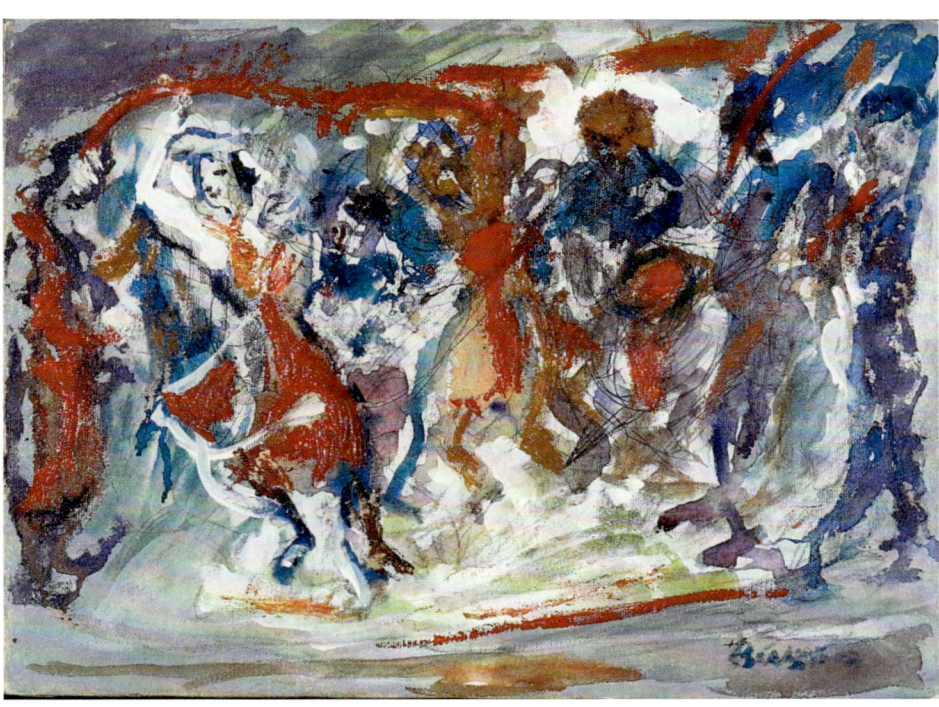

205. *Swing*, 1980. Oil on canvas, 12 x 6 inches. Martin and Edith Stein Collection.

1970

Travels with Meyerowitz to Israel, where they meet artists Reuven Rubin and Marcel Janco.

1972

Travels with Meyerowitz to Israel.

North Shore Arts Association asks Bernstein to write its history for its fiftieth anniversary.

1973

Travels with Meyerowitz to Israel.

November: Exhibits fifteen paintings in *Theresa Bernstein* at Butler Institute of American Art, Youngstown, Ohio.

1976

Has show with Meyerowitz in the Friend Room of the Sawyer Library, Middle Street, Gloucester, Massachusetts.

1977

Travels with Meyerowitz to Israel.

1978

Travels with Meyerowitz to Israel; they visit Gaza.

1979

January 16–February 10: Exhibits in *Paintings: Theresa Bernstein*, Summit Gallery, 101 West 57th Street.

1980

Travels with Meyerowitz to Israel for their last time.

Takes last trip with Meyerowitz to Gloucester.

1981

May 28: William Meyerowitz dies at age ninety-three.

1983

Has show *Themes of New York: Paintings and Prints by William Meyerowitz and Theresa Bernstein*, at The New-York Historical Society.

1984

June 10–October 20: Has essay "William Merritt Chase (1849–1916)" published in *Etchings and Paintings: William Meyerowitz/Theresa Bernstein*, Patterson Public Library, Patterson, New Jersey.

1985

Summer: Diane Dawson and Sylvia Selfridge become custodians of Gloucester Studio.

1986

Her book *The Artist Speaks*, about William Meyerowitz, is published.

Begins an inventory of William Meyerowitz's etching plates with the help of Meyerowitz's nephew Keith Carlson, anticipating show of his prints at the Library of Congress in 1987.

Has joint exhibition of New England motifs by Bernstein and Meyerowitz at the Cape Ann Historical Association, Gloucester, Massachusetts.

1987

April 1–May 23: Shows eight works in *The Genius of the Fair Muse: American Women Artists, 1875–1945*, Grand Central Galleries.

1988

July–September 1988: Shows *American Womanhood: Sketch for a Mural* in exhibition *Painting America: Mural Art in the New Deal Era*, Wichita Art Museum, Kansas (and traveling).

1989

Her book *The Poetic Canvas* is published.

February 26–March 30: *Expressions of Cape Ann and New York* tours to Simmons College and the Crane Collection, both in Boston.

November 19–January 7: Shows in *Theresa Bernstein: Expressions of Cape Ann and New York, 1914–1972, A Centennial Exhibition* at the Stamford Museum and Nature Center.

1990

November 20, 1989–March 31: Has solo show of thirty-nine paintings, *Echoes of New York: The Paintings of Theresa Bernstein*, at the Museum of the City of New York.

August 21–November 4: Is included in *Cornell Collects: A Celebration of American Art* from the Collections of Alumni and Friends at the Herbert F. Johnson Museum of Art, Cornell University, Ithaca, New York.

December–January 1991: Has solo show *Theresa Bernstein: A Salute to Her 100th Year*, Gloucester/New York, Ellen Sragaw Gallery, 73 Spring Street.

1991

January: Shows *Elsa von Freytag-Loringhoven*, 1917, in *Within Bohemia's Borders: Greenwich Village, 1830–1930*, Museum of the City of New York. Is chosen by the Women's Caucus for Art as a recipient of one of its five annual Honor Awards for Outstanding Achievements in the Visual Arts.

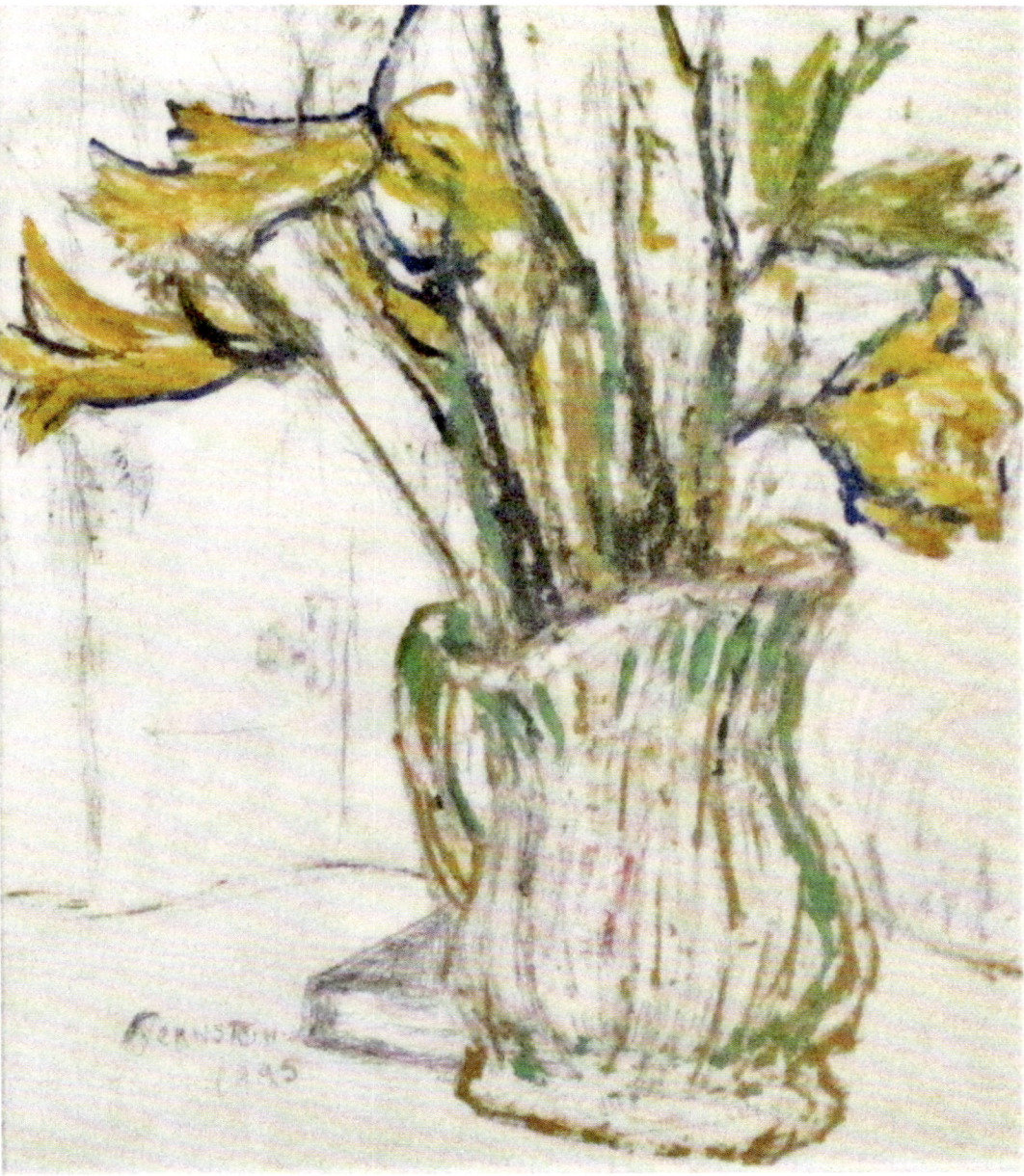

206. *Pitcher with Flowers*, 1995. Pen and ink and acrylic on paper, 16 x 13½ inches. Private collection.

1992

Her book *The Sketchbook* is published with the assistance of her friends.

1995

Shows *Parade* in *A View of One's Own*, an exhibition of eighty works drawn from the collection bestowed by the National Association of Women Artists (formed in 1889 at Douglas College at Rutgers University) at Zimmerli Art Museum in New Brunswick, New Jersey.

February 10–June 10: Has show *Theresa Bernstein—People and Places, A Retrospective*, at the Philadelphia Museum of Judaica Congregation Rodeph Shalom.

1998

January 23–March 15: Exhibits in *The Philadelphia Ten: A Women's Artist Group, 1917–1945*, at Moore College of Art and Design, Philadelphia, in celebration of the founding of the college (touring show).

February: Participates in group show *Self-Revelation: Artist Confrontation* at Krasdale Gallery in White Plains, New York.

February–April: Has solo show at Joan Whalen Fine Art at 24 West 57th Street.

October: Travels with companions Diane Dawson and Sylvia Selfridge to visit Girard Jackson in Sugar Land, Texas

1999

March: Signs copies of her new book, *Rabbitville*, at a reception at Joan Whalen Fine Art, 24 West 57th Street.

2000

Shows *Bryant Park* (1914) in *Painting the Town: Cityscapes from the Museum of the City of New York* at the Paine Webber Art Gallery in midtown Manhattan. Last solo show takes place at Joan Whalen Fine Art.

2002

February 13: Dies at her studio at 24 West 74th Street just two weeks before her 112th birthday.

Contributors

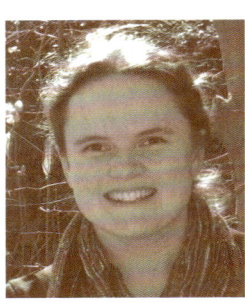

Sarah Archino received her PhD from the Graduate Center of the City University of New York. Her dissertation, "Reframing the Narrative of Dada in New York, 1910–1926," examined the development of an American Dada aesthetic. She is currently a postdoctoral teaching fellow at Millsaps College in Jackson, Mississippi.

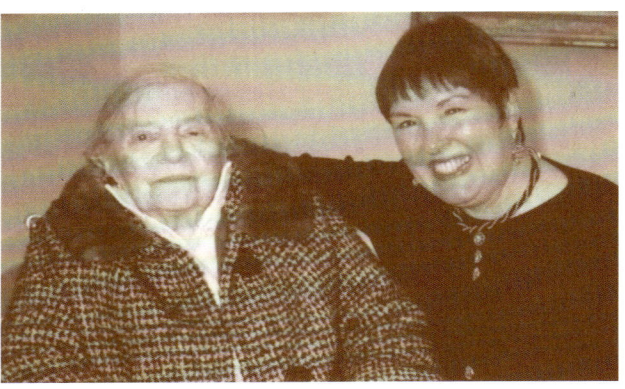

Patricia M. Burnham retired from teaching at the University of Texas at Austin. She knew Theresa Bernstein well, lectured and wrote essays about her art, and organized an exhibition of her work at the Philadelphia Museum of Judaica in 1995. She spoke at the memorial service that took place after Bernstein's death. Dr. Burnham has also written about American History Painting and the early artist John Trumbull.

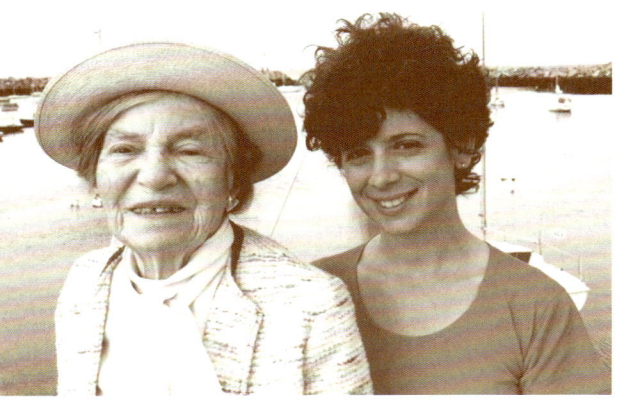

Michele Cohen, who received her PhD from the Graduate Center of the City University of New York, founded and directed New York City's Public Art for Public Schools program from 1989 to 2009. She has written and lectured widely on public art and women artists and is currently an independent public art consultant, curator, and visiting professor. She knew Theresa Bernstein well and in 1990 organized a major exhibition of Bernstein's New York paintings for the Museum of the City of New York. In 2009 she published the first history of New York City public school art and architecture, *Public Art for Public Schools*.

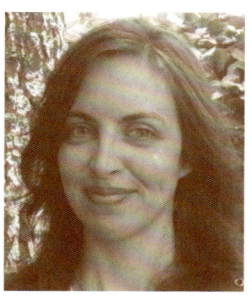

Stephanie Hackett is a doctoral student in art history at the Graduate Center of the City University of New York. She is specializing in Art of the United Sates, 1750–1945. Previously, she worked at Childs Gallery in Boston where she catalogued, curated, and installed nine shows in the Prints, Drawings, and Watercolors Department.

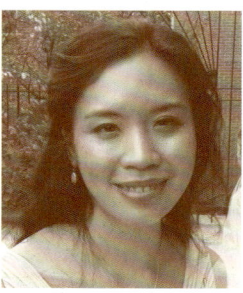

Elsie Heung is a doctoral candidate in art history at the Graduate Center of the City University of New York. Her work focuses on twentieth-century urban realism. Her dissertation is entitled "Portraying Women's Suffrage: Visual Arts and the Vote in the United States, 1900–1920."

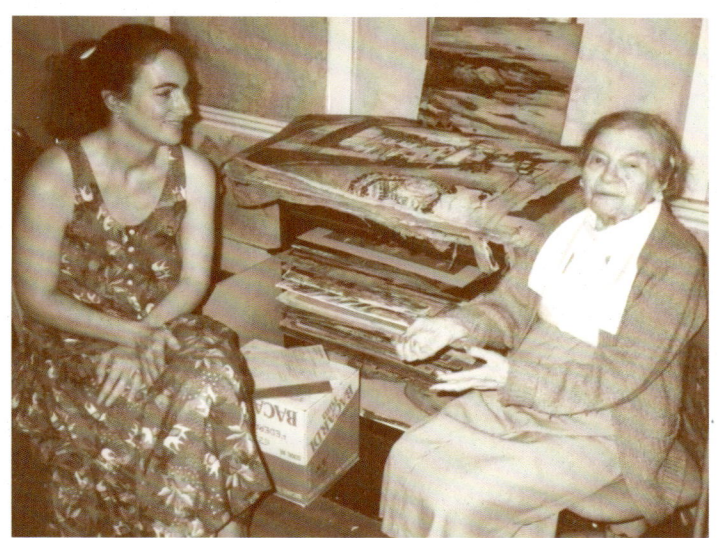

Photo: John Van Sickle

Gail Levin is Distinguished Professor of Art History, American Studies, and Women's Studies at the Graduate Center and Baruch College of the City University of New York. Her many books range from her most recent, *Lee Krasner: A Biography* (2011), to a well-known series on Edward Hopper that culminated in 1995 with both a four-volume catalogue raisonné and *Edward Hopper: An Intimate Biography* (1995, 2007). For this latter book, she interviewed Theresa Bernstein, who imagined the present volume but did not live long enough to see it. This book is part of Levin's project to inscribe erased women artists into history.

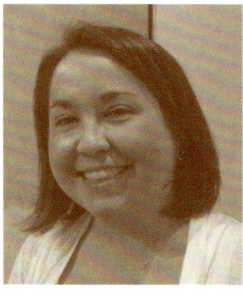

Gillian Pistell is a doctoral student in Art History at the Graduate Center of the City University of New York. She received her BA from Colgate University in 2008, double majoring in History and Art History, and her MA from the Graduate Program in the History of Art at Williams College in 2010.

Index of People Who Appear in *Theresa Bernstein: A Century in Art*

To New York

The city of all Nations
The City of all Creeds
From the wide ends of earth
To the friendly Port they come

Cities within the city
A hundred merged in one
A refuge-tent for all
To find their own again

Here happily they mingle
To strive - to find new aim
Here to build new futures
To strive afresh again

The city of all nations
The city of all creeds
Here under the free flag unfurled
The refuge-tent for all the world -

I. B